112B

R6.15

Sinclair

1973

A FIELD GUIDE TO THE
BIRDS OF SOUTHERN
AFRICA

A FIELD GUIDE TO THE
BIRDS OF SOUTHERN AFRICA

O. P. M. Prozesky

*with 32 colour plates and
8 black-and-white plates by*
DICK FINDLAY

Foreword by
ROCCO KNOBEL
*Director of National Parks,
Pretoria*

COLLINS
St James's Place, London

TO MARIE

ISBN 0 00 212026 7

CONTENTS

FOREWORD 11

INTRODUCTION 13

Ostrich: *Struthionidae* 21
Penguins: *Spheniscidae* 21
Grebes: *Podicipidae* 22
Albatrosses: *Diomedeidae* 24
Petrels: *Procellariidae* 25
Pelicans: *Pelecanidae* 30
Gannets: *Sulidae* 31
Cormorants: *Phalacrocoracidae* 31
Darters: *Anhingidae* 35
Herons: *Ardeidae* 35
Hamerkop: *Scopidae* 40
Storks: *Ciconiidae* 40
Ibises and Spoonbills: *Threskiornithidae* 44
Flamingoes: *Phoenicopteridae* 47
Ducks and Geese: *Anatidae* 50
Secretary Bird: *Sagittariidae* 57
Vultures: *Aegypiidae* 57
Falcons: *Falconidae* 60
Kites, Eagles, Buzzards, Hawks and allies: *Aquilidae* 67
Game Birds: *Phasianidae* 85
Guinea-Fowls: *Numididae* 91
Button-Quails: *Turnicidae* 93
Crakes, Rails, Moorhens and Coot: *Rallidae* 94
Finfoots: *Heliornithidae* 100
Cranes: *Gruidae* 101
Bustards and Korhaans: *Otidae* 103
Jacanas: *Jacanidae* 107

Painted Snipes: *Rostratulidae* 108

Oystercatchers: *Haematopodidae* 109

Plovers: *Charadriidae* 110

Snipes and Waders: *Scolopacidae* 118

Dikkops: *Burhinidae* 126

Coursers and Pratincoles: *Glareolidae* 127

Skuas: *Stercorariidae* 131

Gulls: *Laridae* 132

Terns: *Laridae* 134

Skimmers: *Rhynchopidae* 138

Sandgrouse: *Pteroclidae* 139

Doves and Pigeons: *Columbidae* 141

Fruit Pigeons: *Treronidae* 147

Parrots: *Psittacidae* 148

Louries: *Musophagidae* 150

Cuckoos: *Cuculidae* 151

Owls: *Strigidae* 157

Nightjars: *Caprimulgidae* 163

Swifts: *Apodidae* 165

Mousebirds: *Coliidae* 168

Trogons: *Trogonidae* 169

Kingfishers: *Alcedinidae* 170

Bee-eaters: *Meropidae* 174

Rollers: *Coraciidae* 178

Hoopoes: *Upupidae* 181

Hornbills: *Bucerotidae* 182

Barbets: *Capitonidae* 185

Honey-Guides: *Indicatoridae* 188

Woodpeckers: *Picidae* 190

Wrynecks: *Jyngidae* 194

Larks: *Alaudidae* 195

Swallows and Martins: *Hirundinidae* 202

Cuckoo-Shrikes: *Campephagidae* 207

Drongos: *Dicruridae* 211

Orioles: *Oriolidae* 212

Crows: *Corvidae* 213

Tits: *Paridae* 215

Babblers: *Timaliidae* 217

Bulbuls: *Pycnonotidae* 219

Thrushes, Chats and Robins: *Turdidae* 222

Warblers: *Sylviidae* 235

Flycatchers: *Muscicapidae* 250

Wagtails, Pipits and Longclaws: *Motacillidae* 259

Shrikes: *Laniidae* 264

Starlings: *Sturnidae* 276

Oxpeckers: *Buphagidae* 281

Sugarbirds: *Promeropidae* 282

Sunbirds: *Nectariniidae* 283

White-eyes: *Zosteropidae* 292

**Sparrows, Weavers, Waxbills, Widow-birds, Whydahs
and related species:** *Ploceidae* 293

Canaries and Buntings: *Fringillidae* 324

BIBLIOGRAPHY 333

INDEX 335

ILLUSTRATIONS

1. Penguin, grebes, gannet, cormorants, darter   *facing page* 32
2. Herons and egrets   33
3. Hamerkop, spoonbill, storks, ibises   48
4. Geese and ducks   49
5. Ducks and geese in flight   64
6. Albatrosses, petrels, shearwaters   65
7. Vultures, secretary bird and eagles in flight   80
8. Smaller birds of prey in flight   81
9. Vultures, eagles, secretary bird   96
10. Kestrels and falcons   97
11. Sparrowhawks, goshawks, harriers   112
12. Francolins, partridges, quails, button quails   113
13. Kites, buzzards, gymnogene and osprey   128
14. Oystercatcher, plovers   129
15. Sandpipers, stint, greenshank and ruff   144
16. Dikkop, coursers, pratincole, coot, moorhen, avocet, curlew   145
17. Crake, flufftail, snipes, gallinule, sandgrouse, jacana   160
18. Cranes, bustard, korhaans, storks, crows   161
19. Skuas, gulls, terns, skimmer   176
20. Doves, pigeons, parrots, lovebird   177
21. Lourie, cuckoos, coucal, trogon   192
22. Owls, owlets, nightjars   193
23. Swifts, swallows, spinetail   208
24. Mousebird, kingfishers, bee-eaters   209
25. Rollers, hornbills   224
26. Barbets, honeyguides, woodpeckers, wryneck   225
27. Larks, cuckoo-shrikes, drongo, babblers, hoopoes   240
28. Orioles, rockjumper, bulbuls, tits   241
29. Thrushes, chats, wheatear   256
30. Robins, scrub robins, apalis, prinias   257
31. Warblers, grassbird, crombec, cisticolas   272

32. Flycatchers 273
33. Wagtails, pipits, longclaw, starlings, oxpecker 288
34. Shrikes 289
35. Sugarbird, sunbirds and white-eye 304
36. Weavers, sparrow-weaver, sparrows, widow-birds 305
37. Weavers 308
38. Whydahs, bishops, amadinas 309
39. Mannikin, waxbills, twinspot, firefinch, finches 316
40. Canaries, buntings 317

FOREWORD

It is a pleasure indeed to introduce this publication to all who are interested in South African birds, professional ornithologists and amateur bird watchers alike. This field guide is exactly what especially the latter have been wanting for a long time, viz. a proper introduction to our bird life, and not just another check-list or scientific treatise on a special group.

The more common species are illustrated and described fully while the rare ones are named only. With our more than 800 species, any publication which tries to give illustrated descriptions of them all, becomes too bulky to be used in the veld.

The illustrations by Dick Findlay are excellent, and the silhouette of a well-known bird with each plate, to give some means of comparison as to size, is particularly welcome. The choice of the Cape Sparrow for the smaller, and the Guinea Fowl for the larger species, could hardly have been better.

The descriptions leave nothing to be desired and any bird watcher using both eyes and ears will be able to identify any bird described in this publication. The Author is known for his knowledge of bird-calls, and the reader is well advised to give special attention to these, because it is sure to be of importance at one or other stage in the identification of a lesser-known bird.

May this publication help to introduce many a reader to the wonders of our bird life.

ROCCO KNOBEL
Director of National Parks

Pretoria
28. 10. 1968

INTRODUCTION

The greater part of Southern Africa, at least 75% of it, enjoys more than 270 sunny days a year. No wonder the southern tip of the African continent is called "sunny South Africa". What is more, the winters are so mild that the soil never freezes. A prolific fauna and flora has developed as a result of this stable and moderate climate. Not only do we find many local species of birds in Southern Africa but most of the species are numerically well represented.

During the southern summer the vast number of palaeoarctic migrants moving southwards over the whole of Africa are funnelled into the tip of this large continent. In suitable localities these intercontinental migrants can be seen in their tens of thousands.

This rich and varied bird life has fired the imagination of the resident Bantu tribes. The beautiful glossy starling with its iridescent blue-green plumage and shiny orange-coloured eyes is known by the Zulus as "iKwezi" the "Morning Star". They, the Zulu, even understand the calls of the numerous dove species attracted to their cultivated maize and kaffir corn (a type of millet) fields. While cooing "coor-coor-coo; coor-coor-coo" the Cape Turtle dove is heard to say: "Amdogwe, amdogwe, amabele avutiwe". (Amdogwe is a fermented porridge made from the kaffir corn, amabele). So the dove is looking forward to a feast of porridge and ripe kaffir corn. The female Red-eye dove laments "Upi umhlobo wami?" (Where is my companion?). The male reassures her with "ngi-lapa, ngi-lapa" (I'm here, I'm here).

The purpose of this book is to enable anybody who is interested in birds, but has no specialized knowledge, to identify them in the field "at a glance".

Until recently, Roberts' *Birds of South Africa* was the only book found in Southern Africa readily available to knowledgeable ornithologists and bird-watchers alike. This excellent work was largely responsible for awakening interest in our avifauna, and is still used as the main reference book.

This Field Guide aims to be as authoritative and as complete as any of the books published on birds of Southern Africa, and, being of 'pocket' size, can be used in the field. Whereas many of the recently published bird books cover only a specific field consisting of a limited number of species, the composition of this Field Guide has made it possible to incorporate all the species found in Southern Africa.

Area covered. Southern Africa is the southern tip of the African continent lying south of 17°. This arbitrary line drawn across the continent coincides roughly with the Cunene River in the west and the Zambesi River in the east. It does not represent a clearcut faunal boundary between Southern and Central Africa and hence an overlap is found between the birds in this Field Guide and the birds in the *Field Guide to the Birds of East and Central Africa* by John Williams. Southern Africa has mainly a temperate climate and lies outside the tropics. We do not find such a large variety of habitats in Southern Africa as in Central and Eastern Africa. Therefore there are only about 900 species of birds here, compared to well over 1,200 farther to the north.

Southern Africa can be divided into three main climatic zones. Firstly the moister eastern part with its relatively high rainfall, which commences in the early summer months, September and October. Secondly, the dry western part with its low rainfall, commencing during late summer, usually in February. Lastly, the south-western tip, which also has a relatively high rainfall. This is a winter rainfall region, the rains commencing at the beginning of the southern winter, usually April. These three zones each have their particular vegetation.

The accompanying vegetation map is a simplified version of the one specially prepared by Drs L. Codd and D. Killick of the National Herbarium, for this publication. The numbers used for the different types of habitat have been taken from the vegetation map of Africa by R. W. J. Keay known as the AETFAT map. When considering Southern Africa as a whole, we must exclude the very arid regions and the south-westerly tip (denoted by numbers 32, 28 and 15), and the small patches of evergreen forest, coastal bush, swamps, mountain complexes and the areas with succulent shrubs which together comprise about 20% of the total area. The remaining 80% consists mainly of open savanna, of which the eastern parts are heavily forested. These trees are large, losing their leaves during the winter months. The rainfall in the western regions, being much lower than in the East, results in a sparser and more stunted vegetation.

Throughout Southern Africa the vegetation bordering the permanent rivers in the east and the dry river beds in the west, is much more luxuriant than the vegetation found away from the rivers. The riverine vegetation in the east can be compared to that of the coastal bush and evergreen forest. The result is that we find louries, mousebirds and many other fruit-eating birds (which we would expect to be confined to the more restricted habitats) far inland along these rivers. Similarly, dry river beds in the western regions, even in the Namib Desert, act as 'arteries' along which the birdlife 'flows' from the interior right across the arid areas to the Atlantic Ocean.

The grassland area (number 6) has during the last hundred and fifty years undergone a remarkable change. Before the advent of the colonist very few trees were found in this area and thus mainly terrestrial birds such

Voice. Many people, especially from other countries, are under the impression that the song of the birds of Southern Africa cannot compare wit[h] that of the birds of their own countries. This is a matter of opinion; wher[e] else in the world does one hear birds with such clear loud whistles and duet[s] as those of our shrikes, and many people consider that the power of imita[-]tion of our robins is not equalled anywhere in the world. The Choriste[r] Robin is known to imitate at least 20 different birds perfectly. The Pal[m] Thrush's song compares favourably in tone and repertoire with that of th[e] nightingale.

The calls and songs of birds play an important role in identifying them in the field. Many of our shrikes have specific notes, and being skulkers they are more readily identified by their whistles. Some of the Cisticolas probably the most difficult group of birds to identify in the field, are very often identifiable only by their calls. This also applies to the nocturnal nightjars and owls.

The calls of most birds are given in the text. It should however be remembered that these calls are heard wholly subjectively. It is thus extremely difficult to describe them in a manner acceptable to everyone as each gives his own interpretation to what he hears. The numerous records of birdcalls already available are a great help; and he is fortunate indeed who can spend some time in the field with a knowledgeable person.

Distribution. This Field Guide covers close on 900 species but no distribution maps are given owing partly to lack of space and partly to the fact that very few species are restricted to a particular habitat. For instance, of the numerous larks only a single species, Gray's Lark, is endemic to the Namib Desert.

Before the Colonists reached and settled in Central Southern Africa, certain eastern and western as well as certain northern and southern regions were separated by the grassland plateau, known as the Highveld. However, during the last hundred and fifty years or so, many species of birds such as doves, sparrows, shrikes and numerous others that depend on trees for shelter and nesting sites, have invaded this plateau as a result of all the exotic trees that have been planted there. The result is that this former barrier has disappeared, and now many species of birds are found in their suitable habitats throughout Southern Africa.

Many species of birds are local migrants moving to different parts of the country not only during the summer and winter months, but also at other times, depending on climatic conditions. This is especially true of insect- and fruit-eating birds, more particularly the palaeoarctic migrants found in Southern Africa during the southern summer. For instance, the swallows congregate in large numbers a day or two after a shower of rain has fallen in a certain area. They feed on small flying insects which emerge

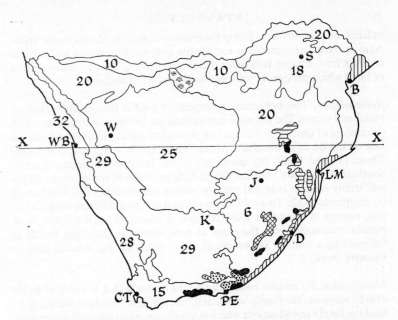

VEGETATION MAP OF SOUTHERN AFRICA

■ *Evergreen Forest*
▥ *Coastal Forest*
▤ *Woodlands (southern type)*
▨ *Semi- to succulent thicket*
🌿 *Swamps*
6 *Grassland*
10 *Dry Deciduous Forest*
15 *Cape Macchia*
28 *Karoo Succulent Steppe*

▩ *Montane Communities*
18 *Woodlands, Savannas (& Steppes)* with *Brachystegia* & *Julbernadia*
20 *Woodlands, Savannas (& Steppes) dry types & with mopane*
25 *Wooded Steppe* with *Acacia* & *Commiphora*
29 *Subdesert Steppe*
32 *Desert*

B	Beira	LM	Lourenço Marques
CT	Cape Town	PE	Port Elizabeth
D	Durban	S	Salisbury
J	Johannesburg	W	Windhoek
K	Kimberley	WB	Walvis Bay

XX *Tropic of Capricorn (23° 30'S)*

as larks were found there. Today the entire area is covered with exotic trees. Among them the Australian eucalyptus and wattle trees as well as the conifers from Europe now offer shelter and nesting sites to many species of birds which previously were confined to the forested area.

Nomenclature. The systematic arrangement used is that of Roberts and Praed and Grant. The scientific names used are those proposed by the List Committee of the South African Ornithological Society in their new Check List of the Birds of Southern Africa. The English, Afrikaans, Zulu (Z), Xhosa (X) and Sotho (S) names are given. The popular names used in Southern Africa vary considerably in different parts of the country. As no uniformity exists it is hoped that the names used in this Field Guide will be acceptable to all. To avoid any confusion due to a different vernacular, and, bearing in mind that Roberts' *Birds of South Africa* is still the most popular reference book, the name of each species in this Field Guide is followed by a number (in brackets) which refers to that specific bird in Roberts' book.

Identification. To be able to identify a bird in the field it is essential to be able to recognise the family to which it belongs. It is therefore necessary to read the family introductions which stress the common characteristics such as the shapes of the bills, length of the legs, etc. of the birds belonging to that specific family.

The illustrations are not intended to be portraits of the birds but are patternistic with the emphasis on outstanding field characteristics. These are indicated by a bar in the illustrations and are printed in italics in the text. The lengths referred to represent the bill-to-tip of tail measurement in centimetres. All the birds are drawn to scale, and as it is often extremely difficult to judge the size of a bird seen from a distance, the well-known Cape Sparrow (15 cm) or the Helmet guinea-fowl (46 cm) is shown in silhouette on the plates for comparative size.

Because the closely related species and seasonal plumages of certain species and the plumages of sub-adults are not illustrated for lack of space, it was found necessary to give a detailed description of these birds in addition to those illustrated. The diagnostic features are in each case given in italics. These detailed descriptions could be useful if ever a bird should come to hand, or when closely studied through fieldglasses.

Certain terms used in the text have a specific meaning. When giving the colour of the eye for instance, the colour of the iris is referred to. The legs include both the tarsus and the toes if not otherwise specified. The chest refers to the upper part of the breast and the cere is the bare wax-like skin found at the base of the bill of certain birds.

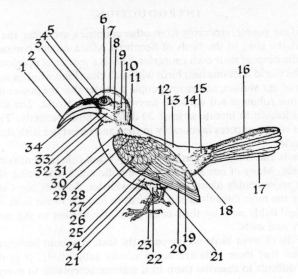

TOPOGRAPHY OF A BIRD

1	*Upper mandible*	18	*Under tail-coverts*
2	*Casque*	19	*Secondaries*
3	*Nostril*	20	*Primaries*
4	*Lores*	21	*Belly*
5	*Forehead*	22	*Thigh (tibia)*
6	*Eye*	23	*Tarsus*
7	*Crown*	24	*Flank*
8	*Ear-coverts*	25	*Primary wing-cove.*
9	*Nape*	26	*Alula*
10	*Neck*	27	*Median wing-cover*
11	*Mantle*	28	*Lesser wing-covert*
12	*Scapulars*	29	*Breast*
13	*Back*	30	*Shoulder*
14	*Rump*	31	*Throat*
15	*Upper tail-coverts*	32	*Cheek*
16	*Central tail feather*	33	*Chin*
17	*Outer tail feather*	34	*Lower mandible*

immediately after such a rain. The larger birds such as the storks, buzzards and other birds of prey usually appear in these areas about ten days later when larger insects, such as locusts, have had a chance to develop. These regions may be far apart. The distribution of the birds has been given as widely and generally as possible because birds are continually being recorded in regions where they had not previously been found.

Nesting. The nests and clutch-sizes have not been described for each species, but the typical nest and eggs of the birds belonging to the different families have been described in the introduction to each family. The identification of birds by their nests and eggs is extremely difficult and does not lie within the scope of this Field Guide.

Allied species. This Field Guide had to include all the 900 species found in Southern Africa but only half the number could be illustrated; it was therefore difficult to choose which species should be illustrated. Eventually the most common and widely distributed species was shown on the plates and the other members, if well-known, were described in detail. Rarer members of the family were merely listed. A typical example is the mouse-birds. The family consists of only three species of which the Red-faced Mousebird is illustrated. There is no chance of mistaking a mousebird, so the other two species, the Speckled and the White-backed, can easily be identified from the description.

If, on the other hand, the family consisted of a large number of birds comprising a few genera, the best-known or most common member in each genus was chosen for the plate. The shrike family is a good example of this case. The Fiscal Shrike was chosen from the genus Lanius, the Bou-bou Shrike from the genus Laniarius and the Black-crowned Shrike from the genus Tchagra, etc. The other well-known members were described as allied species and the rarer one, such as the Souza's Shrike and the Marsh Shrike, amongst others, only listed.

Flight. Flight as a field character for identifying small birds is in most cases only reliable to the family level; for instance the undulating flight of woodpeckers, the erratic wing beats of certain waders, the gliding flight of swifts and the slow, deep wing beats of herons. On the other hand the flight patterns of the larger birds of prey, the oceanic birds and that of the ducks and some of the waders is an important field character and is shown on the respective plates.

Sub-species. The birds depicted on the plates are the typical and not the extra-limital forms; for instance the Fiscal Shrike is shown without an eye-stripe, although these shrikes found in the western parts of Southern

Africa possess one. This method has been used because of its simplicity and also because sub-specific characters are usually trivial and often involved and very difficult to spot in the field. Readers who are interested in the sub-specific status of certain species of birds occurring in Southern Africa are referred to the Check List issued by the List Committee of the S.A.O.S.

Sub-adult. This term can apply to the juvenile as well as the immature bird. The juvenile plumage is retained until the first autumn moult, whereas the immature plumage is the plumage between the first autumn moult and the assumption of the adult plumage. This may cover a period of four to five years in the case of the large birds of prey. This is the reason why the identification of sub-adult birds of prey in the field is extremely difficult because of the variety of their immature plumages. In Southern Africa very few, if any, birds have an 'eclipse plumage'. This term refers to the moult plumages of male ducks and of some game-birds in the late summer and early autumn. Most of the weavers and whydahs have a summer breeding dress and a winter dress which is assumed after breeding. These have either been depicted or described in detail.

Acknowledgements. It gives the author pleasure to record his appreciation and gratitude to all his colleagues and many others, too numerous to name individually, who have assisted in many different ways in making this publication possible. A special word of thanks to Drs L. Codd and D. Killick of the National Herbarium for preparing the vegetation map of which the simplified version appears in this book, Clem Haagner for making available all his bird recordings and Peter Milstein in helping with the English and Afrikaans popular names. Above all, the author wishes to express his deep appreciation for the many pleasant hours spent together with Dick Findlay in preparing the excellent plates.

O. P. M. PROZESKY

Transvaal Museum, Pretoria
December 1969

OSTRICH: Struthionidae

The largest living bird; flightless, with long, powerful legs; only two toes on each foot, the largest having a nail. Long neck and relatively small head, covered with short, tufty down. Runs at more than 40 m.p.h., with *wings* held free.

OSTRICH   *Struthio camelus* (1)

    Afr Volstruis   *X* Inciniba

    Z 'Ntje   *S* Mpse

Identification: 213-244 cm. Adult male black and white. Female pale brown, with wing-feathers a dirty white. Subadult has greyish brown feathers with a lighter edging. Young bird has a fawn head and neck with longitudinal black streaks; rest of body covered with hedgehog-like black and white bristles.

Polygamous; usually found in small scattered flocks. Half-grown chicks gather in flocks of up to 100 individuals, and are cared for by a few old birds. Strictly vegetarian. As a rule males incubate at night and females by day.

Voice: Male utters a hollow booming note, easily mistaken at a distance for the roar of a lion, but without the characteristic grunting with which a lion concludes its roar.

Habitat: Open thornveld and semi-desert.

Distribution: Mostly in the dry west and locally over the rest of Southern Africa, with the exception of the eastern coastal strip.

PENGUINS: Spheniscidae

Flightless birds of the southern seas. Flippers used for swimming under water. Web-footed; legs extremely short. On land have a peculiar upright waddling gait. Body feathers short, furry and close-fitting.

JACKASS PENGUIN   *Spheniscus demersus* (2)   p. 32

    Afr Brilpikkewyn   *X* in-Guza

Identification: 60 cm. Forehead, crown and most of upper parts, sides of face, chin, throat and inverted horseshoe on chest, black. Lower back and rump washed with silvery grey. *Broad stripe from nostril to over the eye white*, as well as the whole of the underparts. Bill black with greyish band near tip. Sexes alike. Subadults have sides of face a dusky black, with only a trace of the white stripe above the eyes. Chin and upper throat white. Nestlings a sooty brown above; chest and belly off-white.

Breeds in large colonies on coastal islands. Swims very low in the water; dives quickly and quietly. Feeds on small fish and marine crustacea.

Voice: Silent by day; at night utters a loud bray like that of a donkey.

Habitat: A common resident of the coastal islands; wanders irregularly to the mainland.

Distribution: Along the entire western and southern coast, and sometimes the south-eastern coast.

Allied species:

ROCKHOPPER PENGUIN (*Eudyptes cristatus*) (3). Slightly smaller than Jackass Penguin and has a longer tail. *Stripe above eye pale yellow and narrow*, extending as far as the plumes. Subadult lacks dusky black on front lower neck. A rare visitor to the Cape coast.

GREBES: Podicipidae

A group of swimming and diving birds, with spatular toes, straight pointed bills and only short plumes for tail-feathers. Found only on water, mainly fresh-water lakes. Nest on floating or semi-floating islands built of dead water-plants and reeds. Parents invariably cover eggs with nesting material before leaving the nest.

CRESTED GREBE *Podiceps cristatus* (4) p. 32
    Afr Kuifkopduiker

Identification: 51 cm. In breeding plumage, adult has conspicuous *chestnut and black frills on either side of the large head*, and a black tuft on either side of the crown. Flanks tinged with chestnut. In non-breeding plumage birds have only a trace of the frills and tufts, and no chestnut on the flanks. General colour of upper parts brown; underparts a silky white. Eyes red; bill a reddish brown; legs black. Sexes alike. Subadult has bare patch on crown and lacks the frills. Head and neck have longitudinal brown stripes.

Found singly, in pairs or in small family parties, usually swimming far from the water's edge. Duck-sized, but readily distinguished from ducks by their long, thin necks and large heads. In flight the long legs project far beyond the short tail, and a *distinct white bar is seen across base of wing*. These birds have an elaborate courtship display, swimming with their bills skimming the water, plumes and frills raised and heads moving jerkily.

Voice: Usually silent, but during the breeding season utter a low-pitched '*keek, keek*'.

Habitat: Prefer large sheets of open fresh water.

Distribution: The southern two-thirds of Southern Africa, but not the arid central regions.

BLACK-NECKED GREBE *Podiceps nigricollis* (5) p. 32
Afr Swartnekduiker

Identification: 23 cm. Adult in breeding plumage has head slightly crested; *neck and upper chest black* with *patch of golden chestnut feathers on the side of the head and neck, behind the eye.* Flanks tinged with chestnut. In non-breeding dress the throat, chest and sides of neck are white; no chestnut patch on side of head; no chestnut on flanks. Upper parts blackish; a silvery white below. Secondaries mainly white. Eyes crimson; bill and legs black. Sexes alike. Subadult similar to adult in non-breeding plumage but browner above and streaked on head, neck and body.

A not common migrant, usually seen in flocks numbering from a few individuals to many hundreds. While preening, *floats on its side, exposing its silvery white flanks.* White secondaries conspicuous in flight. *Shape of lower mandible gives the impression of an upturned bill.*

Voice: Rather silent. Alarm-call a sharp '*whit-whit*'. Also gives a trilling call during the breeding season.

Habitat: Large sheets of water, salt as well as fresh. Also found just offshore. Prefers largish reed-fringed lakes.

Distribution: The southern and south-eastern parts of Southern Africa. Also along the southern and central western coasts.

CAPE DABCHICK *Podiceps ruficollis* (6) p. 32
Afr Kaapse duiker (Dobbertjie)   *X* u-Nolwibili
S le-Fuli

Identification: 15 cm. Adult (breeding dress) has *cheeks, sides and front of neck rufous.* Chin, face, top of head and hind neck black. Chest and flanks have a blackish tinge. In non-breeding dress, rufous is replaced by a brownish white and the black is duller. Flanks and chest have a greyish tinge and appear almost white. General colour a blackish brown above; belly a silvery white or white tinged with brown. Secondaries mainly white. Eyes brown; bill black (gape greenish); legs black. Sexes alike. Subadult similar to adult in non-breeding plumage but has neck and head streaked and blotched with sooty black.

A common resident species, usually found in pairs or small family parties but sometimes also in fairly large flocks, during the non-breeding season. Often seen 'standing' on the water, vigorously flapping its wings, or 'running' on the water in partial flight, during which the *white secondaries* are conspicuous. When feeding undisturbed, it will often bob forward and disappear, creating hardly a ripple; but when alarmed it crash-dives with a flick of its wings. Prefers to escape from danger by diving.

Voice: A loud, often prolonged trill, which can be compared to a rippling musical laugh. Alarm-note a soft whistle or a loud, sharp '*chick*'.
Habitat: Open sheets of water and also quiet streams and pools.
Distribution: Throughout Southern Africa.

ALBATROSSES: Diomedeidae

Large marine birds. Long, narrow wings and gliding flight are characteristic. Bills strong and hooked. Nostrils open through prominent tubes. Hind toes absent. Webbed feet carried open on either side of relatively short tails. Settle gently on water with wings raised. Float very high when wings are closed. To become airborne, they run on the water, stretching out their wings and flapping them vigorously to get clear of the waves.

WANDERING ALBATROSS   *Diomedea exulans* (7)   p. 65
     Afr Grootalbatros
Identification: 137 cm. Wing-span about 365 cm. Adult male mostly white; *primaries black*. Usually some of the feathers on back and sides have dark narrow zigzag cross-bars. Bill yellow or pinkish white, feet a pale flesh-colour. Adult female resembles male, but smaller and has a dark cap on the crown. Subadult mainly a dirty brown. Wings almost black above, white below except at the tips. Face and throat white, abdomen mottled whitish. Feet brownish. bill a pinkish white.
Frequently follow ships in sight of shore, which they approach only if weather is stormy. Feed mainly at night, taking cuttlefish and other marine animals near the surface. Feed on refuse from ships. Breed on islands in the southern seas.
Distribution: Antarctic and neighbouring seas.

BLACK-BROWED ALBATROSS   *Diomedea melanophris* (8)   p. 65
     Afr Malmokalbatros
Identification: 81 cm. Wing-span about 244 cm. Adult birds have head, neck, upper mantle, rump, underparts and under wing-coverts (except the leading edge) white. Wings black on top; back and tail slaty black. *Dark line through eye; bill golden with rose-pink tip.* Feet yellowish. Sexes alike. Subadult has a grey head and neck. Bill a dusky olive with a dark tip; underside of wings dusky with a lighter centre line.
Common pelagic species, often following ships into bays. Large numbers congregate on trawling-grounds, feeding on offal from trawlers.
Distribution: Southern oceans.

YELLOW-NOSED ALBATROSS *Diomedea chloro-*
rhynchos (10) p. 65
Afr Geelbekalbatros

Identification: 89 cm. Wing-span 192-213 cm. Head and neck white, nape sometimes suffused with grey. Usually has a dark-grey patch above and behind the eye. Rump, upper tail-coverts, underparts and under wing-coverts white, except for a narrow strip of brownish black on the leading edge of the wing. Back a slaty brown; tail an ashy brown; upper wings a brownish black. Slender *bill black with a yellow line down the centre of the upper mandible*, which has an *orange tip*. Sexes alike. Subadult birds resemble adults except that their bills are a uniform black.

A pelagic species, commonly found on trawling-grounds, where they feed on offal. Seldom observed near the shore.

Distribution: Southern oceans. Ranges farther north than its congeners.

Allied species:

SHY ALBATROSS (*Diomedea cauta*) (11). 117 cm. Slightly smaller than Wandering Albatross (wing-span 335 cm). Similar underwing pattern. Cheeks and nape suffused with grey. Mark in front of eye and line over eye a greyish black. Bill a bluish grey; lower mandible tipped with black.

SOOTY ALBATROSS (*Phoebetria fusca*) (12). 84 cm. Dark brown; body feathers slightly lighter; incomplete white ring round eye; long *wedge-shaped tail*. Bill black; groove along lower mandible orange or golden. Wings appear narrower than those of other albatrosses. Wing-span about 213 cm.

LIGHT-MANTLED SOOTY ALBATROSS (*Phoebetria palpebrata*) (12X). 71 cm. Body feathers ashy grey. Black bill shows no yellow, groove along lower mandible being pale blue or pearl-grey. Approximately same size as Sooty Albatross.

Rarer species:

GREY-HEADED ALBATROSS (*Diomedea chrysostoma*) (9)

PETRELS: Procellariidae

Members of this large family of marine birds vary greatly in size. The bill of the petrel is characteristic, being hooked at the tip and somewhat compressed at the base, with the nostrils opening together at the end of a double tube on the upper mandible. Petrels are black, brown, grey or white, or a combination of these colours. They have a rapid, gliding flight, resembling that of the albatrosses except in that it is more often interrupted by the flapping of their wings. Except when breeding, petrels spend most of their time at sea. Their food consists of small fish, squids and other floating or surface-living animals. They also feed on refuse from ships. Usually silent at sea but at night during the breeding season loud, mournful wails can be heard at the nesting colonies.

GIANT PETREL *Macronectes giganteus* (13)   p. 65
Afr Reusestormvoël (Nellie)

Identification: 91 cm. Wing-span about 244 cm. Dark phase: General colour a sooty-black, dark chocolate-brown or dark grey, with a lighter head. Light phase: Wholly white or sparingly and irregularly flecked with black. Bill relatively large and light-coloured. Tail wedge-shaped; broad wings relatively short. Head bent downwards in flight, giving a humped-shoulder effect. Sexes alike. Subadult a shiny black.

A marauding species, feeding on carrion and offal and even killing penguins and small petrels. Breeds on most southern oceanic islands during the southern summer.

Voice: Utters a croaking note at night. Voice has been described as 'diabolical'.

Distribution: Southern oceans. Common near the coast during the non-breeding season. In the temperate seas the dark phase is the commoner. The white phase is mostly confined to the Antarctic regions.

CAPE PIGEON (PINTADO PETREL) *Daption capensis* (14)   p. 65
Afr Spikkelrugstormvoël

Identification: 36 cm. Head to upper mantle, sides of face and neck a sooty black; *mantle, scapulars, wing-coverts and upper tail-coverts mottled black and white. Base of tail white;* tip a sooty brown. Basal half of secondaries and inner primaries white; rest of flight-feathers black. Underparts and under wing-coverts white. Bill and legs a blackish brown. Sexes alike. Sub-adult birds similar to adults.

In flight, the *large white patches on the wings* of these pied petrels are unmistakable. Make more use of active flying than of sailing. The sudden upward 'bumps' of from 9-12 m, while sailing over the sea, are very typical. Feed like gulls, picking up food from water while flying or swimming. Not often seen from the shore, but freely approach boats. Nest on islands in the Antarctic.

Voice: A grating, squeaking call.

Distribution: Southern oceans. A common winter visitor all along the coast of Southern Africa.

CAPE HEN (WHITE-CHINNED PETREL) *Procellaria*
aequinoctialis (23)   p. 65
Afr Witkenstormvoël (Bassiaan)

Identification: 56 cm. Sooty black, tending to chocolate brown on mantle and underparts. Chin white; white sometimes extends to sides of face and crown, but is sometimes entirely absent. *Bill a yellowish green.* Feet black. Sexes alike. Subadults similar to adult birds.

Fearless birds, commonly found throughout the year. Scavengers, following boats for refuse and even coming into harbours. Capable divers, can catch fish under water. Breed on southern oceanic islands.

Distribution: Southern oceans. Found along the entire coast of Southern Africa.

GREAT SHEARWATER *Puffinus gravis* (25)   p. 65
    Afr Grootpylstormvoël

Identification: 46 cm. Upper parts brown, darker on wings and tail. Darkest on head, including lores and ear-coverts. *White collar round greater part of neck makes dark cap very conspicuous.* Most of the feathers of the back have pale edges. *Upper tail-coverts have whitish tips;* underparts white, flecked with sooty brown on the abdomen and under tail-coverts. *Under wing-coverts white,* streaked with brown. *Bill a dark horn-colour;* feet brown. Tail slightly graduated. Sexes alike. Subadult similar to adult birds.

Fast flight, very low over water; rapid wing-beats followed by long periods of gliding. Will fly straight into the water for food. In winter large numbers are found on trawling-grounds. Unafraid of boats; even go into harbours. Breed on islands in the southern seas.

Distribution: A pelagic species, common offshore. During southern winter migrates as far north as Greenland.

Allied species:
GREAT GREY SHEARWATER (*Procellaria cinerea*) (24). 46 cm. Similar in size to Great Shearwater. General colour above ashy grey; sides of face pale grey; cap *not* conspicuous. Underside of wing ashy grey (not white or streaked). *Bill a greenish white, with a black tip.*

MEDITERRANEAN SHEARWATER (*Calonectris diomedea*) (26). 46 cm. Similar in appearance to Great Shearwater, but *cheeks and sides of neck a mottled grey.* Crown does not appear as a conspicuous cap. *Bill yellow.* In flight shows white wing-patches.

DOVE PRION *Pachyptila desolata* (22)
    Afr Duifwalvisvoël

Identification: 26 cm. Blue-grey above. Darkish line through eye; top of head darker; shoulder (lesser wing-coverts) to end of scapulars a dusky slate, *looking in flight like a dark horse-shoe bent across back and wings.* Outer primaries and tip of wedge-shaped tail a blackish slate. Stripe over eye and sides of face white. Whole underside, including underside of wings, white. Sides of chest, lower flanks and under tail-coverts blue-grey. *Bill* *light blue with a black tip.* Legs light blue. Sexes alike. Subadult birds similar to adults.

Flight very irregular. Often fly with stiff wings, like waders. Dive and swim under water. Follow ships, but do not feed on refuse. Generally found in flocks. Breed on southern oceanic islands.

Distribution: Southern oceans. Found along the coast during the winter months. Often driven ashore by stormy weather.

Allied species:

WHALE BIRD *(Pachyptila vittata)* (21). 30 cm. Slightly larger than the Dove Prion. Bill much broader; *upper mandible a brownish black, lower mandible blue.* Difficult to distinguish from the Dove Prion in the field.

SOOTY SHEARWATER   *Puffinus griseus* (29)   p. 65
   Afr Donkerbruinpylstormvoël (Malbaartjie)

Identification: 46 cm. Upper parts a blackish brown, underparts ash-brown. *Underside of wings mainly a light greyish white.* Bill black to horn-colour; feet slate-grey. Sexes alike. Subadult birds similar to adults.

In flight, the elongated body with narrow, sharp-pointed wings, showing whitish under wing-coverts and pale underside of primaries, is characteristic. Flight moderately fast; birds sail on bent wings with twists and rises. A southern breeding species.

Distribution: Southern Atlantic and Pacific Oceans to the Arctic Circle. Found in the Cape seas during the winter months (their non-breeding season).

COMMON STORM PETREL   *Hydrobates pelagicus* (30)   p. 65
   Afr Gewone stormswawel

Identification: 16 cm. Sooty black; *white upper tail-coverts* very noticeable in flight; *tail nearly square.* Bill, legs and webs black. Sexes alike. Subadults similar to adults.

These dainty little birds have a swallow-like flight, gliding close over the water and disappearing in the troughs. In flight, their short legs *do not extend beyond their tails;* under wing-coverts appear lighter. Breed mainly in northern hemisphere.

Voice: Normally silent at sea.

Distribution: Common; often close inshore along the entire coast of Southern Africa during summer.

WILSON'S STORM PETREL   *Oceanites oceanicus* (33)   p. 65
   Afr Wilson-stormswawel

Identification: 19 cm. Upper parts a sooty black, darkest on wings and tail. Chocolate tinge on back paler than in the Common Storm Petrel. Upper tail-coverts white; *tail square*. Bill and *relatively long legs black*. Sexes alike. Subadults similar to adults.

In flight, *legs extend beyond end of tail*. This is not always seen, however, for the bird sometimes flies with its legs carried forward, tucked against the side of its body. These birds regularly follow ships. They sometimes hop along the water with their wings raised, or fly so close to the water that their lowered legs trail along the surface. Breeding range extends to Antarctica.

Distribution: Common in Cape seas during the winter months.

Allied species:

LEACH'S STORM PETREL (*Oceanodroma leucorhoa*) (31). 23 cm. Sooty black with white tail-coverts. *Tail deeply forked*. In flight the lighter secondary coverts show as a lightish curved wing-bar from above.

Rarer species:

ANTARCTIC PETREL (*Thalassoica antarctica*)

ANTARCTIC FULMAR (*Fulmarus glacialoides*)

GREAT-WINGED PETREL (*Pterodroma macroptera*) (16)

WHITE-HEADED PETREL (*Pterodroma lessonii*) (17)

SCHLEGEL'S PETREL (*Pterodroma incerta*) (18)

SOFT-PLUMAGED PETREL (*Pterodroma mollis*) (19)

BLUE PETREL (*Halobaena caerulea*) (20)

FAIRY PRION (*Pachyptila turtur*) (22X)

SLENDER-BILLED PRION (*Pachyptila belcheri*) (22Y)

FLESH-FOOTED SHEARWATER (*Puffinus carneipes*) (26X)

MANX SHEARWATER (*Puffinus puffinus*) (26Y)

LITTLE SHEARWATER (*Puffinus assimilis*) (27)

WHITE-FACED STORM PETREL (*Pelagodroma marina*) (34)

BLACK-BELLIED STORM PETREL (*Fregetta tropica*) (36)

WHITE-BELLIED STORM PETREL (*Fregetta grallaria*) (37)

RED-TAILED TROPIC BIRD (*Phaëthon rubricauda*) (39)

WHITE-TAILED TROPIC BIRD (*Phaëthon lepturus*) (40)

BROWN BOOBY (*Sula leucogaster*) (46)

FRIGATE BIRD (*Fregata minor*) (53)

PELICANS: Pelecanidae

Large aquatic birds of the shallow coastal and inland waters. Characterized by their short legs, webbed toes, long bills and the naked pouch suspended from the lower mandible and upper part of the throat. (The pouch may be folded up almost completely.) Feed on fish. Large flocks usually drive the fish into shallow water, where they deftly scoop them up into their pouches. Pelicans fly strongly, with slow, regular wing-beats. During flight they draw their heads back against their shoulders like herons. Often seen soaring in thermals.

PINK-BACKED PELICAN   *Pelecanus rufescens* (41)
Afr Kleinpelikaan

Identification: 137 cm. General colour of adult is greyish. *Primaries slightly darker than rest of plumage:* **not** *black*. Back and rump a vinous pink. Well-developed crest on nape. Bill a yellowish flesh-colour; pouch flesh-coloured; legs orange. Sexes alike. Subadult brownish above; head and neck a greyish white; back and rump white; underparts white.

Usually found fishing singly or in small parties in open water. Sometimes dive for fish while swimming. Resident, and breed in colonies. *In flight, underwing a uniform buff, bisected lengthwise by a broadish paler streak.*
Voice: Clucking guttural croaks at nesting sites.
Distribution: Mainly along the southern and eastern coastal belt, but occasionally found on suitable inland waters in any part of Southern Africa.

WHITE PELICAN   *Pelecanus onocrotalus* (42)
Afr Witpelikaan

Identification: 147–182 cm. General colour white. In breeding season has a pinkish tinge and develops a slight crest. *Primary wing-coverts and primaries black*. Bill grey with pinkish or reddish edges, pouch yellowish. Legs pink or orange. Sexes alike, but crest of female relatively larger. Subadult has brownish upper parts, head and neck. Mantle and rump white, sometimes flecked with brown. Underparts white.

Catch fish by driving shoals to shallow water. Birds at the rear will 'leap-frog' over those in front, and crash-dive into the fleeing fish. Also feed on young birds. Resident and migratory; colonial nesters. *In flight, leading half of underwing white, trailing half black*.
Voice: Usually silent, but grunt or snarl at nesting sites.
Distribution: Found along the entire coast of Southern Africa, and occasionally on inland waters.

GANNETS: Sulidae

Fairly large white or brown marine birds having completely webbed toes, long pointed bills, pointed wings and pointed tails. Characteristic habit of flying at some height above the water and diving down vertically with wings half closed. Reappear on surface a few seconds later, swallow the impaled fish and flap heavily off again. When not fishing glide swiftly, close to the surface of the water, with only occasional unbending wing-beats.

CAPE GANNET *Sula bassana* (44) p. 32
   Afr Gewone malgas
Identification: 89 cm. The adult bird is wholly white, with *black tail and flight feathers*. Distinct *yellow wash on head and neck*. Bare skin on face and neck black; light blue ring round eyes. Bill bluish; legs black. This bird's white plumage has a peculiarly gleaming quality, even at a considerable distance. Sexes alike. Subadult has dark-brown upper parts and neck, speckled with white. Underparts variegated white and sooty brown.

Large flocks can sometimes be seen following shoals of fish. Nest in colonies, on guano islands off the coast.
Voice: A goose-like honking: '*kara-kara-kara*'.
Distribution: Along the coasts of Southern Africa.

CORMORANTS: Phalacrocoracidae

A group of water-birds with long necks, slender bodies, short legs, all the toes webbed and long, stiff tail feathers. Mostly black in colour. Bills slender and hooked at the tip. Expert swimmers and divers. Live on fish and amphibians, caught not by diving, but by under-water pursuit.

WHITE-BREASTED CORMORANT *Phalacrocorax carbo* (47) p. 32
   Afr Witborskormorant   *X* U-Gwidi, um-Xwiga
Identification: 89 cm. The largest cormorant. Tail relatively short. In breeding plumage cheeks, *entire throat and upper breast are white. Two white flank patches conspicuous*. Rest of plumage a glossy greenish black. Non-breeding birds are brownish. Sexes alike. Subadult: underparts off-white. Nestlings a sooty brown.

Swims low in water with body submerged. Often perches with wings held half-open. Feeds on fish. Flies with rapid wing-beats and neck stretched out to its full extent.

PLATE 1

PENGUIN, GANNET, CORMORANTS, DARTER AND GREBES

1 **JACKASS PENGUIN**   *page* 21
   White stripe from nostril over the eye.

2 **CAPE GANNET**   31
   Flight and tail feathers black, yellow wash on head and neck.

3 **DARTER**   35
   Long, slender, pointed bill and slender head.

4 **CAPE CORMORANT**   34
   Short tail and yellow lores.

5 **WHITE-BREASTED CORMORANT**   31
   Large size and white breast.

6 **REED CORMORANT**   34
   Long tail.

7 **CRESTED GREBE**   22
   Chestnut and black frills and black tufts.

8 **BLACK-NECKED GREBE**   23
   Black neck and golden ear tufts.

9 **CAPE DABCHICK**   23
   Rufous on head and neck.

PLATE 2

HERONS AND EGRETS

1 **NIGHT HERON** *page* 38
Head large and eyes red.
a Sub-adult; sooty brown, streaked and blobbed.

2 **CATTLE EGRET** 38
Distinctive heavy jowl. Summer plumage; buff plumes on crown,
chest and back.

3 **GREAT EGRET** 37
Legs and bill black, no real crest.

4 **GOLIATH HERON** 36
Enormous size; crown, neck and underparts rufous-chestnut.

5 **GREY HERON** 35
Head and neck white, streak through eye and crest black; yellowish
green bill long and dagger-shaped.

6 **LITTLE EGRET** 37
Long, slender bill and legs black, feet yellow.

7 **GREEN-BACKED HERON** 38
Crown, plumes and back glossy dark green, rufous streak down centre
of breast.

8 **BLACK-HEADED HERON** 36
Head, plumes and back of neck black, chin white. Bill dark and
shortish.

Voice: Series of guttural croaks at nesting sites.
Habitat: A common resident along the coast and inland, where it is found on dams and other large sheets of water. Social in habits; nests in colonies.
Distribution: Throughout Southern Africa.

CAPE CORMORANT *Phalacrocorax capensis* (48)   p. 32
    Afr Trekkormorant
Identification: 66 cm. A uniform black in breeding plumage. *Bare patch on throat and lores are yellow. Short-tailed* in appearance. Sexes alike. Non-breeding and subadult birds are a brownish black, with lighter brown throat and breast.

Most often seen sitting on rocks, with wings spread out to dry. During the summer months large numbers can be seen flying, or trekking in long, straggling lines low over the sea. When the birds come upon a shoal of fish, they dive and surface with great activity. When about to dive, they jump almost out of the water, to take a 'header'. Feed on pelagic surface fish and have been known to eat mussels and crabs.
Voice: Silent.
Habitat: Found only on salt water. Gregarious as a rule, though solitary specimens are often seen flying among the breakers, close inshore. Breed in immense numbers on guano islands.
Distribution: Along the entire coast of Southern Africa, the eastern and north-eastern sections excepted.

REED CORMORANT *Phalacrocorax africanus* (50)   p. 32
    Afr Rietkormorant   *Z* um-Pishamanzi
Identification: 58 cm. The only *long-tailed* cormorant. In breeding plumage, a glossy black with bronze-grey reflections on the shoulders, and crested. In non-breeding plumage the bird is brown and has a shorter crest. Sexes alike. Subadult brownish, with off-white underparts and a light-brown throat.

Bill shorter than that of other cormorants. Feeds on fish and frogs, especially *Xenopus*. On land waddles quite briskly. Also hangs out wings to dry. Social in habits but usually found only in small numbers.
Voice: Usually silent, but sometimes makes a hissing sound when nesting.
Habitat: A common resident. Inland birds found on dams, lakes, rivers and even small gravel quarries when these have been filled by the summer rains. Coastal birds found mainly near islands, where they breed.
Distribution: Throughout Southern Africa.

Allied species:
BANK CORMORANT (*Phalacrocorax neglectus*) (49). 76 cm. *Totally black*, even to the bare patch on the throat. Larger than the Cape Cormorant and heavy in body. More 'woolly' and less sleek than the other

cormorants. Found only from the Cape Peninsula northwards along the west coast.

DARTERS: Anhingidae

Resemble cormorants but are generally more slender. Bills long and pointed, not hooked at the tip. Tail-feathers stiff and longer than those of cormorants; heads and necks very slender. Legs short; feet webbed. Swim so low in the water that only the neck and head are visible—hence the name Snake Bird. All flight-feathers are dropped during the annual moult, with the result that the birds are for some time unable to fly.

DARTER *Anhinga rufa* (52) p. 32
   Afr Slanghalsvoël

Identification: 86 cm. Adult male has crown and back of neck black and chestnut, with white stripe from chin one-third of the way down. Except for longitudinal white streaks on wing-coverts and scapulars the rest of the body is black. In the breeding season the plumes of the white neck-stripe become longer. Adult female: crown and back of neck brown; lower neck fawn. White stripe less distinct. Bill greenish with yellow tip. Subadult has throat and underside of neck off-white; rest of body fawn or buff; flanks dark. Some individuals a very light fawn.

Usually social, but solitary birds may be found perched over water. At rest and in flight there is a curious kink in the neck. Often seen sitting with wings spread out to dry and tail hanging down. Fly very strongly and are often seen soaring. Feed on fish and frogs caught under water. Nest in the company of other water-birds.

Voice: A harsh, croaking quack.

Habitat: Permanent waters, inland rather than coastal, but sometimes found on coastal lagoons.

Distribution: Throughout Southern Africa.

HERONS: Ardeidae

Tall, slender wading birds with longish pointed bills. Plumage is long and lax; the adults have ornamental plumes during the breeding season. In sustained flight, heads are tucked in between shoulders. Flight is buoyant, with typically large, slow wing-beats. Sexes usually alike.

GREY HERON *Ardea cinerea* (54) p. 33
   Afr Bloureier   *X* u-Ndofu, u-Cofuza

Identification: 102 cm. Upper parts grey; *head and neck whitish* with *broad* *black streak from above the eye to the tip of the long black crest.* Black flecks on neck, from chin downwards. Black markings on breast and underparts not conspicuous in the field, the general impression being grey. *Underwing flight-pattern a uniform grey. Long, dagger-shaped bill yellowish,* legs brownish. Sexes alike. Colour pattern of subadult similar to that of adult except that the white is replaced by grey, and bill and legs are a dull greenish colour.

Flies with head drawn back between shoulders and legs extended. Although its wings are broad the bird glides comparatively seldom. Its flight is powerful, with slow, deep wing-beats. Found near or in shallow water, where it will stand for long periods with neck erect or head sunk between shoulders. Sometimes wades cautiously through water in search of fish and frogs.

Voice: Alarm-note a harsh '*kaark*'; various guttural croaks uttered at nest.
Habitat: Commonly found near water; rarely seen in open grassland. Solitary in habits; rather shy. Birds sometimes hunt at night. Colonial nesting in high trees near water, or in reed-beds.
Distribution: Throughout Southern Africa.

BLACK-HEADED HERON *Ardea melanocephala* (55)   p. 33
   Afr Swartkopreier   *Z* u-Klonke
   X u-Ndofu

Identification: 96 cm. *Head, plumes and back of neck black, chin white* and lower neck streaked. Body slate-grey, darker on back than underparts. Bill *dark and shorter* than that of the Grey Heron. In flight shows *white under wing-coverts and black flight-feathers.* Legs black. Sexes alike. Subadult similar to adult but dark-grey instead of black on head and neck.

Typical heron-flight. This bird is not a good fisherman and is mostly found on dry land, hunting for insects, rodents and lizards. It should be regarded as extremely useful to man. Probably the least shy of the herons.
Voice: A loud, guttural '*kuark*'; a large variety of croaking sounds uttered at nest. Nestlings utter an incessant '*cack, cack, cack*'.
Habitat: May occur either near or away from water. Rather solitary in habits. Colonial nesting, mostly in trees, sometimes far from the nearest water. Has even been found to nest in towns.
Distribution: Throughout Southern Africa.

GOLIATH HERON *Ardea goliath* (56)   p. 33
   Afr Reusereier

Identification: 140 cm. Distinguished from the other herons by its *large size.* Upper parts slate-grey; *crown, neck and underparts mainly a rufous chestnut.* Chin and throat white; black lines down front of lower half of neck. Long, dagger-like bill that of the true fish-eater. Sexes alike. Subadult birds are browner above, and the rufous colouring below has a brownish tinge.

Flight more ponderous than that of other herons; legs tend to sag in flight.

Voice: When flushed, usually utters a loud, raucous *'arrrk'*.

Habitat: More solitary than most herons; nowhere common; very rarely seen on dry ground. A shy bird, usually frequenting estuaries, large inland vleis and pans and quiet stretches of the larger rivers. Solitary nests in trees or reed-beds.

Distribution: Eastern and central northern areas of Southern Africa.

GREAT EGRET *Egretta alba* (58)   p. 33
Afr Grootwitreier

Identification: 91 cm. Largest of the African egrets. Entire plumage white. *Legs black.* In breeding plumage the bill is either black, or black and yellow; non-breeding birds and subadults have yellow bills. Sexes alike. Plumes confined to back; *no real crest.*

While feeding, tends to keep neck stretched out and leaning slightly forward.

Voice: A harsh, deep, guttural *'aahr'*, rarely uttered.

Habitat: Usually found feeding on the margins of flooded pans, vleis and rivers. A wandering species, usually solitary, but nests and roosts among other birds such as cormorants.

Distribution: Throughout Southern Africa, except in the dry west.

LITTLE EGRET *Egretta garzetta* (59)   p. 33
Afr Kleinwitreier

Identification: 63 cm. A graceful, slender bird with snow-white plumage. *Long slender bill black; legs black. Yellow toes* conspicuous in flight. In breeding plumage assumes plumes on back and *two long, slender, white plumes on nape.* Sexes alike. Subadult similar to adult in non-breeding plumage.

Usually solitary when feeding but sometimes gregarious when flying to roosting-places. Unlike other herons very alert while feeding, making swift movements, spreading its wings and darting to and fro with great agility. Very seldom found away from water. Feeds on fish, frogs, aquatic animals and insects caught at the water's edge.

Voice: A brief, hoarse *'kraak'* or a bubbling *'wulla-wulla-wulla'*.

Habitat: Resident and not uncommon. Found on dams, marshy rivers, estuaries and along the sea-shore. Gregarious while breeding in mixed heronries, either in trees or reed-beds.

Distribution: Throughout Southern Africa.

CATTLE EGRET   *Ardeola ibis* (61)   p. 33
   Afr Veereier   *Z* i-Landa

Identification: 51 cm. Stockier and thicker-necked than the Little Egret, and has a distinctive *heavy jowl*. Looks white at a distance. In breeding plumage, *long buff plumes are visible on crown, back and chest*. Bill yellow; legs yellowish brown, but sometimes flesh-coloured. Sexes alike. Non-breeding birds and subadults are white, with yellow bills and legs a greenish brown.

Sociable, usually found catching the insects that have been disturbed by grazing cattle or game. Also found on cultivated fields, following the plough or the hoe. Often seen perched on the backs of animals. Towards evening large numbers may be seen flying in formation towards a meeting-place some distance from their roost.

Voice: A harsh '*kraak*' when alarmed; various croaking notes in the breeding season.

Habitat: The least aquatic of the herons, mostly found feeding away from water, although its colonial nests are usually in the vicinity of water, in a mixed heronry.

Distribution: Throughout Southern Africa, except in the dry west.

GREEN-BACKED HERON   *Butorides striatus* (63)   p. 33
   Afr Groenrugreier

Identification: 41 cm. *Crown, ornamental plumes, back and tail a glossy dark green;* underparts ash-grey except for a *rufous streak down the centre of the breast*. Chin white; centre of throat and front of neck a buffish white. *Light-edged feathers of back and wing-coverts* characteristic. Sexes alike. Subadult generally browner; head and back washed with green; wing-coverts have fawn edgings and white blobs. Underparts streaked with dark brown.

A shy bird, usually nocturnal. Mostly seen in a hunched-up position, cautiously climbing about on low branches and bushes by the waterside, but sometimes found stalking on sandbanks and rocks.

Voice: A loud squawk when flushed, and a high-pitched monosyllabic '*chuck*'. Also a trilling '*kek-kek-kek*'.

Habitat: Resident, and of a solitary disposition. Found in reed- and bush-bound rivers, streams and mangrove swamps. Nests are well concealed and almost always solitary.

Distribution: Eastern and north-central Southern Africa.

NIGHT HERON   *Nycticorax nycticorax* (69)   p. 33
   Afr Nagreier

Identification: 58 cm. A stocky, short-legged heron with a *large head, stout bill* and *big red eyes*. In breeding plumage the crown, nape, mantle and scapulars appear black. Long white plumes on nape. Other upper parts grey; underparts white. Sexes alike. Subadult a *sooty brown above, streaked and blobbed with fawn and white; underparts streaked brown and white.*

Crepuscular and nocturnal, except in breeding season. Most often seen on the outer branches of a tree overhanging the water. Found in groups or singly. Lives on fish and frogs, but lies in wait for rather than stalks its prey. Large rounded wings present a *stumpy silhouette in flight.*

Voice: When disturbed, utters a sharp *'kwak'*. At dusk the note is a hoarse *'quark'*.

Habitat: A common resident, found on dams and rivers where there is sufficient cover. A colonial nester, usually in mixed heronries.

Distribution: Over the greater part of Southern Africa, except in the dry central and western areas.

Allied species:

PURPLE HERON *(Ardea purpurea)* (57). 89 cm. About the size of the Black-headed Heron but has a more snake-like appearance when perching. *Long thin bill* distinctive. General appearance rufous; long, thin chestnut neck boldly striped with black. In flight, the downward bulge of the neck is lower than that of other herons. Found throughout Southern Africa, except in the dry west.

YELLOW-BILLED EGRET *(Egretta intermedia)* (60). 63 cm. Medium-sized egret with *long slender neck and very short yellow bill.* Legs and feet black, the greenish yellow portion above the tarsal joint not being conspicuous in the field. Never found away from water. Found throughout Southern Africa, except in the dry central and western regions.

SQUACCO HERON *(Ardeola ralloides)* (62). 43 cm. A small, skulking, stocky, thick-necked heron. When perched, looks *pale buff;* in flight resembles the Cattle Egret. Has a very long, drooping crest and a dark-tipped, horn-coloured bill. Found throughout the eastern half of Southern Africa.

CAPE BITTERN *(Botaurus stellaris)* (71). 63 cm. A medium-sized, brown, heron-like marsh bird, richly barred and mottled. Legs and feet are green and very large; has a distinctive *booming* voice. Found only in permanent marshes in the eastern parts of Southern Africa.

LITTLE BITTERN *(Ixobrychus minutus)* (67). 36 cm. Mostly nocturnal; very small; *deep chestnut on neck;* upper wing-coverts buff. The migrant race is paler. Found along the eastern coastal belt.

DWARF BITTERN *(Ixobrychus sturmii)* (66). 25 cm. Even smaller; upper parts a *dark slate-grey.* Northern Southern Africa.

Rarer species:

BLACK HERON *(Egretta ardesiaca)* (64)

RUFOUS-BELLIED HERON (*Ardeola rufiventris*) (65)

WHITE-BACKED NIGHT HERON (*Gorsachius leuconotus*) (70)

HAMERKOP: Scopidae

This family contains only one genus and is distantly related to the Herons and Storks. It is peculiar to Africa, southern Arabia and Madagascar. The Hamerkop is the same size as the Cattle Egret and a sombre brown in colour; has a fairly long, deep bill, hooked at the tip, and a longish crest on the back of its head.

HAMERKOP   *Scopus umbretta* (72)   p. 48
    Afr Hamerkop   *Z, X* u-Tekwane
    S   Masianoke

Identification: 56 cm. A sombre brown all over, with a *blackish bill* and relatively thin blackish legs. *Crest always in evidence:* cannot be raised or lowered at will. Sexes alike, but females rather smaller. Subadults similar to adults.

Flies slowly but well. In flight, wings are notably broad and head is not drawn back. Feeds mainly on frogs and other animals captured in shallow water. When feeding, deliberately shuffles its feet to disturb creatures lying in the mud. When standing at the water's edge, sinks its head between its shoulders. Semi-nocturnal: often feeds until very late. Usually found in pairs. Courting display curious and elaborate. Enormous nests in trees or on ledges have a small entrance on the most inaccessible side.

Voice: Squeaky and reedy. Utters a yapping cackle when courting. Often calls when flying.

Habitat: Builds only near permanent water, but is found feeding even in small, temporary pools of rain-water. Often seen on highways early in the morning, picking up insects and small animals killed during the night by fast-moving traffic—but this is a very recent adaptation.

Distribution: Throughout Southern Africa, except for the north-western coastal belt.

STORKS: Ciconiidae

Tall, long-legged, long-necked birds. Their long bills are usually straight and always longer than their heads. Fly with outstretched necks. Two species, the White and the Black Storks, are palaeoarctic migrants; other members of the family confine themselves to extensive local migration. With the exception of the Marabou, which is mainly a carrion-feeder, storks are usually found near water, and particularly in vleis. Most storks have no voice, but clap their bills instead.

MARABOU STORK   *Leptoptilos crumeniferus* (73)   p. 161
   Afr Maraboe-ooievaar   *Z* Igababa
   X Inkosiamadlanga
Identification: 137 cm. Upper side a dark slate, washed with iridescent green. Underparts and ruff at base of neck white; *head, neck and chest bare*, except for a few hairlike feathers. Head a dusky crimson; neck blue; air-filled pouch in front of neck a bluish pink. *Enormous, straight, sharp bill a light horn-colour.* Legs black, often powdered white by the bird's own excrement. Sexes alike. Subadult birds similar to adults, but have more hairlike down on the bare skin.

Have a very upright stance when walking, or when standing with their heads tucked between their shoulders. *In flight, very broad wings and white bodies contrasting with dark wings* are unmistakable. Experts at soaring. Omnivorous, but feed mainly on carrion. Drive vultures off carcass without any trouble—hence the Xhosa name 'King of the Vultures'. Food picked up in tip of bill and thrown back into throat, hornbill-fashion. Usually migrate to Northern Africa, but individuals have lately been found to nest in Southern Africa.
Voice: Usually silent, but guttural croaks and squeaks are uttered by nesting colony. Clap bills freely.
Habitat: Prefer open thornveld.
Distribution: Throughout Southern Africa, except in the western and southern regions.

OPENBILL STORK   *Anastomus lamelligerus* (74)   p. 48
   Afr Oopbekooievaar
Identification: 94 cm. Adults a brownish black. Feathers of back, wing-coverts and breast have tips of shafts flattened and broadened, giving the appearance of jet or sequin ornamentation. During the breeding season these feathers have a greenish bronze gloss. *Bill heavy, and open for part of its length near the tip.* Bill dark, but whitish near base. Legs black. Sexes alike. Subadults lack ornamentation; more brown in appearance; head and neck slightly mottled with white.

Sailing flight and broad, rounded tail and projecting legs are characteristic. Feed on small aquatic animals, mainly freshwater mussels. The smaller mussels are crushed with their bills under water and washed, the larger are carried on to the bank and left in the sun to open. Birds do not return to specific mussels but eat whatever open mussels they find as they wander about. Most of the mussels are not found again by their catchers.
Voice: None.

Habitat: Always found near water fringed with grass and reeds. Also found on coastal lagoons.

Distribution: Along the eastern coastal belt and bushveld, and across the whole extreme northern part of Southern Africa.

SADDLEBILL STORK *Ephippiorhynchus senegalensis* (75) p. 161
    Afr Saalbekooievaar

Identification: 152 cm. Adults have head, neck, upper and under wing-coverts, scapulars and tail black, with a blue and green iridescence during the breeding season. Rest of the body, *including secondaries and primaries, white*. Naked crimson spot on breast. Long, bright red bill has a black band and a *yellow frontal saddle*. Legs black; joints pink. Sexes alike. Subadult has dull grey markings instead of black; back and flight-feathers mottled with sooty black; bill dark grey; legs a dull green, but with pink joints.

In its ponderous flight, in which the legs and head are kept lower than the body, the *white flight-feathers*, shoulders, back and rump, and the *black under wing-coverts* and rump are characteristic. Feeds on any small animals and insects it can find. Feeds like a heron, moving with slow, measured gait and striking at its prey with lightning speed.

Voice: None, except for bill-clapping.

Habitat: Usually found solitary or in pairs in marshy areas or on rivers. Recently found breeding on tall trees in the Kruger National Park during winter.

Distribution: In suitable localities throughout the eastern and northern regions of Southern Africa.

WOOD STORK *Ibis ibis* (76) p. 48
    Afr Geelbekooievaar (Nimmersat)   *S* Levlosyane

Identification: 96 cm. Adults white with *black flight-feathers and tail*. During breeding season mantle has a crimson fringe, and upper and under wing-coverts and inner secondaries are edged and tipped with crimson. *Long yellow bill* has slightly downward-curved orange tip; *red facial patch;* legs pinkish. Sexes alike. Subadult has head, neck and upper wing-coverts brownish; general plumage a dull grey.

Food consists mainly of aquatic animals. Bird wades through shallow water, probing with its long bill, often with its head submerged. Usually migratory from the north, but a few resident breeding colonies recently found.

Voice: Generally silent, but loud, squeaky, nasal sounds are uttered by nesting colonies.

Habitat: Usually found in small parties near water, beside rivers, dams and estuaries.

Distribution: In suitable localities throughout the greater part of Southern Africa, except in the dry western and most southerly regions.

WHITE-BELLIED STORK   *Ciconia abdimii* (78)   p. 48

Afr Kleinswartooievaar   *S* Lekololoane

Identification: 76 cm. *Breast, belly, under and upper tail-coverts, rump and lower back white;* rest of upper parts, including head and neck, black. *Bare cheeks grey* and throat-patch crimson. *Bill a greenish horn-colour,* with carmine base. Legs olive-green; joints crimson. Sexes alike. Subadults similar to adults but have dull reddish bills.

Non-breeding migrants, during the summer months found in large flocks scattered over open veld, feeding mainly on insects. Very tame, even found on playing-fields in built-up areas. Often seen soaring in thermals. Seen from the back, the bird has a very conspicuous *white lower back* when taking off. Communal roosts in trees. When resting, bird shows a white line, which is part of the upper breast, between its black neck and shoulder.

Voice: Usually silent, but flock sometimes utters a feeble peeping call.

Habitat: Frequents open veld; constantly on the move, looking for possible sources of food.

Distribution: Throughout Southern Africa, except for arid western coastal belt.

BLACK STORK   *Ciconia nigra* (79)   p. 48

Afr Grootswartooievaar   *X* u-Nocufu

Identification: 122 cm. General colour a glossy brownish black, including the whole back. *Breast, belly and under tail-coverts white.* Bill crimson; legs scarlet. Sexes alike. Subadult generally a sooty brown; head and neck grey-brown; bill and legs pale.

A shy and solitary bird, though sometimes seen in small parties. Feeds on insects and small animals. Usually a palaeoarctic migrant, although small resident populations, breeding on ledges and cliffs, have been recorded.

Voice: None.

Habitat: Prefers marshy ground, dams, rivers and estuaries.

Distribution: Throughout Southern Africa, except for the central and north-western arid regions.

WHITE STORK   *Ciconia ciconia* (80)   p. 48

Afr Witooievaar   *Z* in-Golantete

X u-Godoyiya   *S* Mokotatsie

Identification: 117 cm. Wholly white, except for *black flight-feathers and scapulars. Bill red and straight.* Red legs often powdered white with bird's own excrement—a phenomenon connected with the mechanism that regulates the bird's body temperature. Distinguished from the Wood Stork by its *white tail* and the colour and shape of its bill. Sexes alike. Subadult resembles adult, except that the black is tinged with brown.

A palaeoarctic migrant, usually found on the open veld and grassland, feeding on insects and small animals. Outbreaks of locusts and caterpillars sometimes attract very large flocks. Wintering individuals not uncommon. Often seen soaring in thermals. Not very shy. Gather in large flocks before migrating to the northern hemisphere. A few breeding pairs have recently been recorded.

Voice: None, but considerable bill-rattling.

Habitat: Most commonly found on open grassland and in vleis, also on cultivated land.

Distribution: Throughout Southern Africa, except along the arid western coastal belt.

Allied species:

WOOLLY-NECKED STORK (*Ciconia episcopus*) (77). 86 cm. Slightly larger than the White-bellied Stork. *Head and neck a woolly white;* belly white; breast and upper parts, including crown, a glossy black. In flight, under wing-coverts black: central white under tail-coverts project beyond black tail, resulting in black and white tail-pattern. Bill black with red tip; legs black. Found in the eastern and south-eastern coastal regions.

IBISES and SPOONBILLS: Threskiornithidae

Ibises are fairly large wading birds with relatively short legs and longish necks. Their long, slender, down-curved bills have a blunt tip. They are often gregarious and may nest in colonies or singly in trees, reed-beds or on ledges. Spoonbills are placed in the same family as Ibises because the young bird has an ibis bill: this only develops the characteristic spatulate tip as the bird reaches maturity. These birds extend their necks during flight and do not tuck them in between their shoulders.

SACRED IBIS *Threskiornis aethiopicus* (81) p. 48
    Afr Heilige ibis (Skoorsteenveër)   *X* um-Cwangele
    Z   um-Xwagele   *S* Lehalangone
Identification: 89 cm. Adult birds pure white, with a *bare, leathery black head and neck.* In flight, the glossy green-black tips of the flight-feathers form *a narrow trailing edge to the wing,* and a stripe of red naked skin is sometimes seen from below, at the base of the wing. In breeding plumage the innermost secondaries and scapulars end in fluffy plumes of a glossy violet-blue. Long, blunt, curved bill and legs black. Sexes alike. Subadults

have head and neck covered with short, mottled, black and white feathers, and have no plumes.

Feed mainly on insects and small animals, also carrion and offal. Obtain most of their food by probing in soft soil. Often wade in shallow water in search of food and aquatic vegetation. Ibises usually fly in V-formation. Their wing-beats are fast, and they seldom resort to gliding or soaring. Colonial nesters, often in company of Herons and Egrets. Also breed on coastal islands.

Voice: Occasionally utters a harsh croak.
Habitat: Found on coastal and inland waters. Usually feeds near water or on cultivated land. Restless, but not a regular migrant.
Distribution: Throughout Southern Africa, except in the dry western regions.

BALD IBIS *Geronticus calvus* (82)   p. 48
  Afr Rooikopibis   *S* mo-Khootlo

Identification: 79 cm. Adult birds iridescent dark green, blue and violet; iridescent coppery shoulder-patch. *Long curved bill and bony swelling on top of head a conspicuous red;* bare face and upper neck bluish. Legs a dull red. Sexes alike. Subadult has head and neck covered with short feathers, mottled in dark grey and white. Bill a dark slate, red at the base.

In flight shows pointed wings. Flight is light and buoyant, interspersed with much gliding, especially at nesting sites. Birds are gregarious and feed mainly on beetles and other insects, which they dig out of holes, even in hard soil away from water. Nest in colonies on ledges.

Voice: Noisy at nesting site, where they utter a loud, high-pitched '*keeauu-klaup-klaarp*'.
Habitat: Found in mountainous country or at sandstone krantzes, always in the vicinity of their feeding-grounds on the short grass of the open veld.
Distribution: Very limited; mainly inland, in the eastern and central regions of Southern Africa.

HADEDA IBIS *Bostrychia hagedash* (84)   p. 48
  Afr Hadida-ibis   *Z* in-Kankane
  X I-Ngagane

Identification: 76 cm. General adult plumage olive-grey, with a *greenish metallic sheen on shoulders and wings.* Head and neck a light grey; under-parts darker. Bill black, with basal half of upper mandible crimson. *Legs a dull red.* Sexes alike. Subadult similar to adult, but duller; bill shorter and straighter.

Found foraging in small parties near wooded water-courses. Feed mostly on insects and their larvae, found in soft, damp soil. Their flight is heavy; their broad, rounded wings and relatively short tail (*beyond which their legs do not extend*) are characteristic. Usually call when flying, especially when leaving communal roosts in the morning. Split up in pairs to breed; nest in trees.

Voice: A very loud '*ha-ha, ha-de-dah*', uttered in flight, and also a loud, long, mournful '*haaa . . .*'.

Habitat: Always near streams and rivers, both inland and coastal.

Distribution: Eastern half and central northern regions of Southern Africa.

GLOSSY IBIS   *Plegadis falcinellus* (83)   p. 48
     Afr Glansibis   *Z* in-Kankane

Identification: 46 cm. Head, neck, mantle, wing-shoulder and underparts a chestnut-brown; rest of plumage an iridescent green, shot with purple and bronze. In non-breeding plumage head and neck are streaked with black and white; the crown has a greenish sheen and the underparts are greyish. Eyes brown; *bills and legs a dark brownish olive*. Sexes alike. Subadult a more sooty brown; head streaked with white.

A fairly rare bird; until recently believed to be a non-breeding migrant, but breeding colonies have now been found. Sociable, usually seen in flocks. Their long, slender down-curved bills and relatively long legs are similar to those of the Curlews. These ibises, with their slender bodies, long, projecting necks and bills, and legs projecting beyond their tails, are unmistakable when seen flying in close formation. From a distance they appear to be black.

Voice: Rather silent, but sometimes utter a harsh '*kaaa-raaa*'.

Habitat: Marshy vleis and along quiet shallow waters.

Distribution: Along the eastern coastal belt and in the south-eastern regions of central Southern Africa, as well as in the central northern regions.

AFRICAN SPOONBILL   *Platalea alba* (85)   p. 48
     Afr Lepelaar   *Z* in-Kenkane

Identification: 90 cm. Adult wholly white, with a crest at the back of the head. Distinguished from the White Egrets and Herons by the characteristic *greyish-red spatulate bill*, red legs and face. Sexes alike. Subadults have brown tips on outer primaries, black legs, and heads streaked with blackish brown.

Usually seen in small parties, wading in shallow water and sweeping their bills to and fro. Also probe in soft mud. Feed chiefly on small aquatic animals and insects. When resting or sleeping, stand on one leg with head tucked back into scapulars. Usually fly in formation; flight strong and slow; head and neck extended. Colonial nesters, but keep to themselves even when breeding with other species.

Voice: A double '*aark-ark*' and a nasal '*kor*' uttered in flight.

Habitat: Always frequent lagoons, dams, and vleis.
Distribution: Throughout Southern Africa, except for the very dry western regions.

FLAMINGOES: Phoenicopteridae

Flamingoes are highly gregarious long-legged, long-necked birds, whose plumage is mainly white and pink. The scarlet and black on their wings can only be seen when the birds spread their wings or fly. Their toes are webbed; their bills are flattened on top and bent down at an angle. Feed mainly on algae and plankton found in brackish water. Fly with rapid wing-beats, necks and legs fully extended. The two species of Flamingoes in Southern Africa are often found in loose association with each other.

GREATER FLAMINGO   *Phoenicopterus ruber* (86)
Afr Grootflamink

Identification: 140 cm. General colour white, with a *slight* pink wash, not discernible from a distance. Wings crimson; flight-feathers black. *Bill pink with terminal third black.* Legs pink. Sexes alike. Subadults lack crimson on wings, which are streaked with blackish brown. Neck brownish; general appearance a dirty grey.

Feed mainly on plankton, which they sift from mud in shallow water. Head often submerged while feeding. Frequently seen standing in one place, but rotating and stamping their feet; the mud thus disturbed is sifted through the lamellae of the bill. Largely a summer migrant, but resident in suitable areas. Small nesting colonies recently found.

Voice: When disturbed, gaggle like domestic geese; also utter a harsh '*honk*', like geese.

Habitat: Shallow coastal lagoons; permanent or temporary brackish waters and pans in the interior.

Distribution: Throughout Southern Africa.

LESSER FLAMINGO   *Phoenicopterus minor* (87)
Afr Kleinflamink

Identification: 102 cm. General colour *not white but a deep pink*. Flight-feathers black; darker crimson blotches superimposed on the crimson of the wings. From a distance a flock of these birds has a definite pinkish hue. *Bill a dark carmine* with a light band near the small black tip. From a distance this band cannot be seen, and *the whole bill looks dark*. Legs a reddish pink. Sexes alike. Subadults lack pink of adults, and are a light greyish brown all over.

Feed mainly on algae found on the surface of the water. Seldom feed

PLATE 3

HAMERKOP, SPOONBILL, IBISES AND STORKS

1 **GLOSSY IBIS** *page 46*
Long slender bill and legs greenish.

2 **HADEDA IBIS** 4
General colour olive-grey with metallic reflections on the shoulder, legs dull red.

3 **BALD IBIS** 45
Long curved bill and bony swelling on top of head red.

4 **HAMERKOP** 40
Crest always evident, bill blackish.

5 **OPENBILL STORK** 41
Heavy bill open near the tip.

6 **WOOD STORK** 42
Tail and flight feathers black, long bill yellow, facial patch red.

7 **SACRED IBIS** 44
Bare leathery head and neck black.

8 **WHITE-BELLIED STORK** 43
Breast and belly white, bare cheek grey, bill horny-green.

9 **AFRICAN SPOONBILL** 46
Spatulate bill greyish-red.

10 **BLACK STORK** 43
Belly white, bill and legs red.

11 **WHITE STORK** 43
Flight feathers black, tail white, longish bill red.

PLATE 4

GEESE AND DUCKS

1 **EGYPTIAN GOOSE** *page* 51
  Patch on the breast and ring round the eye chestnut.

2 **CAPE WIGEON** 53
  Head light greyish, speculum mainly white and surrounding small
  glossy green square.

3 **SOUTH AFRICAN SHELDUCK** 52
  Male; head and neck ash-grey. Female; white on forehead, face
  and chin.

4 **WHITE-FACED DUCK** 55
  Face white, flanks barred black and white.

5 **SOUTHERN POCHARD** 55
  Eyes red, wing bar white. Female has white on face.

6 **CAPE SHOVELLER** 52
  Dark spatulate bill and yellow legs.

7 **RED-BILL TEAL** 53
  Bill reddish and cap dark.

8 **HOTTENTOT TEAL** 54
  Small size; cap very dark and bill bluish.

9 **YELLOW-BILL DUCK** 53
  Bill bright yellow.

10 **SPURWING GOOSE** 50
  Bill, frontal knob and bare skin on face red, wing shoulder white.

with heads submerged and seldom disturb mud by tramping with their feet.
Usually walk through shallow water, skimming the surface with their bills
and moving their heads to and fro in short arcs. Resident in certain
localities; breeding colonies recently found.

Voice: A goose-like '*honk*', and low croaking.

Habitat: Shallow coastal lagoons and the more permanent brackish
waters in the interior.

Distribution: Throughout Southern Africa.

DUCKS and GEESE: Anatidae

A well-known family of aquatic birds with webbed toes and relatively
short legs adapted to swimming. All these diving or surface-feeding birds
feed on animal and vegetable matter sifted through the lamellae along the
edges of their bills, and also on grass and young shoots. In most cases they
lose all their flight-feathers during the moult that succeeds the breeding
season, and become flightless for a short period. The resident species do
not have an 'eclipse' dress like those of the palaeoarctic regions. Most
species are restless or migratory, and are always on the move in search of
suitable feeding-grounds. Gregarious in habits, but do not nest in communities.

SPURWING GOOSE   *Plectropterus gambensis* (88)   pp. 48, 64

    Afr Wildemakou   *Z* i-Itoye

    S   mo-Salamotlaka

Identification: 102 cm. A large, long-legged, long-necked goose. Adult male
has upper parts black, shot with bronze and green. Underparts white. The
amount of white on face, neck, breast and shoulders varies greatly in
different individuals. Shoulders, tipped with a spur, show white in flight.
Bill, frontal knob and bare skin on face red. Feet a pinkish white. Colouring
of female generally duller. Subadults are browner and have faces wholly
feathered, and no frontal knob.

In the field this large goose appears black and white. Often found in large
numbers. Usually feed in the morning and evening, but may even feed at
night. Rest on dams and pans during the day. Often seen flying in a skein
to their feeding-grounds. Flight powerful but not fast. Very shy and wary.

Voice: A weak, whistle-like '*ker-whit*' while flying.

Habitat: Common on the larger stretches of water, and on streams and
rivers that have sheltering vegetation and are in the vicinity of open grassy
flats and cultivated land.

Distribution: Throughout Southern Africa, except in the arid western
regions.

EGYPTIAN GOOSE   *Alopochen aegyptiacus* (89)   pp. 49, 64
  Afr Kolgans   *X* i-Longwe
  S le-Faloa

Identification: 71 cm. General colour of adult male buff. Primaries, rump and tail black; outer secondaries an iridescent green; inner secondaries chestnut-olive. Upper side of wing white; underside black and white. Distinct *chestnut ring round eye; chestnut patch on breast*. Bill a mottled, pinkish flesh-colour; legs flesh-coloured. Female distinctly smaller; colouring less bright. Subadult bird has no eye-ring or spot on chest, and white has a sooty tinge. Bill and legs a greyish brown.

During the breeding season found in pairs, even on the smallest and remotest pools of water. Often nest in the old, deserted nests of larger birds, in trees or on ledges. Males very aggressive during this period. Diurnal feeders; often feed far away from water. Roost in trees or on ledges and sandbanks. After the breeding season congregate in large numbers to cast their flight-feathers.

Voice: Female a loud '*honk-honk*' and male a softer '*haah-haah*'. Often call together in duet.

Habitat: Wherever there is water.

Distribution: Throughout Southern Africa.

KNOB-BILLED DUCK   *Sarkidiornis melanotos* (91)   p. 64
  Afr Knobbeleend

Identification: 79 cm. Adult male in breeding plumage has orange-yellow patch on sides of lower belly; white of head and neck tinged with orange-yellow; *enlarged flat black knob on bill*. Upper parts black, shot with green, violet and bronze. Underparts white. *Head and neck white with black spots*. Bill and legs black. During non-breeding season knob on bill all but disappears. Female similar to male, but much smaller, and has no knob. Subadult similar to female, but has no metallic gloss.

In flight the dark under and upper wings and black tail form a sharp contrast to the white underparts, and are characteristic. Wing-beats rather slow. Often perch on trees and fly in V-formation, with an audible swishing sound. Partial to grass and water-lily seeds; also feed on aquatic and other insects.

Voice: Usually silent, but sometimes makes a short, hoarse, whistling sound when flying.

Habitat: Numbers fluctuate considerably, but in flooded shallows and marshes flocks are not uncommon. During the breeding season pairs are found on small pools in the eastern bushveld.

Distribution: North-eastern half of Southern Africa.

Allied species:

AFRICAN PYGMY GOOSE (*Nettapus auritus*) (92). 33 cm. May be identified by its very small size, greenish-black upper side, bright rufous flanks and white face and belly. In flight shows distinct white line down centre of wing. Usually found swimming among surface vegetation. Occurs in the south-eastern coastal belt and north-eastern parts of Southern Africa.

SOUTH AFRICAN SHELDUCK   *Tadorna cana* (90)   pp. 49, 64
Afr Kopereend

Identification: 63 cm. Adult male has *head and upper neck ash-grey*. Rump, tail and primaries black; secondaries green; upper and under wing-coverts white; rest of body chestnut, but lower neck, breast and under tail-coverts somewhat paler. Distinct line of demarcation between the chestnut of the body and the grey of the head. Bill and legs black. Females similar to males but have *varying amounts of white on forehead, face and chin.* Subadults generally duller in colour, with grey-brown heads and necks.

Flight pattern, especially of wings, much the same as that of Egyptian goose, but *breast without brown mark* distinctive. Feeds chiefly on vegetable matter. Gregarious except in breeding season. Spends most of the day on islands or mud-banks, sleeping or preening. Nests in burrows.

Voice: Normal call of male a sonorous '*how*'; that of female harsher and more high-pitched. Male said to give shrill screech during courtship display, and also a soft, goose-like hiss.

Habitat: Partial to dams and vleis with shallow water and wet mud.

Distribution: Confined to the southern and central regions of Southern Africa.

CAPE SHOVELLER   *Anas smithii* (94)   pp. 49, 64
Afr Kaapse slopeend

Identification: 53 cm. General body-colour of adult male a slightly mottled dark brown. Head much paler than rest of body. Blue shoulder and white-edged green speculum conspicuous in flight. *Large dark-slate spatulate bill and yellow legs* characteristic. Adult female has back more decidedly mottled, head darker and blue on shoulder duller than those of the male. Subadult similar to female, but paler underneath.

The shoveller is a very fast flier, and the wings, which are placed far back, are characteristic. When disturbed, takes off vertically from the water before flying forward. When 'shovelling' in the mud in shallow water, the head is kept well forward, and the bill virtually horizontal. Shovellers have the curious habit of swimming rapidly round each other in small circles when feeding. Gregarious out of breeding season; mix freely with other ducks.

Voice: Often utters a soft, quacking call when flying.

Habitat: Mostly found in shallow waters, especially those rich in plankton and aquatic vegetation. These waters include temporary pans and vleis.

Distribution: Throughout Southern Africa, except the north-eastern tip.

YELLOW-BILL DUCK   *Anas undulata* (96)   pp. 49, 64
    Afr Geelbekeend

Identification: 58 cm. Adult male greyish, mottled all over. *Underside of wing white, except at the base, where it is brown.* Narrow white bands above and below the greenish speculum. *Bill a bright yellow*, with black patch on ridge. Legs brown. Sexes alike. Subadult is duller above, whiter underneath; breast tinged with reddish pink.

The commonest duck in Southern Africa. Restless and highly gregarious, except when breeding. Swims high in the water; often seen up-ending while feeding. Flies with head held high. Readily resorts to 'broken-wing' display when attempting to divert attention from nest or ducklings. Active during the day; sometimes found feeding on vegetable matter and seeds on dry land near water.

Voice: A series of loud, prolonged quacks, hoarse and raucous.

Habitat: Frequents estuaries and all open inland waters, but seldom found on rivers.

Distribution: Throughout Southern Africa.

RED-BILL TEAL   *Anas erythrorhyncha* (97)   pp. 49, 64
    Afr Rooibekeend

Identification: 48 cm. Adult male a light brownish grey, slightly mottled, and darker on top. The light-coloured sides of head and throat set off the *dark cap*. The *reddish bill* is also characteristic. Legs slate-coloured. In flight, the light chestnut speculum shows a narrow dark brown line, running through it near the leading edge. Underwing grey. Sexes alike. Subadult very similar to adult but has narrower markings on underside.

Also highly gregarious, though pairing off in the breeding season. Often found in the company of other ducks. Swims fairly low in the water. Usually feeds among vegetation in shallow water. When approached a flock will close its ranks and swim away rapidly rather than take to the air. Not shy, but very active.

Voice: Male utters a soft, whistling '*whizzt*', and female a long-drawn-out '*quaaak*'.

Habitat: Found on all open inland waters, even small temporary pools. Common in flooded grasslands.

Distribution: Throughout Southern Africa.

CAPE WIGEON   *Anas capensis* (98)   pp. 49, 64
    Afr Bleekeend

Identification: 48 cm. Adult male very light in colour. *Head, neck*, upper back and underparts *a dirty white, finely speckled with black*. Lower back barred with blackish brown. Upper wing-coverts brown. In flight, *speculum is mainly white, surrounding a small, glossy, green rectangle.* Underside of wing dark. Bill pink, but black at base; legs yellowish. Sexes alike. Subadult very similar to adult, but markings on upper parts duller and smaller.

In the field this medium-sized duck appears light grey, with an even lighter head. Resident; usually found in small flocks, often in the company of other ducks. Feed by diving and up-ending. Nests often found close together.

Voice: Male utters a high-pitched whistle, usually while flying. Female gives a nasal '*quurk*'.

Habitat: Frequents large sheets of shallow water: temporary vleis, salt-pans, estuaries, and even coastal waters.

Distribution: Throughout Southern Africa.

HOTTENTOT TEAL *Anas hottentotta* (99) pp. 49, 64
Afr Gevlekte eend

Identification: 36 cm. Adult male small and dark brown, with blackish spots and mottles. *Dark cap* enhanced by buffish cheeks and throat. *Bill a bluish grey.* Wings a dark bottle-green and black, with a distinct white bar below the green speculum. *Underside of wing black and white.* Legs lead-grey. Adult female similar to male, but underparts lighter. Subadults have still lighter underparts, with markings smaller and paler.

This teal is the smallest duck found in Southern Africa. It is retiring and unobtrusive. When disturbed, will rather take shelter in the vegetation bordering the water than seek safety in flight. *Flight fast; dark back with white wing-bar very conspicuous during flight.* Usually found in pairs, but sometimes in small flocks.

Voice: A soft, high-pitched quack, and a short shrill whistle given on the wing.

Habitat: Sheltered water-ways, dams and flooded marshy ground.

Distribution: Throughout the greater part of Southern Africa, the whole southern region excepted.

BLACK DUCK *Anas sparsa* (95) p. 64
Afr Swarteend *Z* and *X* i-Dada

Identification: 56 cm. Adult male a sooty black, with *a few white spots on the back.* Neck sometimes has a white band, varying in width. *Narrow white bands above and below the bluish-green speculum. Whole underside of wing white.* Bill a bluish slate with a black saddle. *Legs yellow.* Sexes alike. Subadult browner, with buff and off-white spots on back; underparts a dirty white, mottled with sooty black.

Most active at dusk and dawn; usually rest or sleep under overhanging branches during the day. Very difficult to flush. When not obstructed by vegetation, fly very low over the water, with wing-tips all but touching the water. Fast fliers, in spite of their plump appearance in flight. Found only in pairs or small family parties. Feed mainly on small aquatic animals, but also on seeds.

Voice: A fairly loud '*quack*'.

Habitat: Seldom found elsewhere than in well-wooded mountain streams or rivers.

Distribution: In any suitable locality, but not in the north-western arid region of Southern Africa.

WHITE-FACED DUCK *Dendrocygna viduata* (100) pp. 49, 64
Afr Nonnetjie-eend

Identification: 48 cm. In the adult male the *front half of the head and throat is white;* remainder of head and neck black. White patch on underside of neck. Lower neck and shoulders a rich chestnut. *Flanks barred in black and white;* remaining underparts, rump, tail and *underside of wing, black.* Back and scapulars olive-brown, edged with buff. Bill black; legs a bluish black. Female similar to male, but has white on head; neck tinged with rust-brown. Subadult has head and neck mainly buff, and buff underparts instead of black, except under the wing.

In the field this bird looks tall, owing to its long legs and neck, and its upright stance when alarmed. Swims high in the water with head held high. Flight heavy and slow. *Rounded wings, long thin neck and feet projecting beyond the tail* are characteristic. Spends much time wading in shallow water, feeding on small aquatic animals, weeds and seeds. Usually found in large flocks, which circle around whistling when disturbed. Seldom perches in trees; prefers resting on sand-banks during the day.

Voice: A clear, high-pitched whistle: '*sip-sip-sien*'.

Habitat: Usually frequents open waters, but subject to local movements.

Distribution: Northern, central and eastern regions of Southern Africa; very rare in the south.

Allied species:

FULVOUS DUCK (*Dendrocygna bicolor*) (101). 47 cm. Similar to White-faced Duck in size and shape, but general colour (including that of the face and head) a bright tawny, with a *black line running from the nape down the back of the neck.* A blackish collar round lower neck. Perches freely in trees; in flight utters a feeble whistle consisting of two (and not three) syllables. *In flight, upper and under tail-coverts are white.*

SOUTHERN POCHARD *Netta erythropthalma* (102) pp. 49, 64
Afr Bruineend

Identification: 50 cm. General colour of adult male *a very dark blackish* *brown.* Dull chestnut sides of head and neck visible only at short range. Underparts, including underside of wings, are dusky. *Broad white wing-bar.* Bill a slate-blue, *eyes red*; legs slate-coloured. Adult female is a lighter brown; throat and feathers at base of bill are white. *A curved white line* from the eye passes behind the ear-coverts to meet the white of the throat, thus *forming a ring.* Amount of white varies in different individuals. Subadult similar to female.

This diving duck looks almost black in the field and tends to remain on deeper water, though sometimes seen in shallow water near the water's edge. Swims fairly low, with tail turned downwards and submerged, but with head held fairly high. *Wing-bar shows as a conspicuous white patch in flight.* Like all diving ducks, takes a run along the water before becoming airborne. Flight relatively fast for a diving duck. Gregarious, but pair off during the breeding season. Subject to considerable local seasonal migrations.

Voice: A low, nasal *'par-ah-ah'.* Sometimes a low-pitched quacking on the wing. During courtship male gives an explosive snorting whistle, and female a short *'quarrk'.*

Habitat: Partial to open deep water and flooded areas in the interior.

Distribution: Throughout Southern Africa.

MACCOA DUCK   *Oxyura punctata* (103)   p. 64
Afr Makoueend

Identification: 46 cm. Adult male a bright chestnut, with black head and dark-brown wings and tail; abdomen light brown. *Bill a bright cobalt-blue*; legs ash-grey. Adult female a mottled brown, slightly darker on upper side. *Chin and upper throat white. A nearly straight white line runs below the eye* from the base of the bill to behind the ear-coverts. Bill a dark greyish brown; legs a dark slate. Subadult similar to female.

Swims very low in the water; when alarmed, submerges even farther, until only the head, thick neck and back are visible. *The pointed tail is then held perpendicular to the water.* Partial to deep water near aquatic vegetation. An expert diver, feeding largely below the surface. Reluctant to fly, but flies strongly when once airborne. Gregarious, but pair off during the breeding season.

Voice: A low, wheezy, snoring *'purr-rr-rr'.* Courting call a grating *'charr'.*

Habitat: To a large extent resident; found on large and small inland waters, mostly in the vicinity of reeds and rushes.

Distribution: Throughout Southern Africa, except for the north-western and north-eastern coastal belts.

Allied species:

WHITE-BACKED DUCK (*Thalassornis leuconotus*) (104). 43 cm. Thickset; general colour ochre, barred with black. Face blackish; *white spot at base of bill.* Neck ochre. White rump mainly visible during flight. Avoids open water. Not gregarious; found only in pairs or family parties.

Rarer species:

MUTE SWAN (*Cygnus olor*) Eastern Cape; introduced.

GARGANEY (*Anas querquedula*) (97X)

EUROPEAN SHOVELLER (*Anas clypeata*) (93)

PINTAIL (*Anas acuta*)

SECRETARY BIRD: Sagittariidae

This remarkable family of birds of prey comprises only one species, characterized by terrestrial habits to which the long legs and short toes of the bird are an adaptation. Bill is of the usual hooked eagle-type. Its name is derived from the similarity of the crest feathers to the quill pen stuck behind the ear of a clerk in days gone by.

SECRETARY BIRD   *Sagittarius serpentarius* (105)   pp. 80, 96
   Afr Sekretarisvoël   *X* i-Nxanxosi
   Z u-Doye   *S* Mamalangoane
Identification: 152 cm. General colour grey; flight-feathers and feathers on tibia black. *Central tail-feathers elongated.* Multiple crest on head; bill a bluish brown; bare skin round eye orange-red. Long legs flesh-coloured. Sexes alike, but female slightly smaller. Subadult duller.

Usually seen striding about the veld alone or with its mate near by, looking for snakes or other reptiles, small mammals and insects. Kills its prey with violent blows of the feet. Can run very fast, with wings half-spread. Flies strongly and is expert at soaring. In flight, the light-coloured body and under wing-coverts, the black flight-feathers, long legs and two central tail-feathers projecting far beyond the rest of the tail, are unmistakable. Runs with outstretched wings when taking off or landing. Stick nests usually built on flat-topped acacia trees.
Voice: A deep, frog-like croak. Alarm-call a sharp '*oo-ook*', frequently repeated. Utters a high-pitched scream on the wing.
Habitat: Open savanna and grassveld, including semi-arid desert regions.
Distribution: Throughout Southern Africa.

VULTURES: Aegypiidae

Vultures are scavenging birds of prey. Most of them are large or very large, with long, broad wings required for soaring. Their powerful hooked bills and nearly bare heads and necks are an adaptation to their feeding habits. Although they live chiefly on carrion, insects like locusts are also eaten. They have excellent eyesight and can spot a carcass while soaring at a great height. The larger species have a downy ruff at the base of the hind neck, into which their heads are withdrawn when they are at rest. They nest in trees or on ledges, and usually lay a single egg.

CAPE VULTURE *Gyps coprotheres* (106) pp. 80, 96

Afr Kaapse aasvoël   *Z* Inqe
S   Rantsoe or le-Tlaka   *X* i-Hlanga

Identification: 107 cm. Adult bird has *upper parts a pale buffish white* (some specimens appear almost white). Ruff at base of neck a dirty white. Underparts a creamy white. *Head and neck bluish.* The head is covered with hair-like feathers, the neck with a sparse whitish down. Primaries and tail black; secondaries ash-brown. Under wing-coverts white. Bill horn-coloured; crop patch brown; legs bluish. Sexes alike. Subadult birds browner above and streaked below. Crop patch buffish. Ruff consists of lanceolate feathers, not down. Upper wing-coverts paler than flight-feathers.

Formerly the commonest vulture in the more southerly regions. Numbers greatly depleted by poisoned bait put out for jackals and other carnivores. At a carcass, these birds fight by taking great bounds at one another, with wings outstretched. Colonial nesters; nest on ledges. Lay a single egg.

Voice: Squealing and squabbling around a carcass.

Habitat: Partial to mountainous regions, where they roost and nest, but are found widely dispersed in search of food.

Distribution: Mainly in the southern half of Southern Africa.

WHITE-BACKED VULTURE *Gyps africanus* (107) p. 80

Afr Witrugaasvoël

Identification: 84 cm. General colour of adult male a light tawny brown, with a distinct *white rump and back* (the white is seldom seen except in flight). Bluish head and neck covered with white down; ruff fairly long and a dirty white. *Inner under wing-coverts white.* These appear as a much narrower white leading-edge in the wing-pattern, as compared with that of the Cape Vulture. Crop patch and bill dark brown; legs lead-coloured. Adult female much paler than the male. Subadult brown all over; *no white on back*. Crop patch a pale mouse-colour. Underwing pattern uniformly dark, with light streaks on coverts.

May be distinguished from the Cape Vulture by its dark face and crop patch, light neck, more uniform brownish colouring and *smaller size*. Pairs nest in loose association with others or singly in tall trees.

Voice: Squeals and hisses when fighting over carcasses.

Habitat: Mostly found in the savanna bushveld.

Distribution: Over the greater part of Southern Africa, but not the southern third.

BLACK or LAPPET-FACED VULTURE *Aegypius tracheliotus* (108)

pp. 80, 96

Afr Swartaasvoël   *X* u-Silwangangubo
S le-Tlakapipi

Identification: 109 cm. Adult birds a blackish brown. Folds of *bare skin on head and face vermilion to flesh-colour.* Underside covered in thick white down and sparse, long, narrow, dark-brown feathers. Ruff dark brown, crop patch nearly black. *Heavy bill* a greenish brown; tip yellowish. Cere blue; legs bluish. Females similar to males, but said to be larger. Subadults similar to adults but with a certain amount of white down on head and neck.

This large vulture, with a wing-span of over 284 cm, is nowhere common. Less gregarious than other vultures; usually seen singly or in pairs. Other vultures make way for it at a carcass. Having had its fill it holds aloof from the others. Nests in pairs, building a large stick nest on the crown of a tall tree. Often seen soaring with legs dangling.

Voice: A sharp, yelping call, seldom uttered.
Habitat: Partial to the savanna bushveld.
Distribution: Not in the southern third of Southern Africa. The most common vulture in the arid west.

WHITE-HEADED VULTURE *Aegypius occipitalis* (109)

p. 80

Afr Witkopaasvoël

Identification: 81 cm. General colouring of adult bird black and white. Crown, crop patch, belly, under tail-coverts and *inner secondaries white.* Bill red with dark tip, cere bluish; bare skin of head and neck lilac. Legs a pinkish flesh-colour. Ridge of white feathers at back of head gives head an angulated appearance. Sexes alike, but males slightly smaller. Subadults resemble young White-backed Vultures but are generally darker, unstreaked and have a brown head and red bill. Inner secondaries brown or parti-coloured.

Usually seen singly or in pairs, but often assemble at carcasses in fair numbers, together with other vultures. In flight, these vultures look more like eagles. Chiefly carrion-eaters, but are said to hunt and kill birds and small antelopes also. Pairs nest singly in tall trees.

Voice: A shrill chittering.
Habitat: The savanna bushveld.
Distribution: Not found in the southern third of Southern Africa.

Allied species:

HOODED VULTURE (*Neophron monachus*) (110). Length about 66 cm. This small vulture is *dark brown all over*. Down on back of head and neck a silvery brown. *Rather short rounded tail and thin, slender dark bill*. Feeds on offal rather than carrion. Tends to hang around the other vultures at a carcass and filch what small pieces it can. Sexes alike; subadults very similar to adults. Common and widely distributed over the northern regions.

EGYPTIAN VULTURE (*Neophron percnopterus*) (111). 71 cm. Slightly larger than the Hooded Vulture, but the adult bird is *wholly white, with black and grey flight-feathers*. Bill slender; bare face yellow; *tail wedge-shaped*. Subadults resemble young Hooded Vultures but have *feathered necks*. Nowhere common.

Rarer species:

PALM-NUT VULTURE (*Gypohierax angolensis*) (112)

FALCONS: Falconidae

Falcons have thickset bodies, relatively long pointed wings, exceptionally muscular feet with strong curved talons, and powerful hooked beaks in which the cutting edge of the upper mandible is notched behind the downcurved tip. The projection behind the notch is known as the 'tooth'. The true falcons catch their prey on the wing by striking with the hind claw in a swift downward stoop, but the kestrels hover over and drop on their prey. The smaller falcons are largely insectivorous. Falcons are usually found in pairs, but some species become highly gregarious during migration.

LANNER FALCON *Falco biarmicus* (114) p. 97
    Afr Edelvalk   *X* u-Ketshana
    S Phakoe

Identification: 43 cm. Adult male dark grey with darker bars above; wings and mantle blackish; *crown and nape rufous*, moustache-stripes black. A pinkish buff below. Dark, narrow, pear-shaped markings confined to flanks and under wing-coverts. Bill black with blue-grey base. Cere and legs yellow. Sexes alike, but females much larger than males. Subadults a blackish brown above, and broadly and heavily streaked below. Head a paler rufous than that of adult; moustache-stripes black.

Usually hunt in pairs, using a cliff or clump of trees as base. During normal flight *the wing-beat is relatively slow*. Active flight interspersed with short spells of gliding. Usually nest in holes in cliffs or on small thick bushes growing from cliffs. Feed mainly on small birds, but also take reptiles and insects.

Voice: A loud, metallic '*chack-chack*' and a shrill, piercing scream. A plaintive '*kweeep*' recognition call.
Habitat: Common in mountainous or open country. Less dependent on cliffs than the Peregrine.
Distribution: Throughout Southern Africa.

PEREGRINE FALCON   *Falco peregrinus* (113)
   Afr Swerfvalk

Identification: 36 cm. Adult male a dark slate above with traces of bars. *Crown a blackish slate, not rufous;* no great contrast between colour of crown and that of upper parts. Moustache-stripes black and distinct. Undersides a buffish white, heavily spotted and barred. Bill a slate-blue; cere and legs yellow. Sexes alike, but females much larger than males. Subadults a brownish black above; heavily streaked below.

Although the Peregrine is smaller than the Lanner, their markings are so similar that it is virtually impossible to distinguish between them in flight. But the *wing-beats of the Peregrine are much faster* than those of the Lanner. Usually seen sitting on a high tree or rock; often not shy. Feed mostly on medium-sized birds. Said to stoop at about 250 m.p.h. Not common; found singly or in pairs. Nest on cliffs.
Voice: A shrill, piercing '*kek-kek-kek*' and sometimes a hoarser '*kwaahk*'. Also gives a plaintive call during the breeding season.
Habitat: Prefers mountainous or hilly country, but sometimes found in large towns.
Distribution: In suitable localities throughout Southern Africa.

HOBBY FALCON   *Falco subbuteo* (115)   p. 97
   Afr Europese boomvalk

Identification: 36 cm. Above, slate-coloured and blackish, wings included. Central tail-feathers slate; rest of tail slate barred with pale chestnut. Inner webs of flight-feathers also barred with pale chestnut. Below, chin and throat whitish; moustache-stripe black. Chest to belly buff, broadly streaked with black. *Flanks and under tail-coverts chestnut.* Eyes brown; bill black; cere, eyelids and legs yellow. Sexes alike, but female slightly larger. Subadult is darker above, and the feathers have buff edges.

A relatively common palaeoarctic migrant, usually associating with Lesser Kestrels. *Very similar in appearance to the Peregrine, especially in the markings of the head* (*black crown and nape and moustache-stripe*), but much smaller and more slender-looking. Unmistakable in flight, looking almost like a swift with its long, narrow, pointed wings. Extremely agile and fast in the air; can even catch swallows and bats in flight when it feeds late in the evening.
Voice: Usually silent in winter quarters.

Habitat: Wherever there are trees.

Distribution: The greater part of Southern Africa except the south-western third.

RED-NECKED FALCON   *Falco chicquera* (117)   p. 97
Afr Rooinekvalk

Identification: 33 cm. Adult dark-grey above, finely barred with black; below, barred in black and white. *Top of head and nape chestnut. Thin black line over eye. Moustache-stripe black with chestnut tip.* Throat and chest a very pale chestnut; bill blackish; cere and legs yellow. Sexes alike, but females much larger than males. Subadult browner above, with broad black streaks on nape, and broken bars on breast and flanks.

This slender, long-tailed falcon is mostly seen on the wing. In flight the *broad black subterminal tail-band* and darkish flight-feathers are conspicuous. During the greater part of the day it shelters in the thick foliage of large trees, only becoming active towards dusk, or in the early morning. Very restless while hunting; never sits on a look-out perch for any length of time. Feeds mostly on small birds but will also take doves, reptiles and insects. Found in pairs; usually nests in Borassus Palms. Of late nests have also been found in large acacias.

Voice: A shrill, high-pitched '*kek-kek-kek*', usually uttered at dusk.

Habitat: Savanna veld, including western semi-desert regions.

Distribution: The northern half of Southern Africa.

Allied species:

AFRICAN HOBBY FALCON (*Falco cuvieri*) (116). 30 cm. Slightly smaller than the Red-necked Falcon. A dark slate above; *the whole of the underside chestnut*, with a few narrow black streaks. Distinct black moustache-stripe. Long narrow wings; appears swift-like in flight. A rare bird, seen singly or in pairs on the outskirts of forests. Largely insectivorous.

Rarer species:

TAITA FALCON (*Falco fasciinucha*) (116X)

MERLIN (*Falco columbarius*)

EASTERN RED-FOOTED KESTREL   *Falco amurensis* (119)   p. 97
Afr Oosterse rooipootvalk

Identification: 30 cm. Adult male slate-grey all over, with head and mantle blackish. Under tail-coverts and tarsal feathers chestnut. *Under wing-coverts white* (very noticeable in flight). Bill horn-coloured; legs orange. Adult female has upper parts slate-grey, faintly barred with black; throat, under tail-coverts and thighs buffish; chest, belly and under wing-coverts a buffish white, heavily streaked with black; distinct black moustache-stripe. Subadult very similar to adult female.

A winter migrant from Manchuria and Siberia. Often seen in large numbers, usually in the company of other kestrel species. Feeds mainly on the wing, and has a swift-like appearance. Captures insects such as flying termites in its claws; also feeds on small mammals.

Voice: A shrill '*ki-ki-ki-ki*'.

Habitat: Open savanna and grassveld.

Distribution: Eastern, central and northern regions of Southern Africa.

DICKINSON'S KESTREL   *Falco dickinsoni* (121)   p. 97
Afr Grysvalk

Identification: 30 cm. Above, head, back of neck, chin and throat light grey, finely streaked with black. *Rump and upper tail-coverts a uniform light grey*. Rest of upper side a blackish slate; inner webs of flight-feathers and *tail distinctly barred*. Below, chest to under tail-coverts a blackish grey, finely barred with black. Large eyes red-brown; bill slate; cere and legs yellow. Sexes alike. Subadult browner than the adult, particularly below.

A not very common kestrel, usually found singly or in small parties, sitting on the branches of dead trees or on palms standing in the open. Perches very upright. Normally drops on to its prey or hawks insects in the air, but can fly very fast. Has been seen catching bats long after sunset. The size of the eyes is probably related to its crepuscular habits. Although it occasionally hovers, its general behaviour is not that of a kestrel. A reasonably tame bird that can be approached fairly closely.

Voice: Call a curious '*lill-loo*', rarely heard, and uttered on the wing.

Habitat: Low-lying country, especially places in which tall palms grow.

Distribution: In the north-eastern third and central northern regions of Southern Africa.

GREATER KESTREL   *Falco rupicoloides* (122)   p. 97
Afr Grootrooivalk

Identification: 36 cm. General colour of adult male tawny. Head and nape streaked with black; remainder of upper side broadly barred with black. Chin uniformly tawny; sides of face, throat and upper chest streaked with black. Under wing-coverts whitish. In flight, primaries appear black. Bill bluish; legs yellow. Sexes alike. Subadults usually look darker than adults.

The streaked appearance of this bird is unmistakable. Found singly or in pairs. Spends most of its time sitting on trees or telegraph poles, on the look-out for its prey, which consists chiefly of insects. Seldom hovers; flies strongly with rapid wing-beats, and can take small birds on the wing. Not dependent on cliffs; usually nests in trees, and sometimes on old nests of larger birds. Usually not shy.

Voice: Usually silent, but sometimes utters a weak whistle at its nest.

Habitat: Open savanna.

PLATE 5

FLIGHT PATTERNS OF GEESE AND DUCKS

1 **SOUTH AFRICAN SHELDUCK** *page* 52
(From below). Male. Body uniform brown, paler on breast. White of under wing-coverts forming greater part of the wing. (Female has white head.)

2 **KNOB-BILLED DUCK** 51
(From below). Dark wings uniform, neck spotted.
2a, male in breeding plumage.

3 **SPURWING GOOSE** 50
(From below). Amount of white on body variable. White of under wing-coverts broadening towards the body.

4 **CAPE SHOVELLER** 52
(From above). Heavy bill and light-blue wing shoulders.

5 **WHITE-FACED DUCK** 55
(From above). Head white and feet projecting beyond the tail.

6 **EGYPTIAN GOOSE** 51
(From below). Dark spot on the chest. White of under wing-coverts less than half the wing.

7 **CAPE WIGEON** 53
(From above). Speculum mainly white and surrounding glossy-green rectangle.

8 **YELLOW-BILL DUCK** 53
(From above). Bill yellow, speculum green with white edge in front and at the back.

9 **SOUTHERN POCHARD** 55
(From above). White window stretches across greater part of the wing.

10 **HOTTENTOT TEAL** 54
(From above). (Small size.) Dark cap, green speculum with white trailing edge.

11 **RED-BILL TEAL** 53
(From above). Dark cap, speculum light chestnut with narrow dark-brown line in front.

12 **BLACK DUCK** 55
(From above). Back has white spots, speculum green with white edge in front and at the back.
12a, white spots on back conspicuous.

13 **MACCOA DUCK** 56
(From above). Short wings uniform brown.
13a, pointed tail held vertically; female has white on the side of face.

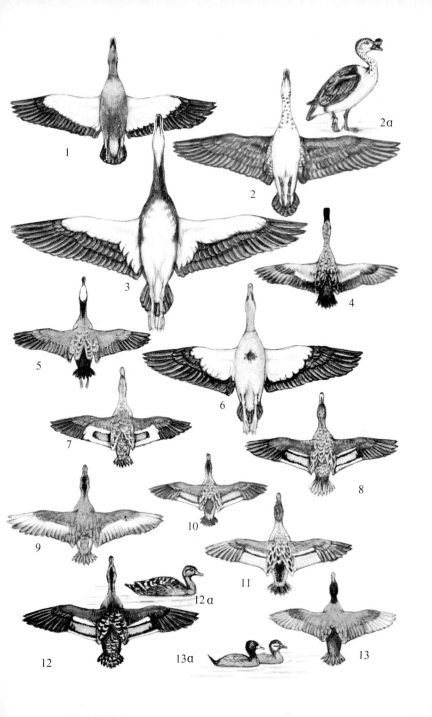

PLATE 6

ALBATROSSES, SHEARWATERS AND PETRELS

1 **WANDERING ALBATROSS** *page* 24
Adult male: primaries black.
a, sub-adult; brownish with white face mask.

2 **GIANT PETREL** 26
Bill with large tubular nostrils.

3 **YELLOW-NOSED ALBATROSS** 25
Bill black with yellow line down centre of upper mandible.

4 **BLACK-BROWED ALBATROSS** 24
Bill yellow, dark line through eye.

5 **GREAT SHEARWATER** 27
Dark cap set off by white collar; upper tail-coverts tipped whitish.

6 **SOOTY SHEARWATER** 28
Under wing-coverts whitish.

7 **CAPE HEN (WHITE-CHINNED PETREL)** 26
Bill yellowish-green; chin usually white, may be brown.

8 **CAPE PIGEON (PINTADO PETREL)** 26
General appearance mottled. Head to mantle and sides of face sooty
black, base of tail white.

9 **COMMON STORM PETREL** 28
In flight legs do *not* extend beyond tail. Tail squarish.

10 **WILSON'S STORM PETREL** 28
In flight legs extend beyond tail. Tail square.

Distribution: Throughout Southern Africa, except for the southernmost tip.

ROCK KESTREL   *Falco tinnunculus* (123)   p. 97

Afr Kransvalk   *Z* u-Matebetebeni
X   in-Tambanana   *S* Seotsanyana

Identification: 30 cm. Adult male has top of head to nape, sides of neck, moustache-stripe, rump, upper tail-coverts and tail a dark blue-grey. Tail-feathers have black ends tipped with white. *Other upper parts chestnut and spotted.* Below, a pale rufous chestnut, with black streaks and spots. Bill greyish; legs yellow. Adult female larger than male, and has less blue in the grey of the head. Tail distinctly barred. Subadult similar to the female but has a rufous crown.

Not gregarious; pairs never stray far from their usual haunts. Often seen hovering or sitting at some vantage point. Feeds mainly on insects, mice and small lizards. When feeding on the wing, holds its prey in both feet, in the true falcon manner. Prefers to nest on ledges.

Voice: Alarm note '*kir-r-r-re*'; also a plaintive '*klee-klee*' and a shrill '*kek-kek-kek*'.

Habitat: Mostly hilly or mountainous country, but in populated areas may even be found in towns, where it nests on tall buildings.

Distribution: Throughout Southern Africa.

LESSER KESTREL   *Falco naumanni* (125)   p. 97

Afr Kleinrooivalk

Identification: 28 cm. In the adult male *top of head, nape, rump and upper tail-coverts are dove-grey.* Tail dove-grey with broad black subterminal band and white tip. Wing-coverts and secondaries grey; primaries black. *Other upper parts a pale chestnut, without spots.* Underparts a pale pinkish buff, sparingly spotted; underside of wing white. Bill bluish; legs yellow. The only kestrel with white and not black claws. Adult female looks much larger than the male. Above, a light brown barred with black. Tail also has a black subterminal band but is brown and barred. Rump grey; all flight-feathers black. Below, buff-coloured, with elongated black spots. Subadult similar to female.

A winter migrant from Europe and Asia. Gathers in huge flocks to roost in tall trees, usually in towns. During the day birds disperse over the open countryside, foraging mainly for insects. Sometimes hover, but prefer to hunt from perches—particularly telegraph poles. When feeding on the wing, convey food to bill with one foot, not both.

Voice: A high-pitched, chattering '*chik, chik, chik*'.

Habitat: Prefers grassveld and open savanna.

Distribution: Throughout Southern Africa, except the very arid western coastal belt.

PYGMY FALCON *Poliohierax semitorquatus* (126) p. 97
   Afr Dwergvalkie

Identification: 18 cm. Adult male blue-grey above, with a white rump; collar on hind neck and ear-coverts white; *tail- and flight-feathers black with white spots and bars*. Below white. Bill yellowish, with a darker tip; legs orange-yellow. Adult female has a maroon mantle. Subadult birds have feathers of crown, neck and back edged with a brownish red.

This very small shrike-like falcon is found in pairs, and usually nests in active Sociable Weaver nests. It has the typical woodpecker flight, using fast wing-beats and gliding up to its perch. Usually perches on the topmost branches of dead trees. Has the habit of sunning itself during the first few hours of the morning, and is completely inactive during this time. Feeds mainly on insects and lizards.

Voice: A high-pitched '*ti-tirr-tirr-tr*', often repeated.
Habitat: Dry thornveld.
Distribution: Semi-arid and arid central, northern and western regions of Southern Africa.

Allied species:
WESTERN RED-FOOTED KESTREL (*Falco vespertinus*) (120) 30 cm. Adult male similar to Eastern Red-footed Kestrel male, except that the head and mantle are not blackish and the *under wing-coverts are a dark grey*. The adult female differs from the Eastern species in that the underside is pale chestnut and *not spotted*; head and nape chestnut. A winter migrant.

CUCKOO FALCON (*Aviceda cuculoides*) (127). 41 cm. The same size as a Lanner Falcon. Easily distinguished by the slight crest at the base of the crown. Grey throat and chest; other *underparts boldly barred with chestnut*; tail broadly barred with black. Found only in the southern and eastern forested areas.

Rarer species:
GREY KESTREL (*Falco ardosiaceus*)

KITES, EAGLES, BUZZARDS, HAWKS, and ALLIES: Aquilidae

Kites have long wings and as a rule forked tails. Their feet are weak. They have a graceful flight and are often seen soaring. Often associated with human habitations. The local species is usually solitary, but the migratory species is often seen in large flocks.

Eagles are the largest diurnal birds of prey. They have feet feathered to the base of the toes, only snake-eagles having bare legs. Most eagles live in mountainous and more open country, although some are forest-dwellers.

As a rule the females are larger than the males. Before reaching maturity, subadults pass through various plumage phases, only one of which will be described.

Buzzards are medium-sized birds with bare legs, broad wings and shortish square tails. They are conspicuous birds, as they spend much time in the air.

Sparrow-hawks and goshawks are mainly birds of the woodlands and forests. They have broad rounded wings, long tails and long legs. They fly rapidly and with great agility through the trees in pursuit of their prey.

Chanting goshawks live in more open country and are usually seen sitting on some exposed perch.

Harriers are slender birds with long wings and tails. Usually seen flying low and gracefully, with slow, regular wing-beats, over open or marshy ground. When they spot their prey on the ground, they twist suddenly, and drop on to their prey with talons extended.

BLACK KITE   *Milvus migrans* (128)   pp. 81, 128
Afr Swartwou

Identification: 56 cm. General colour brown; underparts more chestnut, sparsely streaked with black. Conspicuous *pale head* with black streaks. Body relatively small; wings long and, in flight, bent back at the carpal joint. *Tail long and slightly forked*; bill black. Cere and legs yellow. Sexes alike. Subadult paler, with broad streaks of buff on the underparts and the brownish head.

A non-breeding summer migrant from Europe; found in very variable numbers. Usually seen sailing gracefully overhead, though often on the ground. Feeds on insects, small mammals, carrion and offal. Roosts in flocks in large trees.

Voice: Alarm note a shrill '*queeu-kiki-kiki-kik*'; also has a high-pitched wavering call like that of a gull.

Habitat: Not selective.

Distribution: Throughout Southern Africa, except along the western coastal belt.

YELLOW-BILLED KITE   *Milvus aegyptius* (129)   pp. 81, 128
Afr Geelbekwou   *Z* i-Nkoinyana
X u-Tloyile   *S* Mankloli

Identification: 56 cm. General colour, including that of head, brown. In flight the long wings are bent back at the carpal joint. *Long tail distinctly forked. Bill of adult yellow.* Cere and legs also yellow. Sexes alike. Subadult lighter in colour and has a brown bill tipped with black.

Head pulled back in flight; bird has a distinctive habit of steering with its tail, and twisting it from side to side. Often feeds on the wing, bending its head to reach the food held in its talons. Feeds on insects, small animals and carrion. Resident; usually seen singly. Often seen on the ground.

Voice: A plaintive mew, ending in a trill. The alarm-note is a grating 'chew-chi-chi'.

Habitat: Prefers open to mountainous country.

Distribution: Throughout Southern Africa.

(Considered by some authors to be a race of the Black Kite.)

BLACK-SHOULDERED KITE *Elanus caeruleus* (130)   pp. 81, 128

Afr. Blouvalk   *Z* u-Kholo

X isa-Gogonda   *S* Matlakokoane

Identification: 30 cm. Adult bird grey above and white below, with *black shoulders and primaries*, and a *short square tail*. Eyes crimson; bill black; cere and legs yellow. Sexes alike. Subadult bird has breast and sides of neck a pale chestnut. Flight-feathers tipped with white; back darker than that of adult.

A very common bird of prey, of very un-kitelike habits. Slow flight like that of a gull. At each slow wing-beat the bend of the wing comes far forward. When gliding, holds its outstretched wings slightly above the horizontal. Hovers over its prey like a kestrel, checking its descent a few times before finally dropping on to its prey with outstretched legs. Very conspicuous on the exposed perches, e.g. telegraph poles and wires, that it prefers. When the bird is sitting its wing-tips droop below the short tail, which is often moved rhythmically up and down. Silhouette of perching bird seen from the back is triangular, the wing-tips forming the apex. Feeds mainly on insects and rodents; rarely attacks other birds, which show no fear of it. Seen singly or in pairs.

Voice: A loud, clear piping whistle; alarm-note a harsh scream.

Habitat: Prefers open country to thick bush; often found in cultivated areas and sometimes even on the outskirts of towns.

Distribution: Throughout Southern Africa.

Allied species:

BAT HAWK (*Macheirhamphus alcinus*) (131). Buzzard-like in appearance and size. General colour almost black; nape slightly crested. Bases of head- and nape-feathers white; bill small and black; *large gape and enormous yellow eyes*. Crepuscular habits: lives in dense trees and usually emerges only at dusk, when it pursues bats, swifts and swallows in a dodging, falcon-like flight.

HONEY BUZZARD (*Pernis apivorus*) (132). General colour variable. Similar to Steppe Buzzard, but head smaller and more slender. Tail longer and more rounded. Lores *not* bare with bristles, but covered with small, scale-like feathers. Legs *feathered in front half-way down tarsus*. In flight, tail shows two dark bands near its base.

BLACK EAGLE   *Aquila verreauxi* (133)   pp. 80, 96
    Afr Witkruisarend (Dassiearend)   *Z* and *X* n-Kozi
    S Ntsu

Identification: 86 cm. Totally black, except for a *white back and rump*. Cere, toes and bare skin around the eyes yellow. Legs feathered to the base of the toes. Since the inner web of the primaries is white, *light windows are seen in the wings in flight*. The spear-shaped wings are narrower at the base and at their broadest about one-third of the distance from their tips. Sexes alike. Subadults first fawn-coloured; then dark brown with a light tawny crown; nearly black below except that feathers have broad tawny tips.

Experts at soaring. When displaying execute tight 'loops' after a dive or a vertical climb. A pair will sometimes fall spiralling earthwards with talons interlocked. Single birds or pairs are usually seen soaring along cliffs, or sitting on high rocks. Feed mainly on rock rabbits but will also take game-birds.

Voice: A loud, yelping cry, usually uttered at the nest.

Habitat: Found only in mountainous country.

Distribution: Throughout Southern Africa.

TAWNY EAGLE   *Aquila rapax* (134)   pp. 80, 96
    Afr Grootbruinarend   *Z* n-Kozi
    S Ntsukobokobo

Identification: 69 cm. A fairly uniform rufous brown; the head, abdomen and thighs a brighter rufous. (*Plumages vary from dark to pale brown.*) Primaries a bronzy black; *tail dark brown, relatively short and rounded.* Cere, gape and toes yellow. The tarsi are feathered. Sexes alike. Subadults paler in colour; often very light below. Two pale wing-bars are shown in flight.

This eagle is very sluggish. Largely a carrion feeder, although it sometimes kills small animals. Usually seen in the company of vultures and other carrion-feeders at carcasses.

Voice: A high, rasping '*cow*' or a raucous yelping cry.

Habitat: Not found in heavily-forested regions; prefers any type of open or lightly-wooded country.

Distribution: Throughout Southern Africa, but rare in the southern regions.

WAHLBERG'S EAGLE   *Aquila wahlbergi* (137)   p. 80
    Afr Kleinbruinarend

Identification: 58 cm. Medium-sized; uniformly dark and bronzy, except for the crown, which is greyish. Slight crest on nape. Cere, gape and toes yellow. Tarsi feathered. Plumages vary from dark to light brown, the light cream-coloured phase being very rare. *Tail relatively long and squarish.* Sexes alike. Subadult browner above; more tawny below.

In flight appears slender, with long narrow tail and wings. Although an expert soarer, it often forages on the wing. Large numbers are attracted by insects disturbed by veld fires. Often found sitting on tree-tops. Feeds mainly on insects and small animals.

Voice: A melodious two-noted whistle '*pay-pay*'; a rapidly-repeated greeting call '*kyip-kyip-kyip*' and a harsh, screaming alarm-call.

Habitat: Frequents wooded regions in which there are open spaces.

Distribution: In suitable localities throughout Southern Africa, except the southern third.

AFRICAN HAWK EAGLE *Aquila fasciata* (141) p. 81
Afr Grootjagarend

Identification: 66 cm. Upper parts a brownish black; mantle and rump have a more or less mottled appearance, since the white bases of the feathers show through. Underside white with black streaks. *Tail barred, with a broadish black subterminal bar.* Feathers on tarsi white. Vicious yellow-brown eyes. Cere and toes a yellowish green. Female much larger than male and usually more heavily streaked. Subadult has several intermediate plumages but is generally a blackish brown above, with head a rufous brown, and streaked. Underside a tawny rufous, with thin dark shaft-streaks. These are often confined to the lower throat and flanks.

Found in pairs. This fearless bird is a true hunting eagle and normally hunts from low altitudes, surprising its prey (which consists chiefly of game-birds) with a low rush in the open, and killing it on the ground. It is an expert soarer, and shows a *prominent white window in the wing.* Sometimes hovers like a kestrel.

Voice: A melodious double-noted '*kluee-kluee*' and, more rarely, '*klu-klu-klu-kluee*'. The alarm-note is a yelping cry.

Habitat: Usually found near high trees along water-courses or high wooded hills.

Distribution: Along the southern and eastern coastal belt and in the eastern and northern regions of Southern Africa.

MARTIAL EAGLE *Polemaëtus bellicosus* (142) pp. 80, 96
Afr Breëkoparend

Identification: 86 cm. A large, fierce, powerful bird with a *short rounded crest that is not always conspicuous.* Upper parts, including flight-feathers, ash-brown. The throat and chest to the level of the crop and the under wing-coverts are also ash-brown. *Chest, belly, flanks and tarsal feathers white, but sparingly spotted with dark ash-brown.* Eyes yellow, bill black, cere a yellowish green and toes whitish. Sexes alike, but male much smaller than female. Subadult grey-brown above; *underside, including tarsal feathers, white.*

Usually seen alone, perched on a dead tree. Dropping from the tree, it skims over the ground to strike its unsuspecting prey, which is instantly killed. Also stoops from a great height to take larger animals like small antelope. Feeds chiefly on game-birds and small animals. In flight the tail looks relatively short, and the wings long and narrow. Under wing-coverts spotted. Occasionally hovers facing the wind.

Voice: A ringing call, long drawn out: '*kloo-ee-kloo-ee-kloo-ee*'. Also a low growling '*quolp*'.

Habitat: Mountainous and open wooded country.

Distribution: Throughout Southern Africa.

CROWNED EAGLE *Polemaëtus coronatus* (143)   pp. 80, 96
    Afr Kroonarend   *Z* u-Kozi
    S mo-Koatatsi

Identification: 90 cm. A powerfully built eagle with a *long rounded crest* (like a halo), a relatively long tail and thick legs. Upper side blackish. *Flight-feathers ash-coloured, barred and tipped with black.* Tail broadly barred. Underparts white, heavily barred and mottled with pale brown and black. Tarsal feathers finely mottled. Eye and gape yellow; bill black, cere dusky. Toes yellow. Sexes alike, but female larger than male. Subadult very pale: mottled light ash-brown above and white tinged with light chestnut below. Head whitish. *Tarsal feathers and flanks have small black spots.* Passes through darker intermediate stages.

In flight, the long tail and relatively short, broad, rounded wings are like those of a giant sparrow-hawk. Often seen soaring above the trees, folding up and dropping like a stone into the trees below. A very agile flier, in spite of its size, and can thread its way through tall trees with great skill. A very noisy bird. Feeds chiefly on monkeys, game-birds and small antelope caught in open glades.

Voice: A large variety of musical whistles. While perching, gives a loud melodious '*koi-koi-koi*' or '*kee-kee*'. During display, male utters a shrill, high-pitched '*keewik-keewik*'.

Habitat: A true forest eagle, but also found in open country with patches of forest on rocky hills.

Distribution: In suitable localities along the southern and eastern coastal regions of Southern Africa.

Allied species:

LONG-CRESTED EAGLE (*Lophaëtus occipitalis*) (138). Medium-sized: 56 cm. Looks almost black. *Long lax crest, which can be erected, unmistakable.* Underside of wing white; ends of flight- and tail-feathers distinctly barred. Found in forest strips and well-watered park-like country, usually sitting at some exposed vantage-point.

BOOTED EAGLE (*Aquila pennata*) (139). Medium-sized: 56 cm. A summer migrant, occurring in two colour phases: both dark brown above, and below either brown or white, tinged with buff and streaked with dark brown. In its dark phase very similar to Wahlberg's Eagle but smaller, and more thick-set in appearance. In flight, light phase shows a row of black spots at end of under wing-coverts.

AYRES' HAWK EAGLE (*Aquila dubia*) (140). Medium-sized: 56 cm. *Smaller and paler than African Hawk Eagle;* underparts more heavily blotched, with heavy drop-like spots. Nape distinctly crested. Underwing shows a series of conspicuous bars; tail shows narrow bars in flight. Some individuals have white foreheads and eye-stripes. A forest-dweller, found in the eastern coastal belt and central northern regions.

LIZARD BUZZARD   *Kaupifalco monogrammicus* (144)   pp.81, 128
    Afr Akkedisvalk

Identification: 36 cm. Thickset. General colour grey, finely barred below. *Throat white with a conspicuous longitudinal black line down the middle.* Under wing-coverts and *rump white. Tail dark with one or two white bands only visible from behind.* Eye chestnut; bill black; cere, bare skin around eye, and legs orange. Sexes alike. Subadult has brown chest and upper parts slightly darker, mottled with pale buff.

Sedentary habits. Flight (during which *white rump* is conspicuous) very direct, with alternate flapping and gliding. Usually flies low and glides upwards to perch. Occasionally soars. Feeds mainly on insects and lizards. Small birds appear to show no fear of it.

Voice: A clear, ringing '*kluh* . . .' followed by a quick succession of '*klu-klu-klu*' notes.

Habitat: Open park-like country, even semi-desert bush, and edges of forests.

Distribution: The eastern, central and northern regions of Southern Africa.

BROWN SNAKE-EAGLE   *Circaëtus cinereus* (145)   p. 80
    Afr Bruinslangarend

Identification: 76 cm. Dark brown all over. *Under wing-coverts dark brown*; flight-feathers a silvery grey, and unbarred. When sitting upright has a frill of feathers at the back of the head that gives it an *owl-like* appearance. Eyes large and yellow; bill black; cere greyish. *Unfeathered legs off-white.* Sexes alike. Subadult a paler brown. The bases of the feathers, including those of the under wing-coverts, white, producing a mottled effect.

Usually seen singly, sitting on an exposed perch, and easily identified by its *whitish bare tarsi* and owl-like head. Occasionally soars but habitually flies low. Flight rather clumsy. Feeds mainly on reptiles, especially snakes.

Voice: A loud, low-pitched '*kok-kok-kok-kauuw*', uttered while flying or sitting.

Habitat: Savanna and thorn-tree country.

Distribution: Eastern, central and northern Southern Africa.

BLACK-BREASTED SNAKE-EAGLE   *Circaëtus*
     pectoralis (146)   pp. 80, 96
     Afr Swartborsslangarend

Identification: 66 cm. Upper parts, including large head and chest, dark brown. Underparts white; throat whitish. Large eyes yellow; bill blackish; cere olive-yellow. *Unfeathered legs off-white.* Sexes alike. Subadult has several intermediate plumages. The young birds are a tawny brown above and mottled cinnamon below. Throats and heads finely streaked with black. At a later stage the underside is white with a few dark spots.

This bird looks like a smaller edition of the Martial Eagle, except that its *legs are unfeathered, and its breast not spotted.* Hunts mainly by soaring. When perched, with feathers on nape erected, it *resembles an owl.* Hovers like a kestrel. Tail has three dark bands and a white tip. *Under wing-coverts white and not spotted* like those of Martial Eagle. Trailing edges of wing barred with black. Diet not restricted to reptiles but includes small animals.

Voice: A loud shriek while soaring.

Habitat: Prefers open country, even arid regions. Avoids heavily wooded areas.

Distribution: Throughout, except the extreme south-western tip of Southern Africa.

FISH EAGLE   *Haliaëtus vocifer* (149)   pp. 80, 96
     Afr Visarend   *Z* i-Nkazi
     X   i-Nkwaza

Identification: 74 cm. Adult strikingly coloured in white, black and chestnut. *Head, chest, tail and back white; flight-feathers and scapulars black; abdomen, upper and under wing-coverts dark chestnut.* Eyes, cere and legs yellow. Bill black. Sexes alike. Subadults have several intermediate plumages. General colour of young bird a blackish brown, head included. All the feathers are tipped with chestnut-brown, which gives the bird a mottled appearance. Older birds have buffish white chests, heavily streaked with black; blackish brown abdomens and off-white legs.

These beautiful birds are invariably found in pairs where large trees grow, and are still fairly common. Usually seen flying over the water or perched on a dead bough over the water. Though subsisting mainly on dead or stranded fish this bird can also execute a magnificent stoop and take fish that are swimming near the surface in its talons. Usually checks the stoop before striking the water, but sometimes submerges before catching the fish. Mobs other fish-eating birds and robs them of their prey. Has been known to catch water-birds and small mammals.

Voice: A wild, yelping cry with great carrying power. Calls with head thrown back, even on the wing. Pair often calls together.

Habitat: Found along rivers, dams, lakes, and even the seashore (preferably where large trees grow).

Distribution: Throughout Southern Africa.

BATELEUR EAGLE *Terathopius ecaudatus* (151)   pp. 80, 96
    Afr Berghaan (Stompstertarend)   *Z* i-Ngqungulu
    X i-Ntakayimpi   *S* 'Ntsu

Identification: 60 cm. Adult male has upper parts black and chestnut, with ash-brown shoulders. Underside black with *white under wing-coverts. Very short chestnut tail. Secondaries wholly black* (see flight pattern). Nape crested. Eyes brown; bill black and reddish orange; *cere and legs reddish orange.* Adult female similar to male except that secondaries are *tipped with black, grey above and white below* (see flight pattern). When perched, *female has folded wing grey*, not black. Subadults pass through several intermediate plumages. Young birds wholly brown; tail relatively long. Older birds a darker brown, mottled with black; tail shorter. Bill black and greenish yellow; legs a bluish white, subsequently turning reddish.

These eagles are nearly always on the wing. Their very short tails (in the adult the feet project a little beyond the tail) and long, upswept, pointed wings are unmistakable. While soaring the bird always keeps its *head well down*, as if looking behind it. Usually seen travelling at great speed, but not too high, across country, and not soaring aloft in circles. In flight often rocks from side to side; is capable of remarkable aerobatics. Feeds mainly on carrion, especially small dead animals; rarely seen in the company of vultures at a carcass. Also takes small animals, and even flying termites.

Voice: A loud, explosive, yelping '*caw*'—almost a bark. Also a loud, high-pitched scream.

Habitat: Not found in cultivated areas; prefers open wooded country, even semi-desert regions.

Distribution: Throughout Southern Africa but not in the extreme west.

JACKAL BUZZARD *Buteo rufofuscus* (152)   pp. 81, 128
    Afr Jakkalsvalk   *Z* in-Hlandhlokazi
    X in-Hlandhlokazi   *S* Khayoane

Identification: 53 cm. Colour variable. Adult black above. The *chestnut tail* has a single black bar near its tip, visible only from above. Sides of face, chin, throat or upper breast black (some individuals have a white chin and throat); breast and chest chestnut, with or without black. Other underparts may be nearly black, or else barred or streaked with chestnut or black. Secondaries a pale grey, barred and tipped with black. Primaries black with basal half greyish. Bill dark; cere and legs yellow. Sexes alike. Subadult mottled with brown above; flight-feathers brown to ashy brown. Tail a brownish chestnut, barred with black. Underside variable; some have brown streaks. Thighs chestnut and dusky brown.

Usually seen perched motionless on some vantage-point or soaring with stiffly-spread wings. In flight tail appears shortish and wings broad. Feeds mainly on small animals and insects. Often seen feeding on small animals killed on the roads.

(The AUGUR BUZZARD is a race of the Jackal Buzzard and is *wholly white* below. Found only in the dry western regions).

Voice: Call said to resemble that of a jackal. Also has other, twittering calls.

Habitat: Prefers mountainous country, but its range extends to the neighbouring plains.

Distribution: Throughout, except for the central and north-western regions of Southern Africa.

STEPPE BUZZARD   *Buteo buteo* (154)   pp. 81, 128
    Afr Bruinvalk   *X* u-Magoloda
    S   Nkholi

Identification: 50 cm. *Adult plumage very variable.* Generally dark brown above; feathers edged with chestnut. Below, chestnut or ashy brown, more or less barred. Underside of flight-feathers white; under wing-coverts ash-brown or chestnut, more or less barred. Several bars on tail. Eyes, cere and legs yellow. Bill a bluish horn, with a black tip. Sexes alike. Subadults much browner; underside a deep buff with dark-brown blobs and streaks.

A very common summer migrant; usually seen singly, sitting on telegraph poles and other vantage points, scanning the ground for insects. While flying and soaring, shows the *broad wings* typical of buzzards. *Tail longer than that of Jackal Buzzard.* Also feeds on small animals taken on the ground.

(The MOUNTAIN BUZZARD, which has a broad light band across the lower chest, is a local resident race found only in the southern and south-eastern forested regions.)

Voice: A shrill, squeaky, mewing *'kee-you, kee-you'*.

Habitat: Open woodland, even semi-desert regions.

Distribution: Throughout, except the western coastal belt of Southern Africa.

KITES, EAGLES, BUZZARDS, ETC 77

Allied species:
FASCIATED SNAKE-EAGLE (*Circaëtus fasciolatus*) (147). 60 cm. General colour a blackish brown above; sides of face, chin and chest ash-brown; breast and belly broadly barred with whitish and greyish brown; *tail with two distinct pale bars*. Confined to the northern half of the eastern coastal belt.

LAMMERGEYER (*Gypaëtus barbatus*) (150). Upper parts, wings and tail (above and below) a dark ash-grey with light streaks. Head, nape, neck and underparts a golden brown. *Black beard-tufts, long wedge-shaped tail and long wings unmistakable*. When the bird is diving, its wings are pointed and it looks like an enormous falcon. Only found in the high mountains of the central south-eastern region. Length 112 cm.

Rarer species:
STEPPE EAGLE (*Aquila nipalensis*) (135)

LESSER SPOTTED EAGLE (*Aquila pomarina*) (136)

BANDED SNAKE-EAGLE (*Circaëtus cinerascens*) (148)

LONG-LEGGED BUZZARD (*Buteo rufinus*)

LITTLE SPARROW-HAWK *Accipiter minullus* (158) p. 112
   Afr Kleinsperwer
Identification: 25 cm. Above, anything from slate to almost black; *upper tail-coverts white*. Throat white; flanks washed with chestnut; rest of underparts whitish, with close, narrow, grey and rufous bars. Underside of wing barred. *Tail has two white 'eye'-spots* when seen from the back. Eyes orange-red; bill black; cere and legs yellow. Sexes alike. Subadult a dark brown above; feathers edged with buff. Upper tail-coverts white, tipped with black. Buff or white below, streaked or spotted with dark brown drop-like blobs.
   Mostly seen in flight, as it is inconspicuous when perched. A very fast flier, catching its food, which consists mainly of small, seed-eating birds, in flight.
Voice: A high-pitched '*kik-kik-kik-kik*' and a sharp '*kee-kee-kee-kee*' at the nest.
Habitat: Found mainly in thick bush or isolated stands of large trees, even near built-up areas.
Distribution: In the eastern, central and northern regions. Not found in the extreme south or in the western arid region of Southern Africa.

BLACK GOSHAWK *Accipiter melanoleucus* (159) p. 112
   Afr Swartsperwer
Identification: 58 cm. *A large black-and-white bird*; black above and white below, with *only flanks mottled in black and white*. Tail has narrowish bars.

Underside of wing barred. Eyes orange; bill black; cere and legs yellow. Sexes alike. Subadult mottled with dark brown and buff above; *below* a deep tawny buffish colour *streaked all over with black. Legs are bare, not feathered* like those of subadult African Hawk Eagle. Chin and throat of subadult often white. (The black colour-phase has the underparts black, except for a white throat.)

A rare and local forest species, also venturing into open wooded country, including plantations near built-up areas. A fast, dashing flier, feeding on medium-sized birds (including poultry) and small mammals. In flight tail appears long. Bird is said to fly with slow wing-beats while displaying.

Voice: A ringing '*ku-ku*' during the breeding season. Its other call, '*keep-keep-keep*' has great carrying power.

Habitat: Found in wooded and forested areas.

Distribution: Locally, in the eastern third of Southern Africa.

AFRICAN GOSHAWK   *Accipiter tachiro* (160)   p. 112
   Afr Afrikaanse sperwer

Identification: 43 cm. *Dark grey to blackish above;* feathers on nape have white bases, sometimes giving a mottled appearance. Cheeks grey. Tail has indistinct broad bars (some individuals have *faint white spots on tail*). *White, narrowly barred with chestnut and grey, below.* Eye a brownish yellow; bill a bluish horn; cere and legs yellow. Sexes alike, but female much larger than male. Subadult a brownish black above; feathers tipped with buff; head mottled white and dark buff. Below, a pale tawny blobbed with black. Throat has black streaks.

A forest bird that attacks from cover and can follow its prey through thick foliage at full speed. In the early morning it circles high up, alternately flapping its wings and gliding while uttering its shrill cry or making a clicking sound every few seconds. This display often lasts for many minutes. Sometimes seen soaring over mountainous country. Perches on tops of trees.

Voice: A shrill, often repeated '*wut-wut*' and a harsh '*scree*'.

Habitat: Found in wooded and forested country, and even in towns; can be a menace to poultry.

Distribution: In the south-eastern, eastern and north-western regions of Southern Africa.

GABAR GOSHAWK   *Melierax gabar* (162)   p. 112
   Afr Witsperwer   *S* Mamphoko

Identification: 36 cm. Grey above, including sides of face and upper wing-coverts. *Upper tail-coverts white.* Flight-feathers brownish and barred; tail an ashy grey with a white tip, and broadly barred with black. Below, chin, neck and chest a paler grey; other underparts, including under wing-coverts, barred with dark grey and white. Eye crimson; bill a bluish horn with a black tip; cere and *legs orange-yellow*. Sexes alike. Subadult a blackish brown above; feathers tipped with buff; *rump white*. Below, throat and chest streaked and remainder barred with russet-brown. Tail and wings barred like those of adult.

A much more *slender* bird than the Lizard Buzzard. (Black phase completely black, even to upper tail-coverts. Tail and underside of flight-feathers distinctly barred.) A common species, which keeps to cover and sits on the inside of trees. More sluggish than the other goshawks. Feeds on small birds, lizards and insects.

Voice: A high-pitched, chattering '*ki-ki-ki-ki*', and a tinny cry, kept up for long periods.

Habitat: Thorn-tree and park-like savanna, not dense forest.

Distribution: Throughout, except in the extreme south-western part of Southern Africa.

PALE CHANTING GOSHAWK *Melierax musicus* (165) pp. 81, 112
Afr Bleeksingvalk

Identification: 63 cm. Upper parts, including the head and neck, a darkish grey. Breast, belly and thighs barred in white and grey. *Secondaries whitish*, with grey bars and vermiculations. *Upper tail-coverts white*. Central tail-feathers a uniform grey; others white, tipped with broad blackish bars. Under wing-coverts mainly white. Eyes reddish; *bare facial skin and cere a reddish orange*; bill blackish; *legs red*. Sexes alike. Subadult grey-brown above, including the wings; rump white with brown spots or streaks; tail broadly barred. Sides of face brown, streaked with black; chin and throat white and streaked; chest brown and streaked; rest of underparts broadly barred—almost blobbed—with brown and white.

A pale, long-legged, inoffensive hawk, found in open country. Usually seen sitting very upright on tall dead trees or telegraph poles. Flight slow and deliberate, almost gull-like. Looks very large and light-coloured on the wing, but relatively slender when perched. A sluggish bird, obtaining most of its food on the ground. Hunts walking about, like a small edition of a Secretary Bird. Feeds mainly on lizards, snakes and insects, including termites.

Voice: A peal of clear, beautiful notes, usually uttered during a dipping display-flight executed at daybreak at a great height, but also while perched. Alarm-note a short, high-pitched '*wheee*' and also '*kek-kek*'.

Habitat: Open country, including very arid areas.

Distribution: Confined to the drier western and southern regions of Southern Africa.

PLATE 7

SECRETARY BIRD, VULTURES AND EAGLES
(FLIGHT PATTERNS OF ADULTS)

1 **SECRETARY BIRD** *page* 57
Central tail feathers projecting beyond long legs.

2 **BATELEUR EAGLE** 75
Legs project beyond short tail. Black trailing edge of wing is broader
in male than in female.

3 **WAHLBERG'S EAGLE** 70
Tail fairly long and squarish. General impression is that of a slender
bird.

4 **BLACK VULTURE** 59
Under wing-coverts show distinct, thin white line. (Often soars with
legs dangling).

5 **WHITE-HEADED VULTURE** 59
Secondaries white.

6 **WHITE-BACKED VULTURE** 58
Under wing-coverts form fairly narrow, whitish leading edge of
uniform width.

7 **CAPE VULTURE** 58
Under wing-coverts form whitish edge broadening towards the body.

8 **FISH EAGLE** 74
Head and tail white.

9 **BLACK-BREASTED SNAKE-EAGLE** 74
Under side of wing mostly white; tail has *three* distinct dark bands.

10 **TAWNY EAGLE** 70
Heavy brown bird, no distinct wing pattern.

11 **BROWN SNAKE-EAGLE** 73
Under wing-coverts dark brown, tail banded.

12 **CROWNED EAGLE** 72
Wings broad; entire under side mottled. Tail relatively long.

13 **MARTIAL EAGLE** 71
Head and breast blackish, general impression of under wing darkish.
Tail with numerous bands.

14 **BLACK EAGLE** 70
Distinct large window extending towards body. (White rump often
visible in flight).

PLATE 8

KITES, BUZZARDS, GOSHAWKS, HARRIERS
(Flight patterns of adult birds)

1 **AFRICAN HAWK EAGLE**   *page* 71
Conspicuous white windows, broadish black subterminal tail-bar.

2 **BLACK KITE**   68
Head pale and bill black—long tail slightly forked.

3 **STEPPE BUZZARD**   76
Underside of flight feathers whitish, tail fairly long.

4 **YELLOW-BILLED KITE**   68
Long tail distinctly forked—bill yellow.

5 **JACKAL BUZZARD**   75
Shortish tail chestnut; underside variable.

6 **PALLID HARRIER**   83
Ends of primaries black, rump white.

7 **BANDED GYMNOGENE**   84
White bar on black tail; broad wings have black trailing edge.

8 **PALE CHANTING GOSHAWK**   79
Rump white, primaries black, secondaries whitish.

9 **AFRICAN MARSH HARRIER**   82
White shoulder patch—wings broad.

10 **BLACK HARRIER**   83
Rump white, tail barred with ashy grey.

11 **DARK CHANTING GOSHAWK**   82
Rump barred, primaries black, secondaries uniform grey.

12 **LIZARD BUZZARD**   73
Black line down centre of throat, white bar on tail.

13 **OSPREY**   84
Blackish triangular wrist patch, tail heavily barred.

14 **BLACK-SHOULDERED KITE**   69
Wing shoulders and primaries black.

DARK CHANTING GOSHAWK *Melierax metabates* (163) pp. 81, 112

Afr Donkersingvalk

Identification: 56 cm. Very similar to the Pale Chanting Goshawk, but *general colour darker. Secondaries and upper wing-coverts a uniform grey*, not speckled. *Upper tail-coverts barred* with grey. Eyes brownish; bill a blackish horn; cere, facial skin and legs vermilion. Sexes alike. Subadult differs from that of the Pale Chanting Goshawk in that its upper tail-coverts are not streaked and spotted, but barred in black and white. Brown streaks on chin and chest extend to breast. Narrow bars on belly, not blobs.

Usually found sitting at the top of a tree or flying low, like a harrier, in search of its prey. Feeds on lizards, small rodents and insects, which it catches on the ground. Less sluggish than the Pale Chanting Goshawk.

Voice: A prolonged, musical piping. Alarm-note a loud '*kek*'.

Habitat: Found in well-wooded country.

Distribution: Confined to the north-eastern parts of Southern Africa.

Allied species:

RED-BREASTED SPARROWHAWK (*Accipiter rufiventris*) (156). 41 cm. Above, dark slate to blackish, including upper tail-coverts. Below, tawny rufous, faintly barred with darker rufous—including sides of face. Flight-feathers dusky and barred. Tail has a white tip and is barred in dusky black and grey. Cere and legs yellow. Found along the southern and eastern coastal belt, and from there northwards.

OVAMBO SPARROWHAWK (*Accipiter ovampensis*) (157). 36 cm. Above, a pale grey; feathers on nape have a white base, occasionally giving a mottled effect. *Little or no white on rump*. A darker grey on throat and rump. White below, *distinctly* barred with grey. Under tail-coverts not barred. White-tipped tail distinctly barred. Cere and legs a reddish orange. Found in the dry thornveld along streams and rivers in the northern third of Southern Africa.

LITTLE BANDED GOSHAWK (*Accipiter badius*) (161). 36 cm. Above, a pale blue-grey, cheeks included. Feathers on nape have white bases that are sometimes visible. Below, white and *faintly* barred with pale grey. *Upper tail-coverts grey*. Tail barred in black and white (but outermost tail-feathers often unbarred). Cere and legs a yellowish orange. Often sits on exposed perches. Partial to leafy trees near water. In flight, tail looks rounded and wings relatively long. Not found in the dry western and south-western regions.

AFRICAN MARSH HARRIER *Circus ranivorus* (167) pp. 81, 112

Afr Afrikaanse vleivalk   *S* Mankholi

Identification: 48 cm. Above, a darkish brown with white flecks. Flight-feathers ashy grey, barred with blackish. Underside of primaries whitish and barred. *Upper tail-coverts a pale chestnut.* Under wing-coverts checkered in chestnut and white. Tail barred. Underparts brown, indistinctly streaked with dark rufous. Eyes yellow; bill black; cere and legs yellow. Sexes alike. Subadult a blackish brown with pale chestnut markings on nape, mantle and upper wing-coverts. *White band across chest;* flight-feathers not barred. Some individuals are a dark brown all over.

In flight, the harrier shows a *whitish shoulder-patch.* It seldom alights on the ground. It is usually seen flying low, with slow wing-beats, skimming over vegetation and pouncing on its prey in a somersault-like twist. Feeds mainly on small birds, rodents and frogs. Also eats birds' eggs. Can soar to great heights. Although very local it sometimes strays far from its usual marshy habitat.

Voice: A mewing cry.

Habitat: Local; prefers marshes and the margins of lakes.

Distribution: Throughout Southern Africa, except in the dry central region.

PALLID HARRIER   *Circus macrourus* (168)   pp. 81, 112

Afr Bleekvleivalk

Identification: 48 cm. Adult male a uniform pale blue-grey above; *upper tail-coverts white,* barred with pale grey. Below, white; neck and chest tinged with grey. *Ends of primaries a dark slate, almost black,* but not the first and second, which are greyish. Eyes yellow; bill black; cere a greenish yellow; legs yellow. Female and subadult both brown above and light tawny below, streaked with brown. *Rump white.* (In the field the female and subadult cannot be distinguished from those of Montagu's Harrier.)

A non-breeding migrant, mostly found over dry grassland and not confined to marshy ground. Hardly ever perches in trees. Spends a good deal of time on the ground and is often seen flying very close to the ground, which it systematically quarters. Feeds mainly on grasshoppers, other insects and small animals. In flight the blackish wing-tips and long tail are unmistakable. (Black wing-tips less conspicuous than those of Montagu's Harrier.)

Voice: A shrill, querulous '*kek-kek-kek*'.

Habitat: Prefers dry grassland to swampy areas.

Distribution: In suitable localities throughout Southern Africa except the dry western and southern regions.

BLACK HARRIER   *Circus maurus* (169)   pp. 81, 112

Afr Swartvleivalk

Identification: 53 cm. General colour black; feathers of nape have white bases, which sometimes give it a mottled appearance. Primaries edged with silvery grey. *Upper tail-coverts white.* Tail has a white tip and is broadly barred with ashy grey. Below, a blackish brown, with a few white spots on lower breast and under tail-coverts. Under wing-coverts black. Underside of flight-feathers mainly white, but have black tips. Eyes yellow; bill black; cere and legs yellow. Sexes alike. Subadult a chocolate brown above; feathers have broad buff tips. Below, tawny; chest and flanks broadly streaked with dark brown. Rump white; tail and wings like those of adult, but under wing-coverts tawny and mottled with brownish black.

This harrier is a fairly rare resident species, usually found near dams, vleis and rivers, but in somewhat drier areas than the Marsh Harrier. Also flies close to the ground when hunting. Is sometimes seen soaring over breeding territory. Feeds mainly on small animals and insects.

Voice: A shrill, jarring cry when calling its mate.

Habitat: Any open country, not necessarily marshland.

Distribution: Confined to the southern third of Southern Africa.

BANDED GYMNOGENE   *Polyboroides radiatus* (171)   pp. 81, 128
     Afr Kaalwangvalk

Identification: 66 cm. A long-legged, long-winged, long-tailed bird, with a narrow, rather vulturine head. Above, grey with black spots. Scapulars and inner secondaries show broken black and white barring. *Long tail black with a broad whitish bar*, conspicuous in flight. Long nape-feathers form a lax crest. Below, throat and chest grey; belly, flanks and under tail-coverts distinctly barred with black and white. Tips of flight-feathers black; under wing-coverts grey and mottled. Eyes dark brown; bill blackish; *cere, bare face and feet yellow*. Sexes alike. Subadult wholly brown; generally paler below; mottled off-white and brown. Distinguished from other subadult raptors by its lax crest and long tail, wings and legs.

This curious long-legged hawk has *broad wings*; in flight these make it look much larger than it really is. It has a slow, floppy flight, and seldom soars. Often seen clinging to tree-trunks and scrambling about with flapping wings, in search of lizards. Also raids weaver nests by hanging upside down, flapping its wings and robbing the nests with its feet. Also hops along the ground with wings outspread, chasing insects and other small animals. While displaying, flies in circles with fast wing-beats, calling shrilly.

Voice: A shrill, mewing '*peee-wooo*', long drawn out.

Habitat: Prefers park-like country, and is found in cultivated areas.

Distribution: In suitable localities in the eastern half of Southern Africa.

OSPREY   *Pandion haliaëtus* (172)   pp. 81, 128
     Afr Visvalk

Identification: 63 cm. Above, a dark ashy grey to blackish brown; *head and nape whitish* and blackish brown. Below, throat, lower breast, belly and thighs white. *Chest brownish and spotted*. Tips of flight-feathers a dark slate (appear as dark trailing edge in flight pattern). Underside of wing mottled in brown. In flight, *dark triangular wrist-patch conspicuous from below.* Eyes yellow; bill black; cere blue; legs a bluish slate. Sexes alike. Subadult similar to adult but has less white on crown and nape. Feathers of upper parts broadly tipped with buffish white.

A cosmopolitan bird, but not at all common in Southern Africa. It may have migratory habits. Usually seen perched on a dead tree or branch overhanging the water. When fishing, alternates flapping flight with spells of gliding. Hovers for a few seconds before dropping on to fish, disappearing in a cloud of spray. Carries fish in talons to nearby perch. Often victimised by Fish Eagles. Eats only fish.

Voice: A descending whistle '*tchip, tchip, tchip*' and a clacking '*chick-chick*'.
Habitat: Found only on rivers, dams and coastal lagoons.
Distribution: Throughout Southern Africa, except the dry western regions.

Allied species:
MONTAGU'S HARRIER (*Circus pygargus*) (170). 43 cm. Adult male grey above, white below. Under wing-coverts and belly streaked with chestnut. *Primaries black;* distinguished from Pallid Harrier by *blackish band on secondaries.* Female and subadult similar to those of Pallid Harrier. Habits similar to those of other harriers, but does sometimes perch in trees. A summer migrant, seldom found in the dry western and southern regions.

Rarer species:
EUROPEAN MARSH HARRIER (*Circus aeruginosus*)

GAME BIRDS: Phasianidae

Francolins, partridges and quails are chicken-like terrestrial birds, with shortish tails. Sexes generally alike. Some of the species take to trees to roost, and when threatened by their enemies. The larger species, the francolins and partridges, are resident and local in their distribution; the smaller, the quails, are restless and make extensive local migrations. They nest on the ground and lay fairly large clutches. They feed on seeds, insects, molluscs and bulbs, which are obtained by scratching. Most of the species are gregarious outside the breeding season and have distinctive call-notes. The former range of certain species has been radically reduced by cultivation and shooting. Quails are skulking little birds, generally seen only on the wing, after having been flushed. The cryptically coloured partridges tend to squat when disturbed, but francolins usually take to the wing.

COQUI PARTRIDGE   *Francolinus coqui* (173)   p. 113
   Afr Swempiepatrys   *Z* i-Swempe
Identification: 28 cm. Above, the adult male is black, chestnut and greyish

brown, streaked and barred. *Head and neck a rufous yellow*; top of head darker. Chest and lower neck barred in black and white; other underparts more buffish, and barred with black. Primaries grey. Only the male is spurred. Adult female has a white throat bordered by a thin black line. A second thin black line runs above the eye and halfway down the neck. General colour, *especially on chest, a brownish wine-colour*. Eyes orange-red; tip of bill blackish and base yellow. Legs yellow. Subadult resembles adult female, but is more buffish below, with paler barring, and has no chestnut above.

The smallest of the partridges, usually found in small coveys. Difficult to flush, but when once airborne fly a considerable distance before settling again. In flight *dark chestnut outer tail-feathers* are distinctive. When crossing open ground move very slowly and stealthily, with bodies pressed close to the ground so that the feet are not visible. Feathers on head can be raised to form a short crest. Feed mainly on seeds and insects.

Voice: A loud, penetrating '*kwee-kit, kwee-kit*' or '*swem-pi, swem-pi*', can be heard throughout the day. Alarm-call a softish '*chirr-rrrrr*'.

Habitat: Prefers grassy country with trees and shrubs.

Distribution: Throughout the northern half of Southern Africa, but not in the north-western coastal belt.

CRESTED PARTRIDGE   *Francolinus sephaena* (174)   p. 113
Afr Bosveldpatrys   *Z* isi-Kehle

Identification: 36 cm. Adult male has grey-brown feathers on top of head that can be raised to form a *short inconspicuous crest. Distinct white line above the eye*. Neck and upper breast whitish, with triangular chestnut spots. Upper wing-coverts and scapulars a pale chocolate-brown, with broadish white shaft-stripes. Lower back and upper tail-coverts a pale olive-brown. Belly and flanks buffish, with dusky vermiculations. Flight-feathers olive-brown. Eyes hazel; bill brown; legs red. Adult female similar to male but has mantle, scapulars and rump barred. Has no spurs. Subadult similar to adult but has a buff eyebrow, and chest more finely streaked.

Perch freely in trees and have the habit of *folding their tails double vertically and cocking them at an angle over their backs*. This makes them look like bantams. Not easily flushed, preferring to slink off into cover when danger threatens. *Tails look dark in flight*. Feed on bulbs, seeds, berries and insects.

Voice: The loud, ringing call of the male sounds like '*kwerri-kwetchi*' and is very often answered by the female. Call repeated over and over again. Birds especially noisy at dawn and dusk.

Habitat: Found only in matted bush, particularly in the vicinity of koppies and dry water-courses. Venture into the open to feed.

Distribution: In suitable localities in the northern half of Southern Africa, but not in the north-western coastal belt.

GREY-WING PARTRIDGE   *Francolinus africanus* (176)   p. 113
   Afr Bergpatrys   *Z* in-Tendele
   S   Khuale

Identification: 33 cm. Adult male has top of head and nape mottled black and tawny. *Upper wing-coverts greyish*, barred with buff. Flight-feathers a dusky grey, more or less barred with tawny. Rest of upper side mottled in grey and black, with narrow buff bars and whitish shaft-streaks. Relatively broad streak from behind the eye down side of neck, moustache-stripe and chin to lower neck are all finely mottled in black and white. Throat whitish, mottled with grey. *Central streak down side of neck tawny*. Below, *chest is chestnut, mottled in tawny and grey*; other underparts have narrow bars and mottles in black, white and buff. Chestnut spots on flanks. Tail blackish. Eyes brown; bill a darkish slate; legs a yellowish brown. Sexes alike, but female not spurred. Subadults buff or white below; belly and breast barred rather than mottled with black. General colour duller.

In flight, the wings of this thickset partridge are not wholly grey, for the bases of the flight-feathers are rufous. Usually found in large coveys. *When flushed the birds rise separately, squeaking shrilly* and scattering in different directions. Outer tail-feathers show black in flight. Feed on seeds, bulbs and insects.

Voice: A penetrating, clear, ringing call, often repeated: '*pip-pip-pleu*' or '*squee-eee-kee-oo*'.

Habitat: Confined to grassy patches on hillsides in mountainous areas.

Distribution: Southern third of Southern Africa.

REDWING PARTRIDGE   *Francolinus levaillantii* (178)   p. 113
   Afr Rooivlerkpatrys   *Z* in-Tendele
   X   isi-Kwatsha   *S* Khoale

Identification: 38 cm. Adult male has top of head brown and tawny, bordered by a thin, speckled, black and white streak. *Sides of face and neck tawny.* A speckled black and white streak runs from the gape through the dark ear-coverts and down the side of the neck, broadening to form a *black and white patch round the base of the neck*. Mantle, scapulars and rest of upper side a mixture of black and brown, with buff barring and shaft-streaks. *Flight-feathers a pale chestnut with dusky tips*. Chin and throat white with a tawny border. Chest and flanks a rufous brown with buff markings. Belly and under tail-coverts brownish and barred. Tail dusky. Eyes brown; bill dusky but yellowish at base. Legs a dull yellow. Sexes alike, but females not spurred. Subadult has the black and white mottles of patch on lower neck replaced by brown spots, so that the 'necklace' is less distinct. General colour paler.

Commonly found in family parties. Fly strongly and far when flushed, swerving along the contours of the terrain. Are not easily flushed a second time. Fond of sunning, drying and preening themselves in dry open patches. Feed on seeds, bulbs and insects.

Voice: A shrill and often-repeated '*chirrya-cheep, chirrya-cheep*'.

Habitat: Frequent long grass in sheltered valleys in moist and preferably mountainous regions.

Distribution: The south-eastern third of Southern Africa.

RED-BILLED FRANCOLIN   *Francolinus adspersus* (182)   p. 113
Afr Kalaharifisant

Identification: 38 cm. In the adult male all the upper parts, including tail and top of head, are earth-brown, *finely barred and vermiculated* with lighter and darker colours. Flight-feathers earth-brown. *Lores black.* Below, finely barred in black and white, except for under tail-coverts, which are barred in brown and buff. Eyes brown; *bare skin round eye yellow; bill red*; legs orange-red. Sexes alike, but females not spurred. Subadults have some black markings on mantle and scapulars. Below, ashy brown with white spots and indistinct dusky bars. Bill a dark purple.

Very difficult to flush; run for thick cover rather than fly. Often found in large coveys. Feed mostly in the open, on insects, seeds and young shoots.

Voice: Extremely noisy, especially in the mornings and evenings, when their harsh crowing call increases in volume and tempo.

Habitat: Dry wooded regions; partial to the thick bush in dry watercourses. Seldom found far from water.

Distribution: Central, northern and north-western regions of Southern Africa.

NATAL FRANCOLIN   *Francolinus natalensis* (183)   p. 113
Afr Natalse fisant   *Z* isi-Kwehle

Identification: 38 cm. Adult male: top of head a dark earth-brown; nape, sides of face and throat finely mottled in blackish and white. Other upper parts vary from greyish brown to dark brown, with variable buffish and black markings and chestnut shaft-streaks. Primaries earth-brown. Below, chest to belly brown, the feathers having buffish edges and bars that become larger on the belly. Chest sometimes barred. Flanks and under tail-coverts brownish, with darker markings. *No bare skin round eye*, but a *dark-brown line from the nostril through the eye includes the ear-coverts.* Eyes brown; *bill orange-red;* legs a bright red. Sexes alike, but females not spurred. Subadult has more black above and below; chest and upper parts tinged with chocolate.

A common but shy francolin, usually found in small family parties. Although a strong flier it is not easily flushed, for when threatened it takes refuge in trees, in which it also roosts. *When surprised and flushed, flies up with a loud, harsh 'kek-kek-kek'*. May feed in cultivated fields if cover is at hand, but usually feeds in dense shrub, on seeds, berries, insects and molluscs.

Voice: A harsh *'kwaali-kwaali-kwaali'*; several birds may often be heard calling together.

Habitat: Found mostly in acacia scrub; partial to dense riverine vegetation and bush-covered outcrops of rock.

Distribution: In suitable localities in the eastern third of Southern Africa.

Allied species:

SHELLEY'S PARTRIDGE (*Francolinus shelleyi*) (177). 33 cm. Similar to the Redwing Francolin, but *lacks the broad black and white 'necklace'* and has throat a uniform white. *Flanks a bright chestnut*, with buffish shaft-streaks. Flight-feathers chestnut, with grey tips. Tail and bill grey; legs yellow. Sexes alike, but females not spurred. Found only in the eastern parts of Southern Africa.

ORANGE RIVER PARTRIDGE (*Francolinus levaillantoides*) (179). 36 cm. Similar to the Redwing Partridge, but the thin black and white streaks over the eye and down the side of the neck *broaden into a patch, but do not join* either on nape or on lower neck. Chin and throat white. Rest of underparts buffish, with large dark chestnut marks on chest and flanks. Bill greyish; legs lemon-yellow. Sexes alike. Found in the drier central and north-western regions.

CAPE FRANCOLIN (*Francolinus capensis*) (181). 43 cm. A large dark francolin, general colour earth-brown. All the feathers have thin whitish edges and markings. Chin and throat appear to be spotted with dark brown. *Flanks have broad white shaft-stripes*. Flight-feathers earth-brown. *Bill and legs a dullish red*. Sexes alike. Confined to the south-western tip of Southern Africa.

Rarer species:

KIRK'S PARTRIDGE (*Francolinus rovuma*) (175)

HARTLAUB'S FRANCOLIN (*Francolinus hartlaubi*) (184)

SWAINSON'S FRANCOLIN   *Francolinus swainsonii* (185)   p. 113

Afr Bosveldfisant

Identification: 41 cm. Adult male: above, general colour a dark earth-brown, with blackish markings and shaft-stripes. Nape, sides of face and neck lighter; appear to be mottled in buffish and black. Underparts lighter than upper; feathers have dark shaft-stripes and are sometimes edged with chestnut. Eyes brown; *upper mandible black, lower reddish. Bare skin round eyes and on chin and throat red; legs black*. Sexes alike, but females not spurred. Subadults have broad darker markings on scapulars, and sides of face more buff. Below, a deep buff with blackish bars and whitish tips to feathers. *Chin and throat* are partially feathered and *whitish, not red*.

Usually found singly or in small family parties. Have a very *upright stance*. They are great runners, and when alarmed, run with snakelike movements through the grass. During the late afternoon, often found in the open—for example on the roads in the game reserves. Males can be seen at sunrise and sunset, sitting on an elevated perch and crowing. Usually dig for their food, and are often seen in cultivated fields bordered by sheltering vegetation. Roost in trees. When startled, fly up with a loud whirring of wings.

Voice: A harsh crowing: '*kwahli-kwahli*' repeated five or six times, decreasing in volume, but increasing in tempo. A harsh '*kek-kek-kek*' in flight when startled.

Habitat: Mostly near water in the bushveld.

Distribution: In the northern half of Southern Africa, except in the coastal regions and the very arid central western area.

RED-NECKED FRANCOLIN *Francolinus afer* (188) p. 113
Afr Rooikeelfisant *Z* and *X* i-Nkwali

Identification: 41 cm. Adult male: top of head earth-brown; sides of face and neck finely mottled in black and white. Moustache-stripe blackish; rest of upper parts earth-brown with blackish brown shaft-stripes. *Bare skin round eye and on chin and throat red*. Other underparts *broadly streaked with black or chestnut and white*. (Shaft-stripes are black, with white edges.) Eyes brown; *bill (both upper and lower mandibles) and legs red*. Sexes alike, but females not spurred. Subadults have feathers of underparts edged with chestnut. Chin and throat slightly feathered and whitish.

Usually found in small family parties. Often seen in clearings and on the road in the early morning and late afternoon. Strong, fast fliers, seeking refuge in the thick foliage of trees when alarmed. When startled into flight, utter a harsh, unmusical '*kek-kek-kek*'.

Voice: Very noisy. The cock crows at sunrise and sunset: a harsh '*koraki-koraki-chorrr-chorrr*', fading away at the end. A clucking alarm-call when roosting in trees.

Habitat: Found in thick bush at the edge of forests or cultivated land and in savanna country with plenty of cover.

Distribution: In the south-eastern and eastern coastal regions of Southern Africa.

HARLEQUIN QUAIL   *Coturnix delegorguei* (190)   p. 113
Afr Bontkwartel

Identification: 18 cm. Adult male brown above, with buff bars and distinct straw-coloured shaft-stripes. Distinct white line above the eye. Below, *throat white*, with broadish black centre line and girdle, and a *white bib on lower neck. Underparts mainly black, but sides of chest and flanks are a bright chestnut, with black markings.* Under tail-coverts a bright chestnut. Eyes chestnut; bill blackish and legs pinkish. Adult female has a white chin and throat. Cheeks and sides of neck buffish, spotted with black; eye-stripe buff. Underparts a dull chestnut with scale-like markings; usually a blackish bib on lower neck. Subadult similar to female, but has black spots on chest.

A summer migrant from tropical Africa, appearing sporadically in different localities throughout its range. May descend on an area, breed and disappear again within a few weeks. When flushed, utters a low-pitched *'peet'* and flies quite a distance before settling again. Feeds mainly on seeds, but also on insects and young shoots.

Voice: Male gives a loud, ringing call: *'twee-twit, twee-twit'* that is often repeated.

Habitat: The drier treeless grassveld, particularly near vleis.

Distribution: Throughout Southern Africa, except the southern, western and arid central regions, and along the western coastal belt.

Allied species:
AFRICAN QUAIL (*Coturnix coturnix*) (189). About 18 cm. Adult male is paler above, with a distinct straw-coloured streak down the crown of the head. Has a buffish eye-stripe. The throat, which has a black centre patch, and the cheeks are chestnut; the chest and belly buffish. Flanks and sides of chest a light chestnut, with broad off-white streaks. Female similar to male but throat is whitish, without black patch; chest-feathers have blackish edges. Also a summer migrant with irregular local movements. Found throughout in suitable grassy areas. Distinctive call: *'quit----quit-quit'*, often repeated.

Rarer species:
BLUE QUAIL (*Coturnix adansoni*) (191)

GUINEA-FOWLS: Numididae

Guinea-fowls are larger than francolins but similar in shape, also having drooping hindquarters. They are blackish in colour, with small white or pale blue spots. They have no spurs, and except for some hairy bristles, their heads and necks are naked. They have either a casque or a topknot of feathers. Highly gregarious, but pair off during the breeding season. Roost in trees and nest on the ground. Feed mainly on insects, grubs, bulbs and seeds.

HELMET GUINEA-FOWL   *Numida meleagris* (192)

(See silhouette)

Afr Gewone tarentaal   *Z* and *X* i-Mpangele
S   Khaka

Identification: 58 cm. Adult male: general colour blackish, thickly spotted with white. Chest usually finely barred and lightly spotted. Eyes a reddish brown; *bare skin on head and neck blue*; penduline wattles blue with red tips. Bony part of head and base of casque a reddish brown; tip of casque horn-coloured. Bill reddish to light horn. Legs blackish. Sexes alike. Subadults more brown than black, with white streaks on the neck-feathers. Casques shorter and blackish.

In breeding season found only in pairs; when chicks are about half-grown, the birds congregate in large flocks, sometimes numbering several hundred. Strong fliers but prefer to run. Take refuge in trees when threatened. Their value in the control of weeds and insects has lately been realized, and large flocks are now protected in cultivated areas.

Voice: A bisyllabic whistle '*too-teu*', often repeated at roosting time, and a grating '*chit-chit-tchirrr-tchirrr-tchirrrrrr*'.

Habitat: In wooded country and grassland, always near water.

Distribution: Throughout Southern Africa, except in the dry central and western regions.

CRESTED GUINEA-FOWL   *Guttera edouardi* (193)

Afr Kuifkoptarentaal   *Z* i-Mpangele
S   Khaka

Identification: 50 cm. Adult male: general colour black with small pale blue spots. Underlying chestnut spots on scapulars, mantle and underside create the impression of a chestnut wash. Collar adjoining bare skin lacks blue spots and is black and chestnut. *Head crested with thin, curling black feathers.* Outer primaries a light chestnut; secondaries have blue streaks. Eyes red; bill a yellowish green. Bare skin on head and neck a blackish blue; folds on back of neck a whitish ochre. Legs black. Sexes alike. Subadult barred above with chestnut, buff and black, and a mottled buff and black below.

Shy forest-dwellers, seldom seen in the open. Excellent fliers; when alarmed, seek shelter in the thick foliage of tall trees, rather than run away from danger. Gregarious even during the breeding season, but never found in large flocks. Forage amongst dead leaves for insects (mainly termites) and molluscs; also feed on seeds and young shoots.

Voice: A not unmusical '*tút-tút-tút-tirrr-tirrr-tirrr*', varying in rhythm and volume.

Habitat: Found only in dense scrub and riverine or rain forest.

Distribution: Very local, in the central eastern and north-eastern regions of Southern Africa.

BUTTON-QUAILS: Turnicidae

Small quail-like birds having very much the same markings and characteristics as game-birds, but differing from them in that they have no hind toe. The females are larger and more brightly coloured, and leave the incubation of the eggs and care of the chicks to the males. Found in open grassland and light bush. They are reluctant to fly, and when flushed at one's feet, fly only a short distance before settling again, and disappearing in the grass.

KURRICHANE BUTTON-QUAIL *Turnix sylvatica* (196) p. 113
Afr Bosvelddrietoonkwartel   *X* i-Ngolwane

Identification: 15 cm. Adult female: top of head black and russet. Feathers on hind neck russet, with creamy edges. Rest of upper parts russet, barred with black; feathers edged with cream. Upper wing-coverts cream, the russet centre-spots having black margins. Cheeks creamy, with minute black spots. *A line of heavy heart-shaped black spots down sides of chest and breast.* Chest tawny. Other underparts a creamy white. Eyes yellow; bill bluish; legs pinkish. Sexes alike, but male paler and smaller. Subadult has the whole chest spotted, and smaller spots on the wings.

These small birds behave exactly like quails. Usually found singly or in pairs. Given to irregular wanderings. Do not call when flushed, but fly low and rather noisily for only a short distance before settling. When they alight, often stand bolt-upright for a few seconds before disappearing in the grass. Not easily flushed a second time. Feed on insects and seeds.

Voice: A resonant, frog-like '*oo-úp, oo-úp*'. This monotonous call is often heard on clear nights and is ventriloquial. Also a '*burring*' call.

Habitat: Found in open bush country where there is abundant grass cover —even in semi-desert. Also in fallow fields.

Distribution: Throughout, except the south-western third and western coastal regions of Southern Africa.

Allied species:

HOTTENTOT BUTTON-QUAIL (*Turnix hottentotta*) (194). 15 cm. Differs from the Kurrichane Button-quail in that it has a *dark blackish rump*, *tawny cheeks*, and sides of chest barred with black and tawny (*not heavily spotted with black*). Seldom seen, as it skulks in the grass of the moister grasslands and more mountainous parts of the southern and eastern coastal regions. Flies fast and straight; on alighting, instantly disappears in the undergrowth. Call said to be lower-pitched than that of the Kurrichane.

CRAKES, RAILS, MOORHENS and COOT: Rallidae

The members of this family are mostly waterside birds with laterally-compressed bodies that enable them to move easily through dense reed-like vegetation. Their long toes are an adaptation for supporting them on marshy ground and aquatic vegetation. Coot and moorhens are good swimmers and are often seen on open water, but the rest are skulkers. They vary considerably in size and appear to be weak fliers, although there is evidence to show that long migrations have taken place. In flight their rounded wings and dangling legs are distinctive. Since all the flight-feathers are dropped simultaneously, the birds become flightless for a short period. Their short tails are often cocked up. They feed on water insects, molluscs, young shoots and seeds. Their presence is often made known by loud distinctive call-notes.

BLACK CRAKE *Limnocorax flavirostra* (203)   p. 160
   Afr Swartriethaan

Identification: 23 cm. A blackish slate all over. *Bill a bright greenish yellow; eyes red; legs a bright orange-red.* Sexes alike. Subadult olive-brown above, with white on throat; bill black with whitish tip; legs brownish.

A very common bird that may be found in any marshy area, feeding at the water's edge or among water-lily leaves, and jerking its tail up and down. In spite of its colour it can hide in even the smallest piece of cover. Less skulking than most other crakes. Is often seen climbing about in the vegetation, well above the surface of the water. A fast runner, and very reluctant to fly. Flies with very rapid wing-beats low over the water.

Voice: A duet, each bird uttering a deep growling '*churr*', interspersed with a shrill, rapid, high-pitched, trilling '*rrrrr*'. Individuals make a number of clucking sounds when they walk about.

Habitat: Found in marshes and along any stretch of water, provided there is sufficient vegetation to give the necessary shelter.

Distribution: Throughout Southern Africa.

BUFF-SPOTTED FLUFFTAIL *Sarothrura elegans* (206)   p. 160
   Afr Gevlekte vleikuiken

Identification: 15 cm. Adult male: *head, neck and upper chest chestnut;* remaining *upper parts black, thickly spotted with buff.* Below, black with white spots. Eyes brown; bill and legs a reddish brown. Adult female brownish above, with small black and buff spots; below, barred black and off-white. Subadult unrecorded.

A not uncommon bird, but rarely seen because of its skulking habits. Darts into cover like a mouse at the slightest sign of danger. Not dependent on water. Would probably be overlooked, were it not for its typical call.

Voice: A loud whistle, long drawn out and gradually dying away, with many conversational crooning and juggling notes. Usually heard at night.

Habitat: Forests, vleis and fallow land adjoining forests.

Distribution: In suitable localities in the south-eastern and eastern regions of Southern Africa.

LESSER GALLINULE *Porphyrio alleni* (209) p. 160
Afr Kleinkoningriethaan

Identification: 28 cm. Adult male is a striking bird: a glossy bluish purple, with *back and upper side of wings green*. Head and upper neck appear darkish. *Under tail-coverts white.* Eyes and *bill red; legs a brownish red. Frontal shield green.* Sexes alike. Subadult a pale brownish above; buffish below; flight-feathers have a greenish tinge. Legs and frontal shield brown.

The strong feet and long toes are well adapted to climbing about on reeds and bulrushes, to reach flowers and young shoots; and for walking on aquatic vegetation. The white under tail-coverts are always conspicuous, as the bird flicks its tail up and down while walking about. Very shy: seeks cover at the slightest sign of danger, either hastening along with a curious high-stepping gait and constant flicks of its tail, or—more reluctantly— flying, with heavy wing-beats and dangling legs, to the nearest cover. A good swimmer. Chiefly vegetarian, but also feeds on insects.

Voice: A sharp, clucking alarm-call and a rolling, frog-like *'gurrr'*.

Habitat: Found where there are thick reed-beds and bulrushes standing in water.

Distribution: Throughout, except in the extreme southern and western arid regions of Southern Africa.

COMMON MOORHEN *Gallinula chloropus* (210) p. 145
Afr Gewone waterhoender *S* Khokhonoka

Identification: 36 cm. Adult male: general colour a dark slate; mantle and upper side of wing olive-brown. Shortish tail black. Flanks have a few broad white streaks. Under tail-coverts black and white: the white ones as long as the tail itself. Eyes reddish; *bill red with a yellow tip; frontal shield red.* Legs olive-green, with a dark red band above the tarsal joint. Sexes alike. Subadult paler and more brown; streaks on flank buff; bill and shield greenish.

Not as skulking as the crakes. Often seen wading in the shallows or even

PLATE 9

VULTURES, EAGLES, SNAKE-EAGLE AND SECRETARY BIRD

1 **BLACK EAGLE** *page* 70
Rump and back white.

2 **FISH EAGLE** 74
Head, chest and tail white, flight feathers black, abdomen chestnut.

3 **CROWNED EAGLE** 72
Crest longish and rounded, long tail and flight feathers barred.

4 **CAPE VULTURE** 58
Head and neck bluish, general appearance pale buffish white.

5 **BLACK VULTURE** 59
Folds of bare skin on head and face flesh-coloured, general
appearance black.

6 **MARTIAL EAGLE** 71
Crest short and rounded, chest and belly white, sparingly spotted
with blackish.

7 **BLACK-BREASTED SNAKE-EAGLE** 74
Large head blackish brown, chest and belly white, unspotted; bare
legs whitish.

8 **BATELEUR EAGLE** 75
Tail very short and chestnut, cere and bare legs orange-red.

9 **TAWNY EAGLE** 70
Plumages vary from dark to pale brown, tail relatively short and
rounded.

10 **SECRETARY BIRD** 57
Long multiple crest, central tail feathers elongated.

PLATE 10

KESTRELS AND FALCONS

1 **LESSER KESTREL** *page* 66
Male has top of the head and nape dove-grey, back is chestnut and unspotted. Female has upperparts light brown and barred.

2 **GREATER KESTREL** 63
Whole bird has streaked and barred appearance.

3 **DICKINSON'S KESTREL** 63
Tail distinctly barred, lower back and rump light grey.

4 **RED-NECKED FALCON** 62
Neck red and tail with broad black sub-terminal band.

5 **ROCK KESTREL** 66
Underparts chestnut and spotted.

6 **HOBBY FALCON** 61
Chestnut restricted to thighs, belly and under tail-coverts.

7 **LANNER FALCON** 60
Crown and nape rufous.

8 **EASTERN RED-FOOTED KESTREL** 62
Under wing-coverts white.

9 **PYGMY FALCON** 67
Small size unmistakable. Underparts white, tail and flight feathers spotted. Back of female chestnut.

venturing short distances away from the water. When alarmed runs for shelter with its head held low. Its normal gait is jerky, like its swimming. Since it flicks its tail while walking or swimming, *the white under tail-coverts are very conspicuous*. Mainly vegetarian, but also feeds on the insects it picks up from the surface of the water. Flies fairly well, with dangling legs.

Voice: Normal call a cheerful, musical, high-pitched '*kur-rrrrk*', descending about a semitone. Also utters various clucks, grunts and croaks.

Habitat: Found wherever there are rivers or sheets of water bordered with reeds and sheltering vegetation.

Distribution: Throughout Southern Africa.

RED-KNOBBED COOT   *Fulica cristata* (212)   p. 145
   Afr Bleshoender   *X* u-Nompemvana
   S Mokhetle

Identification: 43 cm. Adult male: head and neck black; rest of plumage, *including under tail-coverts, a sooty black*. Eyes red; bill a light grey; *frontal shield white*. Knobs red (not conspicuous out of breeding season). Legs a dark greenish grey. Sexes alike. Subadults generally a dark ashy brown, with whitish cheeks and throat and a few white edges to the neck-feathers. Shield inconspicuous.

A common, well-known bird, usually seen on open water but sometimes feeding on land. Mainly vegetarian, but also eats insects. Out of breeding season they gather in large flocks. Very pugnacious during the breeding season, fighting and quarrelling with any bird that comes near the nest. Expert divers and swimmers; swim with a characteristic bobbing movement of the head. Skitter along the surface of the water when taking off. Fly with legs projecting behind their tails. Although their flight looks laboured they can cover great distances.

Voice: A nasal '*coot*' and a strange humming '*vvvvv*'. Alarm-call a snorting '*tcholf*'.

Habitat: Found on any large sheet of water, even those that have no sheltering vegetation. Also on coastal lagoons.

Distribution: Throughout Southern Africa.

Allied species:

CAPE RAIL (*Rallus caerulescens*) (197). 28 cm. Above, umber-brown; below, slate, except for *belly and flanks, which are black, distinctly barred with white*. Under tail-coverts white. Eyes a dark red; long bill and legs bright red. Sexes alike. Not often seen, as it seldom ventures out of the shelter of marginal vegetation, but has a distinctive call. A loud, high-pitched '*creeea*' is followed by a rapid, harsh '*crak, crak, crak*'. Found throughout, except in the central and north-western arid regions.

CORNCRAKE (*Crex crex*) (198). 28 cm. General colour a pale tawny. Feathers of upper parts have black centres; flanks barred with light buff. *Upper and under wing-coverts chestnut* (conspicuous in flight). Eyes and *short bill a light brown;* legs flesh-coloured. Sexes alike. A summer migrant, not necessarily dependent on water. Found in the eastern half of Southern Africa.

AFRICAN CRAKE (*Crex egregia*) (199). 23 cm. Above, mottled brown and black; sides of head, neck and chest a pale slate. Remaining underparts black, distinctly barred with white. Eyes a bright orange. *Short bill a yellowish green*, with base of lower mandible red. Legs a dull red. Sexes alike. Found along grass- and weed-fringed streams; not dependent on reeds or rushes. When flushed, flies low for a short distance before diving into cover again. Call a high-pitched, whistling trill of eight or nine notes. Found in the north-eastern half of Southern Africa.

BAILLON'S CRAKE (*Porzana pusilla*) (202). 18 cm. Similar to African Crake, but smaller. Upper parts a darker brown and black, with *white flecks on mantle, lower back and scapulars*. Below, a dark slate, except for lower flanks and under tail-coverts, which are barred in black and white. Eyes orange-red; *short bill dark green*; legs olive. Female a buffish brown below, with a white throat. Found on marshy ground with short vegetation, in which it runs like a rodent. When flushed, flies only a short distance before diving for cover. Call a low, piping '*quick-quick*' and a husky '*churr-churr*'. Found throughout, except in the southern, western and central arid areas.

RED-CHESTED FLUFFTAIL (*Sarothrura rufa*) (205). 15 cm. Adult male has head, neck, chest and upper back chestnut. Remaining plumage (including tail) black, spotted and streaked with white. Eyes brown; bill bluish; legs grey-brown. Female has head and neck brownish; other upper parts black, spotted and barred with buff; below, pale buff. Found in marshes with rank vegetation; swims well, with tail erect. Call a loud '*dúeh-dúeh*', continued for from ten to fifteen seconds. Also a squeaky '*dui*' repeated rapidly about eight times. Found along the southern coastal belt and in the eastern third of Southern Africa.

PURPLE GALLINULE (*Porphyrio porphyrio*) (208). 46 cm. The general colour of this large bird is a glossy bluish purple. Only the *back is green. Under tail-coverts white* and very conspicuous, for the bird constantly flicks its tail while walking or swimming. *Long legs and toes; stout bill and frontal shield bright red.* Sexes alike; subadult almost brown. Found mainly in reed- and bulrush-beds. Flies with heavy wing-beats and trailing legs. Call a loud, bubbling grunt, also various weird shrieks and groans. Found throughout Southern Africa, except in the arid central and western regions.

LESSER MOORHEN (*Gallinula angulata*) (211). 23 cm. General colour slate; *under tail-coverts white*. Frontal shield and ridge on upper mandible red; *rest of bill yellow*. Eyes red; legs greenish. Sexes alike. Similar to the Moorhen, but much smaller and shyer. Frequents sheets of water bordered by reeds and rushes. Seldom ventures into the open. Voice also similar to that of Moorhen. Found throughout the north-eastern half of Southern Africa.

Rarer species:

STRIPED CRAKE (*Porzana marginalis*) (200)

SPOTTED CRAKE (*Porzana porzana*) (201)

WHITE-WINGED CRAKE (*Sarothrura ayresi*) (204)

STRIPED FLUFFTAIL (*Sarothrura affinis*) (207)

STREAKY-BREASTED FLUFFTAIL (*Sarothrura böhmi*) (207X)

CHESTNUT-HEADED FLUFFTAIL (*Sarothrura lugens*)

AMERICAN GALLINULE (*Porphyrio martinica*)

FINFOOTS: Heliornithidae

Aquatic birds with a superficial resemblance to Darters. Their necks however are shorter and stouter; their bills and legs are orange-red, and their toes are lobed instead of webbed. They frequent small streams and rivers with overhanging vegetation, and are of a shy disposition. Feed on small water animals that they catch while swimming or diving.

PETER'S FINFOOT   *Podica senegalensis* (213)
Afr Watertrapper

Identification: 63 cm. In the adult male, crown and back of neck are blackish, washed with iridescent blue-green. Thin whitish line from eye down sides of neck. Sides of face, throat and front of neck a finely mottled slate-blue. Mantle blackish, washed with iridescent blue-green and *spotted with white*. Breast and belly a dirty white; sides of chest and flanks dark brown, heavily barred with light buff. Rump brown; wedge-shaped tail a blackish brown, slightly tipped with light buff. Eyes brown; *bill and legs orange-red*. Adult female smaller than male and browner above. Throat white. *Has a more distinct white line down the side of the neck*. Subadult resembles the female but has fewer spots above and is a distinctly lighter buff below.

These interesting birds are not often seen, as they live among the overhanging branches of the vegetation bordering streams. Swim low in the water and are excellent divers. When alarmed, run like coot on the water, and will dart into cover rather than take to flight. Fly strongly when once

airborne, but seem to have difficulty in taking off from water. Feed on insects and small water animals; nest on a branch overhanging the water.
Voice: A shrill '*keee*', but usually silent.
Habitat: On perennial streams and rivers with well-wooded banks; also
along coastal creeks.
Distribution: The south-eastern coastal belt, and central and north-eastern
regions of Southern Africa.

CRANES: Gruidae

Cranes are large terrestrial birds with long necks and legs. These are fully
extended in flight. They live in open country near water. Although they
resemble storks, their bills and feet are more like those of game-birds; their
hind toes are short and their nostrils are situated in a groove near the
middle of the bill. Whereas storks are usually silent, cranes have characteristic loud, trumpet-like calls. All cranes have short tails and some kind
of ornamental plumage developed from the innermost flight-feathers,
usually hanging over and on the sides of the tail. They often execute
dancing displays. Feed on insects, small animals, seeds and vegetable
matter. Nest on the ground, usually in swamps. Gregarious except in the
breeding season.

CROWNED CRANE *Balearica pavonina* (214)   p. 161
  Afr Mahemkraanvoël   *Z* u-Nohemu
  X i-Hemu   *S* le-Hehemu
Identification: 107 cm. Adult male: general colour slate-grey; *upper and
under wing-coverts white*. Secondaries a dark chestnut; primaries black.
Crown covered in black velvety down. Bird also has a *conspicuous tuft of
stiff, straw-coloured bristles* on the back of its head. Bare skin on face and
neck white and red. Throat-lappet vermilion. Shortish golden-brown ornamental egret-like plumes on upper side of wing near the body. Eyes light
grey; legs and short bill black. Sexes alike. Subadult has a brownish
mottled appearance; cheeks covered in buff down; tuft short and ragged.
   Usually seen in pairs or small family parties, except outside the breeding
season, when flocks of over a hundred may be seen. Walk about in their
stately fashion in open or swampy country. Have the curious habit of
stamping their feet as they walk, thus disturbing insects, which are nimbly
caught. Often perform gyrating gambols and dances, with wings outstretched. Their flight, in which the white wing-coverts are conspicuous,
is heavy and laboured, with the outstretched necks and feet hanging down
at a slight angle to the body. Roost in large numbers, usually in river-beds
but sometimes in trees.

Voice: A not very loud bisyllabic trumpeting '*ma-hém*', with all the stress on the last syllable.

Habitat: Open plains, vleis and cultivated land.

Distribution: The eastern half and central northern regions of Southern Africa.

WATTLED CRANE *Grus carunculatus* (215) p. 161

Afr Lelkraanvoël *Z* u-Mcinsi
X i-Quqolo *S* Mothlathomo

Identification: 127 cm. Adult male: crown slate; neck and chest a uniform white; breast and belly black. Back and wing-coverts grey; flight-feathers a blackish grey. *Long grey ornamental plumes* give the bird the appearance of having a long tail. *Two white, partly feathered pendent wattles* from chin. The base of the bill to the eyes is bare, and covered with red warts. Eyes orange-yellow, *long stout bill a reddish brown*. Legs black. Female has more white on crown, but sexes are indistinguishable in the field. Subadult has a white crown, dark slate belly and breast, no warts and very small wattles.

The largest of the cranes. Usually seen in twos or threes. Uncommon. Very wary: does not allow a close approach. *Long white neck and black underparts* unmistakable on the ground and in flight. Feeds mainly on insects and small animals. Often seen probing swampy ground with its long straight bill, looking for the earthworms to which it is partial.

Voice: A guttural but bell-like '*hornk*', long drawn-out.

Habitat: Moist open grassland and vleis.

Distribution: Very local in the north-eastern half of Southern Africa.

STANLEY or BLUE CRANE *Anthropoides paradisea* (216) p. 161

Afr Bloukraanvoël *Z* i-Ndwa
X i-Ndwe *S* Mokhokoli

Identification: 107 cm. Adult male: top of head, nape, lores and chin a very pale blue-grey. Upper neck slate; lower neck paler; rest of plumage slate-grey. Flight-feathers, including the *long ornamental secondaries that curve and reach the ground, black*. Eyes brown; shortish bill a pinkish yellow; legs black. Sexes alike. Subadult similar to adult but without the long secondaries.

These birds are usually found in pairs, and are often seen stalking over the short veld-grass, far away from water. Feed mainly on insects and small animals, but also on fish, seeds and grain. Except in the breeding season they are highly gregarious, and sometimes gather in flocks of a few hundred. They are wary birds, and often sleep standing in water. Excellent fliers, sometimes giving their familiar call at a considerable height.

Voice: A loud, rattling, very distinctive croak, usually in the form of a

duet. The male gives a low-pitched '*krrurrrrk*', and the female a higher-pitched '*krrirrrk*', repeated several times.

Habitat: Open grassland, cultivated ground and vleis.

Distribution: Mainly confined to the central and south-eastern parts of Southern Africa.

BUSTARDS and KORHAANS: Otidae

These are terrestrial birds, found mainly in the open plains (desert included) and in scrub country, but also in the dry bush-country. They vary in size from the Kori Bustard, which stands about 122 cm high, to others that are the size of domestic fowls. They have long necks and long legs with only 3 toes. Cryptic colouring; upper parts covered with fine vermiculations. Excellent fliers; the flight of the larger species is powerful, with slow, deliberate wing-beats. They feed mainly on insects, especially locusts and other pests, and do farmers a great service. They have distinctive calls and remarkable courtship displays, either in the air or on the ground. Their roundish eggs are laid in a bare scrape.

KORI BUSTARD *Otis kori* (217)   p. 161

  Afr Gompou

Identification: 137 cm. Adult male: *feathers on forehead and crown mottled black and white, and elongated to a crest on the nape.* White stripe above the eye; *chin, throat and the lax neck feathers, front and back, whitish with thin black bands.* Above, mantle, scapulars and upper tail-coverts buffish, finely and closely vermiculated with blackish. Flight-feathers black, broadly banded and mottled with white, except for inner secondaries, which are vermiculated and buffish. Upper wing-coverts white, with sub-terminal black blobs, showing as separate lines on the folded wings. Drooping tail broadly barred in black and white; tip buffish. Below, chest to under tail-coverts and under wing-coverts, white. Eyes yellow; bill horn-coloured; legs yellowish. Sexes alike, but female is much smaller. Subadult paler on the crown; mantle more freckled; has no crest.

These birds can weigh up to 50 pounds, and are probably the heaviest flying birds. Usually seen singly or in pairs. Exceedingly wary; can walk very fast and are reluctant to fly. Usually take off into the wind after a short run and a final kick that launches them into the air. Fly with necks extended but legs folded in under their bodies. Feed on insects, small animals and seeds. Said to be partial to acacia gum. During courtship displays, males erect their body feathers until they look almost white, and puff up their necks to an enormous size.

Voice: Mating call a deep '*woum-woum-woum-woumwoum*', with the emphasis on the last part of the call. Also a loud, nasal '*ka-káh-ká*', repeated several times.

Habitat: Open or semi-open country, also arid bush country with long grass.

Distribution: Throughout Southern Africa, except the southern coastal belt.

KARROO KORHAAN   *Eupodotis vigorosii* (220)   p. 161
Afr Vaalkorhaan

Identification: 60 cm. Adult male: *top of head, sides of face*, neck (front and back), chest, breast and flanks *a pale ashy brown*, finely vermiculated with a darker colour. Belly whitish. Mantle, scapulars, wing-coverts, rump and tail stone-coloured, with blackish vermiculations and a beautiful pink bloom that soon disappears from a preserved skin. Base of feathers a rich wine-red shade. *A black line from the eye to the nape forms a slight crest. Triangular black patch on chin and throat extends a short way down the throat.* Primaries buff with blackish ends, secondaries buffish with black bars. Eyes a light brown; bill slaty; legs yellow. Adult female more clearly vermiculated and broadly barred on the back. Subadult has whitish spots above; also on neck and chest; below, paler buff and barred.

Usually found in pairs, but parent birds often seen with the previous year's chick. Depends on its protective colouring and will often squat if not approached directly. Flies strongly, with peculiar, low, fast, flapping wing-beats. Feeds mainly on insects and seeds.

Voice: Antiphonal call '*squark*'-'*kok*' by male and female.

Habitat: Dry stony ground with scattered stunted bush.

Distribution: South-western third of Southern Africa.

RED-CRESTED KORHAAN   *Eupodotis ruficrista* (224)   p. 161
Afr Boskorhaan

Identification: 50 cm. Adult male: *top of head grey*. Sides of face and back of neck buffish. Chin and throat whitish. Front of neck grey with thin black streak down the centre. *Small tuft of pinkish feathers on nape not always conspicuous.* Rest of upper parts a finely vermiculated tawny, with black arrow-shaped markings bordered with light buff. Tail barred and vermiculated with black and dirty white. *White patch on side of chest.* Flight-feathers a creamy buff, with black bars. *Greater wing-coverts white.* Remaining underparts black. Eyes a pale yellow-brown; bill ashy; legs whitish. Adult female: no crest; no black line on throat; *top of head tawny, speckled with buff;* neck and chest finely barred with a darker colour, breast whitish. *Only belly and under tail-coverts black.* Subadult similar to female but has buff tips to the primaries.

Found singly or in pairs, usually resting in the shade of trees during the heat of the day. When flushed, rises silently and flies at high speed, twisting and swerving through the trees. Soon settles again. When displaying, male flies steeply up to a height of about 12 m, folds himself into a bundle and drops straight down, opening his wings just before striking the ground.

Voice: Call begins with a rhythmic snapping of the bill, followed by a ventriloquial whistle that lasts for half a minute or more, increasing in intensity and then stopping abruptly. This call is often heard during the hottest part of the day. At sunset during the breeding season the whistle of the male is interspersed with the melancholy '*goo-goo*' of the female.

Habitat: Dry bush country or even in thick bush with small open patches.

Distribution: Northern half of Southern Africa, but not in the arid western regions.

BLACK KORHAAN *Eupodotis afra* (225) p. 161
Afr Swartkorhaan

Identification: 53 cm. Adult male: *forehead and sides of face black*. Crown and nape mottled in black and tawny, bordered with light buff. *Ear-coverts white*. Neck and remaining underparts black. Mantle and scapulars black, barred with yellow. Rump to tail finely barred with black and white. Tail has two narrow black bands near the tip. Band at base of neck, sides of chest, *tips of upper wing-coverts, and wing-shoulder white*. Under wing-coverts black; primaries black, sometimes with elongated white markings. Eyes a light reddish brown; bill greyish brown with a pinkish base; legs bright yellow. Adult female has *only the belly and under tail-coverts black*. Chest white; head and neck a pale rufous, finely barred with black. Rest of upper parts mottled and spotted in black, tawny and rufous. Subadult resembles adult female.

Usually found in pairs, occupying a definite territory. Males very noisy and obtrusive, calling in flight or when standing on ant-hills or other slightly elevated posts. Females shy and unobtrusive; difficult to flush. During a display flight the male drops slowly down, usually calling, with dangling legs and fast fluttering wing-beats, looking like a helicopter coming in to land. Feed mainly on vegetable matter, but also on insects.

Voice: A loud, raucous '*krracker-krracker-krracker*'.

Habitat: Open grassland, but also found among scattered trees and bushes.

Distribution: Throughout the central, southern and western regions of Southern Africa.

LONG-LEGGED KORHAAN *Eupodotis melanogaster* (227) p. 161
Afr Langbeenkorhaan   *Z* u-Nofunjwa

Identification: 66 cm. Adult male: *head, sides of face and back of neck buff, finely barred with blackish*. Short crest with black base on nape. Throat a silvery grey. Mantle and scapulars tawny, the black shaft-stripes broadening into arrow-heads. Rump and tail finely vermiculated in black and fawn. White line down side of neck ends in a white patch on side of chest. *Upper wing-coverts mainly white;* flight-feathers black and white. The black of the underparts (including *under wing-coverts*) *extends in a thin black line up the centre of the neck to the throat.* Eyes a light brown; bill yellow; *long legs* a yellowish brown. Adult female differs considerably from the male, having a *white belly* and no black line down the centre of the neck. Neck wholly buff, finely barred with blackish. Upper wing-coverts not white but a light fawn. Subadult similar to female, but flight-feathers are edged with buff.

This long-legged korhaan with its long, thin neck is usually found in pairs. Frequents moist open patches with shortish grass during the cooler hours of the day and seeks shade during the hotter hours. Not wary and rather difficult to flush, since it will often squat and sit tight when danger threatens. *In flight the white in the wings is very conspicuous.* During display flights the male drops like a parachute, with wings held almost vertically above the body.

Voice: The most silent of the korhaans. Call said to be a peculiar whistle, ending after a pause in a '*pop*'. During the breeding season '*or-buk, or-buk*' is repeated at short intervals.

Habitat: Savanna, within reach of water.

Distribution: The eastern and north-eastern parts of Southern Africa.

Allied species:

LUDWIG'S BUSTARD (*Otis ludwigii*) (218). 90 cm. *The whole head to nape, throat, front of neck and chest is brown, finely barred with whitish.* Sides of neck white; *lower part of back of neck and upper mantle a light tawny.* Rest of upper side vermiculated and spotted in brown, black and tawny; *no marked contrast between mantle and upper wing-coverts*, which have *white tips.* Tail slate-grey with narrow whitish and darker bands. Breast, belly and under wing-coverts white. Outer primaries blackish, inner mainly white. Secondaries mottled pale tawny and black. Sexes alike. Usually found in small parties, frequenting the drier regions.

STANLEY'S BUSTARD (*Otis denhami*) (219). 109 cm. *Crown black*, with broken white central stripe. Sides of face, *front of neck and chest a uniform slate-grey.* Throat white. Sides of neck white; *back of neck tawny.* Mantle to upper tail-coverts brown, densely and finely vermiculated in blackish, *strongly contrasting with blackish upper wing-coverts, blobbed with white.* Tail blackish, with broad white bands. Remaining underparts white. Outer primaries black, inner white with black bands. Secondaries black with white tips. Female has front of neck and chest barred and vermiculated in buff and blackish. Found in pairs or small parties on open plains in the southern and south-eastern regions.

WHITE-BELLIED KORHAAN (*Eupodotis cafra*) (222). 53 cm. Forehead and *throat black; crown blue-grey*, bordered with black that ends in short crest on nape. Face whitish. Neck in front grey, hind neck and sides of chest a light chestnut. Rest of *upper side chestnut*, finely vermiculated in tawny and black. *Breast and belly white.* Tail blackish, except for the centre tail-feathers, which are a pale tawny. Primaries black; inner webs a yellowish white; secondaries black and tawny. Female lacks blue-grey crown; neck (front and back) tawny and whitish. Found in small parties in open grass-veld in the south-eastern regions. Loud, rattling, crowing call, given in chorus.

BLUE KORHAAN (*Eupodotis caerulescens*) (223). 58 cm. Forehead, *stripe under eye and throat a blackish slate;* blue-grey crown ends in a slight crest. *Rest of face white. Hind neck* and other upper parts *a rich tawny*, finely vermiculated in black. Neck (front and back) and all the *underparts blue-grey*. Primaries black; inner webs mostly a yellowish white; secondaries vermiculated in black and tawny. Tail has a dark tip. Female similar to male but has brownish cheeks. Usually seen in parties of four or five, walk-ing in the grassveld of the south-eastern regions. Loud call, described as '*knock-me-down*', repeated over and over again.

Rarer species:
RÜPPEL'S KORHAAN (*Eupodotis rüppelli*) (Possibly a race of the Karroo Korhaan.)

JACANAS: Jacanidae

Jacanas or lily-trotters are aquatic birds whose very long toes and claws enable them to walk on water-lily leaves and other floating water-weeds in quiet stretches of water. They feed on insects and seeds, particularly water-lily seeds. Their nests are built on flimsy floating platforms made of water-weeds. During incubation, they lift their beautiful glossy eggs off the nest with their bills and tuck them under their wings to keep them off the cold substratum. Newly-hatched chicks are carried about in a similar fashion. Since all the flight-feathers are simultaneously dropped, the birds are flight-less for a short period.

AFRICAN JACANA *Actophilornis africanus* (228) p. 160
  Afr Gewone langtoon
Identification: 30 cm. General colour a dark chestnut. Chest golden; throat and front of neck white, top of head and back of neck a glossy black. Primaries black. *Frontal shield bluish;* bill greyish; eyes dark brown and legs slate. Sexes alike. Subadult has upper parts tinged with yellowish green;

top of head and back of neck a dull black; whitish below. Frontal shield inconspicuous.

Usually found singly or in pairs, feeding round the margins of stagnant pools or dams, or walking gracefully on floating vegetation. A powerful flier; legs fully extended in flight. Often raises its wings above its body after landing. Sometimes seen swimming and diving. May congregate in large flocks, but not in the breeding season.

Voice: While flying, gives a rattling screech. Also has a coot-like call and a grating '*kyowrr, kyowrr*'.

Habitat: Lagoons, stagnant pools, weed-fringed dams and quiet rivers.

Distribution: Southern and eastern coastal belt, and north-eastern half of Southern Africa.

Allied species:

LESSER JACANA (*Microparra capensis*) (229). 15 cm. Crown, rump, tail and flanks chestnut; back of neck black; rest of upper side a golden buff, washed with green; sides of neck golden. Below, whitish. Under wing-coverts black; legs a greenish brown. Sexes alike. A shy bird, usually seen running on floating vegetation. Also frequents dense vegetation in marshy regions. Has the same distribution as the African Jacana, but is far more rare.

PAINTED SNIPES: Rostratulidae

Though the Painted Snipes look like true snipes, their longish, pointed bills are not pitted like those of the latter. Their rounded wings and slow flight, with dangling legs when flushed, are reminiscent of a rail. The females are more handsomely coloured than the males. During courtship the females are the more active, and do not share in the building of the nest, the incubation of the eggs or the tending of the young. Feed on insects and worms found in marshy ground. Usually nest on dry ground and do not 'drum' with their tail-feathers during display flights.

PAINTED SNIPE *Rostratula benghalensis* (230)   p. 160
    Afr Goudsnip

Identification: 25 cm. Above, adult male is olive-brown, with a bottle-green gloss. Buffish yellow central streak over forehead and crown. *Buffish white ring around the eye extends in a streak behind the eye. Olive-brown back* is widely barred with black and has *two longitudinal golden streaks*; rump a pale grey, barred with black and having round white and pale-yellow spots. Flight-feathers and tail a silvery grey with round golden spots. *Wing-coverts a golden brown with sparse black bars and pale round golden-brown spots.* Below: throat white; *neck and chest a mottled olive-brown*; broken black band on breast; remaining underparts white. Eyes brown; bill a dark reddish brown; legs a dull slaty blue. Adult female has *neck and sides of head a rich chestnut*; broad black band across chest; *wing-coverts green* with fine barring. Subadult similar to male.

Usually found in pairs along the edge of the water-line. When bird alights, hind part of body is bobbed up and down. When alarmed does not always run for cover, but freezes, depending on its camouflage. Sometimes only the white ring around the eye reveals its presence. The two longitudinal golden streaks on the back are distinctive in flight. As a rule, seen only when flushed.

Voice: Usually silent, but sometimes utters a guttural croak.

Habitat: Occurs on the borders of swampy areas, lakes and vleis.

Distribution: Throughout Southern Africa.

OYSTERCATCHERS: Haematopodidae

These are medium-sized plover-like birds of the sea-shore, more or less black and with bills longer than their heads. The mandibles do not meet at the tip, and are vertically flattened to form thin blades at the tip. Feed mainly on mussels; bills seem to be adapted to this diet. Legs relatively short, with only three toes. Nest in depressions on sandy beaches.

BLACK OYSTERCATCHER *Haematopus moquini* (231) p. 129

Afr Swartoestervanger (Tobie)

Identification: 50 cm. Adult male wholly black; *eyes red* with orange eye-lids; *bill vermilion* and *legs a pinkish red*. Sexes alike. Subadult generally a duller black with mottled black and whitish breast and belly; bill orange and legs a greenish brown.

Usually found in pairs inhabiting a well-defined territory, but may also be seen in flocks, probably consisting of subadult birds. Very active birds, moving quickly over exposed rocks or probing the wet sand to the full length of their bills in search of molluscs, whelks, crustacea and annelids. Also feed at night.

Voice: Alarm-call a series of shrill, piping '*pips*', and a clear, shrill '*klee-weep*', repeated several times.

Habitat: Resident. Found only along sandy beaches, rocky coasts, lagoons and estuaries.

Distribution: Along the western, southern and south-eastern coast of Southern Africa.

Rarer species:

EUROPEAN OYSTERCATCHER (*Haematopus ostralegus*) (231X)

PLOVERS: Charadriidae

Plovers are small to medium-sized terrestrial birds with relatively short bills (not longer than their heads), high foreheads and flattened crowns. They have longish legs and rather short toes. They frequent dry open country the sea-shore, or the margins of vleis, lakes and streams. Most of them have distinctive calls. They nest on the ground, in bare or sparsely-lined scrapes and are insectivorous. The migrants usually occur in flocks, and so do some of the resident species out of breeding season.

RINGED PLOVER　　*Charadrius hiaticula* (233)　　　　　　p. 129

　　Afr Ringnekkiewiet

Identification: 18 cm. Adult male, brownish above: forehead black with a white band; sides of face and ear-coverts black, with a white collar that includes the throat. *Single broad black chest-band* extending to the back of the neck. Remaining underparts white. Inner primaries have white patches forming a white bar in flight. Outer tail-feathers white; remaining tail-feathers tipped with white. Eyes brown; bill orange with a black tip; *legs orange-yellow*. Sexes alike. Subadult duller above; feathers edged with pale buff; no black band on forehead. Sides of face and ear-coverts dark brown; chest-band dark brown and not always complete.

A palaeoarctic summer migrant, usually found in small numbers in loose association with other species. Never found in large flocks of its own species. Searches for food on exposed sand- and mud-banks, rarely wading in the water. This plump little wader is neither very shy nor very active and is usually spotted when running rapidly forwards with head held up, and suddenly stopping to pick up an insect. In flight *the white wing-bar and white-edged tail are conspicuous*.

Voice: A mellow, double piping call: '*too-ti*' or '*tiuu-it*'.

Habitat: Found near the water's edge on the shore, and on lagoons, estuaries and dams. Even found on dried-up pans.

Distribution: Throughout Southern Africa.

WHITE-FRONTED PLOVER　　*Charadrius marginatus*

　　　　(235)　　　　　　　　　　　　　　　　　　　　p. 129

　　Afr Vaalkiewiet

Identification: 18 cm. Adult male: mantle, wing-coverts and top of head ashy, washed with tawny. Flight-feathers and rump ashy. *Narrow blackish band on forecrown;* another extending from the lores, through the eyes to the ear-coverts. *White collar on hind neck. Forehead*, sides of face and rest of underparts *white*, except for chest, which is washed with tawny. Central tail-feathers black; rest of tail white. Bases of primaries and inner webs of secondaries white; in flight this forms a white bar. Eyes a dark brown; bill and legs black. Sexes alike. Subadult has no black on forecrown; underparts completely white; wing-coverts edged with buff.

These small plovers are usually found singly or in pairs. Even when very plentiful they do not seem to congregate in flocks. When they run, their legs move so rapidly as to be almost invisible. Often move with a peculiar sideways action. When put to flight, rise with a soft '*twirt*' or '*twit, twit*', fly low and settle a short distance away before running off again. *In flight, feet do not extend beyond the tail.* Feed mainly on insects picked up on the sand. Eggs laid in an unlined scrape and partly covered with sand.

Voice: Alarm-call a short, loud '*kitt-up*' or a '*churrr*', long drawn out.

Habitat: Resident on sandy beaches and dunes; more rarely along sandy rivers.

Distribution: Along the entire coast of Southern Africa and only occasionally inland, along sandy rivers in the eastern region.

KITTLITZ'S PLOVER   *Charadrius pecuarius* (237)   p. 129
Afr Geelborskiewiet

Identification: 16 cm. Adult male is a dark brown above, with a blackish wing-shoulder. The *black band behind the white forehead curves downwards and is extended to meet behind the neck*, forming a border to the white-edged brownish crown and nape. White below; *lower neck, chest and breast washed with a rich tawny.* Eyes brown; bill and legs black. In the adult female the line across the forehead is not black, but a dark brown. Subadult has no black on the head, and the collar on the back of the neck is buff instead of white. The black wing-shoulder is present, however.

Usually found on dry open grassveld, near water. Usually in small flocks, but sometimes in flocks of over 100. These little plovers are not very shy. When disturbed, fly low for some distance before quickly settling again. Often feign injury when nests or chicks are approached. On leaving the nest, even when flushed, they completely cover the eggs with sand. *In flight, feet extend beyond the tail.*

Voice: A plaintive '*pi-peep*' on the wing; alarm-call '*chirrrrt*'.

Habitat: Resident on open flats on the coast and near any inland waters.

Distribution: Throughout Southern Africa.

THREE-BANDED PLOVER   *Charadrius tricollaris*
(238)   p. 129
Afr Driebandkiewiet

Identification: 18 cm. Adult male an umber-brown above. Forehead, stripe above the eye, sides of face and throat white. Chest has *two black bars*

112

PLATE 11

HARRIERS, GOSHAWKS, SPARROWHAWKS AND CHANTING GOSHAWKS

1 **AFRICAN MARSH HARRIER** *page* 82
Pale shoulder patch.

2 **GABAR GOSHAWK** 78
Rump white and legs orange yellow.

3 **PALLID HARRIER** 83
Rump white, ends of primaries blackish.

4 **BLACK HARRIER** 83
Upper tail-coverts white.

5 **LITTLE SPARROWHAWK** 77
Rump white, two white 'eye' spots on the tail seen from the back.

6 **BLACK GOSHAWK** 77
Large black and white bird with flanks mottled black and white.

7 **AFRICAN GOSHAWK** 78
Uniform blackish on upperside and finely barred below.

8 **PALE CHANTING GOSHAWK** 79
Rump white, secondaries and upper wing-coverts whitish with grey barring.

9 **DARK CHANTING GOSHAWK** 82
Upper tail-coverts barred, secondaries and upper wing-coverts uniform grey.

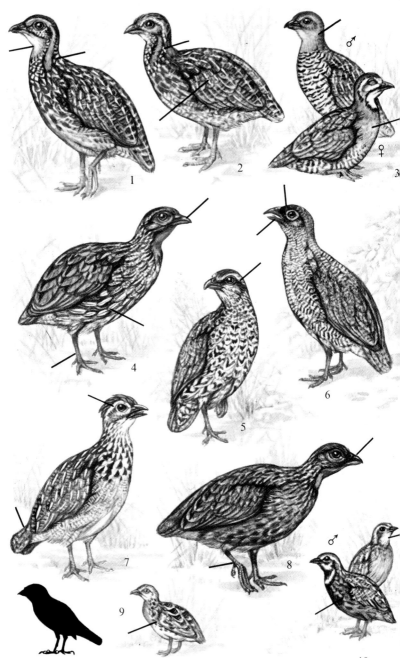

PLATE 12

FRANCOLINS, PARTRIDGES, QUAILS AND BUTTON-QUAILS

1 **REDWING PARTRIDGE** *page* 87
Throat whitish, speckled black and white patch round the base of the neck.

2 **GREY-WING PARTRIDGE** 87
Upper wing-coverts greyish, central streak down side of neck tawny.

3 **COQUI PARTRIDGE** 85
Male has head and neck rufous yellow.
Female is vinous brown on the chest.

4 **RED-NECKED FRANCOLIN** 90
Legs and bill red, belly and flanks streaked with black, chestnut and white.

5 **NATAL FRANCOLIN** 88
Dark brown line from nostril through the eye including the ear-coverts.

6 **RED-BILLED FRANCOLIN** 88
Bill red, lores black and bare skin round the eyes yellow.

7 **CRESTED PARTRIDGE** 86
Slight darkish crest and a conspicuous white eye-stripe.

8 **SWAINSON'S FRANCOLIN** 89
Legs black, upper mandible black and lower mandible reddish.

9 **KURRICHANE BUTTON-QUAIL** 93
Line of heavy heart-shaped black spots down side of chest and breast.

10 **HARLEQUIN QUAIL** 91
Male has flanks and side of chest bright chestnut with black markings.

divided by a white one. Rest of underparts white. Eyes brown and surrounded by a reddish wattle; *bill black with a reddish base*; legs a purplish flesh-colour. Sexes alike. Subadult has feathers on upper side tipped with buff, and black chest-bands narrower and more broken.

Usually in pairs; mainly found at the water's edge, moving about, pecking, and making short flights. Move their tails up and down when alighting. When giving their alarm-calls, stand with their bodies inclined forwards, bobbing up and down at each call. When flushed, give their typical calls as they fly jerkily away. White wing-bar and terminal white bar on the tail conspicuous.

Voice: Alarm-call a loud, high-pitched whistle: '*twi-twi*'. Also utters a loud '*tiuu-it, tiuu-it*', usually in flight.

Habitat: Beside such inland waters, e.g. lakes, lagoons, pans, dams and rivers, as have a clear shore-line. Seldom found on the sea-shore.

Distribution: Throughout Southern Africa.

CROWNED PLOVER *Vanellus coronatus* (242) p. 129

Afr Gewone kiewiet   Z Mbagaqwa
   X i-Gxiya   *S* le-Tetshane

Identification: 30 cm. Adult male stone-brown above. *Crown black, encircled by a broadish white stripe.* Black of forehead extends in a thin line above the eye, to meet on the nape. The stone-coloured chest and breast are divided from the white belly by a thin black line. Under tail-coverts, under wing-coverts and rump white. The white tail has a broad black subterminal band. Eyes orange-yellow; bill red with darker tip; *legs red.* Sexes alike. Subadult has feathers of upper parts broadly edged with buff; crown blackish and finely edged with buff.

This very noisy plover is usually found in pairs or small parties, but becomes gregarious after the breeding season, when fairly large flocks may be encountered. Not dependent on water. Keeps its body horizontal when running or walking, but has a very upright stance when standing still. When pecking, it executes a kind of curtsy, bending its body downwards and taking up the food with a forward thrust of its head. When the nest or chicks are threatened, the parent birds swoop fearlessly on the intruder with wild, loud shrieks. They are very active at night, and their characteristic call can be heard as they fly about.

Voice: A sustained '*kie-wíet*' as a warning call, and '*kree-kree-kree-kreeíp-kreeíp*', usually uttered in flight.

Habitat: Open veld, cultivated land and patches of open ground in wooded areas; even found in arid regions, and particularly if the grass is short or has been recently burnt.

Distribution: Throughout Southern Africa.

BLACK-WINGED PLOVER   *Vanellus melanopterus* (243)   p. 129
   Afr Swartvlerkkiewiet   *Z* i-Titihoya

Identification: 28 cm. Adult male has *white on forehead extending beyond the eye*. Crown and nape a dark greyish brown. Above, brown tinged with bronze. Tail white, with a broad black subterminal band. Secondaries white, but have black tips: this creates the impression of a white bar on the wing. *A broad blackish band* divides the grey neck from the white under-parts. Eyes a pale yellow, with *narrow scarlet eyelids*; bill black; legs a dark scarlet. Sexes alike. Subadult has no dark band on chest.

Usually found in small flocks, but sometimes widely dispersed when feeding in open bush country. White under wing-coverts conspicuous, not only during flight but also when the birds alight with wings raised. In areas still grazed by large herds of game, these birds are often found feeding on the beetles and insect larvae in the game droppings.

Voice: Their typical call '*titihoya*' is often heard at night as they fly high overhead. Also utter a '*che-che-che-chereek*' that varies in pitch and intensity.

Habitat: A local migrant, found in open bush country, usually in moister localities.

Distribution: In the south-eastern and eastern regions of Southern Africa.

BLACKSMITH PLOVER   *Vanellus armatus* (245)   p. 129
   Afr Bontkiewiet

Identification: 30 cm. Adult male has *forehead, crown, back of neck and upper tail-coverts white. Upper wing-coverts and scapulars a pale grey.* Sides of face, nape, throat, front of neck, chest and breast black. Other under-parts, including under wing-coverts, white. Tail white, with broad black terminal band narrowing towards the sides. Eyes carmine; bill and legs black. Sexes alike. Subadult has pattern similar to that of older bird, but is brownish, and the top of the head is mottled with black. Since its feathers are tipped with buff and black the bird has a mottled appearance.

This black and white plover has a sharp black spur on its wing, but this is not easily seen in the field. It is mostly found in pairs or small parties, usually in moist localities in open country, near either sweet or brackish water. Restless out of breeding season, temporarily congregates in larger numbers where conditions are favourable. Its rounded wings, slow wing-beats and bold black-and-white flight pattern are distinctive. Usually silent unless disturbed. Its nest is a scrape ringed with pebbles or small pieces of dry dung.

Voice: A loud, clear '*klink-klink-klink*', like a small hammer hitting an anvil.

Habitat: In open, moist country with short grass, near dams, pans, vleis and rivers.

Distribution: Throughout Southern Africa, but not in the arid central western regions.

WATTLED PLOVER   *Vanellus senegallus* (247)   p. 129
Afr Lelkiewiet

Identification: 36 cm. Adult male an olive-brown above. *Forehead white; crown and nape blackish, with white centre. Neck, front and back, has heavy black streaks.* Chin and throat black. Outer wing-coverts and upper tail-coverts white. Chest, breast and upper belly a pale greyish brown and separated from white lower belly and under tail-coverts by a blackish band. Under wing-coverts white. Inner secondaries white; remaining flight-feathers black. Tail white, with broad black subterminal band. Eyes lemon-yellow; *broad dark red and yellow wattles in front of eye*; bill yellow with black tip; legs yellow. Adult female has much less black on the throat. Subadult has small, inconspicuous wattles; top of head mottled with black; both chin and throat streaked with black and white.

This large plover is never found far from water. Usually found in pairs, but becomes fairly gregarious out of breeding season. The spur on its wing is relatively small. A silent bird, except during the breeding season, when it also calls at night. Less common than the two preceding species.

Voice: A shrill '*peep-peep*', becoming even shriller and louder when the bird is alarmed.

Habitat: Open grassy areas near water; also cultivated ground.

Distribution: The eastern, north-eastern and northern regions of Southern Africa.

WHITE-CROWNED PLOVER   *Vanellus albiceps* (246)   p. 129
Afr Witkroonkiewiet

Identification: 30 cm. Above, *forehead and centre of crown white*; sides of face, neck and upper mantle grey. Grey of upper mantle bordered with white. Mantle and scapulars a pale earth-brown, with a broadish white band along the outer edge of the scapulars. Wing-shoulders black; secondaries and inner primaries white; outer primaries blackish, with basal half white. Tail-feathers white, broadly tipped with black. Below, chin, centre of throat and rest of underparts white. *Long, pendulous triangular wattles in front of the eyes a greenish yellow.* Black spur on shoulder about 15 mm. long, not conspicuous in the field. Eyes yellow; bill yellow with a large black tip; legs a yellowish green. Sexes alike. Subadult resembles adult, but wattles are small, and the black feathers on the wing-shoulders are tipped with white. The brown on the back is faintly barred with darker brown.

A fairly common resident species, usually found singly or in small parties. A nervous bird, readily taking to flight when alarmed, and calling loudly when flying off. Has the habit of shuffling its feet when it becomes aware of impendng danger. This plover is said to peck bits of food from the teeth of crocodiles, as they lie with gaping jaws.

Voice: A staccato '*tee-tee-tip*', which may be either bi- or trisyllabic. This alarm-note is usually uttered when the bird flies off. Normal call an incessant piping cry.

Habitat: Mud- or sand-banks beside permanent rivers, or near pools in dry river-beds.

Distribution: The north-eastern regions of Southern Africa.

Allied species:

TURNSTONE (*Arenaria interpres*) (232) 23 cm. A thickset palaeoarctic migrant. In winter plumage upper parts are a dusky brown, and mottled. Throat, belly, flanks and lower back white. Chest and breast a mottled blackish brown. Upper tail-coverts and broad subterminal band of white tail, blackish. *Short legs a light orange;* short, stout, pointed bill black. *In flight, white bars and patches on wings and back distinctive.* Many individuals are seen in partial breeding plumage (upper parts turning a bright chestnut, and head and underparts black and white) before leaving on their annual migration to the north. Found along the entire coast of Southern Africa, but only rarely inland.

CHESTNUT-BANDED PLOVER (*Charadrius pallidus*) (236). 15 cm. The upper side of this chubby little plover is a pale greyish stone-colour. Forehead, face and underside white, except for a *pale chestnut band on the chest.* Females lack the thin black line on the forehead and through the eye. White bar across primaries conspicuous in flight. Bill black; legs an olive-grey. A shy bird that flies fast and low. Found along the western and southern coast, mainly on the mud-flats of salt-pans and lagoons. Also on large temporary pans in the drier western regions of Southern Africa.

GREATER SAND PLOVER (*Charadrius leschenaultii*) (239). 23 cm. This rather large greyish plover, with white underparts and pale grey patches on the side of the chest, is fairly similar to the White-fronted Plover, but differs from it in having a *much larger and heavier black bill,* and in lacking the white collar on the hind neck. This Asiatic winter migrant is regularly found along the eastern and southern coasts of Southern Africa, but rarely along the western coast.

CASPIAN PLOVER (*Charadrius asiaticus*) (240). 23 cm. Above, a greyish brown; forehead and eye-stripe a light buff. Dark patch behind and below the eye conspicuous. *The broad pale chestnut or pale umber-brown band across the chest may narrow slightly towards the centre.* Throat and rest of underparts white. Longish black bill much thinner than that of Greater Sand Plover. This palaeoarctic winter migrant frequents the dry open plains; not dependent on water. Usually found in small flocks, but often overlooked as they squat when alarmed. Like coursers, they run away from danger rather than fly.

GREY PLOVER (*Pluvialis squatarola*) (241). 30 cm. Above, dark grey and spotted. Chest and lower throat speckled with grey. Rest of underparts white, *except for axillaries (armpits), which are black*. Size, high forehead, shortish heavy black bill and long, ash-grey legs distinctive. A palaeoarctic winter migrant, usually occurring in large flocks, along the entire coast and in the eastern half of Southern Africa. Mainly maritime, but sometimes found inland, feeding on the exposed mud-flats of large sheets of water. Some individuals may be seen in partial breeding plumage (black face, throat, chest and breast) before leaving for the north in the autumn.

SENEGAL PLOVER (*Vanellus lugubris*) (244). 23 cm. Above, brown washed with oily green. *White on forehead does not extend beyond the eye.* A *fairly narrow blackish band* divides the grey neck from the remaining underparts, which are white. White tail-feathers have broad black tips, except for the outer two, which are wholly white. Under wing-coverts ash-brown and white. *Secondaries entirely white*, unlike those of the Black-winged Plovers, which are tipped with black. Eyes orange-yellow; legs a reddish brown. Confined to the extreme eastern regions of Southern Africa.

Rarer species:

MONGOLIAN PLOVER (*Charadrius mongolus*) (234)

LESSER GOLDEN PLOVER (*Pluvialis dominica* (240X))

WHITE-WINGED PLOVER (*Vanellus crassirostris* (248))

SNIPES and WADERS: Scolopacidae

Snipes may be recognized by their very long, straight, slender bills. Probe mud and ooze for the worms and other aquatic animals on which they feed. Quick off the ground; have a fast, twisting, erratic flight. During the breeding season easily identified by their aerial displays over their breeding ground. During these flights a characteristic drumming, caused by a vibration of the outer tail-feathers, is usually audible. Waders are a large group of small to medium-sized birds with long legs, angular pointed wings and slender bills. With the exception of the Avocets and Black-winged Stilts, all are palaeoarctic migrants, differing to a greater or lesser extent in their breeding- and winter-plumages. Always associated with water and, with a few exceptions, highly gregarious in their winter quarters; often found in large mixed flocks. Most of them have the habit of standing on one leg, with their heads tucked in under their wings, while resting.

ETHIOPIAN SNIPE   *Gallinago nigripennis* (250)   p. 160
  Afr Afrikaanse snip   *Z* u-Nununde
  X um-Nqunduluti   *S* Koekoelemao
Identification: 28 cm. Above, a mottled black, dark brown and buff. Crown has longitudinal buff streak down the centre. Buff eye-stripe well-defined. Sides of face buffish and finely streaked; throat buffish. Neck, chest and breast buff-brown with dark streaks; flanks barred. *Belly white.* Narrow outer tail-feathers also white. Eyes brown; long bill, with slightly expanded tip, black; legs a greenish brown. Sexes alike. Subadult similar to adult.

Usually seen only when flushed or when making display flights over their breeding grounds. Usually found singly or in pairs. Resident, but frequently move, probably as a result of the drying up of the habitat.
Voice: When flushed, a soft '*tchek*'; during the breeding season a repeated '*chok, chok, chok*'.
Habitat: Large vleis or stretches of flooded short grass.
Distribution: Throughout Southern Africa.

CURLEW SANDPIPER   *Calidris ferruginea* (251)   p. 144
  Afr Krombekstrandloper
Identification: 20 cm. Winter plumage: above, a greyish brown. Upper tail-coverts white, forming a *conspicuous white patch at base of tail in flight.* Below: white, under tail-coverts included; chest streaked and washed with pale ash-grey. Flight pattern shows a *white wing-bar.* Eyes brown; *blackish bill fairly heavy and curved slightly downward near tip*; legs an olive-brown. Sexes alike. Subadult similar to adult in non-breeding plumage, but mottled buff and white above, and washed with pale buff below. Some birds assume a partial breeding plumage before flying north in autumn (upper parts mottled black and chestnut; underparts bright chestnut, except base of belly and under tail- and wing-coverts, which remain white).

A very common palaeoarctic migrant that arrives at the end of August and departs in late April. Highly gregarious and found in large flocks, mainly on exposed sand- and mud-flats. Very active and restless when feeding. Move about with bodies held horizontally, probing to the full extent of their bills, and lifting their heads after each probe. Rest huddled together; when disturbed, tend to stretch their wings fully above their backs before moving away. Keep together in their flashing flight. Wintering birds are fairly common.
Voice: A single whistled '*tsssip*' and a chittering '*chit-chit-chit*' in flight.
Habitat: Exposed sand- and mud-flats beside inland and coastal waters; not partial to wet grassy localities.
Distribution: Throughout Southern Africa.

LITTLE STINT   *Calidris minuta* (253)   p. 144
   Afr Kleinstrandloper

Identification: 14 cm. Winter plumage: forehead, sides of rump, outer tail-coverts and entire underside white. Sides of chest have a dusky wash. Remaining *upper parts* an ashy grey; darker centres to feathers produce *a slightly mottled effect*. Light eye-stripe conspicuous. Upper tail-coverts, centre of rump and two central tail-feathers blackish. In flight, white wing-bars and two white V's on the back (one fitting into the other) distinctive. Eyes a dark brown; *short bill* and legs *black*. Sexes alike. A few birds show signs of breeding plumage before migrating in autumn (upper parts and innermost secondaries mottled black and tawny).

This *smallest* migrant is very common from September to May. Flocks may number only a few birds, or many hundreds. Often associated with other small waders. When feeding, keeps head down all the time and pecks from side to side while moving forwards rapidly. Flocks bunch together in flight, alternately showing their white undersides and drab backs as they dash past at high speed, twittering all the time.

Voice: A soft, liquid '*wick-wick-wick*' or '*chit-chit-chit*', usually uttered in chorus during flight.

Habitat: Exposed mud- or sand-flats along the coast or even quite small inland waters.

Distribution: Throughout Southern Africa.

RUFF   *Philomachus pugnax* (256)   p. 144
   Afr Kemphaanstrandloper

Identification: Male 30 cm; female 23 cm. Above, general colour a light brown. The darker centres and lighter edges of the feathers present a *distinctly mottled appearance*. Innermost secondaries have some blackish bars. Face white; lower neck and chest tinged with sepia. Rest of underparts white. *Two oval white patches on either side of the dark tail distinctive in flight*. Eyes a dark brown; *shortish bill* a dark brown; legs variable (green, yellow or orange). Sexes alike, but females (Reeves) much smaller than males. Though birds sometimes moult a few winter-plumage feathers and acquire dark feathers, mottled and edged with buff, only very slight signs of the beautiful ruffs the males acquire in the breeding season are ever seen in their winter quarters.

Probably the commonest palaeoarctic migrant. Large numbers may be found from August to May. Not wholly dependent on water, and feed mainly on insects. Can swim fairly well. Distinguished by their size, short-ish bills, fairly rounded heads and the erect stance they adopt when alarmed. At sunset, large flocks are often seen flying to open grasslands or cultivated land, to spend the night away from the water.

Voice: Usually silent in winter quarters.

Habitat: Short vegetation near water; vleis, pans and the mud-banks of any inland waters. Not found on sandy coastal beaches and seldom in saline marshes.

Distribution: Throughout Southern Africa.

COMMON SANDPIPER *Tringa hypoleucos* (258)   p. 144
Afr Oewerstrandloper

Identification: 19 cm. Adult male: above, olive-brown with a bronze-green sheen, and finely barred with a darker olive-brown, especially on the wing-coverts. Secondaries have white tips and bases, forming a white bar on the wing in flight. Central tail-feathers dark; outer ones white, barred with olive-brown. Lower neck and chest washed with olive-brown and finely streaked; remaining underparts white. Eyes and bill brown; shortish legs a greenish grey. Sexes alike. Subadult has upper parts mottled in dark buff. In breeding plumage the mantle and scapulars are broadly streaked and barred with blackish.

Not gregarious. Found singly or in pairs, arriving in August and departing at the beginning of May. At a distance the fine-grained markings on the upper parts cannot be distinguished, and the birds appear to be *a uniform olive-brown above*. At rest, the *white side of the chest is in strong contrast with the dark wing-shoulder and looks like a distinctive white patch*. Skims over the water with *flickering wings*, alternately flying and gliding. Frequents the water-side; is sometimes seen wading, and will perch on low objects, *bobbing both head and tail*.

Voice: A shrill, piping *'twee-tee-tee'* when flushed. Also a twittering call.

Habitat: The margins of dams, lakes, rivers and estuaries; not dependent on sand- or mud-flats; often found on stony ground near the water's edge.

Distribution: Throughout Southern Africa.

MARSH SANDPIPER *Tringa stagnatilis* (262)   p. 144
Afr Moerasstrandloper

Identification: 23 cm. Adult male: above, a uniform ash-grey, except the wing coverts, which have narrow whitish tips. Crown and back of neck sparsely spotted with blackish. Lower back and rump white; tail white, with broken, irregular bars. Shoulder of wing blackish; forehead, sides of face and *underparts pure white*. Eyes brown; *very long, thin bill* brownish; *long, thin, delicate legs* an olive-green. Sexes alike. In the subadult, crown and back of neck have blackish spots and are edged with white; feathers of upper parts clearly edged with white. In breeding plumage, upper parts are mottled in black and buffish; sides of face, neck, chest and flanks are barred and spotted with blackish.

A common migrant, seen from September to April. Usually found singly or in small flocks, wading in shallow inland waters, fresh or saline. In

flight, toes project far beyond tip of tail; white at base of tail and rump extends right up the back; and *wing-bar not in evidence*. This slender-looking wader is a smaller and more delicate edition of the Greenshank. Very active and not too shy. Single wintering birds are not uncommon.
Voice: Alarm-call a single '*tchick*', often uttered in chorus by a flock. On rising, gives a high-pitched '*tuit*'. Usual call a double whistle: '*tee-oo*'.
Habitat: Shallow water (either fresh or saline), mud-flats and vleis. Rarely seen on the coast.
Distribution: Throughout Southern Africa.

GREENSHANK   *Tringa nebularia* (263)   p. 144
   Afr Groenpootstrandloper
Identification: 33 cm. Adult male: above, a pale greyish brown; feathers have white edges and tips, presenting a slightly mottled appearance; crown and neck streaked. Shoulder of wing blackish. *Lower back and rump white.* Central tail-feathers a pale brown; rest of tail white, irregularly barred with brown. White below. *Long, heavy, slightly upturned bill* a bluish brown, tipped with black; long legs greenish. Sexes alike. Subadult has mantle, scapulars and wing-coverts edged with pale buff, and chest peppered with brown. In breeding plumage, upper parts are a mottled blackish, and flanks are spotted with dark brown.
   A common migrant, arriving in late July and leaving at the end of April. Many wintering birds are seen. In the interior, birds are usually found singly or in loose association with other waders; in estuaries, flocks are found. Frequent any waters, from small temporary wayside pools to the open sea-shore, where they feed in rock-pools. Often seen wading to the full length of their legs, keeping their heads up and with rapid movements picking up insects on the surface of the water. Also probe with their long bills in sand or mud. Often only their loud, ringing triple whistle, given on the wing, betrays their presence.
Voice: A clear, flute-like, usually trisyllabic whistle '*téw-téw-téw*' that can be heard at a considerable distance.
Habitat: Found wherever there is water.
Distribution: Throughout Southern Africa.

WOOD SANDPIPER   *Tringa glareola* (264)   p. 144
   Afr Bosstrandloper
Identification: 20 cm. Adult male: above, a sooty brown, edged and tipped with whitish, which gives the upper parts *a spotted appearance. Light eye-stripe conspicuous. Upper tail-coverts white; tail white, barred with blackish.* White below, except for lower neck and chest, which are finely streaked with ashy white. Eyes brown; bill brown with a greenish base; legs a greenish olive. Sexes alike. Subadult has upper parts spotted with a golden buff.

Breeding plumage more blackish above; sides of face, throat, neck and chest streaked with brown; flanks barred.

Usually found singly, though small flocks may also be encountered. A common migrant, arriving at the end of August and leaving in early May. Wintering birds are also found. Usually feeds along the margin of the water, not in the water itself. When alarmed, stretches neck to its full extent and may bob up and down before flying off with its shrill, characteristic triple call. May take refuge in overhanging vegetation. Feeds mostly off the surface, and not by probing.

Voice: When flushed, utters a shrill triple call, '*chiff—iff—iff* ', or '*wit-wit-wit*'.

Habitat: Vleis, dams, estuaries, grassy flooded marshes and pans with marginal vegetation. Seldom found along the margins of streams or rivers.

Distribution: Throughout Southern Africa.

CURLEW *Numenius arquata* (267)   p. 145
    Afr Grootwulp

Identification: 58 cm. Adult male: above, mottled buff and black; *rump white*. Below, neck, chest and breast buffish and broadly streaked; remainder of underparts white. Eyes brown; *very long down-curved bill* a dark horn-colour; legs a greenish grey. Sexes alike, but males much smaller than females. Subadults darker above, with mottling more intense. In breeding plumage the buff above and below is almost cinnamon.

A common migrant, mainly coastal; arrives in August and departs in March. Wintering birds are regularly seen. Inland records are mostly of single birds, but flocks of up to 50 have been recorded at the coast. Usually seen feeding in shallow water, far from the shore, or probing to the full extent of their bills for worms and other small aquatic animals, in marshy ground or mud-flats, and lifting their heads between probes. Flight fast and direct, but wing-beats relatively slow.

Voice: Its typical call, a loud '*cur-lee, cur-lee*', has great carrying power.

Habitat: The sea-shore, estuaries, lagoons and tidal rivers; also large inland waters.

Distribution: The entire coast; also the south-eastern and eastern half of Southern Africa.

AVOCET *Recurvirostra avosetta* (269)   p. 145
    Afr Bontelsie

Identification: 43 cm. Adult male: forehead, crown, back of neck, scapulars, wing-shoulders, bar across wing and primaries black; otherwise white. Eyes crimson; *long, thin, upcurved bill black;* legs a bluish grey; toes webbed. Sexes alike. In the subadult the black is more or less suffused with buffish brown.

The resident birds breed in Southern Africa, but enormous flocks of palaeoarctic migrants are also seen during the summer months. The resident birds are usually seen in small parties that seldom remain in one locality for long. Wade in shallow water, sweeping their upcurved bills from side to side, like scythes. Also swim in deep water, 'up-ending' like ducks. When flying in close formation, call continually.

Voice: Alarm-call a loud '*cwit-cwit, cwit*'; the clear, liquid '*kleeoot*' is usually given in flight, when the birds often call in chorus.

Habitat: Estuaries, lagoons, lakes, dams and temporary pans.

Distribution: Throughout Southern Africa.

BLACK-WINGED STILT *Himantopus himantopus* (270)
   Afr Rooipootelsie

Identification: 38 cm. Adult male: mantle, scapulars and wings (above and below) are blue-black, with a greenish sheen; tail greyish; rest of plumage white. Eyes crimson; *long, straight, thin bill black; very long legs red.* Mantle and scapulars of adult female brownish. Subadult brownish instead of black; crown, nape, sides of face and back of neck a light greyish brown. Legs pinkish.

Resident; usually found singly or in small parties, though flocks of several hundred may be seen. Feed in shallow water or on mud-flats, and pick their food off the surface. Reluctant to swim. Fairly tame, but readily take to the wing when disturbed. Extremely noisy at the breeding ground, screaming continually and dive-bombing any intruder.

Voice: A plaintive, penetrating '*kik-kik-kik*'.

Habitat: Any shallow water, but prefer marshy regions.

Distribution: Throughout Southern Africa.

Allied species:

SANDERLING (*Calidris alba*) (255). 19 cm. Above, general colour a greyish white; forehead white, with *no black bar on forecrown*. Black patch on wing-shoulder; white wing-bar and darkish rump conspicuous in flight. Underside wholly white. Short, heavy bill; feet black; *no hind toe*. Just before birds begin to migrate northwards, individuals may, very rarely, show signs of chestnut and black specks. Usually found in fairly large flocks. Wintering birds common. These plump, tame, drab-coloured waders tend to keep to themselves, and frequent shelving sandy beaches. They move in unison to and fro, as the waves advance and recede, picking up small creatures cast up on the wet sand. From a distance a line of these birds is easily mistaken for the foam of the waves. A very common migrant, found along the entire coast. Seldom recorded inland.

TEREK SANDPIPER (*Tringa terek*) (257). 23 cm. A uniform light greyish brown above, with blackish wing-shoulders. *Light eye-stripe contrasts strongly with darker crown.* Broad white ends of secondaries conspicuous in flight. White below, except for a few grey streaks on the lower neck. *Long, slender, upcurved bill black,* with yellowish base; *shortish legs orange.* Signs of breeding plumage, consisting of black streaks on the mantle and scapulars, may appear before the birds depart in late summer. A coastal migrant, usually found in small flocks but also singly. An active, dumpy-looking bird, probing about to the full extent of its bill as it moves around. Can run very fast. Bobbing of tail characteristic. Often seen perched on dead twigs of partially submerged trees, in estuaries and lagoons.

BAR-TAILED GODWIT (*Limosa lapponica*) (266). 38 cm. Brownish above, with light-edged feathers. Lower back and rump mainly white, but with some black bars and spots. Black barring on tail very variable; only visible at close range. *No wing-bar.* White below. *Very long, straight, blackish bill has flesh-pink base.* Legs a dark greyish green. Entire breeding plumage, except rump, is chestnut, with no barring from chest downwards. Signs of chestnut may appear towards the end of summer. A coastal migrant, very seldom recorded inland. Mostly found singly, though small flocks do occur on the west coast. Usually found on mud-flats or in shallow water. When the birds are probing, their heads are often partly submerged. Keep their heads down while feeding.

WHIMBREL (*Numenius phaeopus*) (268). 43 cm. Above, mottled in black and buff, with a *light streak down the centre of the crown.* Light eye-stripe conspicuous. No wing-bar. White below, but neck, chest and flanks are streaked, and suffused with buff. *Long down-curved bill* a dark horn-colour; legs a blackish green. In breeding plumage streaks appear farther down the breast. This smaller edition of the Curlew is a coastal migrant only. Rather shy; usually seen singly or in small flocks. Call a seven-syllabled rippling whistle and not the double-noted call so typical of the Curlew.

Rarer species:

GREAT SNIPE (*Gallinago media*) (249)

DUNLIN (*Calidris alpina*)

KNOT (*Calidris canutus*) (254)

RED-NECKED STINT (*Calidris ruficollis*)

GREEN SANDPIPER (*Tringa ochrophus*) (259)

BROAD-BILLED SANDPIPER (*Limicola falcinellus*)

REDSHANK (*Tringa totanus*) (261)

BLACK-TAILED GODWIT (*Limosa limosa*) (265)

GREY PHALAROPE (*Phalaropus fulicarius*) (271)

RED-NECKED PHALAROPE (*Phalaropus lobatus*) (272)

CRAB PLOVER (*Dromas ardeola*) (273)

SPOTTED REDSHANK (*Tringa erythropus*) (260)

BAIRD'S SANDPIPER (*Calidris bairdii*)

PECTORAL SANDPIPER (*Calidris melanotos*)

DIKKOPS: Burhinidae

The two species that occur in Southern Africa closely resemble the Stone Curlew or Thick-knee of Europe. They have large heads—hence the Afrikaans name of dikkop—and very large eyes. They have long, *bare* legs and only three toes. Being largely nocturnal, these birds are often picked out by the headlights of a car. They usually frequent dry country, open plains or sparse bush. The Water Dikkop is found on the stony or sandy borders of lakes or rivers. Dikkops feed mainly on insects and their larvae, and other small animals. Their cryptically-coloured eggs are laid in a bare scrape.

CAPE DIKKOP *Burhinus capensis* (275)   p. 145

    Afr Gewone dikkop   *Z* um-Bagaqwa

    X i-Ngqanqola   *S* Tapiane

Identification: 43 cm. Above, a pale tawny buff, heavily streaked and spotted with dull black, wing-coverts included. *No white wing-bar on folded wing.* Whitish below. Chest and lower neck buffish, with broad blackish streaks extending to the flanks. Under tail-coverts a deep buff. *Very large eyes yellow*; bill black but yellow-green at base. Legs yellow. Sexes alike. Sub-adult similar to adult, but more thickly streaked with black above, wing-coverts included.

Though nocturnal, dikkops are often seen during the day. When disturbed, usually run for some distance, with head held low, before flying up silently with curious rapid wing-beats. Upon settling again, spread their wings before quickly folding them. *Small white square near tip of wing and white spot on primary coverts conspicuous in flight.* Very active and noisy on moonlight nights.

Voice: A loud, thin, plaintive piping '*tche-uuuu*', often repeated, long drawn out and gradually dying away. Also an excited '*pi-pi-pi-pi*'.

Habitat: Mostly found in dry open country, sparse bush and scrub.

Distribution: Throughout Southern Africa.

Allied species:

WATER DIKKOP (*Burhinus vermiculatus*) (274). 38 cm. Slightly smaller than the Cape Dikkop. Above, stone-grey with fine, wavering cross-barring or vermiculation, and sparse black streaks. The distinct *whit-*

ish bar near the shoulder is set off by the blackish bar above it. Primary wing-coverts grey. Below, whitish; lower neck to breast streaked with blackish. Large eyes a pale green; bill black, but yellowish at base; legs a greenish slate. Sexes alike. *Always found near water*. Lies up during the day, in shady places near the water's edge. Very noisy at night. Call is a clear, shrill, plaintive whistle *'whee-yu-ee'*, and has a ventriloquial quality. In flight, rapid wing-beats alternate with slower flapping and the small black and white patch at the wing tip and broad grey proximal patch are conspicuous. Found throughout Southern Africa.

COURSERS and PRATINCOLES: Glareolidae

Coursers and pratincoles are medium-sized birds with relatively short, arched bills. They are allied to the plovers. Coursers have short wings, long legs and only three toes. They do not readily take to flight, and can run with astonishing speed. They are mainly insectivorous and resident, and inhabit the drier plains. Certain species of coursers are crepuscular and nocturnal, and lie up during the day.

Pratincoles have long wings and short legs, and do not lack the hind toe. They are migratory, and often follow swarms of locusts, catching the insects either on the wing or on the ground. Both coursers and pratincoles lay their eggs in bare scrapes.

BURCHELL'S COURSER   *Cursorius rufus* (276)   p. 145
    Afr Bloukopdrawwer
Identification: 23 cm. Above, mostly rufous brown, except for the *hind crown, which is blue-grey. White line from behind eye to nape* bordered with black. Chin and throat whitish. *Chest and upper belly a uniform pale brown, divided from the white lower belly by a black bar*. Primaries, primary coverts and underside of wings black; secondaries an ashy grey, with a broad white terminal band. Outer tail-feathers tipped with white. Eyes brown; bill dusky; legs white. Sexes alike. Subadults a pale tawny, mottled with black. Lack black and white markings on side of head.

Usually found in small parties of 5 or 6. Has a very upright stance. When disturbed, runs very rapidly for a short distance, suddenly stopping and bobbing its hindquarters like a sandpiper. Also moves its body backwards and forwards, and swings from side to side.
Voice: A metallic *'kwirt-kwirt'*, usually uttered when the bird takes wing. Also a grunting *'whowk'*.
Habitat: Usually found on barren flats with short grass and bare patches, or on recently-burnt veld.
Distribution: Throughout the drier western regions of Southern Africa.

128

PLATE 13

BUZZARDS, KITES, OSPREY AND GYMNOGENE

1 **JACKAL BUZZARD** *page* 75
Tail and chest chestnut, head and upper breast blackish.

2 **STEPPE BUZZARD** 76
Plumage very variable, cere and legs yellow.

3 **BLACK KITE** 68
Pale head finely streaked, long tail slightly forked, bill black.

4 **YELLOW-BILLED KITE** 68
Bill yellow, long tail distinctly forked.

5 **LIZARD BUZZARD** 73
Throat white with black longitudinal central line, rump white.

6 **OSPREY** 84
Chest brownish and spotted, head and nape whitish with dark line
through the eye.

7 **BLACK-SHOULDERED KITE** 69
Shoulder black, tail short and square.

8 **BANDED GYMNOGENE** 84
Long tail black with broad whitish bar, bare face and feet yellow.

1

2

3

4

5

6

7

8

PLATE 14

OYSTERCATCHER AND PLOVERS

1 **BLACKSMITH PLOVER** *page* 115
Crown and hind neck white, wing-coverts and scapulars pale grey.

2 **BLACK OYSTERCATCHER** 109
Eyes red, bill vermilion and legs pinkish red.

3 **BLACK-WINGED PLOVER** 115
White on forehead extends beyond the eye, chest band broad and blackish.

4 **CROWNED PLOVER** 114
Black crown encircled by broadish white stripe, legs red.

5 **WHITE-FRONTED PLOVER** 110
Forehead white, narrow blackish band on fore crown.

6 **KITTLITZ'S PLOVER** 111
Black bands on sides of neck meet on nape. Lower neck to breast washed with rich tawny.

7 **RINGED PLOVER** 110
Single broad black chest band, legs orange-yellow.

8 **WATTLED PLOVER** 116
Neck and breast heavily streaked, wattles dark red and yellow.

9 **WHITE-CROWNED PLOVER** 116
Crown white, long, pointed wattles greenish yellow.

10 **THREE-BANDED PLOVER** 111
Bill reddish with black tip, two black chest bands separated by a white one.

DOUBLE-BANDED COURSER *Rhinoptilus africanus* (278)　p. 145
　　Afr Dubbelbanddrawwer

Identification: 22 cm. Upper parts, including wing-coverts and rump, tawny, with black crescent-shaped markings. *Upper tail-coverts white.* First few primaries black; rest of wing rufous. Outermost tail-feathers white. Sides of face and neck buff, streaked with black. Rest of underparts buff *with two black bands (upper one narrower) across chest.* Eyes brown; bill black; legs white. Sexes alike. Subadult tawny above, with white edges to the feathers. Chest is speckled and has no black bands.

Usually found in pairs or small parties. Its cryptic colouring makes it almost invisible, unless it starts running. Very reluctant to fly. Active in the day-time and at night.

Voice: A thin, piping *'pee-wee'* when put to flight. Also a *'chickee-chickee-chickee-kee-kee-kee'* when flying at night. The *'woo-oo-oo-ook'* it utters when standing is perhaps an alarm-call.

Habitat: Occurs in rocky country, dry country with scattered thorn, or on dry pans.

Distribution: Throughout the drier western regions of Southern Africa.

BLACK-WINGED PRATINCOLE *Glareola nordmanni* (282)　p. 145
　　Afr Swartvlerksprinkaanvoël　　　*Z* Hlolanvula

Identification: 25 cm. Above, earth-brown; lighter on nape and sides of neck; *upper tail-coverts white.* Below, *light buff throat* is enclosed by a black line running from below the eye. Breast tinged with a brownish buff; belly whitish. *Under wing-coverts and axillaries (armpits) black.* Eyes a dark brown; bill and legs black. Sexes alike. Subadult resembles adult, but lacks black markings on throat, which is fairly heavily streaked.

This swallow-like bird has a *deeply forked tail and a white rump that are conspicuous in flight.* An irregular summer migrant, usually seen in small flocks, but often congregating in very large numbers at locust or army-worm outbreaks. Also found immediately after showers of rain. Take insects on the wing and on the ground. Agile runners, in spite of their short legs. Often seen executing aerial displays over their feeding grounds.

Voice: A loud twittering.

Habitat: Usually found on open grassy plains.

Distribution: Range from north to south in the central parts of Southern Africa.

Allied species:

TEMMINCK'S COURSER (*Cursorius temminckii*) (277). 20 cm. Similar to Burchell's Courser, but slightly smaller and has the *back of the crown rufous*, not blue-grey. Lower chest rufous; black patch on belly extends to between the legs, contrasting with the white flanks. Outer tail-feathers wholly white. Resembles Burchell's Courser in habits and distribution, but is also found along the eastern coastal belt.

THREE-BANDED COURSER (*Rhinoptilus cinctus*) (279). 28 cm. Above, mouse-brown with broadish sandy edges to the feathers; rump white. Throat and upper neck white, with a dark brown V-shaped line forming a necklace. White superciliary streaks meet at the nape. *Chest buff*, with heavy dark brown streaks, *and bordered below by a black band.* Rest of underparts white, with a *chestnut band across the lower breast.* Inhabits the drier bush of the northern regions of Southern Africa.

BRONZE-WING COURSER (*Rhinoptilus chalcopterus*) (280). 25 cm. Above, earth-brown. Upper tail-coverts and tips of tail-feathers white. Superciliary streak (not extending to the nape) and forehead a buffish white. Ear-coverts and sides of face blackish. Throat white with two short blackish moustache-stripes. Chest earth-brown and buffish, with a black band across the breast. Other underparts whitish. *Primaries have iridescent violet tips.* Eyes relatively large. A nocturnal bird, occurring in pairs or small parties in the northern and eastern parts of Southern Africa.

COLLARED PRATINCOLE (*Glareola pratincola*) (281). 26 cm. Very similar to the Black-winged Pratincole, except that the *under wing-coverts and axillaries (armpits) are chestnut,* not black. Usually seen in small flocks near river sandbanks, along the edges of lakes or on the coast. Very swallow-like in flight, catching insects on the wing. A rare visitor to the southerly regions of Southern Africa.

Rarer species:
WHITE-COLLARED PRATINCOLE (*Glareola nuchalis*) (283)

SKUAS: Stercorariidae

These are oceanic birds, whose plumage is largely brown. Their bills are stout, hooked at the tip and have a cere on the upper mandible. Their claws are curved and sharp, and their central tail-feathers elongated. Like other oceanic birds they have long, pointed wings. Usually only seen along the coast during and after storms. All skuas rob gulls, terns and gannets in ruthless fashion, and are mostly seen chasing and mobbing some unfortunate bird until its catch is disgorged. Their dashing, hawk-like flight enables them to fly rings round their victims.

ARCTIC SKUA *Stercorarius parasiticus* (284)   p. 176
  Afr Withalsroofmeeu
Identification: 46 cm. Above, a dark sooty brown. Crown of head much darker: looks like a dark cap. *Cheeks and nape a yellowish white.* Below,

whitish, except for the under wing-coverts and axillaries (armpits) which are a dark sooty brown. *Central tail-feathers straight, elongated and sharply pointed.* Eyes brown; bill a brownish black; legs black. Sexes alike. This bird also has a dark colour phase in which it is a dark sooty brown below and above, except for the basal inner webs of the primaries. These are white and show up as a white patch at the base of the primaries in flight. Subadults are streaked and barred; they lack the dark cap and their central tail-feathers are not much longer than the rest of the tail.

A summer migrant from Arctic and sub-Arctic regions. Seen singly, but more often in pairs or small loose parties. Pairs often combine in attacking their victims. Take offal from line-fishing boats.

Voice: A wailing '*ka-aahr*'.

Habitat: Although a marine bird, it often comes inshore, sometimes into harbours.

Distribution: Along the western and southern coasts of Southern Africa.

ANTARCTIC SKUA   *Stercorarius skua* (286)   p. 176
   Afr Bruinroofmeeu

Identification: 60 cm. Above and below a dark umber-brown, though some birds are reddish at the neck. *Webs at bases of primaries white. Central tail-feathers only slightly longer than the rest.* Eyes brown; bill and legs black. Sexes alike. Subadult very similar to adults.

White 'window' at base of primaries very conspicuous in flight and *visible from above and below.* General impression that of a large, thickset, sluggish bird with a relatively small bill. But its sluggish and inoffensive appearance is belied when it is seen attacking a tern or gull. Then the skua is ruthless strength personified. Present throughout the year, though more common during the winter months. Almost always solitary. Follows ships to pick up offal.

Voice: A plaintive '*queee-kek-kek*'.

Habitat: Occurs out at sea and off-shore; even enters harbours.

Distribution: Along the western and southern coasts of Southern Africa.

Rarer species:

POMARINE SKUA (*Stercorarius pomarinus*) (285)

GULLS: Laridae

Gulls are medium-sized to large swimming birds. Adults are white or white and grey below, and sometimes have some black above. They have long wings, short square or rounded tails, short legs with webbed feet, weak claws and strong bills. Gulls are gregarious, and though mainly birds of the coast, are also found on large sheets of inland water. They are essentially scavengers, feeding on dead fish or any other animal matter that may be floating on the water or lying on the beaches. Also feed on shellfish, and break the shells of molluscs by dropping them from the air on to hard sand or rocks. Steal eggs and chicks from the nests of other birds. Gulls lay two or three eggs in a depression; the eggs resemble those of plovers.

SOUTHERN BLACK-BACKED GULL *Larus dominicanus*
(287)   p. 176
Afr Gewone swartrugmeeu   *X* ama-Ngabongaba

Identification: 60 cm. Adult male: head, neck, upper back, rump, upper tail-coverts and tail white. Below, white. *Mantle, scapulars and wings slate-black.* Scapulars and flight-feathers tipped with white, resulting in a white trailing edge to the wing. Eyes yellow; eyelids red or orange-red; bill yellow, with red or orange spot on lower mandible. Legs bluish yellow, orange, grey or clay-coloured. Sexes alike. *Subadult a mottled brown all over;* flight-feathers not tipped with white; bill black. Transition to adult plumage is gradual, and takes about three years.

A common resident, especially near human settlements where refuse is to be found. This robust species to some extent parasitizes the breeding colonies of other sea-birds, plundering the nests of eggs and chicks.
Voice: A loud, plaintive '*meeoo*' and a deep '*cou-cou-cou-cou*' that accelerates towards the end.
Habitat: Found along the shore, on coastal islands, on estuaries and rarely on inland lakes. May follow ships out to sea for a considerable distance.
Distribution: Along the greater part of the coast of Southern Africa.

GREY-HEADED GULL *Larus cirrocephalus* (288)   p. 176
Afr Gryskopmeeu

Identification: 43 cm. General colour above and below, white and pale grey. During the breeding season *the whole head is grey,* forming a hood that contrasts sharply with the white neck. In non-breeding birds the heads are almost completely white. Outer primaries mainly black, with some white at their bases and a white spot near their tips; inner primaries mainly white, but with blackish ends tipped with white. *Eyes a light greyish yellow*; eyelids red; bill dark red and tip black; legs a dull red. Sexes alike. Subadult has irregular brownish markings on head; mantle and wing-coverts a mottled ashy brown; no white subterminal spot on primaries; legs brown; bill yellowish.

A graceful and fairly tame bird, usually seen singly or in pairs but forming flocks to feed, roost and breed. Tern-like in many of its habits; readily takes insects and offal. The black-and-white design near the wing-tip is conspicuous in flight.

Voice: A laughing, cackling cry. Very noisy at nesting site.

Habitat: Primarily a freshwater gull, found on almost all large inland lakes and pans. Also resident along the coast.

Distribution: Throughout the central and eastern regions and on the eastern coastal belt of Southern Africa. A small, isolated colony on the central western coast.

Allied species:

HARTLAUB'S GULL (*Larus novaehollandiae*) (289). 38 cm. The *head* of this small, graceful gull is *white*, although a few individuals have a faint lavender ring around their necks in the breeding season. Similar to the Grey-headed Gull in non-breeding dress, but bill is rather smaller and a reddish black, not dark red with a black tip. *Eyes brown or a greyish brown*; eyelids red. A local species, abundant along the coast but never found on freshwater inland lakes. Flight-pattern similar to that of Grey-headed Gull.

Rarer species:

LESSER BLACK-BACKED GULL (*Larus fuscus*)

WHITE-EYED GULL (*Larus leucophthalmus*)

SABINE'S GULL (*Larus sabini*)

TERNS: Laridae

Terns are water-birds, medium-sized to fairly large, and found mainly on the sea-coast. Except for a few tropical and freshwater species, virtually all these birds are white and grey. In breeding plumage they have black caps. They are slender, elegant birds with long, pointed wings and a graceful flight. Their legs and feet are relatively small, and their long, slender, pointed bills are more or less straight. Most species have a deeply-forked tail. They are gregarious all the year round, and subsist largely on small fish, which they capture by plunging headlong into the water, like gannets and kingfishers. Often execute a sudden, graceful twist and dive, to pick up a small animal on the surface of the water, after pausing for a moment above it.

CASPIAN TERN *Hydroprogne caspia* (290)   p. 176
Afr Reusesterretjie

Identification: 56 cm. The *largest of the terns*. Above, a pale grey, wings and tail included. Below, white. Adult in breeding plumage has top of head and nape black, with a greenish wash. Non-breeding birds have black streaks and spots on head, nape and sides of face. Eyes a reddish brown; *bill red; legs black*. Sexes alike. Subadult similar to non-breeding adults, but has back and wings mottled and barred with blackish brown, and tips of tail-feathers barred.

This resident species is less gregarious than the other terns, and is usually found hunting singly or in pairs. Nest in large colonies. Feeds on fish and insects, often robbing other terns of their catch. Though rather gull-like in size and flight, its *heavy red bill, long pointed wings and forked tail* are unmistakable.

Voice: A harsh, raucous, heron-like '*kraark*' or '*kwarkwa*'.

Habitat: Mainly along the coast but sometimes found inland. May be seen at some distance from water.

Distribution: Entire coast of Southern Africa, except the extreme north-western section. Also along the larger eastern rivers.

COMMON TERN   *Sterna hirundo* (291)   p. 176
Afr Gewone sterretjie

Identification: 33 cm. Above, a pale grey; below, white. Blackish bar along shoulder of wing. First primaries and outer tail-feathers have blackish outer webs. In non-breeding plumage forehead and base of hind neck are white; *crown is a mottled black* and *nape a sooty black*, and bird has a dark patch in front of the eye. Eyes brown; *bill blackish and legs a reddish brown*. In breeding plumage (seldom seen here since the birds are summer migrants) forehead, crown and nape are black; bill red with blackish tip; legs vermilion; underside washed with pale grey. Sexes alike. Subadult similar to non-breeding adult but upper side mottled buff and ashy: bill reddish at base and legs yellowish.

In summer, seen in large flocks fishing in coastal waters or resting in closely-packed masses on the shore. Flight is swallow-like, and *the inner primaries look semi-transparent against the light*. When at rest, tail-feathers do not project beyond wing-tips. A few individuals may be seen during the winter months.

Voice: A sharp '*pee-err*'.

Habitat: In coastal waters and especially around estuaries.

Distribution: Along the entire coast of Southern Africa, except the north-eastern section.

SANDWICH TERN   *Sterna sandvicensis* (296)   p. 176
Afr Grootsterretjie

Identification: 41 cm. Above, a pale silvery grey, wings included. Below, white. In non-breeding plumage forehead, neck, upper tail-coverts and tail white. Crown and nape a mottled black. In breeding plumage (which these birds attain before migrating northwards at the end of summer) forehead, crown and nape are completely black, and underparts take on a pinkish sheen. Eyes brown; *bill black, with a yellowish tip*; legs black;

soles yellow. Sexes alike. Subadult similar to non-breeding adults, but has blackish markings on wing-coverts and innermost secondaries; tail tipped with blackish.

This is a summer migrant, although wintering birds are sometimes seen. Body looks shorter and plumper than that of other terns. At a distance too great for the *yellow tip to the bill* to be seen, the black portion creates the impression of a short, stout bill. Tail less deeply forked than that of other terns. Feathers of crown and nape form something of a crest. Has a gull-like posture when sitting.

Voice: A grating, strident '*kirrik-kirrik*'. Generally noisy.
Habitat: Only in coastal waters.
Distribution: Along the entire coast of Southern Africa, excepting the far north-eastern section.

SWIFT TERN   *Sterna bergii* (298)   p. 176
Afr Geelbeksterretjie

Identification: 48 cm. Above, a medium grey. Below, white. In breeding plumage forehead, crown and nape are black, with a white band between the base of the bill and the forehead. Non-breeding birds have the crown a mottled black and white, and a blackish band along the wing-shoulder. Eyes brown; *large bill yellow*; legs black or blackish grey; soles yellow. Sexes alike. Subadult also has a yellow bill, but mantle and wing-coverts distinctly mottled in black, white and buff. Primaries blackish.

A large, resident species, usually occurring in parties of up to 50. Often a few individuals are found in loose association with gulls or other terns. Has a graceful flight, chiefly owing to the quick, high action of its very long, pointed wings. Often seen sitting on posts or masts. Dives into the sea from a great height.

Voice: A loud scream: '*kreee-kreee*'. Often calls on the wing.
Habitat: On coastal waters, lagoons or estuaries.
Distribution: Along the entire coast of Southern Africa, excepting the far north-western section.

DAMARA TERN   *Sterna balaenarum* (300)   p. 176
Afr Damarasterretjie

Identification: 23 cm. Above, a pale grey; below, white. In breeding plumage the *forehead, lores, crown and nape are a uniform black*. In non-breeding plumage the forehead is white, the crown blackish and white, and the line through eye and nape black. *Wing-shoulder a uniform grey, like the rest of the wing*. Eyes brown; bill black, with a yellowish base; *legs yellow*. Sexes alike. Subadults similar to non-breeding adults, but have brownish markings on the wing-coverts.

This very small resident tern is a fast and direct flier. Often a party of these terns on the wing resembles a flock of medium-sized waders. Usually hunt apart from other species, although they are communal roosters. Mostly found in small parties, although single birds are also seen. Frequently call while diving for fish.

Voice: A metallic, high-pitched '*tit-tit*' or '*tsit-tit*', repeated several times. When flushed from a roost, their alarm-call is a sharp, grating, squeaking cry.

Habitat: Along the open coast, on sandy bays and lagoons.

Distribution: Along the entire west coast of Southern Africa.

WHITE-WINGED LAKE TERN   *Chlidonias leucoptera* (304)   p. 176
Afr Witkruismeersterretjie

Identification: 23 cm. In non-breeding plumage the forehead, forecrown and hind neck, which forms a collar separating nape from back, are white. Hind crown and nape mottled in black and white; ear-coverts and patch in front of eye blackish. Mantle to *square tail* and upper sides of wings grey; blackish bar on wing-shoulder. Eyes brown; *longish, slender bill black*; legs a purplish brown. *In breeding plumage the whole head, mantle and underparts*, including under wing-coverts, *black*. Wings grey; *wing-shoulder, upper and under tail-coverts and tail white*. Bill a dark crimson; legs orangered. Sexes alike. Subadult has crown, mantle and scapulars mottled in black and buffish; wing-coverts mottled in grey and white; rump and tail grey. Flight- and tail-feathers are tipped with buff or off-white.

A common, but somewhat irregular migrant to freshwater areas. Mainly insectivorous; sometimes seen feeding over dry land, but generally found hawking insects over water, and barely skimming the surface. Usually found in small flocks, but larger numbers may congregate where there is an abundant supply of food. Birds may be seen at the end of summer in partial breeding dress. Wintering individuals are fairly common.

Voice: A rattling '*kerr*'.

Habitat: Inland freshwater lakes, dams and even small pans.

Distribution: Throughout, except the extremely arid western regions of Southern Africa.

Allied species:
ANTARCTIC TERN (*Sterna vittata*) (292). 41 cm. Larger than the Common Tern. In breeding plumage underparts are a dove-grey, and the white on the sides of the face, and also the black cap, are very distinctive. Non-breeding birds have throat, chin and forehead white. Underparts mainly white. Tail white; outer tail-feathers extremely long. Bill and legs cherry-coloured rather than red. Found along the southern coast.

ARCTIC TERN (*Sterna paradisaea*) (294). 33 cm. Same size as the Common Tern, which in non-breeding plumage it greatly resembles. In partial breeding plumage (seen in early summer) it is a very light sooty grey below, and the shortish tail is dark-edged (which distinguishes it from the long-tailed Antarctic Tern). The bill is wholly black in non-breeding and wholly red in breeding plumage, and looks shorter than that of the Common Tern. In flight *all the primaries look semi-transparent* against the light. In breeding plumage forehead and nape are black. Found along the entire coast, except the eastern section.

LITTLE TERN (*Sterna albifrons*) (299). 23 cm. Similar in size to the Damara Tern, but differs from it in having a *white* and not a black *forehead*, and also a *yellow*, *black-tipped bill*. Legs orange. In non-breeding plumage it has *a blackish bar along the wing-shoulder*. Usually the first few primaries are black. Rare along the west coast but a not uncommon migrant along the east coast.

WHISKERED TERN (*Chlidonias hybrida*) (305). 24 cm. Very similar to the White-winged Lake Tern in non-breeding plumage, but bill seems larger and heavier and there is no white collar on the hind neck. In breeding plumage forehead, crown and nape are a deep black; rest of upper side slate-grey. Chin, throat and chest a pale slate; belly blackish. *Sides of face*, *underside of wing*, under tail-coverts and underside of squarish tail *white*. Bill crimson; legs vermilion. An irregular summer migrant from the tropics, sometimes found breeding in Southern Africa.

Rarer species:

ROSEATE TERN (*Sterna dougallii*) (293)

SOOTY TERN (*Sterna fuscata*) (295)

LESSER CRESTED TERN (*Sterna benghalensis*) (297)

WHITE TERN (*Leucanous albus*) (302)

COMMON NODDY (*Anous stolidus*) (303)

WHITE-CAPPED NODDY (*Megalopterus minutus*) (301)

BLACK TERN (*Chlidonias nigra*)

SKIMMERS: Rhynchopidae

Lake- and river-frequenting tern-like birds with a peculiar prolongation of the lower mandible. Being laterally compressed, the whole of the lower and the greater part of the upper mandible are blade-like. These birds have very long wings that project far beyond their forked tails when the birds are at rest, usually on sandbanks.

AFRICAN SKIMMER   *Rhynchops flavirostris* (306)   p. 176
   Afr Waterploeër

Identification: 38 cm. Above, a brownish black; forehead, sides of face and underparts white, except for the underside of the wing, which is grey. Eyes brown; bill red with yellow tip; legs vermilion. During the non-breeding season bird has a whitish collar round the neck. Sexes alike. Subadults have streaked foreheads, and buffish tips to the feathers of the upper parts. Bills blackish, with a yellowish base.

These long-winged, fast-flying birds skim so low over the water when feeding that they plough the surface of the water with their *projecting lower mandibles*. Usually active during early mornings and evenings, and even on moonlight nights. Gregarious; when not feeding, rest on sand-banks. Wary birds, allowing no one to approach them too closely.

Voice: A loud, sharp '*kik-kik-kik*'.

Habitat: Freshwater lakes and large rivers, but may be found on relatively small pools during migration.

Distribution: Generally found on the larger rivers of the northern and eastern regions of Southern Africa. Isolated records from the southern regions.

SANDGROUSE: Pteroclidae

The sandgrouse are a family of medium-sized, ground-living birds. They are thickset, with short, curved bills and short legs feathered to the base of the toes. Their wings are long and pointed. They are exceptionally fast fliers, and come great distances to drink. This they do during the morning or late evening, depending on the species. Highly gregarious, but pair off during the breeding season. Eggs laid in a thinly-lined scrape. The breast-feathers of the males have been modified to retain water when soaked. This water is conveyed by the male to the young chicks, who drink the water from his feathers. This is their only source of water before they can fly. Feed mainly on dry seeds and small bulbs.

NAMAQUA SANDGROUSE *Pterocles namaqua* (307) p. 160

Afr Kelkiewynsandpatrys

Identification: 28 cm. Adult male: head, neck, upper mantle and upper chest khaki. Sides of face, chin, and throat buff. Lower mantle, scapulars and wing-coverts a khaki brown, with buff and lavender spots. Rump and long upper tail-coverts khaki-brown; flight-feathers dusky, with white tips. Tail-feathers a dusky black with buff tips; *central pair elongated and pointed. White and chestnut band across chest.* Lower breast, belly and under tail-coverts a dark rufous. Eyes brown; bill slate; toes lavender. Adult female has head, neck and upper mantle streaked with black; other upper parts mottled and barred with black, chestnut and buff. Underparts barred with black. Subadult mottled with black and chestnut above; buff below, with spots and bars; lower belly blackish.

Resident in the dry west, but a migrant at the extremities of its range. Numbers fluctuate considerably. Usually occurs in small flocks on sandy flats, but very large numbers congregate at water-holes during the morning or at dusk. Usually flies very fast.

Voice: A trisyllabic call, usually heard when flocks are on the wing. Rendered in Afrikaans as '*kelkiewyn*' (pronounced *cal-kee-vane*).

Habitat: Occurs in dry open country where the grass is short and the vegetation sparse.

Distribution: Locally, throughout the western half of Southern Africa.

DOUBLE-BANDED SANDGROUSE *Pterocles bicinctus* (310) p. 160
Afr Dubbelbandsandpatrys

Identification: 25 cm. Adult male: *black band on forehead bordered above and below with white*. Top of head streaked with black and buff. Neck, upper mantle, sides of face, chin, breast and wing-shoulders khaki. Throat yellowish. Other upper parts dusky, but mottled and barred with white. Primary coverts and flight-feathers a dusky black. *Rounded tail* broadly barred with black and buff. Two bands, the upper one white and the lower black, on the breast. Rest of underparts barred in black and whitish. Brown eyes surrounded by bare yellow skin; *bill and legs yellow*. Adult female has whole upper side mottled and barred with black, pale chestnut and buff. Below, neck and chest have no yellow tint but are buff, barred with blackish. Remaining underparts like those of male but more finely barred. Subadult like female, but has buff tips to the primaries.

A fairly common species, usually found in small flocks or in pairs during the breeding season. Fly to water at late dusk and remain near the water all night.

Voice: A loud '*chuck-chuck*' when flushed, and a whistling call on the wing.

Habitat: Occurs in the dry savanna and more open bushveld.

Distribution: Throughout the northern half of Southern Africa.

Allied species:

SPOTTED SANDGROUSE (*Pterocles burchelli*) (308). 25 cm. A short-tailed, compact, khaki-coloured bird, *spotted with white above and below*. Crown streaked. Male has lilac-grey chin, throat and eye-stripe. Breast cinnamon; belly unmarked. Female has throat, chin and eye-stripe buff, with bars on the belly. Usually found in pairs. When disturbed, fly up with a rapid '*kluk-kluk*'. Found in loose association with Namaqua Sandgrouse at drinking places. Confined to semi-arid regions.

YELLOW-THROATED SANDGROUSE (*Pterocles gutturalis*) (309) 33 cm. The largest of the four sandgrouse species, identified by its *conspicuous buff-yellow chin and throat*. The male is olive-brown and unspotted, with a black collar on the foreneck. Upper wing-coverts tipped with light cinnamon. Flight-feathers a blackish brown; thighs and belly a dark chestnut. The female is mottled above and below, with fine black bars on the chestnut belly. Usually found singly, in pairs or family parties on bare ground. Also partial to newly-burnt grassland. May congregate in fairly large numbers at water-holes, but not as regularly as the other species. Confined to semi-arid regions.

DOVES and PIGEONS: Columbidae

Medium-sized to smallish compact birds whose thick, close-lying plumage produces an extremely neat shape. They have small rounded heads. Their bills have a small, hard swelling at the tip and a larger soft one at the base. Their legs are short and strong, and their tails large and rounded. They are fast, strong fliers and occur in every type of country. All the species are resident, the fruit- and berry-eating doves being locally migrant. The term 'dove' usually indicates the smaller species and the term 'pigeon' the larger.

ROCK PIGEON *Columba guinea* (311) p. 177
  Afr Kransduif *Z* and *X* i-Vukutu
  S le-Evakhotho
Identification: 33 cm. Head grey; entire neck chestnut, streaked with grey. Mantle and wings chocolate; wings *speckled with white*. Rump and tail dark grey, but tail has a broad blackish terminal band. Below, slate and unspotted. Eyes yellow, *bare skin around the eyes red*. Bill black; cere blue-grey. Legs a dark crimson. Sexes alike. Subadult similar to adult, but lacks the red skin on the face; spots on wings brownish.

These pigeons are usually found in pairs during the breeding season, but otherwise congregate in large flocks that may cause damage to crops. They are mainly grain-eaters but may also take groundnuts. Can be seen flying fast and high to and from their feeding grounds in the early mornings and late afternoons.
Voice: A hollow, ringing '*voo-voo-voo-voo*'; courting call a trisyllabic '*voo-goo-too*'.
Habitat: Open mountainous country, where they roost and breed on ledges and in caves. Have adapted themselves to human habitations, and in cities breed on the taller buildings. Fly long distances daily to cultivated fields to feed.
Distribution: In suitable localities throughout Southern Africa.

CAPE TURTLE DOVE *Streptopelia capicola* (316) p. 177

Afr Gewone tortelduif   *Z* i-Hope
X i-Kobe   *S* le-Ebana-Khoroana

Identification: 28 cm. Forehead and crown grey; general colour of upper parts a brownish grey (darker along the coastal belt and paler in the more arid regions). *Black half-collar on hind neck.* Flight-feathers dusky. Underside blue-grey, except for *under tail-coverts which are white.* Tail-feathers are slate-grey, and all except the two central ones have white tips. Eyes brown; bill black; legs a purplish red. Sexes alike. Subadult generally duller, with light edges to feathers.

Lives in trees but feeds chiefly on the ground. Found in fairly large flocks at feeding grounds in cultivated areas. During its gliding flight, much white is shown in the tail, which is spread like a fan, and the alighting call is sometimes given.

Voice: The normal call is the well-known '*coor-coorr-coo*' (how's father?), often repeated. The alighting call is a harsh, almost snarling '*kirrrik*', and the courting call, which is given by the male while he bobs up and down, is a rapidly repeated '*kirrk*'.

Habitat: No preference; found wherever there are trees.

Distribution: Throughout Southern Africa.

LAUGHING DOVE *Streptopelia senegalensis* (317) p. 177

Afr Lemoenduif   *X* u-Nonkenke
S le-Evakoko

Identification: 25 cm. Head, neck and chest a rich lilac; mantle mainly rust-coloured; shows much blue-grey on upper side of wing. *Broken speckly black collar on sides and front of lower neck.* Under wing-coverts blue-grey. Belly and under tail-coverts white. Outer tail-feathers mainly white. Eyes brown; bill blackish; legs a purplish red. Sexes alike, but females tend to be duller. Subadults lack speckled collar; head and neck more brownish; generally duller.

This is a common and well-known dove, distinctly smaller than the Cape Turtle Dove, completely adapted to built-up areas and found in almost every garden. Spends much of its time on the ground, in search of weed-seeds. Also flies steeply upwards, gliding down and showing a great deal of white on its outspread tail. Does not call during these flights, as Cape Turtle Doves sometimes do.

Voice: A soft, gentle, lilting '*too-te-loo-te-too-too*'. The courting call, given by the male as he bobs up and down, is similar to the normal call, but faster.

Habitat: Found wherever there are trees; might even be called a 'town dove'.

Distribution: Throughout Southern Africa.

NAMAQUA DOVE   *Oena capensis* (318)   p. 177

   Afr Namakwaduif   *X* isi-Vukazana

   Z i-Gomboza   *S* le-Evanakhoroana

Identification: 26 cm. Adult male has *face, throat and chest black.* Crown, sides of neck and wing-shoulders grey. Violet-blue spots on inner wing-coverts. Underside of wing chestnut; axillaries (armpits) black. Mantle earth-brown; *blackish bands across rump.* Rest of underside white. *Long, graduated tail almost wholly black.* Eyes brown; *bill purple with orange tip;* legs purple. Female differs from male in that face, throat and chest are *not black.* Subadult resembles female, but is barred below; upper parts mottled in black, buff and white.

   This small, long-tailed dove is mostly seen on the wing, flying at great speed. When feeding on the ground, walks about in a hunched-up manner. When alighting, raises and fans out its tail, then lowers it slowly again. Usually perches low, on fences or bushes. In the drier regions, congregates in large numbers at drinking places during the heat of the day.

Voice: A low, soft, mournful '*twooh-hooo*', the first syllable being somewhat explosive. Call is ventriloquial to a certain degree.

Habitat: Prefers more or less dry, open country.

Distribution: Throughout Southern Africa.

EMERALD-SPOTTED DOVE   *Turtur chalcospilos* (321)   p. 177

   Afr Groenvlekduif   *Z* isi-Kombazana

   X isi-Vukazana

Identification: 20 cm. Forehead dove-grey; otherwise earth-brown above, with two broad black bands across the rump. Below, a brownish pink; belly whiter. Underside of wings and flanks a light chestnut. *Emerald-green metallic spots on inner secondaries.* Under tail-coverts dove-grey to blackish brown. Eyes brown; bill a purplish black; legs purple. Sexes alike. Subadult shows more black on the secondaries and has no bands on the rump.

   These small doves are frequently seen singly or in pairs, in clearings or on dirt roads, from which they rise with remarkable suddenness. *The light chestnut in the wing* shows up very clearly in flight. Flight is short, fast and zigzag.

Voice: A long, mournful, characteristic call, the final part being on a descending scale: '*doo, doo-doo; doo-doo, doo-doo, doo-doo, doo-doo, doo, doo, doo, doo, doo*'. Interpreted by the Bantu as a lament for the bird's dead relatives.

Habitat: Frequents wooded country and dry thornveld savanna, always in the vicinity of water.

Distribution: In the northern and eastern regions. Also along the southern coastal belt of Southern Africa.

PLATE 15

SANDPIPERS, STINT, GREENSHANK AND RUFF

1 **WOOD SANDPIPER**   *page* 122
   Rump white and eye-stripe conspicuous.

2 **COMMON SANDPIPER**   121
   White wingbar, back appears uniform olive-brown in the field.

3 **LITTLE STINT**   120
   Bill short and stout; the smallest wader.

4 **GREENSHANK**   122
   Rump white and long bill is slightly curved upwards.

5 **RUFF**   120
   Bill heavy, rump has the same colour as the back. Females rather
   smaller than the males.

6 **MARSH SANDPIPER**   121
   Legs and bill very slender, underparts pure white.

7 **CURLEW SANDPIPER**   119
   Bill slightly curved downwards at the tip, wingbar and rump white.

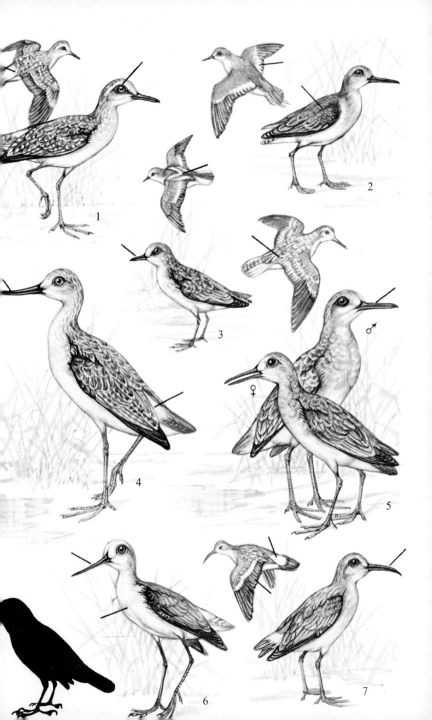

PLATE 16

CURLEW, COOT, MOORHEN, PRATINCOLE, DIKKOP, AVOCET AND COURSERS

1 **CURLEW**   *page* 123
  Bill long and down-curved, rump white.

2 **RED-KNOBBED COOT**   98
  Frontal shield white.

3 **COMMON MOORHEN**   95
  Frontal shield red, under tail-coverts white.

4 **BLACK-WINGED PRATINCOLE**   130
  Under wing-coverts black, throat creamy white.

5 **CAPE DIKKOP**   126
  Large yellow eye and *no* wingbar.

6 **DOUBLE-BANDED COURSER**   130
  Narrow upper and broader lower chestbands both black.

7 **AVOCET**   123
  Bill long and turned up at the tip.

8 **BURCHELL'S COURSER**   127
  Eye stripe white, nape blue-grey. Pale brown breast terminated by
  black band on lower breast.

Allied species:

RAMERON PIGEON (*Columba arquatrix*) (312). 41 cm. Head and neck a vinous grey; nape whitish. General colour of body a dark, greyish maroon, with white spots on chest, belly and wing-shoulders. Eyes grey; *bill, bare skin round eyes and legs yellow*. Sexes alike. The largest of the local pigeons; distribution limited to the southern and eastern heavy woodland and high-land forest. The movements of these pigeons are regulated by the amount of wild fruit and berries available. Form fairly large flocks once the breeding season is over. Seldom come to the ground.

RED-EYED TURTLE DOVE (*Streptopelia semitorquata*) (314). 36 cm. Crown a light grey; nape, neck and throat to belly a pinkish grey. Broadish black half-collar at back of neck has light grey edges. Remaining upper parts umber-brown. Underside of wings slate-grey. *Under tail-coverts grey. Broad terminal band of tail is grey-brown*, not white. Eyes orange-red; *bare skin round eye red*; bill black: legs purplish. Sexes alike. A rather sluggish bird, found in the dense thornveld and riverine forest of the east. Feeds mainly on berries and fruit, but also comes to the ground to feed on seeds. Also has a gliding flight, during which the *broad grey-brown terminal tail-band is conspicuous*.

MOURNING DOVE (*Streptopelia decipiens*) (315). 30 cm. Forehead, crown and sides of face to just behind the eye, dove-grey. Black half-collar on hind neck. Similar to Cape Turtle Dove but distinguished from it by the light orange eye and *the bare red skin around the eye*. Smaller than the Red-eyed Turtle Dove, and differs from it in having a lighter (almost white) belly and the grey under tail-coverts edged with white. Legs not purplish, but a pinkish red. Never found far from human habitations. Usually seen on the ground in the vicinity of houses and domestic animals, searching for seeds. Locally distributed over the northern and north-eastern regions of Southern Africa.

TAMBOURINE DOVE (*Turtur tympanistria*) (319). 23 cm. Above, general colour earth-brown, with blue-black spots on inner secondaries. *Forehead, eye-stripe, cheeks and rest of underparts white*, except for under tail-coverts, which are a dark olive-brown. Underside of wings chestnut. Bars on rump faint, and in the female the white is washed with grey. This small dove inhabits dense bush and is seldom seen in the open. Found singly or in pairs. An expert flier, dodging and darting between the trees at great speed. Feeds entirely on the ground.

CINNAMON DOVE (*Aplopelia larvata*) (322). 28 cm. Forehead, sides of face and throat white. *Hind neck and upper mantle iridescent bronze, green and pink*. Bare skin round dusky eye pink; bill black and legs a dusky pink. Underparts and remaining upper parts cinnamon and russet-brown. This beautiful dove is shy and wary, living in the dense shade of evergreen trees in the southern and eastern coastal belt. Difficult to see when it sits motionless on the ground. When disturbed while feeding, flies off noisily, but is apt to return to the same spot again to feed.

Rarer species:

DELEGORGUE'S PIGEON (*Columba delegorguei*) (313)

BLUE-SPOTTED DOVE (*Turtur afer*) (320)

FRUIT PIGEONS: Treronidae

These arboreal pigeons have green or yellowish plumage. Their stout bills have a soft basal part. Their legs are short and the upper part of the tarsus is feathered. They feed mainly on wild figs and berries. In flight their thickset bodies and relatively short tails are unmistakable. Usually found in small parties.

GREEN PIGEON *Treron australis* (323)   p. 177
    Afr Papegaaiduif   *Z* i-Jubantonto
    X in-Tendekwane

Identification: 30 cm. *Head, neck and underparts yellow-green. Nape grey.* Upper parts mainly olive-green; wing-shoulder mauve. Flight-feathers a dark slate, edged with yellow. Tail grey; under tail-coverts chestnut, with whitish ends. Lower flanks and feathers on tarsi yellow. Eyes blue-grey; bill bluish, with whitish tip and bright scarlet cere. Legs orange to vermilion. Sexes alike. Subadult similar to adult except that wing-shoulder is not mauve, but green.

When these pigeons sit perfectly still in densely foliaged trees, their camouflage is perfect. Often one becomes aware of their presence only when they drop down and streak away with a noisy clatter of wings. While feeding, they clamber about among the branches like parrots, except that they do not use their bills.

Voice: Usual call consists mainly of three parts: a whistle (unusual in doves), followed by a staccato whistling sound that trails off into a series of throaty sounds: '*twee, twee, twee-oo, tiddle-you . . . hrrr-rittit, hrrr-rittit, hrrr . . . rrr . . . rrr . . . rrr-rrr-rrr*'.

Habitat: Found in well-forested areas, and especially in riverine forest that consists mainly of wild fig-trees.

Distribution: In suitable localities in the northern and eastern half of Southern Africa.

PARROTS: Psittacidae

Parrots are medium-sized to small birds with powerful curved bills, sharply pointed at the tip. The short, square lower mandible is adapted to the cracking of hard kernels. Use their bills to grip branches when they climb about in trees. The strong curved claws are longer than the tarsi, and the two outer toes face backwards. Most parrots are green or brown, with yellow or red ornamental patches. They have a fast, direct flight with rapid shallow wing-beats that do not appear to move above the horizontal, and they usually utter their piercing cries while on the wing. They feed on fruit, kernels, berries, young buds and seeds, and nest in holes excavated in trees.

CAPE PARROT   *Poicephalus robustus* (326)   p. 177
   Afr Grootpapegaai   *X* and *Z* isi-Kwenene
Identification: 36 cm. Head and neck greyish; crown dusky and mottled. Mantle, scapulars, wings and tail dusky black, with a greenish wash. Lower back, rump and upper tail-coverts green. Below, green (chest paler). *Leading edge of wing, forehead, chin and lower part of thigh orange-red.* Under wing-coverts green and blackish. Eyes brown; bill whitish; legs slate. Sexes alike. Subadult has edge of wing, forehead, chin and thighs green.

This robust parrot is the largest in Southern Africa. Usually seen in pairs or small parties in thick bush or forest, or flying high overhead with rapid, almost fluttering wing-beats, uttering piercing screams. Their large, conspicuous bills make them look almost top-heavy.
Voice: A single piercing scream, repeated at intervals.
Habitat: Found only in thick bush and forest.
Distribution: In suitable localities in the south-eastern and eastern regions of Southern Africa.

MEYER'S PARROT   *Poicephalus meyeri* (327)   p. 177
   Afr Bosveldpapegaai
Identification: 23 cm. Forehead, hind crown, neck, mantle and scapulars, also tail- and flight-feathers, a sooty brown; *forecrown, wing-shoulders and under wing-coverts yellow*; lower back turquoise; upper and under tail-coverts yellow-green. Below, chin to chest brown; breast, upper belly and flanks blue or a greenish blue, mottled with brown; *lower belly a uniform greenish blue.* Thighs yellow; eyes brown; bill and legs blackish. Sexes alike. Subadult has no yellow on head and only a little on wing-shoulders and wing-coverts; innermost secondaries have blue-green edges.

A common species, usually found in pairs or small parties. Very shy and wary as a rule. When disturbed, dive steeply from their perches before flying off at a great speed, usually keeping well down. Yellow wing-shoulders and under wing-coverts conspicuous in flight. Roost in holes in trees.

Voice: A high-pitched '*chee-chee-chee*', usually uttered on the wing. Also a bisyllabic conversational note, one note being higher than the other.

Habitat: Dry thornveld, usually near water.

Distribution: The northern third of Southern Africa, but not the north-western coastal belt.

ROSY-FACED LOVEBIRD   *Agapornis roseicollis* (330)   p. 177
    Afr Rooiwangparkiet

Identification: 16 cm. A red forehead, sharply demarcated. *Sides of face, chin and neck a reddish pink.* Crown to mantle, upper and under wing-coverts, chest and under tail-coverts green. Flight-feathers mainly dusky. *Rump and upper tail-coverts blue.* Tail multi-coloured. Eyes brown; bill a greenish white; legs a greyish white. Sexes alike. Subadults have paler faces and necks, and foreheads slightly buffish.

This small parrot is locally common and is usually seen in small, fast-flying flocks. May occur in large flocks when certain seeds are ripening; feeds on the ground. A very noisy species, especially when gathering at dusk to roost in rock crevices or weaver nests. Transports nesting material by sticking it into the feathers of the rump.

Voice: A shrill '*skreek*', rapidly repeated on the wing. When sitting undisturbed repeats this single note at intervals.

Habitat: Prefers dry, open or mountainous country, but is dependent on water.

Distribution: The northern half of western Southern Africa.

Allied species:

BROWN-HEADED PARROT (*Poicephalus cryptoxanthus*) (328). 23 cm. *Entire head and neck a dusky brown;* remainder of plumage green, except for the lower back, which is a golden green. Under wing-coverts yellow. Eyes a greenish yellow; *bill a bluish white* and legs black. A noisy, gregarious species, usually seen in small fast-flying flocks and uttering shrill screeches. Found in well-wooded country with fairly large trees, in the north-eastern parts of Southern Africa.

RÜPPEL'S PARROT (*Poicephalus rüppellii*) (329). 23 cm. General colour, including that of breast and upper belly, a dusky earth-brown. Sides of face and throat lighter. Wing-shoulder, edge of wing and under wing-coverts yellow. Feathers on tarsi orange-yellow. Bill and legs a greyish black. *Rump and upper tail-coverts of male earth-brown, washed with blue. Female has rump, upper and under tail-coverts and lower belly a bright blue.*

A local species of the north-western regions. Prefer high trees and are never found far from water. Their flight is fast and short.

Rarer species:

BLACK-CHEEKED LOVEBIRD (*Agapornis nigrigenis*) (331)

LILIAN'S LOVEBIRD (*Agapornis lilianae*) (332)

LOURIES: Musophagidae

Louries or Turacoes are fairly large arboreal birds with long tails and crests. They are confined to Africa, and can be divided into two groups. That which lives in forests or dense bush is richly coloured, mainly green but with crimson wings. These colours are the result of pigmentation and not to any refractory properties of the cells of the feathers. These birds are more often heard than seen. The other species inhabits the more open savannas and is plain grey in colour. Very noisy and always conspicuous. Subsist entirely on fruit and berries and are local in their distribution.

KNYSNA LOURIE   *Tauraco corythaix* (336)   p. 192
    Afr Knysnaloerie   *Z* i-Gwalagwala
    X i-Gologolo

Identification: 46 cm. Head, neck and breast a bright green. *Longish, pointed green crest, tipped with white.* A short white line in front of and a longer one below the eye. Back, wings and tail an iridescent bluish green. *Greater part of flight-feathers crimson.* Belly and under tail-coverts a slaty brown. Eyes brown; bare skin round eyes and bill red. Legs black. Sexes alike. Subadult is duller, shows less crimson in the wing and has a brownish bill.

Usually found in straggling parties, hopping about on the branches or running along them. Difficult to spot when they sit still in dense green foliage. Their flight is heavy, and after a few strong wing-beats they glide to a lower perch some distance away. Their crimson wings show up to the best advantage during such a glide.

Voice: A loud, resonant '*crook-crook-crook*'. Alarm note a soft '*chaaa*' (*ch* as in loch), uttered when feeding birds are disturbed.

Habitat: Evergreen forests.

Distribution: In the south-eastern and eastern coastal regions of Southern Africa.

PURPLE-CRESTED LOURIE   *Tauraco porphyreolophus* (337) p. 192
    Afr Bloukuifloerie   *Z* i-Gwalagwala

Identification: 46 cm. *Short, rounded crest, nape and chin an iridescent violet.* Forehead and line through eye an iridescent green. Throat, neck, breast and upper mantle green, washed with pink. Lower back, wings and tail an iridescent bluish purple. *Greater part of flight feathers crimson*. Belly, flanks and under tail-coverts a dusky brown. Eyes dark brown; bare skin round eye red; bill and legs black. Sexes alike. In the subadult the flight-feathers are a duller crimson.

A very active bird, usually seen singly or in pairs, flying swiftly or gliding from tree to tree. Like all the louries it is very shy, but expert at running along branches and hopping about on them. Less noisy than the Knysna Lourie.

Voice: A long sequence of loud, deep-toned, resonant sounds: '*crook, crook, crook*'. Also a loud hoot.

Habitat: Found in drier country than the last species, and especially in riverine forest. Seldom inhabit true forest.

Distribution: The eastern and north-eastern third of Southern Africa.

GREY LOURIE *Corythaixoides concolor* (339)   p. 192
   Afr Kwêvoël (Grysloerie)

Identification: 50 cm. A long-tailed, *long-crested*, wholly grey bird. Eyes brown; bill and legs black. Sexes alike. Subadult has a shorter crest and is a more ashy grey.

Usually found in small parties, flying rather clumsily from tree to tree, not gliding like the other species of louries. Though wary, they are not as timid as the other species and are often seen perched on the tops of tall trees, from which they have an unrestricted view of the country around. Should they see anything suspicious, their protracted warning calls ring out, alerting all the animals in the vicinity. When alarmed, repeatedly raise and lower their crests. Feed mainly on berries and insects.

Voice: A nasal, penetrating, supercilious '*kweh*' (g'way), and various piercing cries and shrieks.

Habitat: Open thornveld; partial to the taller trees near watercourses.

Distribution: The northern half of Southern Africa, but not along the western coastal belt.

CUCKOOS: Cuculidae

All the cuckoos, except the three smallest, are medium-sized. They have fairly strong, slightly curved, pointed bills. The larger species have long rounded tails and rather pointed wings. The outer toes of cuckoos point backwards. The majority are migratory and parasitic, for all except the coucals lay their eggs in the nests of other birds. Coucals make their own nests and rear their young themselves. Cuckoos subsist largely on caterpillars, and will even feed on the hairy ones that are not taken by other birds. They are usually solitary in habits, and have distinctive calls.

Cuckoos may be divided into four main groups:

(1) The medium-sized *non-crested* cuckoos. These are plainly coloured, being mainly grey, black and white (5 species).
(2) The medium-sized *crested* cuckoos, which are also black, white and grey (3 species).
(3) The small *green iridescent* cuckoos (3 species).
(4) The medium-sized coucals, whose colouring is mainly black, brown and white, though one is green (5 species).

RED-CHESTED CUCKOO   *Cuculus solitarius* (343)   p. 192
Afr Piet-my-vrou   *X* and *Z* Pezukomkono

Identification: 30 cm. Adult male, a dark slate-grey above. Below, throat greyish; *chest chestnut*; breast to belly buff, barred with black. Under tail-coverts buff, but not barred. Underside of wing barred with white. Broad, longish tail has a few white spots. Eyes a reddish brown; eyelids yellow; bill black, with base of lower mandible yellow; legs yellow. Female is paler on the chest. Subadult is mottled black and white above, including throat and chest; breast to belly broadly barred with black.

An extremely noisy summer migrant that calls for hours on end, chiefly in the mornings and evenings but even on moonlight nights. In spite of its noisy habits this bird is rarely seen, for it usually remains concealed in the thick foliage of tall trees. Chiefly parasitizes the Cape Robin, the Cape Thrush, and the Cape Wagtail.

Voice: A loud, trisyllabic call '*whit-whit-whoo*'. When two or three males meet, their usual calls become loud, fast and frenzied and are interspersed with a rapid '*kwik-kwik-kwik*'. Females make low, gurgling sounds.

Habitat: Usually found in forests and wooded kloofs, but has adapted itself to plantations of exotic trees, and even occurs in towns and cities.

Distribution: The eastern half and southern tip of Southern Africa.

GREAT SPOTTED CUCKOO   *Clamator glandarius* (346)   p. 192
Afr Gevlekte koekoek

Identification: 41 cm. Cheeks, crown and crest grey; remaining *upper parts ashy, with white spots*. Below, throat and neck a buffish white; chest to under tail-coverts white. *Long tail-feathers broadly tipped with white*. Eyes brown; eye-ring a dark orange; bill brown, with base of lower mandible yellow; legs a brownish grey. Sexes alike. Subadult has a smaller crest, blackish cheeks and flight-feathers more or less rufous.

A noisy summer migrant, usually seen flying about in the tree-tops. Feeds at lower levels, however, and even on the ground. During its somewhat heavy flight its white-tipped tail is conspicuous. Mainly parasitizes crows and starlings.

Voice: A loud, rasping '*keeeow*', often repeated. Alarm-note a rising screech; also utters a crow-like *'kawk'*. Female gives a bubbling *'burroo-burroo'*.

Habitat: Fairly open wooded country.

Distribution: The northern and eastern half of southern Africa.

JACOBIN CUCKOO   *Clamator jacobinus* (348)   p. 192

   Afr Nuwejaarskoekoek

Identification: 33 cm. Above, longish crest included, a shining blue-black, shot with green and violet. Flight-feathers brownish; *conspicuous white patch at base of primaries* visible from above and below. Below, *varies from wholly black* (entire tail included) *to white*, creamy white or greyish white, with tail-feathers broadly tipped with white. Eyes dusky; bill black; legs a dark grey. Sexes alike. Subadult brownish above; below, varies from dull black to buffish white. Also has the white wing-patch.

A summer migrant, presumably from Central Africa. A restless bird, seldom sitting calling on a perch for any length of time like other species of cuckoos. Usually seen in pairs, flying about. Its flight is swift and straight; when alighting in a tree it swoops up into the branches from below. Mainly parasitizes different species of bulbuls and shrikes.

Voice: Has a large variety of calls: a loud, ringing *'kleeoo-qui-quip'*, an uncontrolled, guttural *'gee-gee-geeegeegee-gee-goo'*, and a querulous *'churr'*.

Habitat: Open thornveld.

Distribution: The eastern and northern half of Southern Africa, including the southern coastal belt.

EMERALD CUCKOO   *Chrysococcyx cupreus* (350)   p. 192

   Afr Mooimeisiekoekoek   *Z* Bantwanyana

Identification: 20 cm. Adult male has the whole head, upper side, neck and chest an iridescent emerald-green, washed with old gold, the dark centres to the feathers giving it a scaly appearance. *Breast to belly and under tail-coverts canary-yellow.* Under wing-coverts white and outer tail-feathers barred with white. Eyes brown; eye-ring and bill a pale green; legs a bluish slate. Adult female an iridescent moss-green above, barred with chestnut; crown of head brown with buff bars. Below, white barred with iridescent moss-green. Subadult similar to adult female but has feathers of crown emerald-green, with a golden sheen and subterminal white bars.

This small cuckoo is one of the most beautiful birds in Southern Africa. Tending to keep to the dense foliage of tall trees, it is more often heard than seen. Dives into cover at the slightest sign of danger. Flight is fast and slightly undulating. Thought to be migratory, but are possibly overlooked owing to their silence during winter. Parasitizes mainly puff-backed shrikes, sunbirds, flycatchers and bulbuls.

Voice: A mellow four-syllabled whistle '*wheeya-whee-whee*' (Pretty Georgie), that has great carrying power and is usually given from the same singing-post in a particular tree.

Habitat: Forested areas with tall, leafy trees.

Distribution: The south-eastern and eastern regions of Southern Africa.

DIDRIC CUCKOO *Chrysococcyx caprius* (352) p. 192
Afr Diedrikkoekoek

Identification: 20 cm. Adult male: above, an iridescent bottle-green, shot with bronze, gold and violet; *white streak behind the eye*, and a certain amount of white on the centre of the crown. *White spots on wing-coverts and secondaries.* Below, white; flanks barred with a bronzy green. Underside of wing barred in black and white; tail a greenish black with white spots. Eyes and eye-rings red; bill blackish; legs blue-black. Adult females duller above; barring on flanks extends to chest and sides of neck. Subadult, iridescent green to cinnamon-brown barred with green. Below, heavily streaked and blobbed with green. *Bill a coral red.*

The commonest of the glossy cuckoos that visit Southern Africa during the summer months. Males very noisy and pugnacious in their established breeding territories. Displaying males chase females in the air with outspread tails and a shivering action of the wings. Not in the least furtive or shy: often heard calling on the wing, or while sitting on an exposed perch. Chiefly parasitizes the Cape Sparrow, weavers and the Red Bishop.

Voice: A plaintive whistle '*dee-dee-deederik*', repeated over and over again. Female answers with a '*deea-deea-deea*'. Subadults can be heard begging all day long, with a monotonous '*cheep-cheep*'.

Habitat: Prefers open thornveld, but has adapted itself to exotic plantations and is found in built-up areas, even in cities.

Distribution: Throughout Southern Africa.

BURCHELL'S COUCAL *Centropus superciliosus* (356) p. 192
Afr Gewone vleiloerie *Z* u-Fukwe
X u-Bikwe *S* Makhofe

Identification: 43 cm. Sides of face and *top of head to upper back a glossy black* (often with a buff eye-stripe). Mantle and wings chestnut; white stripes on nape and mantle. *Rump and upper tail-coverts barred* in green and buff; long tail dark brown with a slight greenish gloss. Below, buff; sides of neck and chest often streaked with buff. *Eyes red*; bill black; legs blackish. Sexes alike. Subadult has head and nape a dull black, and rest of upper side barred with black.

These skulking birds are usually seen creeping about in or under dense bushes. When they reach the top they fly off heavily, with their *short, rounded, chestnut wings conspicuous in flight*, and flop into a nearby bush after a short glide. Sometimes sit drying themselves on low, exposed perches. Usually seen singly or in pairs, and do not appear to be migratory. Not parasitic.

Voice: A series of bubbling, flute-like notes *'doo-doo-doo-doo'*, on a descending scale, often with male and female answering each other. Alarm-call a harsh *'kek, kek, kek,'* often repeated.

Habitat: Common in large reed-beds and the vegetation that borders dams and streams. Also found in gardens and parks in built-up areas.

Distribution: The eastern half and southern tip of Southern Africa.

Allied species:

AFRICAN CUCKOO (*Cuculus canorus*) (340). 33 cm. Not crested. General colour grey, barred from chest to belly with blackish grey. Underside of wing and longish tail also barred. Eyes orange-yellow; bill a dark horn-colour, sometimes with a yellow base. Legs yellow. Call a loud, melancholy, hollow-sounding, low-pitched *'hoop-hoop'*, with the accent on the second syllable. Its flight is fast, and rather like that of an accipiter, except that the cuckoo's wings are long and pointed, not short and rounded. Parasitizes mainly bulbuls. (The European Cuckoo, of which this is a race, is a summer migrant that is silent in Southern Africa.)

BLACK CUCKOO (*Cuculus clamosus*) (344). 30 cm. Not crested. Above, blue-black. Below, varies from plain black to black finely barred with white. A certain amount of rufous on chest and under tail-coverts. Underside of primaries barred. Tail-feathers have very narrow white tips. Eyes brown; bill blackish, legs a pinkish brown. Call is persistent and melancholy, *'who-whee'* or *'who-who-whee'*, with the final syllable a little more highly pitched. A shy, unobtrusive summer migrant, whose presence would often be unsuspected but for its call. *Shows no white window in flight.* Found in open as well as dense thornveld, and also in exotic plantations, in the eastern and northern half of Southern Africa. Parasitizes mainly drongoes and shrikes.

STRIPED-BREASTED CUCKOO (*Clamator levaillantii*) (347). 41 cm. Crested. Very similar to the light-phased Jacobin Cuckoo, but larger, and with *throat and chest heavily streaked.* Base of primaries also white; tail-feathers also broadly tipped with white. A not very common summer migrant, usually found sitting calling in a dense bush or tree. Occasionally seen in small parties, searching for caterpillars. Call a hollow-sounding *'cur, cur, cur'*, abruptly changing into a high-pitched *'kwi-kwi-kwi'*, which is repeated about 20 times. Mainly parasitic on babblers. Not confined to the more open country, but is often found at the edge of thick bush. Distributed over the north-eastern and northern regions of Southern Africa.

KLAAS'S CUCKOO (*Chrysococcyx klaas*) (351). 18 cm. The smallest of the local glossy cuckoos. Adult male an iridescent *dark green shot with bronze above*, sides of face, neck and *sides of chest included. No white eye-stripe and no white spots on upper wing-coverts or secondaries.* Below, white, with flanks slightly barred. Adult female is barred above with bronze, and below with green. Outer tail-feathers mainly white in both sexes. An inconspicuous migrant, easily overlooked. Often seen during the winter months. Female less often seen than male. Call a high-pitched bisyllabic '*klaasi*', sometimes repeated for hours on end. Mainly parasitic on flycatchers and sunbirds. Found in patches of forest as well as open thornveld in the eastern half and along the southern coastal belt of Southern Africa.

BLACK COUCAL (*Centropus toulou*) (353). 33 cm. General colour black; in breeding dress slightly shot with iridescent green. In non-breeding plumage, upper side streaked with tawny. *Wings chestnut;* bill and legs black. A rare species, confined to grassy vleis or open bush with long grass. Only occasionally seen sitting on an exposed perch, and dives into the grass at the slightest sign of danger. Call a rapid bisyllabic '*popop*' and a ventriloquial '*coick*', or a soft bubbling call. Found in the north-eastern regions.

SENEGAL COUCAL (*Centropus senegalensis*) (355). 41 cm. Head, nape, sides of face to upper back black, slightly iridescent and shot with olive-green. No eye-stripe. Wings chestnut; mantle reddish. *Upper tail-coverts greenish and not barred.* Tail an iridescent dark green. Eyes red; bill black; legs lead-coloured. Frequents bush or grassy woodland and seldom leaves thick cover. Rather crepuscular in habits. Call a series of bubbling notes. Found in the northern regions of Southern Africa.

GREEN COUCAL (*Ceuthmocares aereus*) (358). 33 cm. Head olive-grey; back, wings and underside of *long tail* steel-blue, washed with green. Below, green. Eyes red; bare skin round eyes blue; *bill yellow*; legs black. A not very common resident species found in dense bush along the coast, along rivers and also in forest. Shy, and seldom leaves thick cover. Call a series of clicks, becoming more rapid and changing into a wailing '*cheer*' that is repeated several times. Found in the eastern coastal regions.

Rarer species:

LESSER CUCKOO (*Cuculus poliocephalus*) (342)

THICK-BILLED CUCKOO (*Pachycoccyx audeberti*) (345)

COPPERY-TAILED COUCAL (*Centropus cupreicaudus*) (354)

LONG-TAILED CUCKOO (*Cercococcyx montanus*)

OWLS: Strigidae

Owls are nocturnal birds of prey, and vary considerably in size and structure. They have long, curved talons and hooked beaks. Their heads are relatively large; their flattened faces show the familiar 'facial discs' and their eyes face forwards. Some species have ear-tufts. Owing to their soft, downy plumage, and particularly to the downy edges of the primaries, their flight is noiseless. Their calls are specific. They live mainly on rodents and other small animals, and insects. The smaller prey is swallowed whole, the undigested parts, e.g. the hair and some of the bones, being regurgitated in the form of pellets. One species subsists mainly on fish. They occur in all types of country, and lay their plain white eggs on the bare ground, or in the old nests of other birds.

BARN OWL   *Tyto alba* (359)   p. 193
   Afr Nonnetjie-uil   *S* Sephooko
Identification: 33 cm. Above, a golden buff, finely and profusely mottled with grey, and speckled with white. *No ear-tufts; heart-shaped facial disc very distinctive.* Below, white, lightly spotted with dark brown on chest and flanks. Tail and flight-feathers have dusky bars. Eyes black; bill and *long legs* whitish. Sexes alike. Subadult darker above and washed with buff below.
   This virtually cosmopolitan species hunts at night, and occasionally on dull days also. When flying at dusk or in the moonlight it looks pale, almost white.
Voice: An eerie screech, and snores, hisses and bill-clapping at nesting- and roosting-places.
Habitat: Buildings, caves, mine-shafts, holes in trees and deserted Hamerkop nests.
Distribution: Throughout Southern Africa.

MARSH OWL   *Asio capensis* (361)   p. 193
   Afr Vlei-uil
Identification: 36 cm. Upper side and chest sepia. Head slightly barred; secondaries and tail have dusky bars. Facial disc pale, *with blackish rings round the eyes. Short ear-tufts.* Breast to belly paler and vermiculated in brown and buff. Eyes brown; bill and legs black. Sexes alike. Subadult more deeply and warmly coloured than adults.
   Usually found in small parties; rarely seen singly. Often begins to hunt before sunset, and may then be seen sitting on a fence-post or flying low over the ground, which it quarters in harrier fashion. When disturbed

during the day, flies only a short distance before settling on the ground again.

Voice: A frog-like croak, uttered at dusk, while on the wing.

Habitat: Long grass in vleis and on marshy ground.

Distribution: Found in the eastern half, the extreme south, and the northern regions of Southern Africa.

WOOD-OWL   *Ciccaba woodfordi* (362)   p. 193
   Afr Bosuil   *X* i-Bengwana

Identification: 33 cm. General colour brown, varying individually from a blackish brown to a deep russet. Above, speckled with smallish white spots. Large spots on the scapulars and central wing-coverts. *No ear-tufts*; facial disc greyish and indistinct. Below, including wings and tail, broadly barred in brown and white, with the bars narrowing towards the belly. Eyes and bill yellow; legs yellowish. Sexes alike. Subadults generally paler, and more sandy in colour.

A common but local species, usually seen sitting close to the trunk of a tree or bush, and not easily disturbed.

Voice: A cheerful trisyllabic hoot, rendered as '*weh-mameh*' (Oh, my mother!) by the Zulu. Also rendered as 'Who are you?'

Habitat: Frequents forest or dense riverine bush.

Distribution: Found in the southern and eastern coastal regions of Southern Africa.

SCOPS OWL   *Otus scops* (363)   p. 193
   Afr Kleinooruil

Identification: 19 cm. General colour may be grey, buff or tawny, streaked above and below with black, which produces a bark-and-dead-leaf pattern. Wing-shoulder has a band of irregular white spots. *Ear-tufts are small.* Tail barred with white and buffish. Eyes yellow; bill and legs a bluish horn. Sexes alike. Subadult resembles adult.

This small owl is strictly nocturnal, sheltering during the day in holes in trees or sitting pressed tightly against their trunks. Apparently feeds only on insects.

Voice: A monotonous '*kroo, kroo*', uttered at short intervals during the breeding season. Also a melodious chirrup, almost trilled and rather cricket-like.

Habitat: Generally found in the more open thornveld.

Distribution: Over the greater part of Southern Africa, but not in the southern and extreme western regions.

PEARL-SPOTTED OWLET *Glaucidium perlatum* (365)   p. 193
   Afr Dwerguiltjie   *Z* Mundungulu

Identification: 18 cm. General colour of upper parts a warm brown, finely spotted all over with white. Black and white collar round hind neck and two eye-spots on nape create the impression of a second face. Below, white with *chocolate streaks. No ear-tufts.* Eyes and bill yellow; legs yellowish. Sexes alike. Subadults have very few white spots on crown or mantle.

   This small owlet is often active during the day and takes little trouble to conceal itself, although it usually prefers to perch in a leafy tree. Catches rodents as well as insects. It has a dipping flight like that of the barbets. When excited, moves head and body to and fro and flicks tail sideways.
Voice: A series of notes, first ascending and then descending the scale, '*tuu-tuu-tuu-tuu-tiuu-tiuu-tiuu-tiuu-tiuu*'. Call increases in intensity, reaches a climax and gradually subsides. Heard by day as well as night. Subadult has a tremulous high-pitched whistle.
Habitat: A common species of the thornveld.
Distribution: Throughout Southern Africa, except in the southern and south-eastern regions.

SPOTTED EAGLE OWL *Bubo africanus* (368)   p. 193
   Afr Gevlekte ooruil   *X* isi-Huluhulu
   Z   isi-Kova   *S* le-Rivise

Identification: 46 cm. Above, general colour a mottled grey, blackish and white, with rounded white spots on the mantle. *Long ear-tufts.* Below, a mottled whitish, rather finely barred with brown. Eyes yellow; bill and legs blackish. Sexes alike. Subadults similar to adults, but have smoky barring on the head.

   The commonest of the large owls. Usually sleeps in sheltered spots on the ground during the day and emerges at dusk to hunt. Can be seen early in the morning or just before sunset, sitting on telegraph poles or other vantage points. An inoffensive bird for its size. Often killed by cars on the road.
Voice: Usual call a double hoot, '*hu-hoo*'. Also snaps its bill when annoyed.
Habitat: Prefers hilly, bushy country but is also found in fairly open country.
Distribution: Throughout Southern Africa.

Allied species:

GRASS OWL (*Tyto capensis*) (360). 36 cm. A larger, darker edition of the Barn Owl. *Above, a sooty brown* with white flecks; tail not barred. Below, light brown to deep buff, spotted with black. Facial disc whitish; *no ear-tufts.* Eyes black; bill whitish; legs yellowish. Frequents long grass along streams or in vleis; occasionally found in lightly-wooded country. Sits only

160

PLATE 17

JACANA, CRAKE, GALLINULE, SNIPES, FLUFFTAIL AND SANDGROUSE

1 **AFRICAN JACANA** *page* 107
Toes extremely long; frontal shield blue.

2 **BLACK CRAKE** 94
Bill greenish yellow; legs and eyes reddish.

3 **LESSER GALLINULE** 95
Bill and legs bright red, frontal shield green, under tail-coverts white.

4 **PAINTED SNIPE** 108
Female: throat light brown, dark chest-band, upper wing-coverts grey-green and unspotted. Male: throat and chest grey, upper wing-coverts heavily spotted with yellow.

5 **BUFF-SPOTTED FLUFFTAIL** 94
Head and neck red, tail relatively small and short.

6 **ETHIOPIAN SNIPE** 119
Bill long and black, belly white.

7 **DOUBLE-BANDED SANDGROUSE** 140
Legs yellow, bands on forehead and chest, tail rounded.

8 **NAMAQUA SANDGROUSE** 139
Tail long and pointed. Only male has banded chest.

PLATE 18

KORHAANS, BUSTARD, STORKS, CRANES AND CROWS

1 **LONG-LEGGED KORHAAN** *page* 105
Legs long, upper wing-coverts mainly white.

2 **BLACK CROW** 214
Bill relatively long and slender.

3 **RED-CRESTED KORHAAN** 104
Top of head grey, tuft of pinkish feathers on nape *not* always
conspicuous.

4 **KORI BUSTARD** 103
Prominent crest mottled black and white.

5 **BLACK KORHAAN** 105
Ear-coverts, tips of upper wing-coverts and wing shoulder white.

6 **KARROO KORHAAN** 104
Top of head, sides of face pale ashy brown; triangular black patch
on chin and upper throat.

7 **MARABOU STORK** 41
Enormous straight bill. Head, neck and chest bare.

8 **STANLEY OR BLUE CRANE** 102
Long, curving ornamental secondaries black.

9 **PIED CROW** 214
Nape and chest white.

10 **CAPE RAVEN** 214
Nape white, bill heavy.

11 **SADDLEBILL STORK** 42
Bright yellow frontal saddle; flight feathers white.

12 **WATTLED CRANE** 102
Long ornamental plumes grey. Partially feathered pendent wattles
white.

13 **CROWNED CRANE** 101
Tuft of straw-coloured, stiff bristles on crown; upper wing-coverts
white.

on the ground. When disturbed, flies close to the ground for a short distance, turns suddenly and drops into the grass. Found in the southern and eastern third of Southern Africa.

WHITE-FACED OWL (*Otus leucotis*) (364). 25 cm. General colour grey, with fine brownish vermiculations and black streaks above. Below, less closely vermiculated; black streaks longer and more numerous. Shows white line along edge of scapulars. *Facial disc whitish, broadly bordered with black. Ear-tufts long and tipped with black.* Long whiskers around bill. Eyes a bright orange; bill bluish. A common nocturnal species of the thornveld. During the day, hides in trees, particularly those growing along dry water-courses. Usually found in pairs. Largely insectivorous. Call of the male a bisyllabic '*cuc-coo*'; that of the female a stammering trill '*wh-h-h-roooo*'. Snap their bills when alarmed. Found throughout Southern Africa, but not in the southern third.

BARRED OWLET (*Glaucidium capense*) (366). 20 cm. Slightly larger than the Pearl-spotted Owlet and much darker above. *No ear-tufts.* Head barred with white; sometimes has a few small white spots. Mantle and tail barred with tawny. *Chest barred (and not streaked) with chocolate.* Breast to belly spotted with brown. Eyes yellow; bill a bluish horn-colour. A bird of the denser thorn bush; sometimes seen sitting on some exposed perch during the day. Call a low-pitched, penetrating '*kroo-kroo*'. Found in the north-eastern and northern third of Southern Africa.

CAPE EAGLE OWL (*Bubo capensis*) (367). 50 cm. Larger than the Spotted Eagle Owl, and presents a *more spotted* appearance, being more heavily blotched with brown and white on back and chest. General colour blackish brown and tawny. White patch in front of neck. Eyes yellow; bill black. A rare bird, apparently found only in mountainous and forested areas. Has been known to feed by day. Call a deep, resonant, double hoot. Usually found along the southern and south-eastern coastal belt.

GIANT EAGLE OWL (*Bubo lacteus*) (369). 63 cm. Very large; general colour a pale blackish grey, finely vermiculated below. *Ear-tufts long and dark*; ear-coverts fringed with black, *forming a black band on either side of the face*. The long, strong *bill is white*, not black. Eyes brown. Widely distributed but nowhere common; found in acacia savanna where there are large trees. A nocturnal bird, preying on fairly large animals, but also sometimes taking insects. Call a mournful hoot and a deep-throated '*ghuh-ghuh-ghuh*'. Snaps its bill when alarmed. Found throughout Southern Africa, but not in the south-western tip.

Rarer species:
FISHING OWL (*Scotopelia peli*) (370)

NIGHTJARS: Caprimulgidae

Nightjars are medium-sized, long-winged nocturnal birds, feeding on insects caught on the wing. Their weak bills and wide gapes are well adapted to this purpose. Their plumage always has a bark-and-dead-leaf pattern, which gives the birds perfect protection when they rest on the ground or on a sloping branch during the day. They have large eyes and soft plumage, and fly silently like owls. Most of them lay their cryptically coloured eggs on the bare ground. Extremely difficult to identify in the field, except by their calls, which are specific. One's best chance of seeing them is in the headlights of one's car on the less frequented dirt roads.

EUROPEAN NIGHTJAR *Caprimulgus europaeus* (371) p. 193
  Afr Europese naguil *Z* isa-Vola
  X u-Debaya

Identification: 25 cm. Adult male: above, general colour grey, with a bark-and-dead-leaf pattern. Black streaks on the head. First three primaries usually have white spots. Buffish bar on scapulars. Four outermost tail-feathers tipped with white. Chin and breast barred with grey and black, belly with buff and blackish. Moustache-stripe, ear-coverts and patch on either side of lower neck white. Adult female lacks white spots on primaries and has tail-feathers tipped with buff. Eyes brown; bill black; legs brownish. Subadult resembles female, but is tinged with pale brown above.

A common and widely distributed summer migrant. Usually rests on a branch during the day—seldom on the ground.

Voice: While flying and at dusk '*coo-uck*'. Alarm-note of male '*quick-quick-quick*'; that of female '*tchuck*'. Its song is a churring trill, but is probably not heard in Southern Africa.

Habitat: No preference.

Distribution: Throughout Southern Africa.

SOUTH AFRICAN NIGHTJAR *Caprimulgus pectoralis* (373) p. 193
  Afr Suid-Afrikaanse naguil

Identification: 23 cm. Above, general colour stone-grey. Broad black streaks down centre of crown. *Distinct rufous collar on hind neck*. Mantle and rump streaked, barred and spotted with buff and blackish. Primaries blackish, the first four having white spots. Central tail-feathers grey, barred and vermiculated with black. Remainder blackish; the outer two being broadly tipped with white. Below, chin tawny; large white spots on side of neck, with *rufous collar extending beyond them*. Chest barred dusky grey; belly a pale buff barred with black. Eyes, bill and legs brown. Female has white tips of tail-feathers narrower, and white spots on wing tinged with buff. Subadult similar to adult but somewhat paler below.

The commonest resident nightjar, lying up in the shade of bushes during the day. Does not hunt over a large area, but usually hawks from a specific perch.

Voice: A musical whistle; *'fwey-wey-wirrrrrr'*, the third syllable descending, quavering and long drawn out. This call has been aptly rendered as *'Good Lord deliverrrrrrrrr us'*. It is heard mainly at sunset and dusk, but also on moonlight nights. Bird is said to call while perching in a tree.

Habitat: Found mainly in wooded areas, including plantations of exotic trees (pines and eucalyptus).

Distribution: Throughout Southern Africa, but not in the dry central western regions.

FRECKLED NIGHTJAR *Caprimulgus tristigma* (374) p. 193
Afr Donkernaguil

Identification: 28 cm. Whole of *upper side finely speckled dark grey and brown; no collar on hind neck*. First three or four primaries have white spots. Two outermost tail-feathers broadly tipped with white. Below, chin, neck, and chest a dark grey, finely barred with blackish and buff. Belly and upper tail-coverts buffish, sparingly barred with blackish. White spots on side of chest. Eyes brown; bill and legs dusky. Female has buff instead of white tips to tail-feathers. Subadult similar to adult, but spots on primaries buff.

Larger than most nightjars; resident and local in its distribution. Usually found spending the day on rocks, in the shade of bushes and shrubs. When disturbed, rises with a *'cluck'*, almost like that of a game-bird.

Voice: A weird, liquid *'kyoo-kyoo'*, repeated over and over again. Sometimes the call is three- or even four-syllabled.

Habitat: Found in rocky and hilly country.

Distribution: Over the northern half of Southern Africa, but not along the eastern coastal belt.

Allied species:

RUFOUS-CHEEKED NIGHTJAR (*Caprimulgus rufigena*) (372). 23 cm. Similar to the European Nightjar but smaller, and has a *tawny collar on the hind neck*. Distinct tawny spots on wing-coverts. Four outer primaries have white spots. *Tawny collar does not extend to below white patches on side of chest*. Outer tail-feathers broadly tipped with white. Female lacks white on tail and has buff spots on primaries. A summer migrant from equatorial Africa; starts breeding here soon after its arrival in spring. Essentially a bird of the drier west. *Call a prolonged churring*. Also claps its wings audibly.

MOZAMBIQUE NIGHTJAR (*Caprimulgus fossii*) (376) 23 cm. General colour above a brownish grey. Crown streaked with black. *Tawny collar on hind neck does not extend to below white patches on throat.* Below, general colour buff, barred with blackish. First five primaries have white spots; only the two outer tail-feathers are tipped with white, which extends along the whole length of the outer web. In the female all the white in the tail and wings is replaced by buff or buffish white. A resident species of the lower-lying eastern regions. Lives on the ground. *Call a prolonged chuckling* or *gurgling*, reminiscent of a chorus of frogs, and fluctuating in volume.

PENNANT-WINGED NIGHTJAR (*Macrodipteryx vexillarius*) (377). 28 cm. The adult male in breeding plumage, with its long pennants, is unmistakable. Male in non-breeding plumage and female a dark brown, finely mottled with buff above. Distinct collar on hind neck a darkish rufous. White patches on chest relatively small. Throat and breast mottled with brown and grey. Belly whitish, sparsely barred with blackish. *No white spots on primaries or tail.* Primaries blackish, with broad rufous bars; secondaries tipped with whitish. A summer migrant, seldom seen in the southern half of Southern Africa. Usually found on stony, wooded hillsides. Partly diurnal, emerging during the late afternoon to hawk insects. A rather silent bird, said to utter a high-pitched, piping, bat-like call during the breeding season.

Rarer species:
NATAL NIGHTJAR (*Caprimulgus natalensis*) (375)

SWIFTS: Apodidae

Swifts are smallish birds, swallow-like, but non-perching. They have short legs and small feet, with all four toes pointing forwards. Their long, sharp, curved claws enable them to cling to any slightly roughened surface. They are the most completely aerial of all the birds, and are distinguished from swallows by their more slender and scythe-like wings and relatively short tails.

Swifts have a rapid, direct flight, and are often seen gliding for considerable distances. They are generally gregarious, and feed exclusively on insects taken on the wing.

BLACK SWIFT *Apus barbatus* (380) p. 208
Afr Swartwindswawel *S* Lekhaqasi
Identification: 19 cm. General colour a sooty black. *Mantle a glossy black, contrasting with the upper wing-coverts* and secondaries, which are paler and have a greenish bronze sheen. Throat whitish, finely streaked with blackish. Feathers on belly have narrow pale edges. *Tail only slightly*

forked. Eyes, bill and legs black. Sexes alike. Subadult has narrow whitish edges to the feathers, particularly noticeable on the wings.

A resident, gregarious species that rarely settles, but only clings for a few moments to the face of a cliff, or scuttles into its nest. Its rapid, wheeling flight is often seen at great heights. Often seen in the company of other swifts at insect population explosions. Subject to considerable local migration.

Voice: Birds utter a shrill twitter when flying in flocks. This is audible even when birds are flying at a great height.

Habitat: No preference.

Distribution: Throughout Southern Africa.

WHITE-RUMPED SWIFT   *Apus caffer* (383)   p. 208
Afr Witkruiswindswawel   *X* u-Nonqane

Identification: 15 cm. General colour a sooty brown; mantle and underparts have a blue-black sheen. Throat whitish. *White patch on rump relatively narrow and not visible from the side.* Tail longish and forked. Eyes and bill black; legs dusky. Sexes alike. Subadult has white edges to flight-feathers.

Probably only a summer-breeding visitor, although there are some winter records. Generally seen in pairs or small parties. A rather silent bird, usually feeding at a considerable height. Tail appears pointed except when bird banks sharply and reveals the deep fork.

Voice: A low, twittering, bat-like call.

Habitat: Found where there are cliffs, but also in towns. Often evicts swallows from their nests.

Distribution: Throughout Southern Africa.

LITTLE SWIFT   *Apus affinis* (385)   p. 208
Afr Kleinwindswawel

Identification: 14 cm. General colour a sooty brown, with a very slight greenish sheen. Mantle, breast and belly black, with a slight gloss. Forehead lighter; throat to lower neck in front whitish and finely streaked. *Tail short and square*, even slightly rounded when fanned wide open. *White patch on rump broad and plainly visible from the side.* Bill black; eyes and legs brown. Sexes alike. Subadult has white edges to the flight-feathers.

A noisy, gregarious, mainly town-dwelling swift. To a large extent resident throughout the year, building their colonial nests against high buildings or water-towers, but also under overhanging ledges. Their flight is far more fluttering and less dashing than that of the other swifts. Sometimes seen gliding along with their wings held vertically and their tails fanned out.

Voice: A shrill twitter, as flocks wheel about near their nesting-sites.

Habitat: Mainly in built-up areas.
Distribution: Throughout Southern Africa.

PALM SWIFT   *Cypsiurus parvus* (387)   p. 208
   Afr Palmwindswawel
Identification: 18 cm. General colour above and below a uniform dark grey-brown. Throat whitish, streaked with grey-brown. *Very long tail deeply forked.* Wings long and thin. Bill black; eyes and legs brown. Sexes alike. Subadults have buff edges to feathers of upper parts, wings and tail.

These *slender* swifts are colonial nesters and usually build their crescent-shaped nests on the underside of drooping palm-fronds, to which they also cling while roosting at night. Mostly seen singly or in pairs, flying high during the day. Gather in flocks at roosting-places at dusk. Fly into their nests at an incredible speed.
Voice: A thin, high-pitched scream, uttered on the wing.
Habitat: Always found near different species of tallish palm-trees, and also near water.
Distribution: The northern and central eastern regions of Southern Africa.

BOEHM'S SPINETAIL   *Chaetura boehmi* (389)   p. 208
   Afr Boehmstekelstert
Identification: 9 cm. Above, general colour a sooty black, with a slight gloss. Rump white. *Tail very short*, with tail-feathers ending in spines. Below, chin to breast a smoky grey. Belly and under tail-coverts whitish. Eyes brown; bill black; legs purple. Sexes alike. Subadult has light tips to flight- and tail-feathers.

Unmistakable on account of its small size, very short tail and rather erratic, bat-like flight.
Voice: A rather silent bird; call unrecorded.
Habitat: Usually found in clearings in wooded country.
Distribution: North-eastern regions of Southern Africa.

Allied species:
EUROPEAN SWIFT (*Apus apus*) (378). 18 cm. General colour above and below a uniform sooty black, with a slight greenish sheen. *No contrast between mantle and upper wing-coverts.* White patch on throat smaller than in the Black Swift, and tail more deeply forked. A summer migrant, very difficult to distinguish from the Black Swift in the field. Found in the northern, central and eastern parts of Southern Africa.

HORUS SWIFT (*Apus horus*) (384). 15 cm. Very similar to the White-rumped Swift, but less slender. *Tail less deeply forked*; white patch on rump broader and more noticeable during flight. Since its body is plump, its wings appear proportionally larger than those of other swifts. Often seen drinking water from the surface as it skims over it with wings raised at an angle above the horizontal. A summer migrant that apparently nests only in holes in sand-banks. Found in the eastern third of Southern Africa.

ALPINE SWIFT (*Apus melba*) (386). 22 cm. Above, general colour mouse-brown, with a greenish wash. Below, chin and throat white; chest mouse-brown; *breast and belly white*. Under tail-coverts mouse-brown, edged with white. Large size and mouse-brown chest-band, contrasting with white throat and belly, unmistakable. Mainly a mountain species, traversing great distances to feed. Often seen in the company of other swifts, coming down low during overcast weather. Found throughout Southern Africa, but not in the north-eastern tip.

Rarer species:

PALLID SWIFT (*Apus pallidus*) (379)

MOTTLED SWIFT (*Apus aequatorialis*) (382)

SCARCE SWIFT (*Apus myoptilus*) (385X)

MOTTLED SPINETAIL (*Chaetura ussheri*) (388)

MOUSEBIRDS: Coliidae

Mousebirds or colies are smallish long-tailed birds peculiar to Africa. Their body plumage is rather soft and hair-like. They owe their name 'Mousebird' to this characteristic, and also to the way in which they creep about in trees like rats or mice, with their long, stiff tail-feathers pointing downwards. They have tall, hairy-looking crests on their heads and rather short, rounded wings. Their flight is straight and steady, like that of an arrow. They are sociable birds, always found in small parties. Individuals keep in touch with one another by means of their whistling notes, which are specific. To keep warm, they sleep bunched up together, hanging vertically with their tails pointing straight down. Often seen sunning themselves on cold mornings, with their breast- and belly-feathers all puffed up. Their bills are short and stout, like those of finches, and they feed mainly on fruit, berries and young shoots, thus causing a certain amount of damage to gardens. They split up in pairs to breed.

RED-FACED MOUSEBIRD *Colius indicus* (392)   p. 209
    Afr Rooiwangmuisvoël   *Z* um-Tshivovo, in-Dhlazi
    X in-Tshili   *S* le-Tsiavava

Identification: 33 cm. Above, forehead a buffish brown; other upper parts, including crest, ear-coverts and tail, a greenish grey. Chin to belly buff-brown. Underside of wings and tail a light chestnut-brown. Eyes grey; bill black, with cere and base of upper mandible crimson; *bare skin round* *eye red;* legs a dull reddish. Sexes alike. Subadult has buff edges to wing-coverts, and bill and bare skin around eye greenish.

A common and widespread gregarious species. Strong fliers: when disturbed may fly a considerable distance before settling again. Small parties may be seen flying high overhead, giving their familiar call, which is also uttered when the birds are perching. When alarmed, all the members of a party will crawl up to the top of the tree, ready to take off one after the other.

Voice: A clear, melodious whistle: *'tiu-woo-woo'*.

Habitat: Found wherever there are trees. Even found in exotic trees in built-up areas.

Distribution: Throughout Southern Africa, except the central western regions and western coastal belt.

Allied species:

SPECKLED MOUSEBIRD (*Colius striatus*) (390). 33 cm. Above, general colour ash-brown; head and longish crest paler. Mantle and rump finely vermiculated. Sides of face and chin to chest ash-grey. Throat blackish; breast barred; belly to under tail-coverts buff. Bare skin round eye black; *whole of upper mandible black; lower mandible whitish.* Legs wine-coloured. A locally common species, not found in built-up areas, but frequenting scrub and the borders of forests. During their short flight from one bush to another, rapid wing-beats alternate with spells of gliding. Alarm-note a sharp *'tisk, tisk, tisk'*. Keep in touch with one another by means of a short, twittering call. Found in the southern and eastern half of Southern Africa.

WHITE-BACKED MOUSEBIRD (*Colius colius*) (391). 33 cm. Above, general colour ash-grey, sides of face and throat included. Lower breast vinous; belly to under tail-coverts a light buff. Lower back black, with white line down the centre. *Rump maroon* (not easily seen in the field). *Only tip of upper mandible black; rest of bill whitish. Legs a bright red.* A common species, found wherever there are trees—even in built-up areas. Though gregarious, usually found in smaller parties than the other two species. Alarm-note a metallic *'tzik'*. Usual call a rather soft, melodious whistle: *'Tzee, tzit, tzit'*. A bird of the drier west, but also found in the central regions of Southern Africa.

TROGONS: Trogonidae

Trogons are pigeon-sized birds with beautiful soft plumage, a metallic green above and a vivid red on the belly. Their bills are short, heavy and hooked. The first and second toes are turned backwards. Their legs are short and their claws strong and curved. They are usually solitary birds, found in the depths of forests, where they hawk insects in the more open spaces. In spite of their brilliant colouring, they are extremely hard to see when they sit perfectly still. Their rather melancholy call is ventriloquial.

NARINA TROGON *Apaloderma narina* (393)   p. 192
    Afr Bosloerie   *Z* um-Jeninengu
    X in-Tshatshonga   *S* Tzoko

Identification: 33 cm. Adult male has upper parts, sides of face, throat to chest and wing-shoulders a metallic green. Median wing-coverts and inner secondaries vermiculated in grey and black. Upper side of longish tail green and steel-blue. Outer tail-feathers edged and tipped with white. *Breast to under tail-coverts red.* Eyes brown; bill yellow; legs grey. Adult female has sides of face, throat and chest brown. Subadult has throat and breast a mottled brown; belly white with brown and blackish markings, and wing-coverts tipped with white.

Usually seen solitary or in pairs, sitting motionless for long periods. When pursuing insects in the air its flight is fast and twisting. Normal flight is straight and silent, though heavy. Also creeps along branches in search of insects. Is often seen only when it moves.

Voice: A soft, rapidly-repeated '*coo-coo*', gradually dying away. To some extent ventriloquial. Male moves tail up and down while calling, this movement often betraying its presence.

Habitat: Confined to high evergreen or riverine forest.

Distribution: Mainly in the southern and eastern coastal regions of Southern Africa.

KINGFISHERS: Alcedinidae

Kingfishers are small to medium-sized short-tailed birds, most of whom have blue in their plumage. They may be divided into two groups: the 'true fishermen' who live on fish, crabs and aquatic animals, and have long, straight, slender, pointed bills; and the insectivorous kingfishers who are independent of water and have relatively short, stout bills. All kingfishers have rather short legs and the second, third and fourth toes united to a greater or lesser degree. They are hole-nesters, either burrowing in sand-banks or using the old nests of barbets or woodpeckers. Their eggs are round, white and glossy.

PIED KINGFISHER   *Ceryle rudis* (394)   p. 209
    Afr Bontvisvanger   *Z* isi-Quba
    S Seinoli

Identification: 28 cm. Adult male: above, spotted and barred with black and white. Blackish crest, tipped with white; distinct white line above the eye. Below, white, with *two black bands (the upper broader than the lower) across the breast*. Tail mainly white, with broad black subterminal band. Flight-feathers mainly white. Eyes brown; long bill and legs black. Adult female similar to male but with a *single broken black band across the breast*. Subadult similar to adults but has dusky edges to neck- and chest-feathers.

A common resident species, conspicuous owing to its habit of hovering over the water, with fast wing-beats, body held vertically and bill pointing down, before diving head first into the water. When fish is caught it is usually carried to a favourite perch, and beaten to death before being swallowed. Usually seen singly or in pairs, sitting on exposed perches near or over water, raising and lowering its tail.

Voice: A sharp '*kwik-kwik*', or a shrill, rattling whistle when birds are together.

Habitat: Rivers, lakes, dams, lagoons and the sea-shore, where it can be seen fishing just beyond the breakers.

Distribution: Throughout Southern Africa.

MALACHITE KINGFISHER   *Alcedo cristata* (397)   p. 209
Afr Kuifkopvisvanger   *X* in-Dozela

Identification: 13 cm. Upper parts ultramarine; flight-feathers dusky. *Long crest narrowly barred with greenish blue and black*. Below, throat white; sides of face, under wing-coverts and remaining underparts rufous. Smallish white spot on either side of hind neck. Eyes brown; *long bill and legs red*. Sexes alike. Subadult has blackish bill; mantle blackish but mottled with greenish blue; sides of face and chest dusky.

This small, resident kingfisher has the habit of bobbing up and down and raising and lowering its crest while perching low over the water. Catches its prey by diving straight into the water from its perch. Flies very fast, just skimming the surface of the water.

Voice: A shrill '*peep-peep*', usually uttered as the bird darts off. Also said to have a weak song during the breeding season.

Habitat: Any water that is fringed with reeds, bulrushes and other sheltering vegetation.

Distribution: Throughout Southern Africa, but not in the western coastal regions.

ANGOLA KINGFISHER   *Halcyon senegalensis* (399)   p. 209
Afr Angolavisvanger

Identification: 23 cm. Above, forehead and crown greyish; neck and back a greyish blue; rump, wings and tail cobalt to greenish blue. Wing-coverts and ends of primaries jet-black. Below, white; chest and breast a pale bluish grey. Underside of tail blackish. Eyes a dark grey; *bill relatively*

short and stout, with the upper mandible red and the lower black; legs black.
Sexes alike. Subadult has a dusky bill, and blackish barring from neck to
breast.

A summer migrant, common in suitable localities and not dependent on
water, but keeping to the more thickly foliaged trees. Lives mainly on
insects caught on the ground, usually from a fairly low perch. Also takes
reptiles and small animals. A noisy bird, often displaying near its nest-
hole in a tree, stretching out its wings and turning from side to side.

Voice: A loud trill, '*ki-tir-r-r-r-rh*' on a descending scale. Is heard throughout the day and has considerable carrying power.

Habitat: Found in well-wooded areas where there are large trees.

Distribution: In the northern and north-eastern parts of Southern Africa.

BROWN-HOODED KINGFISHER *Halcyon albiventris* (402) p. 209
  Afr Bruinkopvisvanger   *Z* un-Nongozolo
  X i-Ndwazela   *S* le-Inoli

Identification: 23 cm. Adult male: head and sides of face ash-brown, finely
streaked with black; base of hind neck buffish. Mantle, scapulars and
wing-coverts black. *Rump a bright blue*; tail and edges of flight-feathers
blue-grey; tips of flight-feathers blackish. Below, a tawny buff; *breast and
flanks more or less streaked with blackish.* Eyes brown; *bill red but blackish
towards the tip*; legs a dark red. Female differs from male in having mantle,
scapulars and wing-coverts a sooty brown. Subadult is duller, more
streaked below and has almost the entire bill blackish.

The commonest of the insectivorous kingfishers. Resident; nests in
burrows and sand-banks. Usually seen sitting hunched and motionless on
an exposed perch, on the look-out for insects. When disturbed, bobs up
and down before flying off. Males also display by spreading their wings
and turning to and fro. Often found far away from water.

Voice: A shrill, piping '*ki-ki-ki-ki*', often repeated and on a slightly
descending scale.

Habitat: Found in bush country and open woodland where the grass is
short. Even found in gardens in built-up areas.

Distribution: The eastern half of Southern Africa.

Allied species:
GIANT KINGFISHER (*Ceryle maxima*) (395). 46 cm. Adult male: above,
general colour a dark slate; head, longish crest and neck streaked with
white; rest of upper parts spotted with white. Below, throat white; *chest
and breast chestnut; belly and under tail-coverts white, spotted with black.*
In the adult female these colours are reversed: the chest and breast are
mottled in black and white; the belly and under tail-coverts are chestnut.
Long bill black.

The largest kingfisher, usually found sitting on a sheltered perch over or near water. A wary bird, flying off at the least sign of danger. Call a loud, ringing '*kakh-kakh-kakh-kakh*', usually uttered in flight. May hover while fishing, but usually dives straight from its perch into the water. Is sometimes seen catching exotic fish in fish-ponds. Distributed over the greater part of Southern Africa, except in the north-western regions.

HALF-COLLARED KINGFISHER (*Alcedo semitorquata*) (396). 20 cm. Above, a bright cobalt blue; lower back and rump blue-grey; whitish patch forming the half-collar on side of neck. Throat a buffish white, with blue patch on side of breast; rest of underparts a rich tawny. The only 'blue' kingfisher with a *black bill*, which is long and slender. Legs red. A purely aquatic species, preferring large streams and rivers, but also found along coastal lagoons. Usually perches fairly low—even on stones at the water's edge. Call a shrill and not very loud '*seep*' or '*seep-seep*', repeated several times. Found in the eastern half and southernmost tip of Southern Africa.

PYGMY KINGFISHER (*Ispidina picta*) (398). 10 cm. The smallest kingfisher, with a stoutish, relatively short red bill. *Inconspicuous crest* a deep violet, barred with light blue. Forehead and sides of face rufous; *cheeks and nape mauve*. Small white spots on side of neck. Mantle, rump, wings and tail a deep violet. Throat whitish and rest of underparts rufous. Legs red.

Mainly insectivorous, but always found near water, feeding on the insects it takes in the shade of leafy trees. Rarely takes prey from water. A rather silent bird, whose presence is often unsuspected until it makes a sudden dart at its prey on the ground.

STRIPED KINGFISHER (*Halcyon chelicuti*) (403). 18 cm. *Head ashy, streaked with blackish*; hind neck lighter; other upper parts a dark ash-colour. Light bar on wing. Rump a bright blue; tail and edges of flight-feathers bluish. *Distinct black line through the eye*. Throat whitish, rest of underparts a light buff; breast slightly barred and flanks streaked. Bill relatively short. Upper mandible a purplish red and lower mandible a bright red. Legs reddish.

A common resident, insectivorous kingfisher, found in dry, open country. Often attracted to cultivated fields and cattle kraals. Though it shows little fear of man, it is not found in built-up areas. Darts down from its perch to catch its prey, as a Fiscal Shrike does. Its call, an often repeated '*tirrrruh-tirrrruh*', has great carrying power. Bird calls while bobbing up and down, rapidly opening and closing its wings. Found in the northern, central and eastern regions of Southern Africa.

Rarer Species:

MANGROVE KINGFISHER (*Halcyon senegaloides*) (400)

GREY-HEADED KINGFISHER (*Halcyon leucocephala*) (401)

BEE-EATERS: Meropidae

Bee-eaters are medium-sized to smallish birds. The larger species are gregarious, and some are long-distance migrants. The smaller species are found in pairs or family parties. All are insectivorous, and conspicuous on account of their brilliant plumage. They capture insects either on the wing, or else by darting at them from a perch. Their bills are long, slender and slightly curved, and their long wings are pointed. They nest in burrows in sandbanks, excavated by themselves, and their eggs are an immaculate white.

EUROPEAN BEE-EATER *Merops apiaster* (404) p. 209
    Afr Europese Byevreter   *S* Thlapolome
Identification: 28 cm. Above, narrow white band at base of bill is edged with blue and green. Black line through eye. *Crown, mantle and wing-coverts chestnut.* Scapulars and rump a golden yellow. Flight-feathers blue and green; tail a greyish green; *central tail-feathers slightly elongated.* Below, throat yellow, bordered by a *narrow blackish band on the lower neck*; rest of underparts blue and green. Eyes red; bill black; legs a greyish brown. Sexes alike. Subadult has nape, mantle and rump green and the central tail-feathers are not elongated.

A summer migrant, usually seen in flocks, hawking insects while soaring. Their presence is often betrayed by their call, which they give as they fly overhead, sometimes at a great height. Also catch insects by darting at them from perches such as telegraph poles and wires. Often heard on moonlight nights.
Voice: A beautiful, clear, liquid, bubbling '*quilp*', usually bisyllabic and mostly given on the wing. Calls help to keep flocks intact.
Habitat: No preference; move about a good deal in search of food but usually come back to particular trees to roost.
Distribution: Throughout Southern Africa.

CARMINE BEE-EATER *Merops nubicoides* (407) p. 209
    Afr Rooiborsbyevreter
Identification: 36 cm. Above, forehead and crown a dark bluish green; black line through eye; general colour carmine with a brownish wash; wings darker. Flight-feathers tipped with black; rump sky-blue. Below, a bright carmine, with under tail-coverts blue and tail dusky. *Central tail-feathers very much elongated.* Eyes brown; bill black; legs ash-brown. Sexes alike. Subadults have throats pink or pale blue, and central tail-feathers not elongated.

A summer migrant, congregating in large flocks at dusk to roost. During the day seen singly or in small parties, hawking insects from perches. Often feed on insects disturbed by grazing animals, and come freely to grass-fires. Active in the mornings and evenings, but lethargic in the heat of the day.

Voice: A loud, low-pitched '*terk-terk*', often repeated.

Habitat: Usually found near rivers or marshy ground.

Distribution: In the north-eastern regions of Southern Africa.

WHITE-FRONTED BEE-EATER *Merops bullockoides* (409) p. 209
Afr Rooikeelbyevreter   *Z* i-Nkota

Identification: 23 cm. Above, forehead to crown a silvery white; nape cinnamon; black line below eye; back, wings and *square tail* green, with a bluish wash. Secondaries have broad blackish tips. Upper tail-coverts a deep blue. Below, chin and moustache-stripe white; *throat a vivid red*; chest to belly and under wing-coverts cinnamon; lower belly greenish and under tail-coverts a deep blue. Eyes brown; bill black; legs a greenish black. Sexes alike. Subadult has a paler throat and a bluish tinge on the back.

Resident; usually encountered in pairs or smallish flocks. Hawks from a favourite perch and returns to it after each sortie. Often seen picking insects off the surface of the water. Lives chiefly on butterflies. Out of the nesting season gathers in large flocks to roost, in tall trees or on rocks, ledges or sand-banks. A rather noisy bird, usually betraying its presence by its call.

Voice: A sharp, shrill, nasal '*kwannk-kwani-kwani*', or '*waark-aark-aark*'.

Habitat: Along streams and dry rivers.

Distribution: The north-eastern half of Southern Africa.

LITTLE BEE-EATER *Merops pusillus* (410)   p. 209
Afr Kleinbyevreter   *Z* i-Guondwana

Identification: 15 cm. Above, general colour green. Short, thin blue stripe above the eye and a distinct black line below it. Below, throat and sides of neck a bright yellow. Black patch on chest with a thin blue line between the black and the yellow; remainder of underparts chestnut, growing lighter towards the under tail-coverts. *Square tail* saffron, with broad black terminal band. Eyes crimson; bill black; legs dusky. Sexes alike. Subadult has no black patch on neck and is a pale greenish below.

The smallest of the bee-eaters. Resident; usually found solitary, in pairs or in family parties. Hawks insects from a perch that is often quite close to the ground, e.g. the snag of a bush. A pair is often seen sitting side by side on the same perch. Frequent specific territories where they may be found day after day.

Voice: A low squeaky call, but usually silent.

176

PLATE 19

SKIMMER, TERNS, SKUAS AND GULLS

1 **AFRICAN SKIMMER** *page* 138
Projecting lower mandible.

2 **CASPIAN TERN** 134
Large size. Bill red, legs black.

3 **DAMARA TERN** 136
Small size. Forehead, lores, crown and nape uniform black, legs yellow.

4 **SWIFT TERN** 136
Large bill yellow.

5 **WHITE-WINGED LAKE TERN** 137
Tail square, wing shoulder white. (*a*): summer. (*b*): winter.

6 **SANDWICH TERN** 135
Bill black with yellow tip.

7 **COMMON TERN** 135
Crown mottled black, nape sooty black. Bill blackish, legs reddish brown.

8 **ARCTIC SKUA** 131
Cheeks and nape yellowish white. Central tail feathers straight, elongated and sharply pointed.

9 **ANTARCTIC SKUA** 132
Central tail feathers only slightly longer than the others.

10 **GREY-HEADED GULL** 133
Whole head grey. (Only in breeding plumage).

11 **SOUTHERN BLACK-BACKED GULL** 133
Adult: Mantle and wings slate black.
Sub-adult: Brown and mottled all over.

PLATE 20

LOVEBIRD, PARROTS, DOVES AND PIGEONS

1 **ROSY-FACED LOVEBIRD**   *page* 149
Small with rosy face and throat.

2 **CAPE PARROT**   148
Largest parrot, greyish head, leading edge of wing orange-red;
(markings variable).

3 **MEYER'S PARROT**   148
Shoulders yellow and belly green.

4 **CAPE TURTLE DOVE**   142
Black collar, general colour variable.

5 **ROCK PIGEON**   141
Large; red face and speckled wing-coverts.

6 **EMERALD-SPOTTED DOVE**   143
Small with green wing spots.

7 **LAUGHING DOVE**   142
Medium-sized with speckled reddish chest.

8 **NAMAQUA DOVE**   143
Small; long thin tail. Male has black face and throat and red bill.

9 **GREEN PIGEON**   147
Nape grey, face and underparts yellowish. Thighs bright yellow.

Habitat: Usually found near rivers and streams, but may be found quite far from water during the breeding season.
Distribution: The north-eastern half of Southern Africa.

SWALLOW-TAILED BEE-EATER *Merops hirundineus* (411) p. 20?
Afr Swawelstertbyevreter

Identification: 22 cm. Above, general colour a golden green, except for the *deeply forked tail*, which is bluish, tipped with white and blackish. Upper tail-coverts a light turquoise. Black stripe below eye. Flight-feathers have blackish tips. Below, throat yellow, with an ultramarine band across the lower neck. Chest to upper belly green; lower belly and under tail-coverts a light turquoise. Eyes crimson; bill black; legs brown. Sexes alike. Sub-adult lacks the yellow throat and the blue band across the chest.

A common resident, usually found in pairs or, after the breeding season, in family parties. Hawks insects from a conspicuous perch; also takes them from flowers. Nests often burrowed in sandbanks, which are sometimes barely two feet high, or in the sides of abandoned ant-bear burrows.
Voice: A soft, melodious '*deery-deery*', repeated over and over again.
Habitat: Found from moist woodland to semi-desert savanna and even in dry river beds in the most arid regions.
Distribution: The northern two-thirds of Southern Africa.

Allied species:

BLUE-CHEEKED BEE-EATER (*Merops superciliosus*) (406). 30 cm. General colour above and below green. Forehead white and blue; black line through eye bordered with white and blue. Crown brownish; *chin yellow;* rest of throat chestnut. *No black band across chest. Central tail-feathers slightly elongated.* Eyes crimson; bill and legs black. A summer migrant that more often hawks its prey from a perch than while soaring. At dusk, can be seen wheeling and twisting like a flock of waders. Roost mainly in reed-beds. Found in the north-eastern half of Southern Africa.

Rarer species:

BOEHM'S BEE-EATER (*Merops boehmi*) (408)

ROLLERS: Coraciidae

Rollers are pigeon-sized, thickset birds with large heads and brilliant plumage, the blue of the wings being particularly striking. Their tails may be square, or the outer pair of tail-feathers may be elongated. Their bills are strong and crow-like. They feed almost entirely on large insects that they take from exposed perches such as telegraph poles. They nest in natural holes in trees, and are often seen tumbling and 'rolling' over their nesting sites, uttering raucous cries. Usually seen singly or in pairs, but congregate in considerable numbers at grass-fires, and places at which flying termites emerge from their nests. The migratory species also tend to flock before migrating.

EUROPEAN ROLLER *Coracias garrulus* (412) p. 224
Afr Europese troupand

Identification: 30 cm. Head, neck and underparts a *pale azure*; back a tawny brown; upper and under wing-coverts a greenish blue; wing-shoulders and rump purple. Flight-feathers blackish, with a purple tinge. *Longish tail square*; apical half of tail-feathers a light blue; outer tail-feathers slightly pointed but not elongated, and tipped with blackish. Eyes brown; bill blackish; legs yellowish. Sexes alike. Subadult is generally duller, with brown on head, throat and chest. Outer tail-feathers not tipped with blackish.

A summer migrant, usually seen singly, but flocking during migration. Arrive in Southern Africa in about midsummer, temporarily displacing the local roller populations, which tend to move westwards. Like most rollers, sit on exposed perches, flying down to pick up insects from the ground. They are crepuscular feeders, often active even after sunset. Their wings are long and pointed, and their flight is fast and strong.

Voice: A loud, harsh '*rack-kack, kacker*', but bird is rather silent.

Habitat: No preference.

Distribution: The north-eastern half of Southern Africa and more rarely along the southern coastal belt.

LILAC-BREASTED ROLLER *Coracias caudata* (413) p. 224
Afr Gewone troupand   *Z* u-Mziligazi

Identification: 36 cm. Head, nape and upper back a greenish brown; remainder of back and scapulars brown. Wing-shoulders, outer webs of flight-feathers and rump a light blue. Tail bluish, with *outer tail-feathers elongated and blackish*. Below, chin whitish; *breast a rich lilac, lightly streaked with white*. Remainder of underparts blue, with a slight greenish tinge. Eyes a dark brown; bill black; legs a greenish yellow. Sexes alike. Subadult is brownish below; the wing-coverts are greenish and the outer tail-feathers not elongated.

A noisy resident species, usually seen in pairs. The different shades of blue in the wings are very conspicuous, especially when the bird flies down to the ground. From the back the bird appears wholly blue when its wings are spread. Sits on exposed perches while feeding, but moves into the shade during the heat of the day. Noisy display-flights during courtship consist of rolling and twisting at great speed.

Voice: A series of harsh, raucous screams.

Habitat: Thornveld savannas.
Distribution: North-eastern half of Southern Africa.

PURPLE ROLLER   *Coracias naevia* (415)   p. 224
   Afr Groottroupand
Identification: 41 cm. Above, forehead whitish; crown, mantle and scapulars olive-green. *Stripe above eye and variable patch on nape white.* Wing-shoulder and rump lilac; tail-coverts and flight-feathers violet and brownish. *Square tail* violet and blackish, except for the central feathers, which are olive-green. *Below, a brownish lilac to a pure lilac, heavily streaked with white.* Eyes a dark brown; bill black; legs a greenish brown. Sexes alike. Subadult duller above, with no lilac shoulder-patch, and browner below.

   The largest of the rollers. Usually found singly, seldom in pairs. Prefers to perch on tall trees. Though widely distributed is nowhere common. Usually silent and sluggish, but display-flight in which bird flips over from side to side, barely skimming the tree-tops, is very fast.
Voice: A querulous bisyllabic '*huk-uk*', and a raucous '*kra-kra*' during the display-flight.
Habitat: Thornveld savanna; even found in semi-arid regions.
Distribution: The northern half of Southern Africa.

Allied species:
RACQUET-TAILED ROLLER (*Coracias spatulata*) (414). 36 cm. Head and back brown, washed with green. Wing-shoulders, flight-feathers and rump violet. Scapulars and wing-coverts a tawny brown. Forehead and eye-stripe white. Central tail-feathers blue-black; outer tail-feathers a light blue, *the outermost pair being elongated and having racquet-shaped ends.* Opened tail slightly forked. Below, a pale greenish blue and brownish lilac, streaked with pale blue. The general impression made by the bird is one of soft pastel shades. Frequents well-wooded country and is usually seen in pairs or small parties. Found in the north-eastern regions of Southern Africa.

BROAD-BILLED ROLLER (*Eurystomas glaucurus*) (416). 25 cm. *General colour chocolate*; head, nape and underparts washed with lilac. Flight-feathers violet. Rump a greenish blue. Square tail a light blue, with blackish violet tips. *Broad, short bill yellow.* A summer migrant, breeding in Southern Africa. Feeds from prominent perches; also hawks insects in the air, sometimes at a great height. Prefers the denser to the more open bush-country. Found in the north-eastern and eastern regions of Southern Africa.

HOOPOES: Upupidae

Hoopoes may be divided into two groups, depending on whether they feed on the ground or in trees. Both groups have long, curved, slender bills that enable them to extract their food from holes, cracks and crevices. Hoopoes are hole-nesters, and one of the few bird species that befoul their nests. The terrestrial species are richly coloured in brown, black and white, and have large, long crests of erectile feathers. The arboreal wood-hoopoes are long-tailed birds with beautiful glossy plumage: green, blue and purple. They have specific calls and are noisy during the breeding season.

AFRICAN HOOPOE *Upupa africana* (418) p. 240
  Afr Hoephoep *Z* u-Ziningweni
  X u-Bobye *S* Pupupu

Identification: 28 cm. Above, *long erectile crest rufous, tipped with black*; mantle earth-brown; wings and tail barred with black and white; primaries black; lower back barred with black and buff. Below, chin to breast a reddish buff; belly whitish, with black streaks. Eyes brown; bill a blackish brown; legs slate-grey. Sexes alike, but female generally duller. Subadult even duller than female and has secondaries regularly barred with black and white.

A common, widely distributed resident species, disappearing at times from certain areas, but not a regular migrant. Spends most of its time on the ground, busily probing the ground with its long bill and occasionally raising its crest. Crest is usually erected for a moment when the bird alights. Has large wings and a jerky, butterfly-like flight.

Voice: A melodious '*hoop-hoop*' or '*hoop-hoop-hoop*', repeated at regular intervals. Can be heard at a great distance. Usually uttered while bird is perching. Subadults give begging call, a high-pitched '*sweet-sweet*', while following their parents about on the ground. Alarm-note a grating '*churr*'. Seldom heard out of the breeding season.

Habitat: Savanna veld and built-up areas. Partial to short veld-grass and lawns.

Distribution: Throughout Southern Africa.

RED-BILLED HOOPOE *Phoeniculus purpureus* (419) p. 240
  Afr Kooibekkakelaar *Z* u-Nukana
  X u-Tlekabafazi

Identification: 38 cm. General colour iridescent green, blue and purple. Chin, throat, nape and wings blue; wing-shoulders and graduated tail purple and violet. *Primaries are crossed by a white bar and tail-feathers* *have white spots.* Belly black. Eyes brown; *bill and legs red.* Sexes alike. Subadult has bill and head black; neck and breast washed with brown.

A noisy resident bird, always seen in small parties, flying from tree to tree and chattering loudly. While exploring trees for insects, they adopt attitudes that show off their striking colours. *In flight the white wing-bar and checkered tail are unmistakable.* Often several birds may be seen grouped together, bowing to each other and noisily cackling in chorus. Nest in holes in trees. All the members of a party help to feed the incubating female and the fledglings.

Voice: A large variety of unmelodious, cackling calls, usually started by one individual and then taken up by the rest of the party.

Habitat: Woodland, especially along rivers. Also found in forests.

Distribution: Found throughout the northern half of Southern Africa, except in the extreme west. Also found in the south-eastern coastal region.

Allied species:

SCIMITAR-BILL HOOPOE (*Rhinopomastus cyanomelas*) (421). 25 cm. General colour an iridescent blue-black. *Long, slender, heavily-curved bill and legs black.* Has a white wing-bar; occasionally has small white spots on outer tail-feathers. Usually seen singly or in pairs; often joins mixed bird-parties. Frequently seen feeding while hanging upside-down. They are very restless and have a graceful flight. Their plaintive, high-pitched whistle '*whi-whi-whi*' has great carrying power. Found throughout the northern half of Southern Africa, even in very arid regions.

HORNBILLS: Bucerotidae

Hornbills are medium-sized to large birds with relatively long tails. Their curved bills are laterally compressed, and admirably adapted to their peculiar nesting habits. They nest in natural holes in trees, and imprison the incubating female by plastering up the entrance until only a narrow slit remains, through which they feed the female and young. During incubation the female undergoes an induced moult of her flight- and tail-feathers. In most species the male has an ornamental casque on the upper mandible. They are arboreal, but some feed on the ground. Their food consists of wild fruit, berries, insects and small animals. Their wings are relatively short and rounded, and they fly heavily, alternately flapping and gliding. They all inhabit forest or savanna country where the trees are large enough to afford suitable nesting-holes.

GREY HORNBILL　*Tockus nasatus* (424)　　　　　　　　　p. 224
　　Afr Grysneushoringvoël (Vaalboskraai)

Identification: 48 cm. Adult male: above, *general colour a brownish grey.*

Broad white stripe over the eye to the nape. Wing-feathers and coverts have whitish edges. Outer tail-feathers tipped with white. Below, off-white. Bill black, with a cream-coloured line from the base to halfway along the upper mandible. Lower mandible has a few creamy diagonal lines. Casque black. Eyes a reddish brown; legs black. Female is smaller and has half the upper mandible a creamy yellow, including the small casque. Tip of bill reddish. Subadult browner, and bill generally smaller.

A common species, spending most of its time in trees and very seldom seen on the ground. During its strong but dipping flight *the white line down the centre of the back is conspicuous.* Usually seen in pairs or small parties. Restless, being always on the move from tree to tree.

Voice: A melancholy, penetrating 'pee-u, pee-u', repeated over and over again while the bird flaps its wings and points its bill upwards. Also calls on the wing.

Habitat: Dry savanna bushveld, and even semi-desert.

Distribution: The northern half of Southern Africa, but not in the extremely arid western regions.

RED-BILLED HORNBILL *Tockus erythrorhynchus* (425) p. 224
   Afr Rooibekneushoringvoël (Rooibekboskraai)
   Z u-mKota

Identification: 46 cm. Forehead to nape a greyish black; mantle black with white line down the centre; rump black. Wing-coverts mottled in white a and black; primaries black with white spots. Middle secondaries white; innermost secondaries brown. Central tail-feathers black; remainder black and white or almost wholly white. Sides of face and entire underparts white. *Bill, with only a very slight casque, red,* but adult male has base of lower mandible black. Eyes, bare skin on face and throat yellow; legs brown. Sexes alike. Subadult is mottled with buffish on the wing-coverts and has a smaller bill.

Usually found in pairs or family parties, but congregate in considerable numbers wherever there is an abundance of food. Mainly ground-feeders, following large herds of game and feeding on dung-beetles. Also extract termites from holes in the ground, their long, thin, pointed bills being admirably suited to this purpose. Not at all timid, and are often found near human dwellings.

Voice: A crescendo of monotonous notes '*kuk-kuk*', uttered during display.

Habitat: Found in savanna woodland where the trees are relatively large, and especially near riverine forest.

Distribution: The northern half of Southern Africa, but not in the more arid west.

YELLOW-BILLED HORNBILL   *Tockus flavirostris* (426)   p. 224
Afr Geelbekneushoringvoël (Geelbekboskraai)
Z u-mKota   *S* Kgogoropo

Identification: 50 cm. Plumage identical to that of Red-billed Hornbill. *The greatly compressed bill is yellow*, with the tip and cutting edge a dark reddish. Eyes a yellowish white; bare skin on face and throat red; legs black. The adult male has a narrow casque-ridge running in a smooth arc to the tip of the bill, whereas the casque-ridge of the female terminates abruptly about three-quarters of the way down the bill. Subadults look darker and browner and have smaller, blackish bills.

A common species, usually found in pairs or small parties. Mainly a ground feeder, taking insects and small animals from the surface of the ground, as their bills are less adapted to digging. Become very tame, and are often found near human dwellings.

Voice: Also a monotonous '*kuk-kuk*', uttered in crescendo during display, while the bird stretches its wings upwards.

Habitat: Found in the savanna thornveld, and even in semi-arid regions.

Distribution: The northern half of Southern Africa, but not in the more arid west.

CROWNED HORNBILL   *Tockus alboterminatus* (427)   p. 224
Afr Gekroonde neushoringvoël (Gekroonde boskraai)
Z and *X* um-Kolwane

Identification: 50 cm. Above: general colour, including that of chest, flanks, wings and tail, a brownish black. Sides of head and nape have whitish streaks. *Tips of outer tail-feathers white*. Breast to belly white. Eyes brown; bill, with its fairly pronounced casque, is a dull red and has a narrow yellow band at its base. Legs black. Females have shorter bills than males. Subadult has brownish edges to wing-coverts, and no distinct casque.

Usually seen in small parties. In the field these hornbills appear almost black, and their slow, floppy flight is unmistakable. *No white line down the centre of the back.* Largely arboreal, feeding on fruit, insects and small animals. They are noisy birds, roosting in companies.

Voice: A series of thin, high-pitched, melancholy whistles.

Habitat: Light forest or wooded country, but even venture into towns.

Distribution: The north-eastern regions, and the eastern and south-eastern coastal belt of Southern Africa.

Allied Species:

TRUMPETER HORNBILL (*Bycanistes bucinator*) (422). 66 cm. General colour an iridescent blue-black and white. Above, mainly blue-black, except for the rump, ends of secondaries and outer tail-feathers, which are white. Breast to under tail-coverts white. Bill black; casque pointed in front and about the same size as the bill itself. Eyes red; bare skin round the eyes pink; legs black. A large, arboreal hornbill, usually found in parties in forested areas and riverine forest. Feeds mainly on wild fruit, especially wild figs. In flight its heavy bill and black and white pattern are unmistakable. A noisy bird, making various laughing, braying, trumpeting and wailing sounds. Found only in the south-eastern and eastern coastal regions.

GROUND HORNBILL (*Bucorvus leadbeateri*) (430). 109 cm. General colour black, except for the primaries, which are white. *Bare skin on face and wattles red.* Bill, with small casque, black; eyes greenish; legs black. In the subadult the bare skin on the face and wattles is blackish. The largest of all the hornbills, spending most of their time on the ground, where they waddle about in small parties. Live on insects, reptiles and small animals. Hunt separately but keep within sight of one another. Take to trees when disturbed; also roost and nest in trees. Do not plaster up the natural holes in which they nest. *In flight, their white primaries are quite unmistakable.* Call a succession of deep, booming notes: '*oohmp-oohmp-oohmp*', usually heard in the early morning. Found in the central northern and north-eastern parts of Southern Africa, and also in the eastern and south-eastern coastal belt.

Rarer species:
SILVERY-CHEEKED HORNBILL (*Bycanistes brevis*) (423)

BRADFIELD'S HORNBILL (*Tockus bradfieldi*) (428)

MONTEIRO'S HORNBILL (*Tockus monteiri*) (429)

BARBETS: Capitonidae

Barbets are small, thickset, noisy, conspicuous birds, related to the woodpeckers. They differ from the latter in having soft tails and shorter, stouter bills. Though mainly fruit-eating, they also catch large numbers of insects. They have colourful, variable plumage and specific calls. They nest in holes in trees excavated by themselves. Most of them can be attracted if their calls are imitated.

BLACK-COLLARED BARBET *Lybius torquatus* (431) p. 225
    Afr Rooikophoutkapper   *Z* isi-Kurukuru
    X i-Sinagogo   *S* Kopaopi
Identification: 20 cm. *Face, throat and chest crimson;* crown, hind neck and upper breast a glossy black. Rest of upper parts a greyish brown, with a yellow edging to the secondaries. Below, lower breast to under tail-coverts

a yellowish grey. Under wing-coverts white. Eyes red; heavy bill and legs black. Sexes alike. Subadult has head blackish, with only a little red.

Usually seen in pairs, on the topmost branches of dead trees. Often gather in small parties, making a great deal of noise while bobbing up and down and swaying from side to side. Parasitized by honey-guides.

Voice: A very loud whistle '*too-tiddle-doo, tiddle-doo, tiddle-doo*', repeated several times. Alarm-note a subdued, repeated '*caw*'.

Habitat: Thornveld, but also in riverine and open forest. Even found in built-up areas.

Distribution: Throughout the eastern half of Southern Africa.

PIED BARBET *Lybius leucomelas* (432) p. 225

Afr Bonthoutkapper   S se-Rokolo

Identification: 16 cm. *Forehead and forecrown red*. Black line from base of bill, through eye and down side of neck is bordered above and below by two distinct white lines, the upper being yellowish above the eye. Mantle and wing-coverts black, spotted with white and yellow. Rump lemon-coloured; tail- and flight-feathers blackish, edged with yellowish white. Below, the black on the chin and throat is extended to form a pointed bib on the breast. Remainder of underparts whitish. Eyes a dark brown; bill and legs black. Sexes alike. Subadult has no red on forehead and is more streaked below.

A restless bird, found singly or in pairs. Flight fast and direct. Often sits calling on the top of a tree.

Voice: Courting and breeding call '*poop-poop*', rather like the call of the Hoopoe but more hollow-sounding, and without the definite pauses between the different phrases. Ordinary call a nasal '*tnhar- tnhar*', repeated several times.

Habitat: Found wherever there are trees, even in the very arid regions.

Distribution: Throughout Southern Africa.

YELLOW-FRONTED TINKER *Pogoniulus*

chrysoconus (437) p. 225

Afr Geelbleshoutkappertjie   *X* u-Noqand-ilanga

Identification: 11 cm. Forehead black; *crown yellow to orange-red*. Black stripe through eye and down side of neck bordered by white stripes, above and below. Moustache-stripe black. Nape, mantle and rump black with whitish streaks. Upper tail-coverts a very pale lemon. Flight- and tail-feathers black; secondaries edged with pale yellow. Upper wing-coverts tipped with yellow and white. Below, a dirty greyish olive, washed with yellowish; throat and chin showing slightly more yellow. Eyes brown; bill and legs black. Sexes alike. Subadult has a black crown.

Usually found singly, and often overlooked, as it tends to keep to the thick foliage at the tops of trees. Often its presence is only betrayed by its monotonous call, which is sometimes given for minutes on end. Feeds mainly on berries; when hunting for insects, clambers about on the branches almost like a woodpecker.

Voice: A loud, rapid, monotonous, clinking '*toot-toot-toot*', given only by the male. Ventriloquial and difficult to pinpoint. The notes are uttered at an even tempo. When two birds meet, both give short, low trills while chasing one another.

Habitat: Thornveld and other types of woodland. Not very shy; often found near human dwellings but not in built-up areas.

Distribution: The northern and central parts of Southern Africa.

CRESTED BARBET   *Trachyphonus vaillantii* (439)   p. 225
Afr Kuifkophoutkapper

Identification: 23 cm. Forehead and sides of head lemon-yellow, tipped and streaked with crimson. *Longish crest an iridescent black*; mantle, wing-coverts and tail also an iridescent black, more or less spotted and barred with white. Lower back and rump lemon. Below, chin and throat lemon; chest-band black, spotted with a whitish pink; breast to belly lemon, streaked with crimson. Eyes red; bill a greenish yellow; legs ashy. Sexes alike. Subadults are duller and browner above.

A noisy, conspicuous bird, usually seen singly or in pairs. Often seen on the ground in search of the larger insects. Spends much of its time sitting on exposed perches, calling.

Voice: A loud, heavy trill, like an alarm-clock going off. Call is kept up for long periods without a pause. Alarm-call a loud, strident trill.

Habitat: Wooded country, preferably with heavily foliaged trees, but also found in built-up areas.

Distribution: The eastern half of Southern Africa.

Allied species:
WHITE-EARED BARBET (*Stactolaema leucotis*) (433). 19 cm. General colour a blackish brown. *The broad white stripe from behind the eye and down each side of the neck is very conspicuous.* Breast to under tail-coverts and under wing-coverts white. Bill and legs black. These heavy, thickset birds are usually found in small parties, sitting on dead snags high above the ground. They have a strong, straight flight and a shrill, twittering call. Found in the large trees of evergreen and riverine forests along the eastern coastal belt of Southern Africa.

RED-FRONTED TINKER (*Pogoniulus pusillus*) (436). 11 cm. Very similar to the Yellow-fronted Tinker, except that the *crown is red* and not yellow and the general colouring more vivid. Call similar to that of the Yellow-fronted Tinker, but the 'tinks' are slightly higher pitched, and are uttered in more rapid succession. Usually found in evergreen forests in the south eastern coastal regions.

BLACK-CROWNED TINKER (*Pogoniulus bilineatus*) (438). 11 cm Distinguished from the other two species of tinkers by its golden rump and the *uniform black of its crown and back*. Its call is deeper and fuller and is not given at an even tempo; a few notes, varying from two to six being followed by short pauses. Prefers the denser forests, and is found in the south-eastern and eastern coastal regions.

Rarer species:

WHYTE'S BARBET (*Stactolaema whytii*) (434)

GREEN TINKER (*Pogoniulus simplex*)

GREEN BARBET (*Pogoniulus olivaceus*) (435)

HONEY-GUIDES: Indicatoridae

Honey-guides are smallish, plainly coloured birds with relatively long wings. Their white outer tail-feathers are conspicuous in flight. The larger species have developed the remarkable habit of leading humans and animals to bees' nests. They feed on beeswax as well as on the larvae of bees and other insects. They are parasitic in their breeding habits, their hosts being mainly barbets, woodpeckers and bee-eaters. The sexes live apart, the males as a rule calling from regular sites to attract the females during the mating season. After mating they separate again.

GREATER HONEY-GUIDE *Indicator indicator* (440) p. 22.
   Afr Grootheuningwyser *Z* i-Ngede
   X in-Takobusi *S* Tsese

Identification: 20 cm. Adult male: Above, general colour a sooty grey Upper edge of wing-shoulder yellow (not easily seen in the field). Wing coverts, rump and upper tail-coverts streaked with white. *Ear-coverts white* Below, chin and throat black; remainder of underparts a dirty white. *Three outer tail-feathers white*, with sooty tips. Eyes brown; bill a pinkish white legs lead-coloured. Adult female a uniform sooty grey above, ear-coverts included. Throat whitish instead of black. Subadult similar to female but is tinged above and below, and particularly on the throat, with yellowish Has no yellow on the wing-shoulder.

This bird guides human beings and Honey-badgers to bees' nests by repeatedly calling and flying in short stages from tree to tree until the nest is reached. During this performance the white outer tail-feathers are conspicuous. Males execute spectacular display-flights, swooping up and down while flying in circles and making a whirring sound by means of the flight-

or tail-feathers. Their tough skin appears to be impervious to bee-stings. They have a musty smell.

Voice: A cheery, bisyllabic '*whit-purr, whit-purr*' that is repeated over and over again and has great carrying power. When the bird is guiding it keeps up a continuous chattering '*chǎ-chǎ-chǎ-chǎ*'.

Habitat: Woodland, preferably park-like country in which there are tallish trees.

Distribution: The eastern half of Southern Africa. Also the southern coastal belt.

SHARP-BILLED HONEY-GUIDE   *Prodotiscus regulus* (443)   p. 225
Afr Skerpbekheuningvoël

Identification: 13 cm. A very plain and unobtrusive bird. General colour, including that of the throat and breast, a smoky brown; belly to under tail-coverts a brownish white. Outer two tail-feathers wholly white and the third partly white. Eyes brown; *thin sharp bill* and legs black. Sexes alike. Subadults similar to adults.

This small honey-guide may easily be mistaken for a fly-catcher, since it sometimes hawks insects. Very restless; does not sit on a perch for any length of time. During its dipping flight, in which rapid wing-beats alternate with spells of gliding, its white outer tail-feathers are conspicuous. Does not guide to bees' nests.

Voice: A rasping, high-pitched, often-repeated '*trrip-zeet*', uttered while sitting or flying.

Habitat: Open thornveld; also found in exotic plantations (wattles and eucalyptus).

Distribution: The eastern half of Southern Africa.

Allied species:

SCALY-THROATED HONEY-GUIDE (*Indicator variegatus*) (441). 19 cm. Above, olive-green; central tail-feathers and flight-feathers darker; forehead and crown streaked with whitish. Below, chin and chest a yellowish white, streaked with blackish. Breast has blackish spots. Four outer tail-feathers whitish, with dusky tips. Bill a dark horn-colour. Has also been known to lead the way to bees' nests. Call an ascending, trilling '*churr*' and a high-pitched, whistling '*foyt-foyt-foyt*'. Usually seen in the tall trees of riverine forests, in the south-eastern and eastern coastal regions.

LESSER HONEY-GUIDE (*Indicator minor*) (442). 15 cm. Above, olive-green; central tail-feathers and flight-feathers darker. Head, including chin and chest, greyish. Below, breast olive-grey; belly whitish. Four outer tail-feathers whitish, with dusky tips. *Stout but pointed bill black.* An inconspicuous bird that seems to crouch when perching. Sometimes seen at bees' nests but has not been known to lead the way to them. Call a '*klew-*

klew-klew', with fairly long intervals between the series of notes. Usually
calls from dense foliage. Also has a sharp chirp. Found in various types of
wooded country in the northern, eastern and southern parts of Southern
Africa.

Rarer species:
SLENDER-BILLED HONEY-GUIDE (*Prodotiscus insignis*) (444)

WOODPECKERS: Picidae

Woodpeckers are smallish birds, generally mottled or speckled, and with
black or bright red on the crown. Their straight, pointed bills are stout
at the base and admirably suited to the extraction of insects and insect
larvae from dead wood. Their long tongues, which are coated with a sticky
substance, serve the same purpose. Woodpeckers have powerful feet, with
the two middle toes pointing forwards and the outer toes backwards. The
short, sharp, curved claws enable them to clamber about and cling to the
bark of trees. The stiff shafts of their pointed tail-feathers act as prop
when the birds are clinging to tree-trunks. They have an undulating flight
with fast wing-beats. Most have loud, penetrating calls, and the habit of
drumming with their bills on dead boughs. They nest in holes excavated
by themselves.

GROUND WOODPECKER   *Geocolaptes olivaceus* (445)   p. 22.
   Afr Grondspegt   *X* um-Nqangqandola
   S Uapaleome
Identification: 28 cm. Head and sides of face grey, with a slight olive wash
rest of upper parts olive-brown with small whitish spots. Tail earth-brown
barred with yellowish white; *rump rose-red*. Below, chin and throat off
white; chest to belly rose-pink. Eyes pinkish; bill and legs black. Sexes
alike. Subadult is duller, with belly mottled with olive and buffish white
   This large woodpecker lives entirely on the ground and is very seldom
seen perched on low trees or shrubs. Usually found in small parties
Posture, as it sits on rocks or boulders, very erect. Red rump very con
spicuous during its rather heavy flight. Hops when it moves about on the
ground.
Voice: A sharp, metallic sound, as if the teeth of a saw were being sharp
ened with a file. Also a high-pitched whistle like the alarm-note of a rock
rabbit.
Habitat: Boulder-strewn hillsides and mountain slopes, in more open
country.
Distribution: Confined to the southern and south-eastern parts of Southern
Africa.

CARDINAL WOODPECKER   *Dendropicos fuscescens* (450)   p. 225
   Afr Kardinaalspegt   *Z* i-Nqonqonda
   X   isi-Qola

Identification: 15 cm. Adult male: *forehead ash-brown; crown to nape a bright red; moustache-stripe black;* rest of upper parts a blackish green, barred with white and yellowish. Tail-shafts golden. Below, chin and throat white, heavily streaked with black; chest to belly yellowish, streaked with black. Eyes red; bill black; legs olive-green. Adult female similar to male except that *crown and nape are black.* Subadults resemble males but are duller, and have crown red but nape black.

This *small* woodpecker is probably the most common. Usually found in pairs, often joining mixed bird parties. Unlike most other woodpeckers they feed among the smaller branches. Usually alight in the lower parts of a tree and work their way upwards. Have been observed taking insects from maize-stalks. A rather tame and confiding bird. During the breeding season its drumming is rapid, and less resonant than that of the larger species.
Voice: A quiet chittering, uttered by both sexes. Alarm-note a high-pitched scream.
Habitat: Occurs wherever there are trees, but not in true forests.
Distribution: Throughout Southern Africa.

BEARDED WOODPECKER   *Thripias namaquus* (451)   p. 225
   Afr Grootspegt

Identification: 24 cm. Adult male: forehead black, spotted with white; crown red; sides of face, chin and throat white. Nape, *broad stripe behind the eye and moustache-stripe black.* Below, chest to belly a dull olive-green, *finely barred with whitish.* Tail-shafts golden. Eyes a deep red; bill a greenish grey; legs olive-grey. Adult female similar to male, but the crown is black and not red. Subadult similar to male, but greyer.

This large, noisy, conspicuous woodpecker is usually found in pairs, feeding in dead trees. It has a very fast, undulating flight. Its drumming is very loud and resonant.
Voice: A loud, nasal scream, sounding like '*hare*'.
Habitat: Thornveld and open woodland, even in the drier regions.
Distribution: Over the greater part of Southern Africa, but not in the western and south-western coastal regions.

Allied Species:
BENNETT'S WOODPECKER (*Campethera bennettii*) (446). 20 cm. Above, general colour a dark greenish, barred and spotted with whitish and lighter green. *The forehead, crown, nape and moustache-stripe of the male are crimson.* The forehead and crown of the female are black, spotted with

PLATE 21

TROGON, LOURIES, CUCKOOS AND COUCAL

1 **NARINA TROGON**   *page* 170
   Belly bright red.

2 **GREY LOURIE**   151
   Long grey crest.

3 **PURPLE-CRESTED LOURIE**   150
   Crest purple.

4 **KNYSNA LOURIE**   150
   Crest green with white edge.

5 **RED-CHESTED CUCKOO**   152
   Chest reddish brown.

6 **BURCHELL'S COUCAL**   154
   Head and nape glossy black; back reddish brown and upper tail-
   coverts barred.

7 **GREAT SPOTTED CUCKOO**   152
   White spots on upper wing-coverts, tail long.

8 **DIDRIC CUCKOO**   154
   Eye-stripe white, white spots on upper wing-coverts.

9 **JACOBIN CUCKOO**   153
   Long black crest. (Chest either black or white).

10 **EMERALD CUCKOO**   153
   Belly bright yellow.

PLATE 22

OWLS, OWLETS AND NIGHTJARS

1 PEARL-SPOTTED OWLET *page* 159
Finely spotted with white above, chocolate-brown streaks below.
No ear-tufts.

2 BARN OWL 157
Facial disc heart-shaped.

3 SPOTTED EAGLE OWL 159
Ear-tufts long and appearance spotted. A large owl.

4 WOOD OWL 158
No ear-tufts, bill yellow, barred below.

5 SCOPS OWL 158
Ear-tufts small. A small owl.

6 MARSH OWL 157
Ring round eyes blackish, ear-tufts short.

7 EUROPEAN NIGHTJAR 163
Black streaks on crown; no rufous on hind neck.

8 FRECKLED NIGHTJAR 164
Upperside finely speckled dark grey; no collar on hind neck.

9 SOUTH AFRICAN NIGHTJAR 163
Distinct rufous collar on hind neck.

white; the stripes below the eye and on the sides of the throat are a dark chestnut. Chin and throat whitish, remainder of underparts a pale yellow, spotted and barred with blackish. Call a deep, bell-like note, quite unusual in a woodpecker. Nowhere common. Found in the dry thornveld and confined to the northern and more central parts of Southern Africa.

GOLDEN-TAILED WOODPECKER (*Campethera abingoni*) (447). 22 cm. Very similar to Bennett's Woodpecker, but the *males have the forehead black and red*, not wholly red, and the females lack the dark chestnut stripes on the sides of the head and throat. Below, broadly streaked as a rule from chin to belly, but sometimes chin and throat are not streaked. Tail a golden olive. Call a single loud '*whaa*', uttered by the male, and a screech when alarmed. A common, widely distributed species, found in the dense thornveld and especially along dry river-beds. Also found in mountain forests. A restless species, with a swift and deeply-dipping flight. Distributed over the northern half of Southern Africa, but not in the very arid west.

KNYSNA WOODPECKER (*Campethera notata*) (448). 20 cm. Similar to the Golden-tailed Woodpecker except that male has forehead and crown olivaceous or black, with red tips to the feathers, and female has forehead and moustache-stripe black, with yellowish spots. Both sexes are *heavily spotted below*. Back not barred but spotted with yellowish white. Call said to be similar to that of the Golden-tailed Woodpecker. Found in forests and more open country with large trees. Confined to the coastal and adjoining regions in the south and south-east of Southern Africa.

OLIVE WOODPECKER (*Mesopicos griseocephalus*) (452). 18 cm. *General colour a uniform dull olive* with a yellowish wash. Male has crown, nape and upper tail-coverts red; forehead, sides of face and throat grey. Female has crown and throat grey, and, rarely, a little red on the nape. This smallish woodpecker differs from the others in that its *plumage is plain, not spotted or barred*. Red rump conspicuous in flight. Call is a clear, cheerful, not very loud '*chi-r-r-r-re*'; also a loud '*wer-chick*'. Confined to the thick coastal bush and evergreen forests of the southern and south-eastern parts of Southern Africa.

Rarer Species:

LITTLE SPOTTED WOODPECKER (*Campethera cailliautii*) (449)

WRYNECKS: Jyngidae

Wrynecks resemble woodpeckers in the shape of the bill and the structure of the feet, and also in their habit of climbing about on tree-trunks, extracting insects from the bark. They also do a certain amount of tapping, but are incapable of the heavy chisel-strokes of the woodpeckers. Wrynecks also resemble barbets in that their tail-feathers are soft. Their plumage has the same bark-and-dead-leaf pattern as that of the nightjars. The snake-like movements of their necks are characteristic. They nest mainly in holes in trees not excavated by themselves.

RED-BREASTED WRYNECK   *Jynx ruficollis* (453)   p. 225
Afr Draaihals

Identification: 20 cm. Above, general colour mouse-brown, with arrow-shaped black markings forming a dark stripe down back of neck. Flight-feathers dusky; tail barred with black. Below, sides of throat finely barred with black and whitish; *throat and chest chestnut*; rest of underparts buffish, streaked with black. Under wing-coverts and under tail-coverts chestnut to buffish. Eyes a pale brown; bill and legs a dull greenish colour. Sexes alike. Subadults have duller throats and chests.

Usually seen singly or in pairs, sitting on an exposed perch and giving its characteristic call. Also feeds on the ground. Local in its distribution and not very common. Roosts in holes and crevices in trees.

Voice: A loud, harsh '*kwik-kwik-kwik-kwik*'. Alarm-call a rapid '*choo-choo-choo-choo*', pitched lower than the normal call.

Habitat: In the drier thornveld, and particularly in wooded gorges. Is also found in exotic trees near human habitations.

Distribution: Over the south-eastern coastal and central regions of Southern Africa.

Rarer Species:

Family **Eurylaemidae**

AFRICAN BROADBILL (*Smithornis capensis*) (454)

Family **Pittidae**

ANGOLA PITTA (*Pitta angolensis*) (455)

LARKS: Alaudidae

Larks are smallish ground-living birds with cryptic coloration. They usually present a mottled appearance, for their feathers have darker centres. Very often a rufous phase occurs together with the normally coloured form. The hind claw is well-developed and often elongated, and more or less straight. Their well-made, cup-shaped nests are built on the ground. Some species sing from conspicuous posts; others sing on the wing and sometimes at a great height. They feed on insects as well as seeds. Many species become gregarious out of the breeding season. Larks are extremely difficult to identify in the field, for their general plumage-patterns are often very similar, and are also subject to local and seasonal variation. Certain species may be identified by their song and call-notes, which are often distinctive.

RUFOUS-NAPED LARK　*Mirafra africana* (458)　　p. 240

Afr Rooineklewerkie　　*Z* u-Nongwatshi
X i-Qabatule

Identification: 18 cm. Above, general colour ranges from rufous to greyish brown, and feathers have distinct black centres. Forehead and crown streaked with black; *hind neck rufous-tinged and paler*, with smaller black markings. A distinct light eye-stripe. Tawny basal half of flight-feathers conspicuous in flight. Below, chin and throat a buffish white; chest and breast a pale tawny, heavily spotted with blackish; rest of underparts buff or tawny. Eyes brown; bill horn-coloured and fairly long; legs flesh-coloured. Sexes alike, but female slightly smaller. In the subadults the markings above and on the breast are more diffused.

This large, stockily-built lark is conspicuous as it is often seen calling from fence-posts and other perches, with its short crest slightly raised. It also sings a short, sweet song as it flies low and short, with quivering wings. Also has a flapping, gliding and hovering flight. It can run very fast on the ground, and often crouches to avoid detection. Utters a single sharp alarm-note when flushed.

Voice: A loud, clear, plaintive whistle, usually four-syllabled: '*tseep-tsee-hoooee*'.

Habitat: Grassland with or without scattered trees and bushes, and ranging from desert to mountainous country.

Distribution: Over the greater part of Southern Africa, but not in the south-western region.

SABOTA LARK　*Mirafra sabota* (460)　　p. 240

Afr Sabotalewerkie　　*Ts* Sabota

Identification: 15 cm. A medium-sized to smallish lark with a *not too short, stoutish bill*. General colour grey or tawny rather than rufous. The whole upper side, including the forehead, has a streaked appearance, for the buff feathers have dark centres. *White eye-stripe distinctive. Chest heavily spotted.* Chin, throat and belly white or buffish white. Primaries dusky; secondaries and tail-feathers dusky, edged with buff. Eyes brown; bill dusky; legs flesh-coloured. Sexes alike. Subadults have buff tips to the feathers of the upper parts.

Often referred to as a tree lark, for it perches freely on trees or bushes when alarmed, or when singing its varied song. Sometimes sings while hovering at a low altitude. Common; usually found in pairs or small parties.

feeding in open glades in bush country. When flushed, flies with an undulating flight to the nearest tree or bush.

Voice: Has a shrill, piping song. An excellent mimic; imitations of at least ten species of birds have been recorded.

Habitat: Grassland, with scattered trees and bushes. Partial to acacia veld.

Distribution: Over the greater part of Southern Africa, but not the southern third.

CLAPPER LARK   *Mirafra apiata* (466)   p. 240
Afr Klapperlewerkie

Identification: 15 cm. General colour rufous, but colour becomes more russet towards the north-east and greyer towards the north-west. *Mottled appearance of mantle and scapulars* owing to the black and whitish barring of the feathers. Cap darkish. Chin and throat whitish or buff, spotted with dusky brown; rest of underparts tawny. Flight-feathers dusky; basal half of primaries russet, and seen as a lightish window in flight. Tail-feathers tawny, the outermost feathers having their outer edges whitish. Eyes a light brown; horn-coloured bill narrow and rather sharply pointed; legs a fleshy white. Sexes alike. In the subadults the markings are much more diffused.

A common resident species, easily recognized by its courting display, in which the bird claps its wings and calls during its fluttering flight. Often overlooked during the non-breeding season, when it is silent. Occurs singly, in pairs or in small parties. When disturbed, seeks refuge in trees or bushes.

Voice: Male flies high, rising steeply with a clapping of wings and then dropping straight down with a long-drawn-out whistle: '*frrrr-frrrr-frrrr-phoooeee*'. Several birds may be heard at the same time. Also sings a short, melodious song at dawn.

Habitat: Bush and open country; is partial to rocky slopes.

Distribution: Over the greater part of Southern Africa, except the north-eastern regions and eastern coastal belt.

SPIKE-HEELED LARK   *Certhilauda albofasciata* (474)   p. 240
Afr Vlaktelewerkie   *X* u-Ngqembe
S Motinyane

Identification: 15 cm. Top of head, mantle and back russet-brown, streaked with black. Upper tail-coverts cinnamon-brown. Flight-feathers dusky; *central tail-feathers brownish; remainder blackish, with white tips. Chin and throat whitish;* remainder of underparts russet-brown, with a few dark streaks on chest. Eyes brown; longish curved bill blackish; legs flesh-coloured. Hind claw long and straight. Sexes alike, but female usually smaller. Subadults have a mottled appearance, since their feathers are tipped with white.

Upright stance, longish bill and shortish tail distinctive. *Dark tail with white terminal band conspicuous in flight.* A fairly tame terrestrial species, usually found in small parties, even during the breeding season. When disturbed, fly off for a short distance and turn towards the intruder before settling again. Not easily flushed; usually seen running about, with quick, mouse-like movements.

Voice: A chirruping alarm-call, '*chree-chree*', uttered in flight. Also a soft, melodious '*croo-croo-croo*'.

Habitat: Open, preferably stony country or desert.

Distribution: Over most of Southern Africa, except the northern-central and eastern regions and eastern coastal belt.

GREY-BACKED FINCH-LARK *Eremopterix verticalis* (485) p. 240
Afr Grysrugwitoorlewerkie

Identification: 13 cm. Adult male: top of head, face, ring round neck, throat and entire underside black. *White patch on crown; chest and sides of face white.* Flanks streaked with white. Mantle, scapulars and upper wing-coverts a drab grey, mottled with blackish. Flight-feathers and tail ash-brown. Eyes brown; stout finch-like bill a bluish grey; legs pale flesh to bluish white. Adult female ash-brown mottled with black all over, except for blackish patch on belly. Subadults have greyish feathers of upper parts tipped with buff, presenting a mottled appearance.

These restless little larks look finch-like on the ground, except that they run instead of hopping. Usually found in small parties, but sometimes in fair-sized flocks. When disturbed, take off for a short distance in a low, irregular flight, before dropping suddenly to earth again. Occasionally settle on bushes or trees. Often found in association with other larks, particularly Stark's Lark and the Chestnut-backed Finch-lark.

Voice: A shrill '*cheep*', uttered on the wing or when rising. Also a soft, squeaky chirp when feeding.

Habitat: Sandy or bare stony ground, old cultivations and open areas with thin scrub. Often found feeding on dirt roads.

Distribution: Over the western half of Southern Africa, but not in the southernmost tip.

RED-CAPPED LARK *Calandrella cinerea* (488) p. 240
Afr Rooikoplewerkie   *X* in-Tubane, in-Tutyane

Identification: 15 cm. *Top of head chestnut;* stripe over eye white; upper parts earth-brown and mottled; upper tail-coverts chestnut. Flight-feathers and tail dusky. Outer web of outermost tail-feathers white. Below, whitish, except for distinct *chestnut patch at side of breast.* Eyes brown; narrow, thinnish bill blackish; legs brown. Sexes alike. Subadult presents a highly spotted appearance, since the feathers of the upper parts have whitish tips. Chestnut patches on side of breast are spotted, and join at the centre of the breast.

A resident, ground-dwelling species; found singly or in pairs during the breeding season. After having bred, form small flocks of up to 20. Walk about briskly and twitter as they feed. Can run very fast over open ground. When flushed, fly off low, drop suddenly and run off immediately on alighting.

Voice: Flock-call in flight a short *'chick'*. Male has a short, musical song that he utters high in the air as he hovers and dives. A continuous twittering whilst feeding, and a sharp call when put to flight.

Habitat: Open plains, stubble fields, over-grazed pasture and burnt veld.

Distribution: Throughout Southern Africa.

PINK-BILLED LARK   *Calandrella conirostris* (490)   p. 240
Afr Pienkbeklewerkie

Identification: 13 cm. Upper parts brown, with broad black streaks. Flight- and tail-feathers dusky. Outermost tail-feathers mostly white. Buff stripe over eye. Chin and throat whitish, with black lines running from gape and side of chin to heavily-spotted chest. Rest of underparts a light rufous. Eyes straw-brown. *Pink bill is short, thick and conical;* legs pink. Sexes alike. Subadults have pale buff spots on wing-coverts and their bills are black, not pink.

Apparently resident for the most part, but possibly migratory in certain regions. Usually found in small parties during the non-breeding season, searching for seeds. Otherwise found in pairs.

Voice: A rapid bi- or trisyllabic *'twee-twee-twee'* or *'whee-tee-tee'*, uttered on the wing or on the ground.

Habitat: Short grass or old cultivated fields; partial to burnt areas.

Distribution: The central and north-western parts of Southern Africa.

Allied species:

SINGING BUSH LARK (*Mirafra cheniana*) (456). 14 cm. Upper parts russet, broadly streaked with black. Eye-stripe buff. *Throat and chin whitish; rest of underparts russet and buff.* Chest has black spots. Flight-feathers dusky; *tail a blackish brown, with outermost feathers entirely white*, except at the base. Conical bill dusky, not pink. Sings mostly on the wing, at a great height, often imitating the notes of other birds. Found in open veld and glades in the central parts of Southern Africa. Often perches on rocks and bushes.

MONOTONOUS LARK (*Mirafra javanica*) (457). 15 cm. Upper parts buff, with dark streaks; hind neck paler. Eye-stripe whitish. *Entire underparts, including chin and throat, white or buffish white.* Chest has dusky spots or streaks. Flight-feathers dusky; tail blackish, except for the outermost feathers, which are white. Conical bill horn-coloured. Partly migratory, inhabiting lowland open bush. During the breeding season the males keep up a continuous, monotonous '*aquavit*', even on moonlight nights. Call on the wing or from a tree-top perch. *Hold wings vertically above the body when gliding.* Found in the central and northern parts of Southern Africa.

FAWN-COLOURED LARK (*Mirafra africanoides*) (459). 15 cm. General appearance of upper parts a rufous fawn, broadly streaked with blackish; hind neck lighter; head finely streaked. Below, a buffish white; upper chest has short black streaks; a few black spots on throat. *Folded wing shows a rufous patch.* In flight, tail appears darker than rest of body. Sharp, slender bill horn-coloured. A common resident species of the savanna veld with low scrub and bushes. Not easily flushed; prefers to seek shelter under small bushes. Usually sings its melodious song while perched on the top of a bush. Found mainly in the northern half of Southern Africa. The commonest lark of the dry west.

KARROO LARK (*Certhilauda albescens*) (461). 16 cm. Upper parts vary from greyish to a rich rufous, streaked with black. Underparts white, fairly heavily spotted and streaked with dusky on chest, flanks and under tail-coverts. Face-pattern is distinctive, with a *whitish stripe above and below the eye, in contrast to the dark patch on the ear-coverts.* Horn-coloured bill fairly long and narrow. In flight the shortish square tail appears blackish. A common resident of open scrub with a sandy or gravelly substratum, where it is often seen digging for its food. Found in the south-western third of Southern Africa.

DUSKY LARK (*Pinarocorys nigricans*) (464). 19 cm. General colour of this *large* lark a dark sooty brown, wings and tail included. Black markings on face and chest very similar to those of the Groundscraper Thrush, but the lark is smaller and much more slender. *Does not show light rufous windows in flight.* A migrant, usually seen singly but sometimes in small flocks. Often perches on trees. Usually found on stony ground in open bush country in the northern and north-eastern parts of Southern Africa.

FLAPPET LARK (*Mirafra rufocinnamomea*) (468). 15 cm. Very similar to the Clapper Lark, but the bill is less robust, the tail rather shorter, and the greater part of the outermost tail-feathers light in colour. Also claps its wings during its display-flight, but never whistles while dropping to the ground. The crackling wing-flaps number from 3 to 5 for each display flight. Runs very fast and is not easily flushed. Found in bush or savanna country in the north-eastern regions. Clapper and Flappet Larks overlap only in the northern central region.

LONG-BILLED LARK (*Certhilauda curvirostris*) (475). 20 cm. Upper parts of this *large* lark a slightly russet earth-brown, streaked with black. Below, buffish; chin and throat lighter. Lower neck, chest and flanks streaked with blackish. The dark tail is longish and narrow. *The long, slightly down-curved bill is brown, and the white stripe over and behind the eye is prominent.* Crouches when feeding, and stalks rather than runs. During display-flights, rises nearly vertically and drops straight down, giving a plaintive, long-drawn-out whistle. Found in open country, preferably stony, in the southern and western parts of Southern Africa.

CHESTNUT-BACKED FINCH-LARK (*Eremopterix leucotis*) (484). 13 cm. Adult male: ear-coverts and hind neck white; remainder of head, wing-shoulders and underparts black. *No white patch on crown, and flanks not streaked with white. Mantle, scapulars and wing-coverts chestnut.* Tail dusky; outer web of outermost feathers mainly a buffish white. Female has top of head brown, streaked with black; back a dull chestnut; underparts buffish with black patch on belly. Gregarious; flocks are usually found in open stony or sandy ground, in the central and northern parts of Southern Africa. Found together with Grey-backed Finch-larks in the dry western regions.

BLACK-EARED FINCH-LARK (*Eremopterix australis*) (486). 13 cm. Adult male: *general appearance black.* Head, flight-feathers, tail and whole underside (including wing-coverts) black. Remainder of bird brown, mottled with blackish. Adult female a dark brown above, streaked with blackish. Chin to lower neck white and blackish; rest of underparts a buffish white; chest streaked and spotted with black. Gregarious; small scattered flocks usually found in very barren country in the central western regions of Southern Africa.

GRAY'S LARK (*Alaemon grayi*) (483). 14 cm. Whole of upper side, including central tail-feathers, a pale fawn. Rest of tail blackish, tipped with white. Underside white. Eye-stripe whitish. The dark grey bill is short and narrow. Usually found in small parties. *Confined to the Namib Desert of the central western coastal region.* Cryptic colouring blends with that of the gravel plains. Very difficult to spot when standing still; usually seen only when flying off.

STARK'S LARK (*Calandrella starki*) (492). 13 cm. Upper side a light buffish, with dusky streaks; prominent lightish eye-stripe. *Feathers of striped crown relatively long and often raised to form a definite crest.* Tail-feathers dusky and blackish, except for the outermost ones, which are mainly white. Below, whitish; lower neck sparsely streaked with brown. Bill horn-coloured and fairly stout. A common lark, frequenting open ground with short grass in the central and northern western regions. Gregarious; flocks often number a few hundred.

Rarer species:

THICK-BILLED LARK (*Calendula magnirostris*) (463)

SHORT-CLAWED LARK (*Mirafra chuana*) (465)

BOTHA'S LARK (*Calandrella fringillaris*) (472)

RUDD'S LARK (*Calandrella ruddi*) (473).

RED LARK (*Alaemon burra*) (479)

CALANDRA LARK (*Melanocorypha bimaculata*) (487)

SCLATER'S LARK (*Calandrella sclateri*) (491).

SWALLOWS and MARTINS: Hirundinidae

Swallows and Martins are smallish birds that capture virtually all their food on the wing. Unlike swifts, and notwithstanding the fact that their feet are relatively small, they can perch like other birds. Their bodies are slim and they have a graceful flight, less rapid and direct than that of swifts. Their bills are weak, short and flattened and they have a wide gape. Their tails are usually forked, and in many species the outer tail-feathers are long and slender. Their nesting habits vary considerably. The majority build mud nests, either open or closed, and with or without a long tubular entrance, but some burrow in sandbanks. *In flight they are distinguished from swifts by their wings, which are angular, not sickle-shaped and narrow.* The family is cosmopolitan, and many species are migratory.

EUROPEAN SWALLOW   *Hirundo rustica* (493)   p. 208

    Afr Europese swawel   *X* u-Fabele

    Z i-Nkonyane   *S* le-Fokotsane

Identification: 18 cm. Forehead, chin and throat a dark chestnut. Upper parts a glossy blue-black. Broad, glossy blue-black band across the chest. Rest of underparts whitish. Outermost tail-feathers considerably elongated. All the tail-feathers have large white spots on the inner web. Eyes hazel; bill and legs black. Sexes alike, but adult female has shorter outer tail-feathers. Subadults generally duller, upper parts showing more brownish, and slightly mottled with whitish. Forehead, chin and throat a pale chestnut. Outer tail-feathers only slightly elongated.

This palaeoarctic migrant is probably the commonest swallow to be seen in the summer. Winter records are rare. Usually seen in large flocks, and gather in thousands to roost in reed-beds. Vast numbers can be seen sitting on telegraph wires in late summer, when the birds begin to gather for their northward migration. Often seen flying very low, hovering for a moment and then pecking insects off grass stalks. As a result of moulting, these birds lack the elongated tail-feathers for the greater part of their stay. Only just before migration do the tail-streamers become evident. But the *chestnut chin and throat, and the broad dark band below*, distinguish this swallow, at any stage of its plumage, from all the other species.

Voice: A single, high-pitched '*tswit*' and a rapid twitter. Warbling song, which is sometimes heard just before the northward migration, is usually uttered on the wing.

Habitat: Any type of country.

Distribution: Throughout Southern Africa.

WHITE-THROATED SWALLOW *Hirundo albigularis* (495) p. 208
Afr Witkeelswawel

Identification: 16 cm. Upper parts a glossy steel-blue, except for the *chestnut forehead*, which is more conspicuous than in the European Swallow. Below, *throat a clear white*; blue-black band (often broken at the centre) across the chest. Rest of underparts a greyish white. Outer tail-feathers only slightly elongated; white spots on inner web of tail-feathers conspicuous in flight. Eyes brown; bill black; legs a dark brown. Sexes alike. Subadult generally duller above; chestnut patch on forehead smaller and paler.

A common local migrant, usually breeding in early summer and returning to the same nesting-site year after year. Found singly or in pairs and, after breeding, in small family parties. Flies very fast, slightly bent wings giving the appearance of a prominent shoulder. Often found in urban areas.

Voice: A gentle twitter and a pleasant warbling song.

Habitat: No preference.

Distribution: Throughout Southern Africa.

RED-BREASTED SWALLOW *Hirundo semirufa* (501) p. 208
Afr Rooiborsswawel

Identification: 24 cm. Top of head, mantle, scapulars, wings and tail a glossy blue-black. Lores and ear-coverts a glossy black. *Rump and entire underside chestnut*, extending to the nape. Outer tail-feathers greatly elongated; large white spots on inner web of tail-feathers very conspicuous in flight. Eyes and legs dusky; bill black. Sexes alike. Subadults brownish above, much paler below and have a shorter tail.

This large local migrant is solitary in habits. Very often uses culverts for nesting, and can usually be seen sitting on fences or telegraph wires near the nest. Flies heavily and often resorts to gliding.

Voice: Alarm-note a short '*weet weet*'. Also utters a plaintive '*seeúriseeúr*' and has a soft, pleasant, gurgling song.

Habitat: Open country; prefers fairly level ground.
Distribution: Northern and central Southern Africa.

LARGER STRIPED SWALLOW   *Hirundo cucullata* (502)   p. 20
Afr Grootstreepswawel

Identification: 18 cm. Forehead, crown and rump a deep tawny. Mantle a glossy blue-black; wings and tail blue-black. Outer tail-feathers fairly long All the tail-feathers have white spots on the inner webs. Underparts a ligh fawn, with *narrow blackish stripes that are not easily seen from a distance* *Ear-coverts whitish*, forming a distinct light patch on side of head and distinguishing this species from the Lesser Striped Swallow (see allied species). Eyes and legs brown; bill black. Sexes alike. Subadult duller with some black on the head; underside washed with tawny.

A local migrant that returns to the same nesting-site year after year Usually found in pairs, but several pairs may build their gourd-shaped nests on the same building.

Voice: A pleasant, twittering '*chissick, chissick*'.
Habitat: Usually found near human habitations.
Distribution: Throughout Southern Africa, except in the extreme north easterly regions.

CLIFF SWALLOW   *Hirundo spilodera* (504)   p. 20
Afr Familieswawel

Identification: 15 cm. Forehead, crown, wings and tail brown, with a sligh green sheen. Lores a light chestnut; hind neck and mantle a glossy blue-black. Back streaked with whitish. Rump a light tawny. Chin a ligh chestnut; throat-band brown, mottled with tawny; *chest a light tawny mottled with brown* (amount of mottling variable). Breast and belly a dirty white. Under tail-coverts a light chestnut. *Shortish tail square, with n white spots on tail-feathers*. Eyes and legs dusky; bill black. Sexes alike Subadults not glossy but generally duller and paler.

A local migrant, nesting in large colonies. Birds seldom found far from breeding sites. Their round mud nests are built one against the other or cliffs, under bridges and on many different kinds of buildings.

Voice: A softish, three- or four-syllabled '*chor-chor-choor*', usually uttered in chorus.
Habitat: Prefers high open country.
Distribution: The central south-eastern and north-western parts of Southern Africa.

ROCK MARTIN   *Hirundo rupestris* (506)   p. 208
   Afr Kransswawel   *X* u-Nongubende
   S le-Kabelane
Identification: 15 cm. Entire upper side a dark sooty brown. Chin and neck a pale russet; breast and belly brown, tinged with russet; under tail-coverts a sooty brown. *Tail squarish and fairly short; when fanned out during flight shows conspicuous white spots.* Eyes and legs brown; bill black. Sexes alike. Subadults have russet edging to flight-feathers, mantle, rump and tail-coverts.

A common resident species that has adapted itself to human dwellings. Usually found in pairs or small parties, not far from their nests. In the wilds, never far away from water. Flight slow, and interspersed with twists and turns. Often seen flying about in the half-light of dusk and early morning.
Voice: A high-pitched '*cheep-cheep-cheep-churr*', repeated several times in flight. Also a soft, melodious, twittering song.
Habitat: Near cliffs or in built-up areas.
Distribution: Throughout Southern Africa.

AFRICAN SAND MARTIN   *Riparia paludicola* (509)   p. 208
   Afr Gewone oewerswawel   *S* le-Kavelane
Identification: 11 cm. Above, mouse-brown, including wings and tail. Tail without white spots, and only slightly forked. Below, *chin to upper belly a pale mouse-brown*; lower belly and under tail-coverts whitish (some specimens wholly mouse-brown below). Eyes and legs brown; bill black. Sexes alike. Subadult has dark buff tips to wing-coverts, secondaries, rump and upper tail-coverts. This gives it a mottled appearance.

A common resident species, subject to local migration; in some areas recorded only during the winter months. Usually found where there are sand-banks, since it uses these for breeding purposes. Colonial nesters. Out of the breeding season, roost in large flocks in reed-beds.
Voice: A thin, feeble '*svee-svee*'; during the breeding season a weak, twittering warble.
Habitat: Frequents permanent water (dams, rivers and streams).
Distribution: Throughout Southern Africa.

BLACK SAW-WINGED SWALLOW   *Psalidoprocne pristoptera*
   (511)   p. 208
   Afr Saagvlerkswawel
Identification: 15 cm. Above and below: general colour black, with a bottle-green gloss; under wing-coverts an ashy brown. *Tail deeply forked.* Eyes and legs brown; bill black. Sexes alike, but tail of female slightly less forked. Subadult less glossy above; browner below.

A not uncommon resident species. Usually found singly or in pairs. Bird has a slender build and a swift, graceful flight. Flies with great agility through the trees, hawking insects. Nests in burrows in sand-banks; probably rests in thick foliage during the heat of the day.

Voice: Usually silent, but sometimes utters a soft chirp.

Habitat: Prefers forested regions in which there is water. Also found in kloofs, but always near water.

Distribution: In the southern and eastern coastal regions of Southern Africa.

Allied species:

WIRE-TAILED SWALLOW (*Hirundo smithii*) (496). 13 cm. *Entire top of head chestnut;* rest of upper parts a glossy violet-blue. White spots on inner webs of tail-feathers visible in flight. *Outer tail-feathers elongated and extremely narrow.* Those of the female are shorter, and do not protrude beyond the wing-tips when the bird is perched. Below, wholly white, except for a smallish blue-black patch on either side of the breast. A common resident species, usually found near water. These small swallows occur singly or in pairs, and nest on buildings or bridges. Found in the north-eastern third of Southern Africa.

PEARL-BREASTED SWALLOW (*Hirundo dimidiata*) (498). 14 cm. Above: forehead, crown, sides of face, sides of chest and rump a glossy steel-blue. Below, a pearly white. *Tail forked, but outer feathers only slightly elongated;* no white spots on tail-feathers. A resident breeding species, migratory in some regions. This smallish swallow is usually found in pairs or family parties. Nests on buildings. Found throughout Southern Africa, especially in the dry west, but not in the eastern and north-eastern coastal regions.

GREY-RUMPED SWALLOW (*Hirundo griseopyga*) (499). 14 cm. Above, top of head an ashy brown; lores black; mantle, wings and tail a glossy blue-black. *Rump and upper tail-coverts a greyish brown*, conspicuous in flight. Tail is well forked, with outer tail-feathers elongated. Below, wholly white. This smallish swallow is apparently resident, and is partial to open grass-land. Is usually seen flying about in small parties, occasionally settling on the dry branches of trees. Found in the north-eastern third of Southern Africa.

LESSER STRIPED SWALLOW (*Hirundo abyssinica*) (503). 16 cm. *Top of head to nape, including the ear-coverts, a uniform chestnut.* Rump also chestnut. Below: white, broadly and heavily streaked with blackish. From a distance breast and throat look very dark. Mantle, scapulars and wing-coverts a glossy steel-blue; flight-feathers dusky. Tail-feathers also dusky, and spotted with white; outer tail-feathers elongated. A local summer migrant, occurring in pairs and small parties, and building nests on cliffs, dwellings and bridges. Has a slow flight and often resorts to gliding. Often heard singing and calling on the wing. Found in the eastern half of Southern Africa.

HOUSE MARTIN (*Delichon urbica*) (507). 14 cm. Above, a glossy blue-black; wings and tail dull black; rump and upper tail-coverts white. Below, wholly white, including feathers on tarsi. Tail well-forked, but outer tail-feathers not elongated. This palaeoarctic migrant, with its *conspicuous white rump and underside*, is often seen in the company of other swallows and swifts. Found in fairly large flocks when gathering for the northward migration.

EUROPEAN SAND MARTIN (*Riparia riparia*) (508). 11 cm. Above, including wings and tail, mouse-brown. Below, white, with a *broad mouse-brown band across the chest*. Under wing-coverts and flanks also mouse-brown. This small martin is a rare and irregular palaeoarctic migrant, usually found singly near water in the north-eastern half of Southern Africa.

BANDED SAND MARTIN (*Riparia cincta*) (510). 16 cm. Above, wholly mouse-brown, including wings and *square tail*. White mark in front of eye conspicuous. Lores and ear-coverts blackish. Below, white, with broad mouse-brown band across chest, broadening slightly down centre of breast. This large, breeding migrant is usually seen singly or in pairs. Its flight is slow and deliberate, and it is often seen perched on wire fences and grass-stems. Picks insects off grass-tops. Found in open grassy country, not necessarily near water, throughout Southern Africa.

Rarer species:
BLUE SWALLOW (*Hirundo atrocaerulea*) (497)
MOSQUE SWALLOW (*Hirundo senegalensis*) (500)

CUCKOO-SHRIKES: Campephagidae

Cuckoo-shrikes are medium-sized shrike-like birds with strong bills and short legs. They are largely insectivorous, and live in thick bush or forest. They are usually seen singly or in pairs, very often as members of a mixed bird-party. Most of their plumage is soft, the rump-feathers also having the apical quarter soft and weak but the rest of the shaft hard and stiff, forming blunt spines that can be felt when brushed upwards. In one species the sexes are very dissimilar and might easily be taken for different species in the field.

BLACK CUCKOO-SHRIKE *Campephaga phoenicia* (513)   p. 240
  Afr Swartkatakoeroe   *X* u-Sasa
Identification: 22 cm. Adult male; general colour a glossy blue-black. Some

PLATE 23

SWIFTS, SPINETAIL AND SWALLOWS

1 **PALM SWIFT**
Uniform blue-grey, long, slender tail deeply forked.

page 167

2 **LITTLE SWIFT**
Tail square, rump white.

166

3 **BLACK SWIFT**
Throat whitish. A large swift.

165

4 **WHITE-RUMPED SWIFT**
Tail forked, white band across rump narrow.

166

5 **BOEHM'S SPINETAIL**
Tail very short. Has batlike appearance.

167

6 **WHITE-THROATED SWALLOW**
Throat white, forehead red.

203

7 **BLACK SAW-WINGED SWALLOW**
Uniform black, tail deeply forked.

205

8 **LARGER STRIPED SWALLOW**
Stripes on throat and breast narrow, ear-coverts whitish, rump rufous.

204

9 **EUROPEAN SWALLOW**
Throat reddish, bordered below by blue band.

202

10 **CLIFF SWALLOW**
Tail square, mottling on chest variable.

204

11 **ROCK MARTIN**
Tail square with white 'windows'. Colour uniform brownish.

205

12 **RED-BREASTED SWALLOW**
Underparts and rump red. A large swallow.

203

13 **AFRICAN SAND MARTIN**
Chin, throat and chest brownish. A small swallow.

205

PLATE 24

BEE-EATERS, KINGFISHERS AND MOUSEBIRD

1 **CARMINE BEE-EATER** *page* 174
Throat and breast carmine, centre tail feathers very much elongated.

2 **SWALLOW-TAILED BEE-EATER** 178
Medium-sized with bluish swallow-tail.

3 **EUROPEAN BEE-EATER** 174
Throat yellow, back rufous, centre tail feathers slightly
elongated.

4 **LITTLE BEE-EATER** 175
Small; square tail and black throat band.

5 **WHITE-FRONTED BEE-EATER** 175
Throat red, forehead white.

6 **RED-FACED MOUSEBIRD** 168
Red face, general colour olive-green.

7 **BROWN-HOODED KINGFISHER** 172
Entire head brown, bill reddish.

8 **ANGOLA KINGFISHER** 171
Black legs, black shoulders, upper mandible red, lower black.

9 **PIED KINGFISHER** 170
Male with double black band on chest.

10 **MALACHITE KINGFISHER** 171
Small; long bluish-green crest tipped with black.

individuals have bright lemon wing-shoulders. *Gape a bright orange-yellow.* Longish tail is rounded. Eyes brown; bill and legs black. The adult female is brown or yellowish brown above, indistinctly barred with black on mantle and heavily barred on rump and upper tail-coverts. *Wings brown, with bright yellow edges to all the feathers.* Tail olive-brown and blackish; outer feathers mainly a bright yellow. Below, white with black bars, and sometimes a yellowish wash. Under wing-coverts a bright yellow. Subadults resemble the female but have darker throats, more barring below, and pointed tail-feathers.

Silent, inconspicuous birds, usually found in pairs, restlessly hunting for insects amongst the leaves of densely-foliaged trees. Sometimes hawk insects in the air or feed on the ground. Often seen flying from one bush to another, with a heavy, flapping flight.

Voice: A cricket-like chirp and a low, trilling call uttered at rest or in flight, '*wheeo-wheeo-eee-ee-e*'.

Habitat: Forest, forest strips, thick bush and even lowland scrub in the coastal belt.

Distribution: In the north-eastern third of Southern Africa and along the southern and south-eastern coastal belt.

GREY CUCKOO-SHRIKE   *Coracina caesia* (516)   p. 240

    Afr Bloukatakoeroe   *X* u-Singa
    S Mmaselakhoasa

Identification: 25 cm. *A bluish grey all over;* flight-feathers and tail blackish; lores black; white ring round the eye. Eyes brown; bill and legs black. Adult female differs from male in being slightly paler and having lores grey. Subadult has edges and tips of flight-feathers white; tail-feathers pointed and tipped with white; upper and under tail-coverts barred with black.

Found singly or in pairs in evergreen forests, clambering about on the trunks and thicker branches of tall trees in search of insects. Perches motionless for long periods in one place. Its weak flight is ghostly and silent.

Voice: A thin, mammal-like squeak. Also said to have a whistle.

Habitat: Tall trees in evergreen forests.

Distribution: In the southern and eastern coastal belt and the mountainous north-eastern part of Southern Africa.

Allied species:

WHITE-BREASTED CUCKOO-SHRIKE (*Coracina pectoralis*) (515). 25 cm. Adult male a pale grey above; forehead and eye-stripe lighter; flight-feathers and tail blackish. Below, sides of face and chin to neck a dark slate; rest of underparts white, including underwing. Female has chin to neck a pale grey, or white and grey. Behaviour rather similar to that of the orioles. Found singly or in pairs as members of mixed bird-parties in large trees in open woodland. Often spotted only when they make a gliding or flapping flight to another tree. Not common. Found in the north-eastern and central northern regions of Southern Africa.

DRONGOS: Dicruridae

Drongos are medium-sized, black, shrike-like birds with short, broad, slightly arched bills. Their nostrils are covered by feathers and bristles. They are usually seen perched on some particularly conspicuous spot, from which they hawk flying insects, returning as a rule to the same perch. They also take insects off the ground. These very active and vivacious birds even mob large birds of prey.

FORK-TAILED DRONGO   *Dicrurus adsimilis* (517)   p. 240
   Afr Mikstertbyevanger   *X* in-Tengu
   Z Induna-yezinyoni   *S* Theko

Identification: 25 cm. General colour a glossy blue-black; inner webs of flight-feathers ashy (in flight wings appear light brown and partly transparent). *Fish-like forked tail* in evidence even when bird is perching. Eyes brick-red; bill and legs black. Female has tail less deeply forked. Sub-adult a dull black, with grey edges to the feathers producing a mottled effect.

A common and extremely conspicuous bird, usually found in pairs, sitting on prominent vantage-points from which insects are hawked. Large numbers are attracted to grass-fires. Often found in the company of grazing game, catching insects disturbed by the animals. Even perches on the animals. Has a fast, tumbling, twisting flight. Fearlessly mobs small carnivora and birds of prey, swooping down on them noisily and actually striking them about the head. Often found as a leading member of mixed bird-parties.

Voice: A variety of twanging, rasping, metallic, not unpleasing notes. Sometimes tries to imitate the calls of other birds.

Habitat: Found in open bush country, but not in thick forest. Not averse to exotic trees.

Distribution: Throughout Southern Africa, but not in the southernmost tip.

Allied species:

SQUARE-TAILED DRONGO (*Dicrurus ludwigii*) (518). 19 cm. General colour a glossy blue-black. *Tail is actually not square, but slightly forked.*

Inner webs of flight-feathers blackish. *Eyes crimson*; bill and legs black Not common and very local in habitat, occurring only in forest and dense bush. Sometimes found on an exposed vantage-point at the forest's edge but prefers thick cover. *Differs from the Black Flycatcher in that its eyes are red, its bill stouter, and its tail much shorter and broader.* Often found leading bird-parties and giving its strident alarm-call. Distributed over the eastern and northern coastal regions.

ORIOLES: Oriolidae

Orioles are medium-sized birds, with strong, slightly curved pinkish or reddish bills. The plumage of the adult birds is mainly a bright yellow with black patches and markings. All have loud, clear, melodious whistles They prefer the tops of the taller trees in forests, and are easily overlooked unless they call. Their flight is fast and direct, and they are easily identified in flight by their bright yellow colouring.

EUROPEAN GOLDEN ORIOLE *Oriolus oriolus* (519) p. 241
Afr Europese wielewaal

Identification: 23 cm. Adult male: a golden yellow above and below, with *lores, wings and tail black.* Tail-feathers black, tipped with yellow. Eyes crimson; bill a dark pink; legs slate. Female a greenish yellow above; rump golden; wings a blackish brown; tail blackish and golden. Below, chin to belly whitish, streaked with black. Flanks and under tail-coverts yellow. Subadult resembles female but the yellow is more olivaceous and the wings and tail less black. Below, a yellowish white with dusky streaks. Bill dusky.

A common palaeoarctic migrant, often seen in pairs or small parties, in the tops of tall trees in rather dry areas. Not confined to indigenous bush. Many of these visitors are immature birds.

Voice: A loud, clear whistle: '*weela-weeō*'. Alarm-note a harsh, rattling '*chrrr*'.

Habitat: Woodland and forest.

Distribution: The northern and eastern half of Southern Africa.

AFRICAN GOLDEN ORIOLE *Oriolus auratus* (520) p. 241
Afr Afrikaanse wielewaal

Identification: 23 cm. Adult male a rich golden-yellow above and below. *Black of lores extends around and behind the eye. Only a small amount of black on the wing.* Only central tail-feathers black; others yellow. Eyes blood-red; bill a deep brownish pink; legs a bluish grey. Female has upper parts a more olivaceous yellow and is a less rich yellow below, more or less streaked with olive. Subadult similar to young European Golden Oriole but has an olivaceous stripe through the eye and bright yellow or greenish yellow edges to the upper wing-coverts.

A local migrant, keeping to thick bush, especially along the edges of small hills. Shy and difficult to see in spite of its brilliant plumage. Has a very rapid and direct undulating flight and sweeps sharply upwards before alighting in a tree.

Voice: A clear bisyllabic whistle, repeated two or three times: '*fee-you-fee-you-fee-you*', Alarm-note a harsh '*mwah-mwah*'.

Habitat: Thick bush and riverine forest.

Distribution: The northern and north-eastern parts of Southern Africa.

BLACK-HEADED ORIOLE *Oriolus larvatus* (521) p. 241

Afr Swartkopwielewaal *X* um-Qokolo
Z um-Qoqonga *S* Khulon

Identification: 24 cm. *Head, nape and upper chest black;* hind neck and rest of underside golden-yellow. Flight-feathers blackish, with whitish edges. Wing-coverts black; with white ends and yellow-green edges. Rest of back a yellowish green. Central tail-feathers yellow-green; rest black, tipped with golden-yellow that decreases towards the centre. Eyes red; bill a brownish pink; legs grey-blue. Sexes alike. Subadult has top of head to nape flecked with yellow; ear-coverts blackish; chin to upper chest streaked with black; bill blackish.

A common local migrant, usually found in pairs and comparatively tame, for an oriole. Most often heard calling in the early morning. Flight is swift, direct and undulating.

Voice: A loud, melodious, bisyllabic whistle '*pheeeooo*', with the second syllable much lower in pitch. Alarm-note a harsh '*kweeer*', often repeated.

Habitat: Well-wooded regions such as forests and coastal bush, but even found in gardens.

Distribution: The eastern half of Southern Africa.

CROWS: Corvidae

Crows are the largest of the passerine birds and have glossy black or black-and-white plumage. Their bills are heavy, and vary in shape, the nostrils being covered with forward-pointing bristles. They are omnivorous and feed mainly on the ground. Although they often gather in large numbers they are usually found in pairs. They have loud, raucous calls. Although they do a certain amount of damage to agriculture this is probably more than outweighed by their services as scavengers.

PIED CROW   *Corvus albus* (522)   p. 161

    Afr Bontkraai (Witborskraai)   *X* Gwahube
    Z   i-Gwabayi   *S* Lokhokuba

Identification: 50 cm. General colour a glossy blue-black; *broad collar across base of hind neck, chest and upper belly white.* Eyes brown; bill and legs black. Sexes alike. Subadults a duller black; also black from chin to breast.

A common, widespread, localized species, usually seen in pairs, but sometimes in small parties where food is abundant. Found at refuse dumps near towns and often seen on roads, feeding on animals and insects run over by cars. Can often be seen soaring at a considerable height.

Voice: A loud, raucous, nasal '*kwahk*', repeated several times in quick succession.

Habitat: No preference; often nest in tall exotic trees.

Distribution: Throughout Southern Africa.

BLACK CROW   *Corvus capensis* (523)   p. 161

    Afr Swartkraai   *X* i-Dakatye
    Z   i-Gwababane   *S* le-Khoa

Identification: 50 cm. General colour a glossy black. Eyes brown; *slender bill* and legs black. Sexes alike. Subadult is a duller black and has a brownish wash on head and breast.

A common localized species that replaces the Pied Crow in some areas. Usually seen in mated pairs. Young and unmated birds are sometimes found in large flocks. Often seen perching on telegraph poles beside roads. When calling from a high perch usually arches its neck and puffs out the feathers of its head. A very noisy bird.

Voice: A high-pitched '*kah*' and a bubbling alarm-note.

Habitat: Open country and cultivated land.

Distribution: Throughout Southern Africa but not in the north-eastern tip.

CAPE RAVEN   *Corvus albicollis* (524)   p. 161

    Afr Withalskraai   *X* i-Hwababa
    Z   i-Gwababa   *S* Lekhoaba

Identification: 52 cm. General colour a slightly glossy black. *Broad collar at base of hind neck white.* Head and neck a bronzy brown. Eyes a dark brown; *deep, heavy bill black, with a white tip;* legs black. Female has a smaller bill. Subadult is a dull, sooty black below and the white collar is streaked with black.

A widely-distributed species, usually seen in pairs, and regarded as a pest. A bold, daring but wary bird, well able to look after itself. A scavenger, often arriving at a carcass before the vultures do. White collar invisible in flight, but distinguished from the Black Crow by its *heavy bill*.

Voice: A deep-throated '*kraaak-kraaak-kraaak*' and also a high-pitched nasal call.

Habitat: Mountainous regions, but birds often stray very far in search of food.

Distribution: The southern half of Southern Africa; also the north-eastern regions.

TITS: Paridae

Tits are small, rather plump insectivorous birds with shortish and fairly strong bills. They are extremely active when feeding, and assume all sorts of queer positions—even hanging upside-down. They are usually tame and inquisitive, and often join mixed bird-parties. One very small species, the Penduline Tits, build remarkable, felt-like oval nests, but the other species are hole-nesters.

GREY TIT *Parus afer* (525)   p. 241
    Afr Grysmees   *S* Sekhekha

Identification: 14 cm. Top of head to nape, sides of neck, chin to chest and down centre of belly black. *A conspicuous white line from the gape passes under the eye and down the side of the neck*. Whitish patch on nape; back olive-grey; flight-feathers dusky; tail black, tipped with whitish. Rest of underparts ash-grey. Eyes brown; bill and legs black. Sexes alike. Sub-adult has browner back and top of head also slightly brownish.

Common and well distributed. Found in small, noisy parties, foraging for food in small trees or low bushes. Often join mixed bird-parties and creep restlessly about on the branches, uttering their loud call at intervals.

Voice: A loud, clear '*peet-choe-choe*' and various other calls; '*give-ear, give-ear*' or '*t'wit, t'wit, t'wit*'. Alarm-call a scolding '*titsi-krurkrurkrur*'.

Habitat: Dry bush and acacia country.

Distribution: Throughout Southern Africa, but not along the southern or eastern coastal belt.

BLACK TIT *Parus niger* (527)   p. 241
    Afr Swartmees   *X* isi-Cubujeje

Identification: 15 cm. Adult male: general colour a glossy blue-black; breast to belly rather slaty. *Conspicuous white shoulder*. Edge of flight-feathers and tips of tail-feathers white. Outer web of outer tail-feathers also white. Lower belly and under tail-coverts black. Eyes brown; bill and legs black. Female is duller and paler above and a dull slaty grey below. Subadult similar to female but has the white on the shoulders and flight-feathers washed with cream.

A very noisy bird, found in pairs or small parties that are always on the move. Males often seen sitting on exposed perches, calling loudly.

Voice: The commonest call is a shrill, harsh, '*twiddy*', followed by a rasping '*zeet-zeet-zeet*'. Also utters a loud, buzzing '*zeu-zeu-zeu-twit*'.

Habitat: Forest, thick bush and scrub.

Distribution: The north-eastern half of Southern Africa.

CAPE PENDULINE TIT   *Anthoscopus minutus* (531)   p. 241
   Afr Kaapse kapokvoël   *X* u-Notoyi
   S le-Soarelela

Identification: 8 cm. *Forehead black, speckled with white*; rest of head and back mouse-grey, washed with olive. Flight-feathers and tail dusky. Rump and upper tail-coverts a dull, yellowish grey. Below, *chin whitish and slightly spotted*; throat whitish; rest of underparts a dull, light, brownish yellow. Eyes brown; bill and legs black. Sexes alike. Subadults similar to adults but a yellowish white below.

Usually found in small family parties, looking for insects on the flowers and leaves of trees. When flying from bush to bush they trail one after the other, maintaining a continuous soft twitter to keep in touch with one another. Usually very tame and unafraid of man. When their own nests are not available, they roost in the nests of other birds.

Voice: A twittering '*trrit-trrit*' and a single, sharp mating-call.

Habitat: Bush country, especially in the drier regions.

Distribution: Over the greater part of Southern Africa, except the eastern coastal and far northern and north-eastern regions.

Allied species:

RUFOUS TIT (*Parus rufiventris*) (529). 14 cm. Whole head, nape and chest blue-black. Back grey; flight-feathers black, broadly edged with white; tail black, tipped with white. *Breast to under tail-coverts russet-brown.* Not very common: confined to the forests of the central northern and north-eastern regions of Southern Africa.

GREY PENDULINE TIT (*Anthoscopus caroli*) (530). 8 cm. *Forehead not black, but a buffish white*; top of head, sides of face and back an ashy grey. Flight-feathers and tail dusky. Chin to chest whitish; rest of underparts buff. Habits similar to those of the Cape Penduline Tit described above. Found mostly in the acacia veld of the north-eastern and north-western parts of Southern Africa.

Rarer species:

Family **Certhidae**

SPOTTED CREEPER (*Salpornis spilonata*) (532)

BABBLERS: Timaliidae

The babblers are medium-sized thrush-like birds. They are gregarious and very noisy, keeping up a continuous harsh chattering while looking for insects in the lower parts of bushes or among the fallen debris on the ground. Their plumage is dull: usually brown, grey or rufous. They have rounded wings and strong bills. Though mainly insectivorous, they also feed on fruit and berries.

ARROW-MARKED BABBLER *Turdoides jardineii* (533)   p. 240
   Afr Gewone katlagter   *Z* u-Hlegawedwane
Identification: 24 cm. Above, ash-brown; feathers of head have dark centres; flight- and tail-feathers a bronzy black. Below, a pale ash-colour; *arrow-like white tips to feathers of chin, breast and upper belly* give it a speckled appearance. Eyes orange; bill and legs black. Sexes alike. Subadult has dusky spots below, and brownish flight-feathers.

A common and conspicuous bird, usually seen in parties of about six, clambering about in the lower branches of bushes and maintaining a harsh, unpleasing, continuous chattering. They have the typical 'follow-my-leader' way of moving about, following one another in quick succession from bush to bush with a low, straight, fluttering flight, followed by a glide into cover.
Voice: A chattering, squabbling sound uttered by all the members of a party, working up to a climax and then subsiding again as individual birds stop calling.
Habitat: Bush country, riverine reed-beds and forest undergrowth.
Distribution: The north-eastern half of Southern Africa.

PIED BABBLER *Turdoides bicolor* (536)   p. 240
   Afr Witkatlagter
Identification: 25 cm. *Wholly white, with black wings, wing-coverts and tail.* Eyes orange-red; bill and legs black. Sexes alike. Subadults have greater part of head, neck and back earth-brown; some brown specks on chest and flanks; lower belly buff-brown.

A noisy, sociable, extremely inquisitive species, found in parties of up to a dozen birds. Other habits similar to those of the genus.
Voice: Very similar to that of the Arrow-marked Babbler, but slightly more challenging (like that of the Red-billed Hoopoe).
Habitat: Dry bushveld.
Distribution: Central and north-western Southern Africa.

ROCK-JUMPER *Chaetops frenatus* (540) p. 241
Afr Gewone bergkatlagter

Identification: 23 cm. Adult male: top of head and back streaked with grey and black; rump and upper tail-coverts chestnut. Lores to ear-coverts and chin to throat black. *Moustache-stripe white.* Short wings black; tip of coverts white. Tail black, with tips of all but the central feathers white. Rest of underparts chestnut. Eyes orange-red; bill and legs black. Female generally duller, with ash-grey on chin and throat; underparts more rufous, with sparse black streaks.

Rock-loving birds, rarely using their short, rounded wings, preferring to jump from rock to rock or run across open spaces like a rodent, disappearing and then reappearing some way off. Feed like thrushes, digging spasmodically in the soil and flicking the loose material sideways with their bills. Shy but inquisitive; often peer from behind rocks. More often heard than seen.

Voice: A rapidly repeated '*pee-pee-pee-* . . .', becoming slower and lower, like an alarm-clock running down. Alarm-note a sharp, clicking call, sometimes followed by a '*churr*'.

Habitat: Boulder-strewn mountain slopes.

Distribution: The extreme south and south-west, and up into the central regions of Southern Africa.

Allied species:

BLACK-FACED BABBLER (*Turdoides melanops*) (534). 28 cm. General colour a dusky brown and dusky black. Feathers on top of head have silvery-white tips. *Lores black.* Chest-feathers have light edges, presenting a scaly appearance. Chin and throat a silvery ash-colour. Gregarious and noisy, like typical babblers. Not common, and wary, keeping to thick cover. Found in the extreme north-western part of Southern Africa.

WHITE-RUMPED BABBLER (*Turdoides leucopygius*) (535). 25 cm. Feathers of head, throat and breast have blackish centres and silvery-white edges and tips, giving the bird a markedly *scaly appearance*. Upper side dusky, or a blackish earth-brown; *lower rump white*. Upper belly and flanks earth-brown, but lower belly white. A very noisy babbler, found in thick bush and reed-beds in the central northern parts of Southern Africa.

BOULDER-CHAT (*Pinarornis plumosus*) (538). 25 cm. A sooty black all over, but with thin whitish bars on chin and throat, *a broad white band across centre of flight-feathers*, and *tail-feathers broadly tipped with white*. Found on rocky hills and boulder-strewn slopes, running nimbly over boulders and half-flying, half-gliding from rock to rock, very like the Rock-jumper. Found in the north-eastern parts of Southern Africa.

tarer species:

BARE-CHEEKED BABBLER (*Turdoides gymnogenys*) (537)

DAMARA ROCK-JUMPER (*Achaetops pycnopygius*) (539)

BLACKCAP BABBLER (*Lioptilus nigricapillus*) (542)

BULBULS: Pycnonotidae

Bulbuls are smallish birds, mainly fruit-eating but sometimes feeding on insects also. They sometimes do great damage to orchards. They have green, yellow, grey, brown and black plumage. Most species of bulbuls inhabit bush or forest country and are arboreal in habits, but some are also found in gardens and built-up areas. Most have loud, characteristic, whistling calls.

CAPE BULBUL   *Pycnonotus capensis* (543)   p. 241
   Afr Witoogtiptol

Identification: 20 cm. General colour a sooty brown, head, wings and tail included. Lores blackish. Underparts uniform in colour and very nearly as dark as the back. *No marked contrast between head and breast.* Under tail-coverts yellow. *Wattle round the eye white.* Eyes, bill and legs black. Sexes alike, but subadult is browner.

A locally abundant species, found in pairs or small parties. A lively, noisy bird, often seen perched at the top of a tree or on a low bush, from where it sometimes hawks flying insects. The head-feathers are raised to form a fairly conspicuous crest. A regular visitor to gardens and feeding-tables, becoming gregarious where there is abundant food.

Voice: A very lively, liquid whistle: '*piet-pop-le-wiet*' and '*piet-majol*'. Also has a soft, melodious, bubbling song.

Habitat: Coastal shrub or bushes along rivers. One of the few birds to be found in the dense thickets of exotic wattles along the coast.

Distribution: Very limited; found only in the southern coastal belt of southern Africa.

RED-EYED BULBUL   *Pycnonotus nigricans* (544)   p. 241
   Afr Rooioogtiptol

Identification: 20 cm. General colour above a sooty brown. Entire head and throat blackish; rest of underside a light brown; lower belly whitish. *Marked contrast between black of throat and light brown of chest.* Under tail-coverts yellow. Eyes a reddish brown; *wattle round eye red*; bill and legs black. Sexes alike. Subadult a paler brown above; black on head duller.

Similar in habits to the Cape Bulbul, but perhaps more gregarious. In the very dry regions never found far from water, but often visits wells in dry water-courses.

Voice: Very similar to that of the preceding species.

Habitat: Bush country and riverine forest in the drier western regions.

Distribution: In the western half of Southern Africa, but not the southern coastal belt.

BLACK-EYED BULBUL *Pycnonotus barbatus* (545)   p. 24

Afr Swartoogtiptol   *X* i-Kwebula
Z i-Potwe   *S* le-Koete

Identification: 20 cm. Above, general colour mouse-brown. Top of head face and chin blackish. Throat to breast mouse-brown. Rest of underpart light brown to whitish. *Marked contrast between black on head, and rest of body.* Under tail-coverts lemon. *Wattle round eye black.* Eyes a dark brown; bill and legs black. Sexes alike. Subadults are generally duller including black on head.

An extremely common bird, generally seen in pairs. Habits similar to those of the two preceding species. Cheerful and friendly; often found near human habitations. Makes a great fuss when snakes or small carnivores are spotted, gathering in large numbers and keeping up a ceaseless scolding and chattering.

Voice: The typical bulbul call, which may be rendered as '*cóme báck to Pretoriá*'. Also a bisyllabic '*chit-chit*' or '*gwit-gwit*', repeated over and over again.

Habitat: Wherever there are trees (exotics included) and fairly thick bush

Distribution: Over the eastern half and central northern regions of Southern Africa.

TERRESTRIAL BULBUL *Phyllastrephus terrestris* (546)   p. 24

Afr Bruintiptol   *X* u-Gwegwegwe

Identification: 20 cm. Above, a warm olivaceous brown, wings and tail included. Below, chin and throat white; breast and belly whitish; chest flanks and under tail-coverts a very pale olivaceous brown. Eyes reddish bill brownish; legs grey. Sexes alike. Subadult similar to adults, but wing coverts are narrowly edged with russet, and eyes are greyish.

This dull-coloured species is fairly common, and spends most of its time on the ground, searching for its food amongst the decaying vegetation Usually found in small parties and maintain a low, grating chatter as they scratch noisily about among the dry leaves. Very difficult to see, but can be attracted if an alarm-call is given. When disturbed, the group sounds the alarm and moves deeper into the dense undergrowth.

Voice: A harsh, scolding '*gwe-gwe-gwe*' and a short, warbling song.

Habitat: Forest and thick bush.
Distribution: The southern and eastern coastal belt and north-eastern parts of Southern Africa.

SOMBRE BULBUL *Andropadus importunus* (551)   p. 241
   Afr. Willietiptol   *X* i-Nkwili
   Z   i-Wili

Identification: 20 cm. Above, olive-green, wings and tail included. Below, variable, from a pale olive-green to a pale yellowish green (usually centre of belly is even paler). Under wing-coverts lemon-yellow. *Eyes almost white*; bill and legs grey. Sexes alike. Subadult duller in colour, with yellow ring round eye, and bill horn-coloured.

A very common bird, but solitary and skulking. Though very often heard on all sides, and even at close quarters, it is difficult to spot, as it remains concealed in the thick foliage and is cryptically coloured. Spends most of its time searching for food in the dense foliage of trees and creepers. Flight rapid and direct, with very fast wing-beats.

Voice: A clear, loud whistle *'villi'*, followed by a series of soft notes *'chuke-achuke-achuke'* and ending in a protracted *'pheeoooo'*. (At a distance only the *'villi'* is heard.) Also has a short, cheerful song. Alarm-call a series of *'villi's'*, repeated in quick succession.

Habitat: Found in dense vegetation, in forest and coastal bush.
Distribution: In the southern and eastern coastal regions of Southern Africa, but also coming fairly far inland along riverine forests.

Allied species:

YELLOW-STREAKED BULBUL (*Phyllastrephus flavostriatus*) (547). 20 cm. Top of head a dark olivaceous grey; stripe over eye, sides of face and ear-coverts a light grey. Rest of upper parts olive-green. *Below, chin and throat whitish; remainder a greyish white with clear yellow streaks.* Usually found in small parties, climbing about on the branches of trees or even hanging upside-down in search of insects. Has the curious habit of flicking open first one wing and then the other. Found in evergreen forest along the eastern coastal belt of Southern Africa.

YELLOW-BREASTED BULBUL (*Andropadus flaviventris*) (550). 23 cm. Above, including sides of face, wings and tail, a brownish olive-green; *below*, including under wing-coverts, *sulphur-yellow*, with sides of chest olivaceous. A shy, skulking species, usually found in pairs or small parties in dense coastal bush or the tangled vegetation along rivers. Found in the north-eastern parts of Southern Africa.

Rarer species:

SLENDER BULBUL (*Phyllastrephus debilis*) (548)
STRIPE-CHEEKED BULBUL (*Andropadus milanjensis*) (549)

THRUSHES, CHATS and ROBINS: Turdidae

Thrushes are medium-sized arboreal birds that find their food, consisting chiefly of insects and small molluscs, mainly on the ground. Fruit and berries are also eaten. They have longish, slender bills and sturdy legs. They are frequently found in built-up and cultivated areas. Chats form a mixed group of smallish birds, most of whom have shortish tails and relatively long legs. They are found in rocky or open country, and have the habit of flying from one vantage-point to another. In most species of chats the male is the more brightly coloured. Robins are woodland and forest birds, many of whom live in dense vegetation and are more often heard than seen. The majority have beautiful songs and are excellent mimics.

OLIVE THRUSH   *Turdus olivaceus* (553)   p. 256
    Afr Gewone lyster   *X* um-Swi
    S   u-Muswi

Identification: 24 cm. Above, including sides of face, tail and wings, a dark olivaceous slate. Chin and throat whitish, streaked with dark brown. Chest and breast a dusky olive, shading to orange-rufous on the belly and flanks. Under tail-coverts whitish, with dusky markings. Eyes brown; *stout bill a yellowish orange*; legs yellow-brown. Sexes alike. Subadult has underside spotted with dusky black; upper side has light streaks.

A common, geographically variable species. Originally a shy bird, it has lately become a familiar inhabitant of urban gardens, and tends to dominate most of the other species found there. Often seen scratching among leaves and debris, and digging for earthworms on lawns. Has the peculiar habit of running forward for a short distance, stopping abruptly, cocking its head to one side as if listening intently, and then darting forward and digging vigorously in the soil. It usually succeeds in pulling out a worm. Its flight is fast and direct. When courting, the male puffs himself up, spreads his tail, half opens his wings, and shuffles about on the ground round the female with trailing wings.

Voice: A thin, soft, monosyllabic '*tsit*', usually given when flying off. Alarm-note a lower-pitched '*tschuk-tschuk*'. Has a clear, simple song that varies according to the locality.

Habitat: Evergreen and riverine forest and cultivated land.

Distribution: The southern and eastern half of Southern Africa, but not the north-eastern coastal regions.

GROUNDSCRAPER THRUSH *Turdus litsitsirupa* (557)   p. 256
Afr Gevlekte lyster

Identification: 22 cm. Above, including wings and tail, an ashy brown. *Inner webs of primaries and under wing-coverts mainly orange-buff (seen as conspicuous light-brown window in flight).* Sides of face white, with well-defined black bars on ear-coverts. Below, a creamy white, with black streaks on side of throat and neck, and black, drop-shaped spots on remainder of underparts. Eyes red-brown; bill brown; legs a yellowish brown. Sexes alike. Subadult a lighter brown above, with buff streaks and spots.

A fairly common resident species, found singly or in pairs. Usually seen on the ground, scratching for food among fallen leaves. Short tail gives it a squat appearance. Has a very upright stance and a strong undulating flight. Has the habit of flicking one wing at a time while perching.

Voice: A clear, loud, rather monotonous song, usually uttered from the top of a tall tree. The name '*litsitsirupa*' is onomatopoeic. Alarm-note a series of four or five sharp '*clicks*'.

Habitat: The drier acacia veld where there are fairly large trees. Also found in built-up areas.

Distribution: The northern half of Southern Africa.

Allied species:

KURRICHANE THRUSH (*Turdus libonyanus*) (552). 22 cm. Whole of upper side, including wings and tail, a brownish slate-grey. Chin and throat white, with conspicuous *black moustache-stripes.* Chest a greyish buff; breast and flanks a light tawny; belly and under tail-coverts whitish. Eyes brown; *bill orange-red*; legs yellowish.

A resident species of the acacia savannas, usually found near streams and rivers. Not often found in built-up areas. A shy bird, usually feeding on the ground near tall trees. Found in the north-eastern half of Southern Africa.

NATAL THRUSH (*Turdus fischeri*) (558). 20 cm. Above, including wings and tail, an olivaceous brown. All the tail-feathers except the central ones have white ends. *Upper wing-coverts tipped with white.* Broad black bars on ear-coverts. Thin moustache-stripes black. Whole underside white, with large black spots on chest, breast and flanks. Eyes brown; bill black, but with base of lower mandible yellow; legs a pale brown. A very local species, found singly or in pairs; usually along streams in the coastal forest. Scratches amongst decaying vegetation for its food. Found only in the south-eastern coastal region of Southern Africa.

Rarer species:
GURNEY'S THRUSH (*Turdus gurneyi*) (556)

PLATE 25

ROLLERS AND HORNBILLS

1 **EUROPEAN ROLLER** *page* 17
Square tail; greenish underparts.

2 **LILAC-BREASTED ROLLER** 17
Dark lilac on upper breast, thin straight outer tail feathers.

3 **GREY HORNBILL** 18
Male has dark bill with casque and yellow side-stripe.

4 **PURPLE ROLLER** 18
Large; square-tailed with streaked throat and breast, marked eye-stripe.

5 **YELLOW-BILLED HORNBILL** 18
High yellow bill with small casque.

6 **RED-BILLED HORNBILL** 18
Sharp red bill with no casque.

7 **CROWNED HORNBILL** 18
General colour blackish, dark red bill with casque, outer tail feathers
tipped with white.

2α

2

4

3

5

6

7

PLATE 26

BARBETS, HONEY-GUIDES, WRYNECK AND WOODPECKERS

1 **BLACK-COLLARED BARBET** *page* 185
Face and throat red.

2 **CRESTED BARBET** 187
Black crest and spotted chest-band.

3 **PIED BARBET** 186
Red forehead and spotted back.

4 **YELLOW-FRONTED TINKER** 186
Small with yellow forehead.

5 **SHARP-BILLED HONEY-GUIDE** 189
Drab grey with sharp slender bill.

6 **GREATER HONEY-GUIDE** 188
Adult male has yellow ear coverts.
a Sub-adult: Duller and browner.

7 **RED-BREASTED WRYNECK** 195
Throat light rufous brown, breast streaked.

8 **CARDINAL WOODPECKER** 191
Small. Black moustache-stripes. Crown of adult female black.

9 **BEARDED WOODPECKER** 191
Large, with heavy black moustache-stripes.

10 **GROUND WOODPECKER** 190
Largest woodpecker with rose-pink underparts.

CAPE ROCK-THRUSH *Monticola rupestris* (559) p. 256
Afr Gewone klipwagter *Z* i-Kwelamatsheni
Identification: 22 cm. Adult male: *head, neck, chin and throat slate-grey;*
lores blackish; mantle and scapulars a dark brown; flight-feathers blackish;
rest of plumage (above and below) a deep tawny, except for the central
tail-feathers, which are black. Eyes brown; bill and legs black. Adult
female: head and neck a finely mottled brown; top of head has blackish
streaks; buffish streak down centre of chin and throat. Subadult is barred
and spotted with brown and black, above and below.

A common and not very shy resident species, usually found in pairs or
small scattered parties. Mostly seen sitting on the tops of boulders, aloes
or bushes. Has the habit of flicking its wings when alighting.
Voice: A wild, melodious whistle, usually uttered from the top of a rock:
'*chirreewoo, chirri-weeroo*'. Alarm-note a sharp '*charrr*'.
Habitat: Mountainous country. Occurs even along the sea-shore and has
sometimes adapted itself to human habitations.
Distribution: The southern third of Southern Africa.

Allied species:
SENTINEL ROCK-THRUSH (*Monticola explorator*) (560). 18 cm. Very similar to Cape Rock-Thrush, but slightly smaller. *Chin, throat and chest a uniform slate-grey;* top of head to rump a brownish slate-grey. Female is earth-
brown and has a mottled appearance. A rather uncommon, lively bird
which has *not* adapted itself to human habitations. Usually found in pairs,
often in the company of the Cape Rock-Thrush. Has a very upright stance.
Prefers open hillsides in the southern and eastern coastal regions of Southern Africa.

SHORT-TOED ROCK-THRUSH (*Monticola brevipes*) (561). 18 cm. Similar
to Sentinel Rock-Thrush, except that it has *only the chin and throat a dark
slate-grey.* In some specimens the top of the head is whitish. Back a dark
grey, finely streaked with blackish. Female appears much whiter below.
Not uncommon; usually found in pairs on isolated stony koppies covered
with trees. A very tame bird that often perches in trees. Found in the
western, central and northern coastal regions, and also in central Southern
Africa.

Rarer species:
ANGOLA ROCK-THRUSH (*Monticola angolensis*) (562)

TRANSVAAL ROCK-THRUSH (*Monticola pretoriae*)

MOUNTAIN CHAT *Oenanthe monticola* (564) p. 256
Afr Gewone bergwagter *S.* Khaloti
Identification: 18 cm. Adult male: variable, but the same pattern is ap-
parent in each: *shoulder-patch, rump and outer tail-feathers white;* remainder

wholly black, black and grey or wholly grey, except for the flight-feathers, which are blackish. Belly whitish in all phases. Eyes, bill and legs brown. Adult female either sooty black or sooty brown; upper and under tail-coverts white, and all the tail-feathers except the central ones mainly white, tipped with blackish. Subadult similar to adult female, but young male shows a certain amount of white on shoulders.

A common resident species, usually found in pairs or small parties. Has adapted itself to human habitations. Has the chat habit of flicking its wings and jerking its tail when alighting. A bold bird, usually perching on prominent rocks. Has a short, curious, soaring flight, ending in a sudden vertical drop and a rapid flight just above the ground.

Voice: A beautiful, clear, ringing song, uttered while perched or on the wing, during a peculiar hovering flight. Has a chattering alarm-note and a short, cheerful whistle.

Habitat: Dry rocky or stony places, not necessarily mountainous. Also found in built-up areas.

Distribution: The southern half, and the north-western parts of Southern Africa.

CAPPED WHEATEAR   *Oenanthe pileata* (568)   p. 256
Afr Gewone skaapwagter   *X* isi-Xaxabesha
  S Thoromeli

Identification: 18 cm. Above, russet; *eye-stripe and forehead white.* Crown black or blackish, merging into russet on nape. Upper tail-coverts white. Basal half of all except central tail-feathers white. Lores to ear-coverts and side of neck black. Below, including under wing-coverts, whitish. Flanks and belly buffish. *Broad black band across chest.* Eyes brown; bill and legs black. Sexes alike. Subadult mottled below with tawny and above with buff; no chest-band.

A common resident species, widely distributed but rarely seen in large numbers. Lively and noisy during the breeding season, and hops about with much flicking of wings and jerking of tail. Otherwise rather silent and subdued. Usually perches on stones, fences or low bushes, and has a very upright stance.

Voice: A variety of pretty notes, heard even at dusk. An excellent mimic, imitating not only other birds but also animals.

Habitat: Open savanna country, preferably where the grass is short and the vegetation low.

Distribution: Throughout Southern Africa, but not along the eastern coastal belt.

BUFF-STREAKED CHAT *Oenanthe bifasciata* (569) p. 256
Afr Vaalbruinbergwagter *S* le-Tsoanafika
Identification: 18 cm. Adult male: top of head black: *forehead and broad stripe over the eye and down the side of the neck a light buff.* Mantle a dark brown, streaked with black; scapulars white; rump and upper tail-coverts a light buff; wings and *entire tail black.* Below, chin to upper breast black; remaining underparts a warm buff. (In worn plumage the light buff on the back becomes almost white.) Eyes brown; bill and legs black. Female has scapulars and wing-coverts brown; chin to upper chest buff-brown. Subadult is mottled and streaked with buffish brown and blackish, above and below.

A local migrant, usually seen in pairs. A lively bird, hopping about on the rocks, excitedly flicking its wings and chirping when disturbed. Not shy, but very difficult to approach when alarmed. When the bird is perching, the *large buff-white V on its back is conspicuous from behind.*
Voice: A loud, pleasant song. Often imitates other birds.
Habitat: Stony or rocky outcrops.
Distribution: The central south-eastern parts of Southern Africa.

FAMILIAR CHAT *Cercomela familiaris* (570) p. 256
Afr Gewone spekvreter *S* le-Terenyane
Identification: 15 cm. Above, a dark brown; below, a uniform pale brown, slightly lighter on the belly. Ear-coverts rust-coloured; wings dusky. *Upper tail-coverts a deep russet-brown. Central tail-feathers blackish;* remainder russet, with blackish tips. Eyes brown; bill and legs black. Sexes alike. Subadult generally darker, and indistinctly speckled with buff above, and with blackish and buff from chin to breast.

Probably the commonest of the chats. An active but rather silent bird, becoming very tame around a homestead if not molested. Often flicks its wings and tail. (The wings are flicked sideways and forwards.) Pursues and catches insects on the wing.
Voice: A soft, rather low-pitched '*tjree-tjree-tjree*', repeated several times. Alarm-call a squeaky '*whee-chuck-chuck*'. Also has a short, pleasant song.
Habitat: From rocky mountain-slopes and bush country to cultivated lowlands. Has adapted itself to human habitations.
Distribution: Throughout Southern Africa, but not in the north-eastern tip.

MOCKING CHAT *Thamnolaea cinnamomeiventris* (573) p. 256
Afr Dassiebergwagter (Dassievoël)
Identification: 22 cm. Adult male: whole head, chest, mantle, wings and tail a glossy black; *shoulder white.* Rump, lower breast, belly and under tail-coverts a rich chestnut. Some individuals have a white line on the breast,

dividing black and chestnut. Eyes brown; bill and legs black. In the female, the black of the male is replaced by grey, except in the tail. *No white patch on shoulder*. Subadult duller and more fluffy-looking. Young male has only a little white on the shoulder.

A common local resident species, tending to wander after breeding. Usually seen in pairs or family parties. If unmolested, becomes very tame around dwellings, and even breeds under the eaves. Its flight is low, with many spells of gliding. When alighting after a glide it slowly raises and lowers its tail several times. Often jumps from a high to a low perch with closed wings, but opens its wings at the last moment.

Voice: A loud, attractive, whistling song. Expertly mimics the calls of other birds. Alarm-note a harsh '*kret-kret*'.

Habitat: Usually found near cliffs or on boulder-strewn hillsides, but also in the vicinity of buildings.

Distribution: Over the eastern half of Southern Africa, but not in the north-eastern coastal regions.

ANT-EATING CHAT   *Myrmecocichla formicivora* (575)   p. 256
   Afr Swartpiek   *X* isa-Nzwili
   Z in-Dundumela   *S* Thume

Identification: 18 cm. Adult male: above, a smoky brown; tail slightly darker. *Shoulder and inner webs of basal half of flight-feathers white*. Below, russet-brown, with centres of feathers dusky and belly blackish. Eyes brown; bill and legs black. Female usually lacks white shoulder-patch. Subadult a more reddish brown.

A common resident species, usually found in pairs. Likes perching on ant-hills, on the tops of bushes or on fence-posts. Has a peculiar fluttering flight, with very fast wing-beats giving the effect of a blurred white window. Is often seen hovering and then dropping straight down. Has a very upright stance.

Voice: A shrill '*peek*', The male has a simple, pleasant song consisting of loud, clear, whistled notes.

Habitat: Prefers dry, open country where there are termite mounds.

Distribution: The southern and central parts of Southern Africa.

STONE CHAT   *Saxicola torquata* (576)   p. 256
   Afr Gewone bontrokwagter   *X* i-Ncape
   Z is-Ncapela   S Hlatsinyane

Identification: 14 cm. Adult male: entire head, chin, throat, back of neck, mantle, scapulars, wings and tail black. *White patch on folded wings. Sides of neck, rump and upper tail-coverts also white*. Below, chest, breast and flanks chestnut; belly and under tail-coverts a dirty white. Eyes, bill and legs black. Female tawny; top of head, mantle and scapulars streaked with blackish. Also has white patch on wing, and rump and upper tail-coverts white. Below, tawny, shading to dirty white on belly. Subadults have breast and upper parts speckled.

A common resident species, migrating locally in some areas. Usually found in pairs and relatively tame. Perches on the tip of a dry bush or weed, and hops down to take insects off the ground. Also catches insects on the wing.

Voice: A brief, cheerful song, and a scolding, persistent '*wheet-chak-chak*', usually uttered while the bird flicks its wings and tail.

Habitat: Treeless country with grass and low scrub. Often found in vleis.

Distribution: The southern and eastern half of Southern Africa.

Allied species:

KARROO CHAT (*Cercomela schlegelii*) (566). 15 cm. Above, a yellowish grey. Wings dusky; *tail blackish*, except for the outer webs of the outermost feathers, which are white. Upper tail-coverts white. Below, a uniform colour, but lighter than above. A common resident chat of the drier regions, often seen sitting on telegraph wires. Usually calls while perching on the tops of bushes. *Has a very fast and wavering flight in which it shows only a little white on the back.* Found in the southern central regions of Southern Africa and along the western coastal belt.

LAYARD'S CHAT (*Cercomela tractrac*) (571). 14 cm. Above, ash-grey; whitish ring round eye. Flight-feathers dusky. *Rump and upper tail-coverts white*. Tail white, with broad blackish terminal band. Below, white with an ashy wash on chest and breast. A tame bird that perches freely on small rocks and bushes, with a nervous fluttering of its wings and flicking of its tail. Spends most of its time on the ground, and can run very fast. *In flight, shows much white on the back*. Distribution the same as that of the Karroo Chat.

SICKLE-WINGED CHAT (*Cercomela sinuata*) (572). 15 cm. Very similar to the Familiar Chat, except that *all the tail-feathers are russet, with the apical half blackish*, and the chest and breast are more earth-brown, becoming lighter on the belly. In flight, shows much russet on the back, *with no dark line down the centre of the tail* but with a broad blackish terminal band. Frequents open stony ground where the vegetation is sparse and stunted. Behaviour similar to that of the Stone Chat: flies from one low perch to another, dropping down and picking up insects from the ground. Found in the central southern regions of Southern Africa, but not in the southernmost tip.

ARNOTT'S CHAT (*Thamnolaea arnotti*) (574). 18 cm. *Wholly black*, with a slight gloss, except for the white on the top of the head, and the *large white patch on the wing*. Differs from the black-and-white phase of the

Mountain Chat in having *no white on rump or tail*. Occurs in small parties in the park-like Mopane and *Brachystegia* regions of central-eastern and northern Southern Africa.

Rarer Species:

EUROPEAN WHEATEAR *(Oenante oenanthe)* (563)

WHINCHAT *(Saxicola rubetra)* (577)

HERERO CHAT *(Namibornis herero)* (660)

CHORISTER ROBIN   *Cossypha dichora* (578)   p. 257
 Afr Swartkopjanfrederik   *X* u-Gaga-sisi
 Z i-Binda   *S* Tsakha
Identification: 20 cm. *Top of head*, mantle, scapulars and wing-coverts *a dark slate. Lores to ear-coverts black*. Flight-feathers dusky. Lower rump and upper tail-coverts an olivaceous tawny. Central tail-feathers blackish; remainder mainly tawny. *Whole of underside a rufous brown*. Eyes brown; bill black; legs a yellowish brown. Sexes alike. Subadult spotted above and on the breast.

A not uncommon resident species. Though very noisy, it is rather shy; and is therefore more often heard than seen. More arboreal than most other robins, but also feeds on the ground at certain times of the year.
Voice: An excellent mimic, interspersing its imitations of other birds with its own bubbling phrases, uttered from the tops of forest trees. Alarm-note harsh and ratchet-like.
Habitat: Forest and thick bush.
Distribution: The southern and central eastern coastal regions. Also found inland at the northern end of its range.

HEUGLIN'S ROBIN   *Cossypha heuglini* (580)   p. 257
 Afr Heuglinjanfrederik
Identification: 20 cm. Adult male: top of head to nape, and sides of face black. *A well-defined white line runs from the bill over the eye to the nape*. Mantle an olivaceous brown; wings slate. Rump and upper tail-coverts a tawny brown. Central tail-feathers an olivaceous brown; rest of tail and *entire underside a tawny brown*. Eyes a light brown; bill black; legs brownish. Sexes alike, but female is browner on the mantle. Subadult is mottled above and below and has large tawny spots on the upper wing-coverts.

A common bird, inhabiting thick undergrowth and feeding mainly on the ground. Except perhaps when singing, is seldom found in the higher parts of trees. Pairs are usually found in a very limited locality. Though very retiring, is sometimes found near homesteads.
Voice: A remarkable trisyllabic call, consisting of bubbling, flute-like

notes that increase in tempo and volume. The call is ventriloquial. Male and female sometimes sing a duet, in which the female part is more high-pitched and shrill. Expertly mimics the calls of other birds.

Habitat: Low, dense bush in forests or along streams and rivers.

Distribution: The north-eastern and northernmost parts of Southern Africa.

CAPE ROBIN   *Cossypha caffra* (581)   p. 257

Afr Gewone janfrederik   *X* u-Gaga

Z   u-Gaka   *S* Mokhofe

Identification: 18 cm. Top of head an olivaceous grey. *White streak from bill to over the eye.* Lores to ear-coverts black. Mantle and scapulars an olivaceous brown; wing-coverts slate-coloured; flight-feathers dusky and upper tail-coverts tawny. Central tail-feathers blackish; rest of tail a tawny chestnut. Below, *only the chin and chest are tawny. Breast and flanks grey;* belly whitish; under tail-coverts buff. Eyes brown; bill and legs black. Sexes alike. Subadult mottled above and below with buff and black.

A common resident species, found in pairs where there is sufficient shelter. Has become accustomed to man and is even found in gardens in the centre of cities. Feeds on the ground, hopping about with much nervous jerking of its tail. Never far from sheltering vegetation, and flits out of sight at the slightest sign of danger.

Voice: Has a short, pretty song, with slight variations on the theme '*jan-free-derik*'. Alarm-note a scolding '*wadeda*'.

Habitat: Forest, bush or cultivated areas.

Distribution: The southern and eastern half of Southern Africa, but not the north-eastern coastal regions.

KALAHARI SCRUB ROBIN   *Erythropygia paena* (586)   p. 257

Afr Kalahariwipstert

Identification: 16 cm. Top of head a greyish brown; mantle, scapulars and rump a dull russet; flight-feathers blackish, edged with buff. Basal half of tail-feathers tawny; *apical half blackish, tipped with white.* White stripe over the eye and blackish stripe through the eye. Sides of face and *under-parts a uniform buff or buffish white.* Eyes brown; bill and legs black. Sexes alike. Subadult mottled above and below.

A common resident species that spends most of its time on the ground or creeping about on the lower branches of bushes. A very excitable bird, dancing about and flicking open its tail before flying off into cover. *The broad dark terminal tail-band with the white margin that is shown in flight is characteristic of this species.* A noisy bird that sits on the tops of bushes when it sings, particularly in the early mornings and evenings.

Voice: A low-pitched scolding note and a simple, lively song, repeated without much variation.

Habitat: Prefers relatively open scrub or scattered trees.

Distribution: The central and north-western parts of Southern Africa.

WHITE-BROWED SCRUB ROBIN *Erythropygia leucophrys*
(588)   p. 257

Afr Gestreepte wipstert   *Z* 'Mtcheliswali

Identification: 15 cm. Top of head, mantle and scapulars a rufous brown, faintly streaked with blackish. Rump and upper tail-coverts more russet. *Distinct white stripe over the eye*; ear-coverts brownish. Flight-feathers and wing-coverts dusky. *The white tips of the wing-coverts form distinct white lines on the folded wing.* Tail russet, with a narrow blackish sub-terminal band; white tips form a narrow end-bar. Below, a buffish white, with *heavy blackish streaks on chin, throat and breast.* Eyes brown; bill a dark brown; legs stone-coloured. Sexes alike. Subadult mottled above and below. Bars on wing buffish, not white.

A common resident, usually found singly or in pairs. Though a shy and skulking bird that keeps to thick bush, it can easily be attracted if the alarm-call of any bird is imitated. When flushed, darts for the nearest cover, keeping close to the ground. Feeds mainly on the ground and also has the habit of flicking and fanning its tail when excited. When display-ing to the female, runs along a branch with head held down, tail cocked up and wings drooping.

Voice: Scolding alarm-notes and a loud, penetrating song. Repeats its simple tune again and again as it sits on the top of a tree.

Habitat: Prefers scattered scrub and secondary growth to dense bush or forest.

Distribution: The northern and north-eastern half of Southern Africa, and along the south-eastern coastal belt.

Allied species:

NATAL ROBIN (*Cossypha natalensis*) (579). 19 cm. Above, head and rump cinnamon-brown; mantle a mixture of slate and cinnamon-brown; tail-coverts and tail cinnamon-rufous (except for the central feathers, which are blackish). Wings slate-blue. *Sides of face and underparts a uniform, bright cinnamon-rufous.* An elusive bird, frequenting the dense undergrowth in forests, and more often heard than seen. Becomes active at dusk, and may then be seen hopping about in open glades or on forest paths. An excellent mimic. Found in the eastern coastal belt of Southern Africa.

WHITE-THROATED ROBIN (*Cossypha humeralis*) (582). 16 cm. p. 257. Above, head and mantle a dark slate-grey. Distinct white line over eye. Sides of face, neck and chest black. Wings blackish; lesser wing-coverts white, forming a conspicuous white line from the shoulder. Upper tail-coverts and tail chestnut, but central feathers and ends of all others a blackish brown. Below, *chin to breast a silvery white*; remainder washed with chestnut. A common resident of matted thorn and riverside scrub. Spends most of its time hopping nimbly about on the ground. Although a retiring bird, it is sometimes seen near human habitations. Found singly or in pairs in the eastern half of Southern Africa, but not in the north-eastern coastal regions.

KARROO SCRUB ROBIN (*Erythropygia coryphaeus*) (583). 16 cm. Above, a sooty brown except for the tail, which is black. All except the central tail-feathers have narrow white tips. *White stripe over the eye;* centre of chin and throat white, with *thin blackish moustache-stripes.* Below, a uniform brown. An exceedingly common species of the dry sandy regions. A lively bird, spending most of its time on the ground. When disturbed, dances about with much flicking of its tail before darting into cover. Very noisy when snakes or small carnivores are near. Found in the south-western third of Southern Africa.

BROWN SCRUB ROBIN (*Erythropygia signata*) (584). 18 cm. Above, an olivaceous brown, with a certain amount of white on alulae and primaries. *Eye-stripe and spot below the eye white.* Chin, throat and belly white; moustache-stripe greyish; chest, breast and flanks grey and white. Usually found singly in the undergrowth at the foot of large trees. Feeds only on the ground, scratching about amongst the fallen leaves and other debris. A very active bird that moves about with quick, short hops. Found mainly in the south-eastern coastal belt of Southern Africa.

BEARDED SCRUB ROBIN (*Erythropygia quadrivirgata*) (585). 18 cm. Above, mainly russet-brown, with *distinct black and white stripes over the eye.* Upper tail-coverts rufous. Wings and tail dusky. All the tail-feathers except the central pair have large white tips. A certain amount of white on alulae and primaries. *Chin, throat and chest white, with long, well-defined dark grey moustache-stripes.* Breast and flanks a tawny buff; belly whitish. A shy bird that haunts the more or less dense dry forests. Usually seen on the ground, hopping about with upcocked tail, and scuffling like a thrush in the fallen leaves. Found in the north-eastern parts of Southern Africa.

STARRED ROBIN (*Pogonocichla stellata*) (589). 16 cm. Whole head, chin and throat a dark slate-grey, with *inconspicuous white spots in front of eye and centre of throat.* Mantle, scapulars and rump greenish; wings dusky; shoulders blue-grey. Central tail-feathers blackish; others orange-yellow with blackish tips; *rest of underparts a bright golden-yellow.* A quiet bird, solitary but not shy, usually seen searching for food amongst the dead leaves on the ground or in the lower branches of forest trees. Also hawks insects in the air. Found in the south-eastern and eastern parts of Southern Africa, along the coast and inland.

Rarer species:

SWYNNERTON'S ROBIN (*Pogonocichla swynnertoni*) (590)

GUNNING'S ROBIN (*Sheppardia gunningi*) (591)

THRUSH NIGHTINGALE (*Luscinia luscinia*) (592)

PALM THRUSH (*Cichladusa arquata*) (593)

RUFOUS-TAILED THRUSH (*Cichladusa ruficauda*)

WARBLERS: Sylviidae

The warblers are a very large family of small, slim, active birds, generally of a plainish plumage. As a rule *the sexes are alike and the subadults, having unspotted plumage, resemble their parents.* (This will not be repeated in the text.) Warblers are not terrestrial, and occur in all types of country. All are mainly insectivorous, although the larger species of the family will also eat fruit.

Many species lack distinctive markings and are exceedingly difficult to identify in the field. They appear confusingly similar, but can be identified by their behaviour, calls and habitat. Some of the species are palaeoarctic migrants, found in Southern Africa only during the summer months.

GARDEN WARBLER   *Sylvia borin* (595)   p. 272
   Afr Tuinsanger

Identification: 14 cm. Above, including wings and tail, an olivaceous brown. Lightish stripe over the eye. Below, an olivaceous cream; centre of belly whitish. Eyes brown; bill horn-brown (lighter at base of lower mandible); legs a pale brown.

A common palaeoarctic migrant, usually found singly, in twos or threes. An active, *plump-looking*, rather skulking bird that might easily be over-looked but for its cheerful, subdued, protracted song. Sometimes feeds on fruit and berries.

Voice: A soft, mellow, warbling sub-song, continuously uttered.

Habitat: Woodland, bush, and gardens in built-up areas.

Distribution: The north-eastern half and south-eastern coastal belt of Southern Africa.

WILLOW WARBLER *Phylloscopus trochilus* (599) p. 272
    Afr Hofsanger

Identification: 11 cm. Above, a pale olivaceous green. *Distinct pale yellow eye-stripe. Below, sulphur-yellow*; belly paler and whitish. Eyes and bill brown (base of lower mandible lighter); legs brown.

This small, slender tree-warbler is a common palaeoarctic migrant. Usually heard before it is seen. Appears to spend most of its time scrambling about in the middle or upper foliage of trees in search of insects.

Voice: Usual note a plaintive bisyllabic '*soo-ee*' or '*hoo-eet*'. Also has a pleasing liquid warble, quiet at first and then becoming clearer and more deliberate, until it ends in a flourish.

Habitat: Any type of country in which trees grow. Also found in gardens, plantations of exotic trees and swampy regions.

Distribution: Over the greater part of Southern Africa, but not in the south-western regions.

YELLOW-BELLIED WARBLER *Eremomela icteropygialis*
    (600) p. 272
    Afr Geelpenstinktinkie

Identification: 9 cm. Above, an ashy grey, including wings and tail. *Faint white ring round the eye.* Below, chin to upper belly white; flanks greyish; *lower belly and under tail-coverts a pale yellow.* Eyes brown; bill blackish; legs black.

A not uncommon resident species, usually found in pairs or family parties, actively searching for insects in the lower parts of trees or bushes. This small, lightly-built bird is often found in the company of Penduline Tits.

Voice: A distinctive four-syllabled jingle and a plaintive '*see-see*'. Also a scolding '*chee-chiri-chee-chiri-chit*'.

Habitat: Open bush and low trees, even in very arid regions.

Distribution: Throughout Southern Africa, but not in the southernmost or eastern coastal regions.

AFRICAN MARSH-WARBLER *Acrocephalus baeticatus* (606) p. 272
    Afr Kleinrietsanger

Identification: 11 cm. Above, a russet brown; flight-feathers and tail more dusky. *An indistinct light brown stripe over the eye.* Below, a creamy buff, with chin and throat more whitish. Eyes a pale brown; bill brown and *legs a light greenish yellow.*

A common local migrant, occurring as a summer-breeding visitor. Usually fairly tame. Its sustained song reveals its presence. Not easily seen, as it tends to keep to thick cover.

Voice: A harsh, scolding note, frequently uttered. Also a pleasant warbling song, frequently interspersed with '*kirrrr*' and '*karra*'.
Habitat: Prefers low vegetation near water but is also found quite far from water, and even in gardens.
Distribution: Throughout Southern Africa.

LARGER BARRED WARBLER   *Camaroptera fasciolata* (614)   p. 272

Afr Groot gestreepte tinktinkie

Identification: 14 cm. Above, including wings and tail, russet-brown with an olivaceous wash. Wing-coverts, innermost secondaries and tail-feathers tipped with off-white. *Below, buffish, with neat blackish bars.* Lower belly and under tail-coverts a brighter buff. Eyes orange; bill a brownish black; legs flesh-coloured.

A common resident species that creeps restlessly about in the undergrowth, usually with its tail cocked up like that of a wren. When looking for insects it usually starts at the bottom of a bush, works its way to the top and then flies to the next bush, where it repeats the performance. Commonly found in pairs, but small parties keep in touch with one another by means of a high-pitched '*tsik*'. When displaying, male flies almost vertically upwards before swooping down.
Voice: Call a '*twee-deet*' or '*biririt-biririt*' that has great carrying power and is uttered at short intervals for long periods at a time.
Habitat: Open woodland. Prefers thorny trees and bushes.
Distribution: Over the northern half of Southern Africa, but not in the coastal regions.

GRASSBIRD   *Sphenoeacus afer* (618)   p. 272

Afr Grasvoël   *X* u-Dwenya

Identification: 22 cm. Above, *top of head chestnut, streaked with black.* Lores and eye-stripe white. Mantle and wing-coverts black, edged with buff; flight-feathers dusky. Rump and upper tail-coverts chestnut. *Long tail-feathers a brownish black, narrow and pointed.* Ear-coverts chestnut. Below, buff; chin and throat streaked with black; remainder finely streaked with brown. Eyes a reddish brown; bill black; legs lead-grey.

A common resident, but seen only when sitting on tall grass-stalks or weeds, preening itself or singing. More often remains hidden. When flushed, flies off with an awkward labouring flight, during which the *ragged tail and short, rounded wings* are conspicuous.
Voice: A short, loud, melodious song, with a fixed refrain. Call-note a protracted '*ppee-ee-ee*'. Alarm-note a high-pitched '*chee-chee-chee-* . . .'
Habitat: Coarse vegetation or scrub along streams and vleis, and sometimes on hillsides.
Distribution: The southern and eastern third of Southern Africa.

RUFOUS-BELLIED CROMBEC *Sylvietta rufescens* (621) p. 272

Afr Gewone stompstertjie *Z* Ndibilitshe

Identification: 10 cm. *Above, greyish (very short tail included).* Sides of face, ear-coverts and underside buff. Light buff stripe over the eye and a dusky streak through the eye. Eyes a pale brown, *longish curved bill* a dusky brown and legs a yellowish brown.

A common resident, usually occurring in pairs or small family parties. A very active bird, usually searching for insects among leaves and twigs, and often uttering its rattling, vibrant call. Moves from tree to tree with a rapid, darting flight. Often found as a member of a mixed bird-party.

Voice: A pretty, high-pitched '*peep-peep-peep*' and a simple song '*richitiddlit*', steadily repeated. Also '*krrip-koop-kripkrip-kreee*'.

Habitat: Open savanna, dry thornveld and scrub.

Distribution: Throughout Southern Africa.

BAR-THROATED APALIS *Apalis thoracica* (622) p. 257

Afr Bandkeelkleinjantjie *X* u-Gxakweni
S Setholemoru

Identification: 13 cm. Above, greyish to greenish, sides of face, wings and tail included. *Outermost tail-feathers mainly white*; others have white tips. Lores and *band across chest black*. Rest of underside varies from whitish to light yellowish (*colour above and below chest-band particularly variable*). Eyes a pale yellow; bill black; legs pinkish.

A common resident, usually found in pairs. Not at all shy: continues to creep about in the foliage of trees in search of insects, undeterred by the presence of an onlooker. Often only its loud, whistling call discloses its presence.

Voice: Call-note '*pil-pil*', or '*pilly-pilly*', usually answered by the mate with a similar but softer call. Also a loud, violent '*tic-tic-tic-tic*' by the one bird, sometimes answered with a '*chupe-chupe-chupe*' by the other.

Habitat: Partial to riverine forest and heavily-wooded kloofs.

Distribution: Found in the southern third and eastern half of Southern Africa, but not in the northern coastal regions.

YELLOW-BREASTED APALIS *Apalis flavida* (625) p. 257

Afr Geelborskleinjantjie

Identification: 11 cm. Above, forehead to nape, sides of face and ear-coverts greyish; rest of upper parts, including wings and tail, green. Tail-feathers tipped with yellow. Below, chin whitish; remainder yellow. *In summer males have an inverted brown 'V' on the breast.* Eyes a yellowish brown; bill a dark brown and legs a light brown.

A resident species, locally not uncommon. Usually found in pairs or family parties, creeping through the foliage of tall trees in search of insects.

Voice: A bisyllabic '*chirrer*' or '*chizzick*'. Alarm-note a harsh, buzzing '*churr*' or rapid '*crit-crit-crit*'.

Habitat: Evergreen forest and thick moist bush. Prefers the sunny side of a forest.

Distribution: The south-eastern coastal belt and the north-eastern and north-central parts of Southern Africa.

GREY-BACKED WARBLER *Camaroptera brevicaudata*

(628) p. 272

Afr Grysrugtinktinkie *X* u-Nome

Z i-Mbuzana

Identification: 11 cm. *Head to mantle and rump a dark ashy grey; wings green.* Below, a pale greyish buff; centre of belly whitish. Tail an ashy grey, with very faint barring. *Thighs a brownish yellow.* Under wing-coverts yellow and white. Eyes a pale red; bill blackish; legs flesh-coloured.

A common resident species, found singly or in pairs. Inquisitive small birds that creep about in the dense undergrowth, often with their relatively short tails cocked up. Their weak, bleating call often draws attention to their presence.

Voice: A gentle, bleating, nasal note. During courtship display male utters a high-pitched '*pee*'. This is followed by bill-snapping.

Habitat: Dense patches of bush in woodland and forest (dry bush included).

Distribution: The northern half of Southern Africa.

Allied species:

ICTERINE WARBLER (*Hippolais icterina*) (596). 14 cm. Above, a pale olive-green with a yellowish wash. Wings and tail more dusky. Faint yellow stripe over the eye. *Below, including sides of face, a palish yellow.* A rather retiring palaeoarctic migrant, seen creeping about and hopping actively from branch to branch in search of insects, keeping up a subdued song most of the time. Frequents the thornveld of central and northern Southern Africa.

BURNT-NECKED WARBLER (*Eremomela usticollis*) (601). 11 cm. Above, ash-grey, wings and tail included. Below, a pale creamy buff; throat paler. *There is often only an indication of a rusty wash or bar on the chest.* Resident and usually found in pairs or small family parties, searching for food in the topmost branches of acacia trees. Often found in association with white-eyes or other warblers. Found in the northern half of Southern Africa, but not in the north-western regions.

GREEN-CAPPED WARBLER (*Eremomela scotops*) (602). 11 cm. Top of head and sides of face a pale greenish yellow; *lores a brownish grey*. Rest of upper parts, including wings and tail, a pale ashy grey. Below, chin white; rest of underparts a pale lemon-yellow. Resident; usually found in

PLATE 27

CUCKOO-SHRIKES, HOOPOES, DRONGO, BABBLERS AND LARKS

1 **BLACK CUCKOO-SHRIKE** page 207
   Male: gape orange-yellow. Female: wing feathers with bright yellow edges.

2 **RED-BILLED HOOPOE** 181
   Long, slender bill red; white spots on graduated tail.

3 **AFRICAN HOOPOE** 181
   Large crest brick-red and black.

4 **FORK-TAILED DRONGO** 211
   Tail forked and eyes red.

5 **GREY CUCKOO-SHRIKE** 210
   Uniform grey with white ring round the eye.

6 **ARROW-MARKED BABBLER** 217
   White tips to feathers from chin to upper belly.

7 **PIED-BABBLER** 217
   Wings and tail black.

8 **SABOTA LARK** 196
   White eye-stripe well defined; chest rather heavily spotted.

9 **PINK-BILLED LARK** 199
   Conical bill short, thick and pink.

10 **RUFOUS-NAPED LARK** 196
   Nape rufous-tinged, eye-stripe light. A large lark.

11 **RED-CAPPED LARK** 198
   Cap and patch on side of breast distinctly rufous.

12 **SPIKE-HEELED LARK** 197
   Bill longish, short tail feathers tipped with white.

13 **CLAPPER LARK** 197
   Mantle mottled.

14 **GREY-BACKED FINCH-LARK** 198
   Back grey, white patch on crown and side of face.

PLATE 28

ORIOLES, BULBULS, TITS AND ROCK-JUMPER

1 **BLACK-HEADED ORIOLE** *page* 213
Head black, bill pinkish.

2 **AFRICAN GOLDEN ORIOLE** 212
Black facial stripe extends beyond the eye; wings show only a little
black.

3 **EUROPEAN GOLDEN ORIOLE** 212
Black facial stripe ends at the eye; wings black.

4 **SOMBRE BULBUL** 221
Eyes almost white.

5 **CAPE PENDULINE TIT** 216
Very small. Forehead black and chin spotted.

6 **RED-EYED BULBUL** 219
Eye-wattle red.

7 **BLACK-EYED BULBUL** 220
Eye-wattle black.

8 **CAPE BULBUL** 219
Eye-wattle white.

9 **GREY TIT** 215
Broad white streak below the eye.

10 **BLACK TIT** 215
Upper wing-coverts white.

11 **TERRESTRIAL BULBUL** 220
Throat whitish, contrasting with dark head.

12 **ROCK-JUMPER** 218
Throat black, moustache-stripe white.

small parties, keeping up a continuous piping as they actively search for insects in trees. Fly out from trees to hawk small insects, which they catch with an audible snap of their bills. Often members of mixed bird-parties. Prefer open woodland and are found in the north-eastern parts of Southern Africa.

GREAT REED-WARBLER (*Acrocephalus arundinaceus*) (603). 20 cm. Above, olive-brown, wings and tail included. Rump paler. Light buffish eye-stripe. Below, a pale buff; throat and centre of belly whitish. Tail gradu-ated; *brownish bill rather heavy* for a warbler. A common palaeoarctic migrant that looks rather like a robin and is usually found singly. Not confined to reeds or the vegetation beside streams. Presence usually be-trayed by its very loud, grating, vibrant song; '*karra-karra*', '*krik-krik*' '*gurk-gurk*', etc. Found in the north-eastern half of Southern Africa.

CAPE REED-WARBLER (*Acrocephalus gracilirostris*) (604). 16 cm. Above, an olivaceous brown. Lower rump and upper tail-coverts browner; wings and tail more dusky. Tail slightly graduated. *Eye-stripe whitish; strong legs fairly dark brown.* Below, a creamy or buffish white. A common resident, usually seen in the reeds at the water's edge, exploring the stems for insects. Cheerful song short and complete (not merely a repetition of a simple phrase). Found in the greater part of Southern Africa, but not in the dry central and north-western regions.

AFRICAN SCRUB-WARBLER (*Bradypterus baboecala*) (609). 15 cm. Above, a dusky brown, wings and tail included. *Wing-coverts have brownish-white edges; throat usually faintly streaked.* Eye-stripe and underparts a pale buff. *Tail-feathers broad and graduated, so that tail appears rather rounded.* A resident, skulking bird, always found near water, in matted reeds or weeds. Call a loud rattle, ending with a bubbling trill. Found in the southern and eastern half of Southern Africa.

VICTORIN'S SCRUB-WARBLER (*Bradypterus victorini*) (612). 16 cm. Above, a warm brown; wings and tail also. Sides of face and ear-coverts slightly greyish; tail graduated; feathers not broad. *Below, cinnamon.* A common local resident, frequenting mountain slopes and the rocky kloofs of mountain streams. When disturbed, scuttles through the grass like a mouse. Although fairly tame, does not sit on an exposed perch while singing. Confined to the extreme south-western tip of Southern Africa.

BROAD-TAILED WARBLER (*Schoenicola brevirostris*) (616). 15 cm. Above, olivaceous to russet-brown; *long, broad tail a blackish brown, tipped with whitish.* Below, a buffish white; chest and flanks browner. A resident species that frequents moist reed-beds and flooded grassy marshes. A not very active bird, only occasionally venturing onto an exposed perch in the early mornings. Its short flight is jerky and bobbing, as though the bird were weighed down by its heavy tail. Found in the central and north-eastern coastal regions of Southern Africa.

KARROO GREEN WARBLER (*Eremomela gregalis*) (626). 11 cm. *Above*, including edges of flight-feathers and tail, *olive-green;* upper tail-coverts brighter. Sides of face and hind neck greyish. Below, mainly off-white; under tail-coverts a yellowish green. A not very common local resident, usually found in small parties amongst the twigs of stunted vegetation. Found in the south-western parts of Southern Africa, but not in the southernmost tip.

BLEATING WARBLER (*Camaroptera brachyura*) (627). 11 cm. Forehead a dark grey; rest of *upper parts, including tail, a dark green*. Sides of face and ear-coverts greyish. Below, whitish; chest has a light buff wash; flanks greyish. A common forest species, also found in the dense vegetation beside streams and rivers. Creeps about in the undergrowth and on the ground, attracting attention by its weak, bleating call and noisy scuffling amongst the dry leaves. Usually found in pairs, in the south-eastern and eastern coastal regions of Southern Africa.

Rarer species:

WHITETHROAT (*Sylvia communis*) (594)

OLIVE-TREE WARBLER (*Hippolais olivetorum*) (597)

RIVER WARBLER (*Locustella fluviatilis*) (598)

EUROPEAN MARSH-WARBLER (*Acrocephalus palustris*) (607)

SEDGE-WARBLER (*Acrocephalus schoenobaenus*) (608)

GREATER SWAMP-WARBLER (*Acrocephalus rufescens*)

EUROPEAN REED-WARBLER (*Acrocephalus scirpaceus*)

LESSER BARRED WARBLER (*Camaroptera stierlingi* (614)

FOREST SCRUB-WARBLER (*Bradypterus barratti*) (610)

KNYSNA SCRUB-WARBLER (*Bradypterus sylvaticus*) (611)

CINNAMON-BREASTED WARBLER (*Camaroptera subcinnamomea*) (613)

MOUSTACHED WARBLER (*Melocichla mentalis*) (617)

RED-WINGED WARBLER (*Heliolais erythroptera*) (620)

RED-FACED CROMBEC (*Sylvietta whytii*) (621X)

BLACK-HEADED APALIS (*Apalis melanocephala*) (623)

RUDD'S APALIS (*Apalis ruddi*) (624)

WOOD-WARBLER (*Phylloscopus sibilatrix*)

FAN-TAILED CISTICOLA　*Cisticola juncidis* (629)　　　p. 272
　　Afr Gewone tinktinkie　　　　　*X* u-Noqandula
　　Z　u-Dogwe　　　　　　　　*S* mo-Teane

Identification: 11 cm. Above, male in breeding plumage brown, streaked with blackish; *rump rufous*. Below, whitish; shortish tail a dusky black above; silvery white below. Subterminal spots on tail visible from above and below; tips whitish. Eyes hazel; bill a dark brown, but with lower mandible a pale horn; legs flesh-coloured. Male in non-breeding plumage has feathers of head and mantle more broadly edged with buff, and looks paler. Female similar to male in non-breeding plumage. Subadult a rusty edition of adult, but paler below.

A common resident species, usually found in pairs. Spends most of its time on the ground and is not often seen during the non-breeding season. When flushed makes only short flights. Male very conspicuous during the breeding season, and executes dipping display-flights over the breeding territory. Bird flies high, dipping repeatedly and uttering a 'klink' at each dip. *This species does not snap its wings.* Nest has a remarkable shape, like that of a soda-water bottle.

Voice: An often-repeated '*klink*' or '*tzit*'; alarm-note '*zit-zit-zit*' in excited succession.

Habitat: Open grassland, particularly in moister places, where the grass is longer. Also found at the edges of cultivated fields.

Distribution: Throughout Southern Africa, but localized.

CLOUD-CISTICOLA　*Cisticola textrix* (631)　　　p. 272
　　Afr Gevlekte tinktinkie

Identification: 10 cm. Top of head brown; hind neck, mantle, scapulars and wing-coverts blackish, with relatively narrow buff edges to the feathers. Sides of face mottled with black and white. Rump and upper tail-coverts brown with black streaks. *Very short tail* is blackish and has white tips. Below, whitish, with *black streaks on chest and flanks*. Eyes brown; bill lead-grey; legs flesh-coloured. In non-breeding plumage the blackish centres of the feathers become narrower, so that the bird presents a streaked rather than a mottled appearance. Female similar to male in non-breeding dress. Subadult is washed with yellow below.

A local resident species; during the non-breeding season not very obtrusive. During the breeding season male performs remarkable aerobatics at a great height. Mounts on very rapidly-beating wings until almost out of sight, cruises for a short time in random circles, repeatedly calling '*chick-chick*', Then dives down almost vertically to within a few feet of the ground, checks the dive and lands gently on the grass. *Does not snap its wings as it descends.*

WARBLERS 245

Voice: Song, usually given at a great height: *'u-tic-tic-tick-chick, chick, chick, chick, chick'*. Also a sharp chattering during its rapid descent.
Habitat: Open country covered with short grass; also grassy vleis.
Distribution: The south-eastern third of Southern Africa, including the southernmost tip.

NEDDICKY CISTICOLA   *Cisticola fulvicapilla* (637)   p. 272
    Afr Rooikroontinktinkie   *X* u-Ngcede
    Z i-Ncede

Identification: 11 cm. *Top of head to nape a plain rufous;* rest of upper parts, including wings and tail, a plain earth-brown. Sides of face and stripe over eye buff. *Below*, *greyish*; belly whitish. Tail has indistinct darker subterminal spots, seen from above and below. Eyes hazel; bill a greyish flesh-colour; legs flesh-coloured.

An extremely common resident, usually found singly or in pairs. Song sung by male during the breeding season, from prominent singing-posts, is loud and penetrating and has great carrying power. When alarmed, bird flies into the nearest bush, and watches the intruder intently from its shelter.
Voice: A loud, resonant, ventriloquial, slightly mournful *'weep-weep-weep'* that gradually increases in volume and rises in pitch, and is endlessly repeated. Alarm-note a rapid clicking sound, like that produced by running one's finger over the teeth of a comb.
Habitat: Open savanna with trees or bushes; plantations and even gardens.
Distribution: The north-eastern half of Southern Africa, and the southern coastal belt.

RATTLING CISTICOLA   *Cisticola chiniana* (642)   p. 272
    Afr Bosveldtinktinkie   *Z* i-Nqoba

Identification: 15 cm. *Top of head to nape a pale rufous, with no stripe over the eye.* Rest of upper side dusky, with brownish blotches. Edges of flight-feathers slightly tawny. Tail a dusky brown; black subterminal spots on tail visible from above and below. Below, a pale creamy white. Eyes hazel; bill blackish; legs a dark flesh-colour. In winter both sexes become redder and look streaked rather than blotchy.

A common resident species, conspicuous and fairly large. During the breeding season the male often sits on a high point of vantage, singing his characteristic song. Black palate conspicuous while bird is singing. Very noisy: utters a harsh, scolding alarm-note when disturbed.
Voice: Two or three whistled notes, followed by a trill; *'chee-chee-chee-chirrrrrr'*. Alarm-note a harsh, angry *'churr-churr'*.

Habitat: Savanna bush with scattered trees.
Distribution: The north-eastern half of Southern Africa.

LE VAILLANT'S CISTICOLA   *Cisticola tinniens* (646)   p. 272
Afr Vleitinktinkie   *X* u-Mvila

Identification: 13 cm. Above, top of head to nape a plain, warm russet-brown; *mantle, scapulars and wing-coverts buff, blotched with black*. Flight-feathers dusky. Sides of face and stripe over eye buff. Tail-feathers dusky to blackish, with broad tawny edges. Black subterminal spots visible from above and below. Underside buff; chin, throat and belly slightly paler. Eyes hazel; bill blackish; legs a dark flesh-colour. In winter dress, crown becomes streaky and general appearance is streaky rather than blotched. Subadult shows more rust in winter dress than adults and sometimes has a yellowish tinge on face and breast.

A very common resident species, usually found in pairs. Commonly seen flitting just above the vegetation, with a jerky flight and much flicking of its tail. When disturbed, makes for the highest available perch or flies directly above the intruder, keeping him in view and scolding all the time.

Voice: Alarm-note a high-pitched, moderately loud '*tee-tee-tee*'; song a chirpy, warbling '*chi-chi-chi-cherrrueee*', with the last part a loud warble.
Habitat: Prefers marshes and damp areas with fairly short weeds or reeds. Seldom found beside rivers.
Distribution: Found in the southern tip and the eastern half of Southern Africa, but not in the northern coastal regions.

CROAKING CISTICOLA   *Cisticola natalensis* (647)   p. 272
Afr Groottinktinkie   *X* u-Boboyi
Z u-Boyu

Identification: 18 cm. Entire upper side, including *top of head and nape, earth-brown, with dusky streaks*. No distinct eye-stripe. Flight-feathers dusky. Tail a faint ash-brown; black subterminal spots visible from above and below; tail-feathers tipped with whitish buff. Below, a creamy white. Eyes brown; bill blackish; legs a dull flesh-colour. In winter dress both sexes have longer tails; their general colour becomes more buff, and they are more broadly streaked. Female much smaller than male; bill flesh-coloured. Subadult more rusty and a bright sulphur below.

This very large cisticola, with its strong, almost weaver-like bill, is a common resident. Males often perch on the tops of trees or bushes. They perform courting flights over nesting females, zig-zagging to and fro with a high, jerky, loose-jointed wing-action and uttering guttural, clucking notes.

Voice: A vibrant, unmelodious, monosyllabic '*trrr*', often repeated.

Alarm-note a sharp, frog-like croak, with the accent on the second syllable: 'ee-PRRK'.

Habitat: Rank, open grassland with scattered trees and bushes. Also found on the borders of cultivated areas. Prefers dry country to wet.

Distribution: In the north-eastern parts of Southern Africa; also along the south-eastern coastal belt.

Allied species:

DESERT CISTICOLA (*Cisticola aridula*) (630). 11 cm. Very similar to the common Fan-tailed Cisticola, except that it is *much paler above and the rump is a pale rufous*. Subterminal tail-spots visible only from below. Found in drier and more open country where the grass is short. Spends most of its time on the ground. *Snaps its wings as it swoops downwards during display-flights*. Found throughout the interior of Southern Africa and also in the north-western coastal belt.

AYRES' CISTICOLA (*Cisticola ayresii*) (634). 10 cm. Very similar to the Cloud-Cisticola, but a warmer brown above, especially on crown and rump. Tail shorter; *underside lighter and not streaked*. Also sings from a great height during display-flights, but its notes are more squeaky and highly-pitched. *Song accompanied by wing-snapping*. Unlike the Cloud-Cisticola it prefers long, thick grass. Found in the eastern third of Southern Africa but not in the north-eastern coastal regions.

DANCING CISTICOLA (*Cisticola subruficapilla*) (638). 13 cm. Top of head a dark brown, streaked with black; *no eye-stripe. Back an ashy grey, streaked and not blotched with black*. Tail brown; black subterminal spots visible from above and below; tail-feathers tipped with a lighter brown. Below, a greyish white; chest streaked with blackish. A common species of the drier west; found in a variety of habitats, from the coastal sand-dunes and estuarine flats to mountainous country. Found in the western third of Southern Africa but not in the far north.

WAILING CISTICOLA (*Cisticola lais*) (639). 13 cm. Very similar to the Dancing Cisticola, but broader black markings on back produce a bolder pattern. Underside not greyish but washed with buff. *Shows a greater contrast between the light rufous crown and the light grey back*, than the Dancing Cisticola. Found in mountainous and rocky country where there is plenty of grass. Alarm-note, usually uttered when bird is sitting on a tall grass-stalk, a loud, wailing 'hweeet'. Found in the eastern third of Southern Africa.

TINKLING CISTICOLA (*Cisticola rufilata*) (641). 14 cm. Top of head to nape a plain russet-brown; part of ear-coverts also. *Distinct buffish stripe over eye; lores also buffish*. Dusky brown back heavily mottled. Since the edges of the flight-feathers and the narrow tail-feathers are tawny, the *general appearance of the bird is reddish.* Below, buff; chin, throat and centre of belly whitish. A shy bird that dives for cover at the slightest sign of danger. Prefers more or less dry, open scrub country and is found in the central and north-western parts of Southern Africa.

RED-FACED CISTICOLA (*Cisticola erythrops*) (644). 14 cm. Similar to the Tinkling Cisticola, but since the crown and edges of the flight-feathers are earth-brown they contrast less strongly with the *plain back.* Eye-stripe very indistinct; face a pale reddish buff. Widely distributed; often found in the reeds and other vegetation of subtropical marshes. Though wary, they have *very loud calls* and are therefore easily located. Found in the eastern half of Southern Africa.

LAZY CISTICOLA (*Cisticola aberrans*) (648). 14 cm. Top of head to nape a plain, dull russet-brown. Being a slightly russet earth-brown, with indistinct dark markings, *back appears plain from a distance. Similar to the Neddicky Cisticola, but has a very much longer tail.* Subterminal spots rather indistinct and usually visible only from above. Very much localized; prefers rank weeds and grass beside streams and on stony hillsides. Usually found hopping about, with a flirting tail, in the lower parts of the vegetation. Found in the eastern third of Southern Africa, but not in the north-eastern coastal regions.

Rarer species:
PALE-CROWNED CISTICOLA (*Cisticola brunnescens*) (635)

SHORTWING CISTICOLA (*Cisticola brachyptera*) (636)

SINGING CISTICOLA (*Cisticola cantans*) (643)

BLACK-BACKED CISTICOLA (*Cisticola galactotes*) (645)

CHIRPING CISTICOLA (*Cisticola pipiens*) (645X)

TAWNY-FLANKED PRINIA *Prinia subflava* (649) p. 257
  Afr Bruinsy-langsterttinktinkie
Identification: 10–15 cm. Above, grey-brown; rump, tail (with blackish subterminal spots) and edge of flight-feathers russet-brown. Black spot in front of eye; *distinct eye-stripe.* Sides of face and underside a creamy white, except for under tail-coverts and *flanks, which are a pale tawny.* In non-breeding (winter) dress the upper parts are more rufous and the tail is longer. Eyes hazel; bill black; legs flesh-coloured.

A common, widely distributed species, usually seen in pairs or small parties. Noisy, conspicuous little birds, usually seen hunting for insects in low vegetation. Pipe cheerfully as they move about, with their long tails cocked up like those of wrens.
Voice: Alarm-note a sharp, persistent, weeping '*sbee-sbee-sbee*', uttered

while bird jerks its tail. Several birds may demonstrate jointly against an intruder. Song a monotonous '*przzt-przzt*'.

Habitat: Coarse vegetation along rivers and streams.

Distribution: The north-eastern half of Southern Africa.

BLACK-CHESTED PRINIA   *Prinia flavicans* (650)   p. 257

Afr Swartbors-langsterttinktinkie

Identification: 15 cm. Above, including wings and tail, earth-brown. Sub-terminal spots on tail very indistinct. Eye-stripe, sides of face, chin and throat whitish. *Broad black band across lower neck and chest*; rest of underparts a pale yellow. In winter plumage the black band is replaced by a few blackish spots, or may disappear altogether, and the upper side is a more tawny brown. Eyes a brownish yellow; bill black; legs brown.

A common, lively little bird, found in pairs or small parties. Very noisy when disturbed. Inquisitive and not at all shy.

Voice: Alarm-note a weeping call. Song a clacking warble, of short duration.

Habitat: Thick patches of open thorn bush. Also found in orchards and gardens.

Distribution: Central and north-western Southern Africa.

KARROO PRINIA   *Prinia maculosa* (651)   p. 257

Afr Karoo-langsterttinktinkie   *X* n-Jiza

Identification: 15 cm. Above, a warm earth-brown, including wings and tail. Dusky streaks on crown. Blackish subterminal spots on long, narrow tail very indistinct. Stripe over eye and sides of face whitish; chin and throat whitish, spotted with black; *rest of underparts a yellowish white, broadly streaked with black*. Centre of belly a plain yellowish colour. Flanks and under tail-coverts an olivaceous brown. Eyes brown; bill blackish; legs brown. In the subadult the spots and streaks are dusky, not black.

A common, very active and excitable bird, usually found in pairs and small parties, creeping about in the undergrowth or on the ground. When alarmed, sits on the top of a bush and scolds at the intruder from a distance. When approached too closely, dives into cover and slips away in the undergrowth. Hawks insects in the air. Constantly flirts its tail up and down.

Voice: A long series of different clicking and ringing notes, varying in tempo. Has a dipping display-flight in which each dip is punctuated by a thudding beat of the wings and a loud '*cheenk-cheenk*'.

Habitat: Dry stunted bush, coastal scrub (exotic as well as indigenous) and mountain slopes. Sometimes found beside rivers.

Distribution: The southern half of Southern Africa.

Allied species:

NAMAQUA PRINIA (*Prinia substriata*) (653). 13 cm. Above, including wings and tail, a dull russet-brown; sides of neck a brownish grey; stripe over eye and underparts whitish. *Small dusky streaks on chest and breast;* flanks brownish. *Tail has no subterminal spots.* A small, restless, rather rare bird, occurring in scrub beside streams and rivers. Confined to the southern part of the central western regions of Southern Africa.

RUFOUS-EARED PRINIA (*Prinia pectoralis*) (619). 15 cm. Top of head streaked with pale chestnut and blackish. Back streaked with black and buff. Long, thin tail and flight-feathers a dusky black, edged with buff. *Stripe over eye, lores, sides of face and ear-coverts chestnut.* Underparts a creamy white, with a *narrow black band across the chest.* A common resident species of dry country with low scrub. Flies very low; can run extremely fast. Found in the central western parts of Southern Africa.

Rarer species:

FOREST PRINIA (*Prinia robertsi*) (649X)

FLYCATCHERS: Muscicapidae

Flycatchers are small to medium-sized birds with wide bills that are flattened towards the gape and bordered by stiff bristles. Some have plain colours; others are beautifully coloured or ornamented. Most are rather silent and have feeble songs. They all build cup- or saucer-shaped nests. They are insectivorous, and many catch their prey in the air. They perch upright on some vantage-point, from which they make short, erratic flights after insects. Having caught their prey they return to the same perch. Other flycatchers hunt for insects in the foliage of trees, like warblers. Although most species are resident and very local in habitat, a few are migratory.

SPOTTED FLYCATCHER *Muscicapa striata* (654) p. 273
Afr Europese vlieëvanger

Identification: 15 cm. Above, ashy brown, including wings and tail. Forehead and crown streaked with blackish. Below, whitish; *sides of throat and chest fairly heavily streaked with a dark ash-grey.* Flanks buffish and slightly streaked. Eyes brown; bill black; legs ashy. Sexes alike.

A common, non-breeding palaeoarctic migrant, usually found singly. Perches low as a rule, on bare branches under trees or on fences from which it darts out to catch passing insects. While perching, flicks its wings upwards (unlike the Familiar Chat, which flicks its wings sideways and forwards).

Voice: A thin, weak '*tzee*'. Alarm-note a sharp '*tec-tec*' and a rapid '*tzee, tuc-tuc*'.

Habitat: Wherever there are trees, preferring those that border open spaces.

Distribution: Throughout Southern Africa.

COMMON TIT BABBLER   *Parisoma subcaeruleum* (658)   p. 273
Afr Rooigatvlieëvanger

Identification: 15 cm. Above, a darkish grey, wings included. *The feathers of the alula are tipped with white*, forming a distinct pattern on the folded wing. Tail black; all except the central tail-feathers have white ends. Below, a light grey; chin and throat heavily streaked with black. Belly lighter. *Under tail-coverts chestnut.* Eyes a creamy white; bill black; legs dusky. Sexes alike. Subadult has sparser streaks on chin and throat.

A common resident species, found singly or in pairs. Cheerful, noisy birds, usually seen creeping about in trees, bushes or thickets in search of insects. Work their way carefully through one tree before flying quickly to the next and repeating the performance. *During flight the white tips of the tail-feathers are very conspicuous.*

Voice: While feeding, utters a loud '*cheriktik*', which is answered by the mate. Call-note a string of ringing, sharply-articulated '*ticks*', followed by a rapid run. Has a loud, clear song and often imitates other birds.

Habitat: Acacia country and open bush, especially on sheltered hillsides and along dry river-beds.

Distribution: Throughout the greater part of Southern Africa, but not in the eastern or north-eastern coastal regions.

MARICO FLYCATCHER   *Melaenornis mariquensis* (661)   p. 273
Afr Maricovlieëvanger

Identification: 18 cm. Sides of face and entire upper side fawn. Wing- and tail-feathers have light russet edges. Small darkish spot in front of eye. *Below, white.* Eyes brown; bill and legs black. Sexes alike. Subadult streaked with blackish below, and spotted above.

A common resident, usually found singly or in pairs, but sometimes in small parties when not breeding. Like the Spotted Flycatcher, perches on the lower branches of trees when hunting flying insects. Often feeds on the ground as well. On the ground its body is held high and its longish tail is held up slightly. Bird flicks its tail when settling.

Voice: A soft, piping whistle, not often uttered. Alarm-note a loud chattering '*churr*', rapidly repeated.

Habitat: Open acacia thornveld, in the drier regions.

Distribution: The central and western parts of the northern half of Southern Africa.

FISCAL FLYCATCHER *Melaenornis silens* (665) p. 273
Afr Fiskaalvlieëvanger

Identification: 19 cm. Adult male: head, sides of face, scapulars, mantle and rump a glossy black. Wings black, with white spots on primaries and secondaries; secondaries edged with white. These are seen as *white windows in flight.* Tail-feathers black, but *all the outer feathers have white bases.* Below, white; chest and flanks washed with grey. Eyes brown; bill and legs black. Female brownish or a *dull* sooty black above; dirty white below. Subadult spotted above and mottled below.

A common, somewhat sedentary species, usually found in pairs. Sits on some prominent perch, from which insects are hawked, or caught on the ground. *Similar to the Fiscal Shrike but has a much shorter tail. This is often spread out fan-wise showing the broad black terminal band.* Has the typical flycatcher bill and not the heavy hooked bill of the shrikes. Also distinguished from the Fiscal Shrike by its black back.

Voice: Characteristic call '*zirrrrr*'. Song feeble and long drawn out: '*zirrrr-zirrrr-tit-tit-tewt-tewt*'. Often several birds sing together, with much flitting about and fanning of tails. Alarm-note '*skisk*'.

Habitat: Savanna and low open bush country; also cultivated ground and gardens.

Distribution: The southern and south-eastern parts of Southern Africa.

CAPE FLYCATCHER *Batis capensis* (672) p. 273
Afr Kaapse vlieëvanger   *X* in-Gedle

Identification: 11 cm. Head and nape a dark grey; mantle and rump an olivaceous grey; wings greyish. *Rufous wing-coverts seen as a patch on the folded wing.* Under wing-coverts white. Tail-feathers black, with small white tips. Sides of face, ear-coverts, and line that almost meets at the back of the neck, black. Below; chin, throat, sides of neck and belly white. Broad black band across chest; *flanks rufous.* Eyes yellow or orange; bill and legs black. Female similar to male except that *band across chest is rufous*, not black, and *chin rufous*, not white. Subadult has upper parts streaked with light tawny.

A common resident species, generally found in pairs and often as members of mixed bird parties. Hawk insects; also hunt for them in the foliage of trees. When alarmed, fly about excitedly and make a whirring sound with their wings. Very tame when incubating and can be closely approached.

Voice: A penetrating, monotonous note '*reep-reep-reep*', steadily repeated; also a soft, low-pitched '*wee-warrawarra*'.

Habitat: Prefers the marginal vegetation of moist forest and kloofs.

Distribution: The southern and eastern coastal regions of Southern Africa; also (but more rarely) the evergreen forests of the north-eastern regions.

CHINSPOT FLYCATCHER   *Batis molitor* (673)   p. 273
Afr Keelvlekvlieëvanger   *Z* Matoobane
X   u-Ndyola

Identification: 11 cm. Adult male: top of head and mantle grey; thin white streak from bill, over lores, to the eye; rump black and white. Sides of face, ear-coverts and sides of neck black. Wings and tail black; edges of secondaries white; under wing-coverts black. Tail-feathers have small white tips. *Below, white, including flanks.* Broad black band across chest. Eyes scarlet; bill and legs black. Female similar to male except that *chin is rufous, and band across chest rufous* instead of black. Subadult similar to female, but head, back and chest-band are speckled with buffish.

A common resident, found in pairs, often belonging to mixed bird parties. An active, restless little bird, usually searching for insects amongst the lower branches of trees. Also hawks insects in the air, and often hovers while hunting. Much wing-clapping during display. A not very shy little bird, showing itself in the open far more often than the Cape Flycatcher.
Voice: Three short, flute-like notes on a descending scale: '*whee-who-who*'. This call is remarkably loud for such a small bird. Also utters a squeaky '*chi-chirr*'; alarm-note a harsh, rather low-pitched '*purk-purk-purk*'.
Habitat: Open savanna and the edges of forests. Often found near human habitations.
Distribution: The eastern half and northernmost parts of Southern Africa.

FAIRY FLYCATCHER   *Stenostira scita* (678)   p. 273
Afr Feëvlieëvanger

Identification: 11 cm. Above, a dark grey; sides of face and ear-coverts black. Thin eye-stripe and moustache-stripe white. Wings black. Wing-coverts and inner secondaries white, forming a *conspicuous white line on the folded wing.* Tail black; all feathers except central ones have white tips; outermost feathers almost completely white. Below, chin and throat white, washed with pink; chest, breast and flanks grey; *belly white, with pink centre.* Eyes a dark brown; bill and legs black. Sexes alike. Subadults paler and more brownish above, with little or no pink on chin or belly.

A fairly common local migrant that disappears from certain areas during the non-breeding season. *A slender, graceful little bird with a longish tail,* behaving more like an apalis than a flycatcher. Since it creeps about in low vegetation and the foliage of trees, searching for insects, it is not easily seen. Usually found singly or in pairs; often bobs and fans its tail when excited.
Voice: A twittering, sunbird-like '*kisskisskiss*', and a chirping call ending in '*cheep-cheep*'. Alarm-note a prolonged chattering.
Habitat: Prefers acacia veld and riverine forest. Also found in exotic trees near houses, and in reed-beds.

Distribution: The southern half of Southern Africa, but not along the southern and eastern coastal belts.

BLUE-MANTLED FLYCATCHER *Trochocercus cyanomelas*
(680)   p. 273
Afr Bloukuifvlieëvanger   *X* i-Gotyi

Identification: 16 cm. Adult male: *head crested.* Entire head and chin to upper breast a glossy blue-black. Back and tail grey. Wings dusky; wing-coverts tipped and edged with white, forming *distinct white bars on the folded wing.* Below: flanks grey; belly and under tail-coverts white. Eyes dusky; bill and legs slate-blue. Female: top of head blue-black, only slightly crested; a greyish ash-brown above. Below: mainly white, except for grey chin, throat and flanks. Subadult more ash-brown above (top of head included); bars on wing less distinct.

A not very common species, usually seen singly. A very active bird with a rapid, darting flight; flits through the trees with remarkable agility, chasing insects. Rather retiring; usually feeds at lower levels. When excited, pirouettes along a branch, fanning and closing its tail.

Voice: A short, rasping '*zi-za*' or '*zi-zerdt-zerdt*' and a loud, high-pitched song '*kwew-ew-ew-ew*', sometimes followed by a short series of loud clicks.

Habitat: Forest and evergreen coastal bush. Prefers open shady patches near streams.

Distribution: The south-eastern coastal belt and the eastern and north-eastern coastal regions of Southern Africa.

PARADISE FLYCATCHER *Terpsiphone viridis* (682)   p. 273
Afr Paradysvlieëvanger   *X* u-Jejane
Z Uve   *S* mo-Thoapea

Identification: 20 cm; (41 cm including tail). Adult male: head crested. Entire head, neck and chest either a metallic blue-green or a slightly glossy blue-grey. *Remainder of upper parts and tail a rich tawny chestnut.* Central tail-feathers greatly elongated as a rule. Flight-feathers dusky, edged with chestnut. Underparts mainly grey; under tail- and under wing-coverts white. Eyes brown; wattle round eye and bill cobalt-blue; legs slate. Female is less glossy on head; has only a slight crest; chin and throat a dark grey; central tail-feathers only slightly elongated. Subadult similar to female, but paler.

A common local migrant, usually found in pairs. Catches its prey on the wing. Very noisy and active, flitting about with an undulating flight, its long, conspicuous tail-feathers streaming behind it as it darts after flying insects. A tame, bold bird that will attack any large bird of prey coming near its nest. Male helps to incubate the eggs, and his long tail-feathers, hanging gracefully down, often betray the position of the well-camouflaged, lichen-covered nest.

Voice: Normal call similar to that of the Blue-mantled Flycatcher: a short '*zi-za*', '*swee-swer*' or '*zwa-i-zwer*'. The brief song is a melodious, rippling '*whee-wheeo-whit-whit*', repeated several times.

Habitat: Evergreen and riverine forest. Also found in gardens in built-up areas.

Distribution: The eastern half of Southern Africa and also in the northern-most and southernmost regions.

Allied species:

DUSKY FLYCATCHER (*Muscicapa adusta*) (655). 13 cm. Upper side, in-cluding wings and tail, a dark mouse-colour. Sides of face, *chin, breast and flanks ash-brown, sparsely streaked with whitish*. Throat whitish and not streaked. Belly a light mouse-colour. Catches insects on the ground and off foliage, and also hawks them from low perches. An unobtrusive bird that would often be overlooked if its quiet call '*tsirit-tsit-tsirit*' did not betray its presence. Flicks its wings when settling. Usually found in pairs under large trees or on the edge of forests in the southern and eastern coastal regions.

BLUE-GREY FLYCATCHER (*Muscicapa caerulescens*) (656). 15 cm. Upper side, including wings and tail, grey. Flight-feathers edged with whitish. *No white in the tail*. Lores and narrow ring around the eye white. Below, a uniform light grey; chin and throat whitish. Quiet birds, usually found in pairs as members of mixed bird-parties. Habits similar to those of the Dusky Flycatcher. Found in the drier forests of the eastern coastal regions and in the north-eastern third of Southern Africa.

FAN-TAILED FLYCATCHER (*Myioparus plumbeus*) (657). 14 cm. Above, a pale grey; flight-feathers blackish, with white edges. *Central tail-feathers black; rest of tail-feathers black and white; outer tail-feathers wholly white.* Lores and line above eye white. Eyes red-brown. Chin to upper belly a light grey, not streaked. Lower belly whitish. A not very common species, found in pairs creeping about in the middle parts of trees in search of insects. More like a warbler than a flycatcher. Frequently *fans and raises its open tail, clearly showing the white outer feathers*. Occurs along the edges of dry forests and in open bush, in the north-eastern parts of Southern Africa.

LAYARD'S TIT-BABBLER (*Parisoma layardi*) (659). 14 cm. Similar to the Fan-tailed Flycatcher, but has *chin, throat and chest streaked with black*. Edges to flight-feathers very narrow and not conspicuous. Tail similar to that of the previous species but is never fanned. *Eyes not red-brown but white*. Found feeding in fairly dense cover, moving about wi h a fast, jerky

PLATE 29

THRUSHES, WHEATEAR AND CHATS

1 **GROUNDSCRAPER THRUSH**   *page* 223
Breast and flanks heavily spotted.

2 **OLIVE THRUSH**   222
Bill yellowish, belly and flanks rufous-orange.

3 **MOCKING CHAT**   228
Shoulder-patch white, rump and belly rich chestnut.

4 **CAPE ROCK THRUSH**   226
Head and neck blue-grey.

5 **BUFF-STREAKED CHAT**   228
Eye-stripe and 'V' on back buff-white.

6 **MOUNTAIN CHAT**   226
Shoulder-patch white, rump white. (Colour of head, nape and back of males variable.)

7 **CAPPED WHEATEAR**   227
Throat white, cap black.

8 **FAMILIAR CHAT**   228
Rump rufous, centre tail-feathers dark brown.

9 **STONE CHAT**   229
Breast chestnut.

10 **ANT-EATING CHAT**   229
Small white shoulder-patch. (Male.)

PLATE 30

PRINIAS, APALIS, SCRUB ROBINS AND ROBINS

1 **KARROO PRINIA** *page* 249
Heavily streaked breast.

2 **BAR-THROATED APALIS** 238
Black bar across chest. Outermost tail feathers mainly white.

3 **TAWNY-FLANKED PRINIA** 248
Breast whitish, flanks tawny and wings reddish.

4 **BLACK-CHESTED PRINIA** 249
In breeding plumage well defined black bar across chest, in winter
bar may be absent.

5 **YELLOW-BREASTED APALIS** 238
Size of small brown inverted 'V' on breast variable.

6 **WHITE-THROATED ROBIN** 233
Breast, throat and eye stripe snow white, face blackish.
(See under Allied Species.)

7 **WHITE-BROWED SCRUB ROBIN** 233
Upper breast heavily streaked.

8 **KALAHARI SCRUB ROBIN** 232
Dark terminal tail band has white edge. Breast *not* streaked.

9 **HEUGLIN'S ROBIN** 231
Well defined white eye-stripe.

10 **CAPE ROBIN** 232
Throat and chest dirty orange, light eye-stripe.

11 **CHORISTER ROBIN** 231
Underparts rufous brown, head blackish. Centre tail-feathers dark.

B.S.A. R

flight. Frequents dry scrub country in the south-western parts of Southern
Africa, but not the southern coastal belt.

MOUSE-COLOURED FLYCATCHER (*Melaenornis pallidus*) (662). 16 cm.
Above, including wings, tail and sides of face, ash-grey. Below, *chest and
breast also ash-grey and not white* as in the Marico Flycatcher. Chin, throat
and belly whitish. General impression stoutish. Usually found in pairs;
takes most of its food off the ground. Found in the acacia savanna and
open dry bush of the north-eastern parts of Southern Africa.

CHAT FLYCATCHER (*Melaenornis infuscatus*) (663). 20 cm. Above, a
dusky ash-brown; wing-feathers have conspicuous light edges. Light ring
around the eye. Below, a paler ash-brown; chin, throat and belly a dirty
white. This *large fly-catcher* is usually seen sitting on some prominent perch
(telegraph wires included) from which it drops on to insects on the
ground with a heavy, clumsy flight. May occur in scattered parties. Found
in the dry open country of the western half of Southern Africa, but not
along the southern coastal belt.

BLACK FLYCATCHER (*Melaenornis pammelaina*) (664). 20 cm. General
colour a glossy blue-black; could easily be mistaken for other totally black
species except that *its tail is relatively long, narrow and square*, and not
forked like that of the drongos, or rounded like that of the Black Cuckoo-
shrike. *Eyes black* (not red like those of the Square-tailed Drongo). Has
longer legs, a smaller head and a weaker bill than the drongos. Unlike the
Square-tailed Drongo it prefers open bush to dense forest. Is not always
on the move in the foliage of trees searching for insects like the Black
Cuckoo-shrike. Not as noisy or bold as the drongos. Usually seen in
pairs, sitting on an exposed perch or dropping slowly to the ground to
pick up an insect. Occurs in the north-eastern half of Southern Africa.

YELLOW FLYCATCHER (*Chloropeta natalensis*) (666). 14 cm. Above, olive-
brown, washed with yellow; wings and tail darker. *Below, a bright lemon-
yellow*. Bill blackish, broad and flat, but lower mandible yellowish. Rather
rare; found singly or in pairs in long grass, reeds or weeds near water or on
the borders of evergreen forests; also found in inland riverine forests.
Behaves more like a reed-warbler than a flycatcher and very seldom flies
out into the open after insects. Found in the eastern and south-eastern
coastal regions of Southern Africa. (Also classified as a warbler.)

YELLOW-THROATED FLYCATCHER (*Seicercus ruficapillus*) (671). 10 cm.
Above, top of head to hind neck saffron-brown; rest of upper parts olive-
green. Flight- and tail-feathers dusky, edged with yellowish green. Sides
of face, eye-stripe, *chin to breast and under tail-coverts yellow*. Quiet little
birds, often found in forests, as members of mixed bird-parties. Usually in
the upper parts of trees, looking for insects. Hawk insects in the air, and

hover to take insects off the upper surface of leaves. Found mostly in the southern and eastern coastal regions. (Also classified as a warbler.)

PRIRIT FLYCATCHER (*Batis pririt*) (674). 11 cm. Male similar to that of the Chinspot Flycatcher, but *smaller; flanks not pure white but mottled in black and white*. Has a frog-like croak. Female quite different, and easily identified. Except for her white belly and mottled flanks her underside from *chin to breast is buff*. Habits similar to those of the Chinspot Flycatcher. Found only in the drier central western regions of Southern Africa.

WATTLE-EYED FLYCATCHER (*Platysteira peltata*) (677). 18 cm. Above, including wings and tail, a glossy black. Below, white, with *narrow black band across the chest*. Female has whole head and throat a glossy blue-black. Eyes have a white inner ring, a dark brown outer ring and a conspicuous *crimson wattle over the eye*. Active but rather quiet; usually found in pairs searching for insects in the scrub of evergreen and riverine forests. Occurs in the eastern coastal regions of Southern Africa.

Rarer species:

WHITE-COLLARED FLYCATCHER (*Ficedula albicollis*) (655X)

BLACK AND WHITE FLYCATCHER (*Bias musicus*) (667)

MASHONA FLYCATCHER (*Hyliota australis*) (668)

YELLOW-BELLIED FLYCATCHER (*Hyliota flavigaster*) (670)

WOODWARD'S FLYCATCHER (*Batis fratrum*) (676)

LIVINGSTONE'S FLYCATCHER (*Erythrocercus livingstonei*) (679)

WHITE-TAILED FLYCATCHER (*Trochocercus albonotatus*) (681).

WAGTAILS, PIPITS and LONGCLAWS: Motacillidae

This group consists of small to medium-sized terrestrial birds that walk instead of hopping, and can run very fast. They are mainly insectivorous and build cup-shaped nests, usually on the ground, or in or under concealing vegetation. Most have characteristic call-notes and some a feeble song. A few are palaeoarctic migrants.

Certain wagtails have become closely associated with man, and are probably some of the most familiar species. Wagtails are graceful birds with long, slender tails that they swing up and down, even when walking about. They are usually more boldly patterned than the pipits, two species being black and white, and the migrant species yellow below.

The true pipits are lark-like birds. Most have sober colours, more or less mottled and streaked. *In worn plumage, when the lighter edges to the feathers have mostly disappeared, the birds look darker above than they do in fresh plumage.* They are rather wary and difficult to approach. They are more slender than the larks and have a more upright carriage. Their bills are very slender, and they have the habit of swinging their tails up and down while standing. One species is a migrant from the northern hemisphere. Pipits are extremely difficult to identify in the field and many can only be classified in the hand.

Longclaws resemble larks but are larger and more robust, and have far larger feet. Their underparts are yellow, yellow and orange or pink, and all have a black band across the chest.

AFRICAN PIED WAGTAIL   *Motacilla aguimp* (685)   p. 288

Afr Bontkwikstert   *X* um-Celu
Z   um-Vemve   *S* mo-Selakatane

Identification: 20 cm. Adult male: above, a glossy black, including wings and tail. Since the *upper wing-coverts are white* and the flight-feathers have white spots and edges, the folded wing shows a great deal of white. Two outermost tail-feathers on either side mainly white. *Broad, distinct white eye-stripe.* Sides of face and ear-coverts black. White patch on side of neck. Below, white, with narrow black line from ear-coverts joining broad black band across chest. Eyes brown; bill and legs black. Female a duller black above. Subadult has a more brownish appearance.

A common resident, easily recognized by its bold black-and-white pattern. Tame and confiding; usually seen in pairs near water, feeding along the water's edge.

Voice: A shrill, short '*tsssip*' and a subdued canary-like song.

Habitat: The sandbanks and rocks of the larger rivers. Also found on coastal lagoons and near human habitations.

Distribution: Rather patchy. Most of the eastern half of Southern Africa. Also found along all the larger rivers except those in the south-western regions.

CAPE WAGTAIL   *Motacilla capensis* (686)   p. 288

Afr Gewone kwikstert   *Z* um-Vemve
S   mo-Tjoli

Identification: 18 cm. Above, including wings and tail, a uniform brownish grey. The wing-coverts are tipped with whitish, forming a narrow, indistinct line on the folded wing. Secondaries edged with buffish. Two outermost tail-feathers on either side mainly white, and very conspicuous in flight. Line through eye buffish. Below, a dirty white; sides of breast and flanks greyish. *Blackish band across the chest.* Eyes brown; bill black; legs brownish. Sexes alike. Subadult more brownish.

One of the tamest and most familiar birds in Southern Africa. Less dependent on water than most local wagtail species. Usually found in pairs during the breeding season, but large flocks, numbering several hundred, gather during the winter to roost in trees. Hunts mainly on the ground, flying up to catch disturbed insects. Walks along with bobbing tail, often darting forward to snap up an insect. Not purely insectivorous in built-up areas.

Voice: Normal call a thin, plaintive '*tseep*'. Alarm-note a loud, continuous, sharp, short '*tseep-tseep-tseep*'. Also utters a clear, loud whistle '*ti-wheee*'. Has no regular song.

Habitat: Wherever there is water and a certain amount of shelter. Even found along the coast. Has become very common in cities and towns and on farms.

Distribution: Throughout Southern Africa.

Allied species:

LONG-TAILED WAGTAIL (*Motacilla clara*) (688). 20 cm. Above, a soft blue-grey. Wings black; wing-coverts tipped with white and broadly edged with white. *Tail long*, with three outer tail-feathers on either side wholly white. In flight, white tail shows a dark central line. Conspicuous white eye-stripe. Below, white, with a *thin black band across the chest*. A resident species, occurring in pairs, and found only beside swiftly-flowing mountain streams. When flushed, flies fast and low over the water. Found in the south-eastern coastal belt and the eastern and northern evergreen forests of Southern Africa.

Rarer species:

YELLOW WAGTAIL (*Motacilla flava*) (689)

RICHARD'S PIPIT   *Anthus novaeseelandiae* (692)   p. 288
Afr Gewone koester   *X* i-Cetshu
Z um-Ngcelu

Identification: 16 cm. Above, colour variable but mostly buff to greyish buff. Top of head has dusky streaks; mantle mottled. *Distinct buff eye-stripe. Two outer tail-feathers on either side mainly white.* Below, a buffish white. Chest slightly darker, with distinct blackish spots. Eyes and bill brown; legs yellow-brown. Sexes alike. Subadult more mottled above, since the feathers of the upper parts and wing-coverts have broad whitish edges.

   The commonest pipit; subject to local migration. Spends most of its time on the ground, hardly ever perching on trees or bushes but preferring to sit on upturned sods. Usually crouches when alarmed; difficult to flush. Display-flight a series of dipping undulations, accompanied by a string of repeated notes.

Voice: A loud, double-syllabled '*pip-pip*' or '*chis-sik*'. Simple song uttered during display-flight.

Habitat: Open grassland, preferably short grass near vleis, moist ground and cultivated fields. In the drier regions never found far from permanent water.

Distribution: Throughout Southern Africa.

BUSHVELD PIPIT   *Anthus caffer* (699)   p. 288
   Afr Bosveldkoester

Identification: 14 cm. Above, a tawny brown, broad edges to feathers producing a heavily-streaked effect. Upper tail-coverts more tawny than the back. Outermost tail-feathers of shortish tail mainly white. Below, chin and throat whitish, finely streaked with blackish. *Chest buff, heavily streaked with blackish.* Belly more or less white; flanks streaked and washed with buff. Eyes brown; bill horn-coloured; legs a pale horn-colour. Sexes alike. In the subadult the edges to the feathers of the upper parts are even more tawny.

A common local resident, usually found singly or in pairs. Found mostly on the ground but when flushed darts off with an erratic flight to a nearby tree. Perches freely on trees, from where it calls or sings.

Voice: A bleating '*see-ip*' and a short, twittering song.

Habitat: Prefers open thornveld with short or sparse grass.

Distribution: The north-eastern third of Southern Africa.

Allied species:

NICHOLSON'S PIPIT (*Anthus similis*) (693). 18 cm. Very similar to Richard's Pipit but general appearance a more tawny brown. Can be identified in the hand by the difference in wing-formula. (First primary is not the longest, but is shorter than the second and third.) Tail more blackish; white on outer tail-feathers tinged with buff. Though sometimes found in the same locality as Richard's Pipit it prefers stony, hilly areas with open vegetation. Perches freely on trees, bushes or rocks, calling for long spells. Usually found in pairs. Occurs throughout Southern Africa.

PLAIN-BACKED PIPIT (*Anthus leucophrys*) (694). 16 cm. *Above, a uniform buffish brown;* flight- and tail-feathers darker. Below, more a uniform pale buff, with streaks on the chest indistinct and diffused. Outer tail-feathers a light buff. Truly terrestrial, found in small flocks during the non-breeding season. Prefers open ground with short grass; often found in mountainous country. Occurs in the southern and eastern third of Southern Africa.

BUFFY PIPIT (*Anthus vaalensis*) (695). 18 cm. Very similar to the Plain-backed Pipit, but generally lighter and browner in colour and slightly more heavily-built. Spots on chest more distinct and variable. (Can be identified in the hand by its shorter hind-claw.) When flushed, usually settles for a little while on a small stone or hummock before disappearing into the grass. Sometimes perches on trees or telegraph wires. During the non-breeding season may be found moving about in small, restless flocks. Found in the greater part of Southern Africa, but not in the southern and eastern coastal regions.

STRIPED PIPIT (*Anthus lineiventris*) (696). 19 cm. A large, heavily-marked pipit; an olivaceous brown above and with *yellow-green edges to the wing-coverts, flight- and tail-feathers*. Only the four outer tail-feathers have the inner webs of their apical tips white. The amount of white decreases towards the centre of the tail. *Below: buff, closely and heavily streaked with blackish*, except for the chin and throat. Generally found singly or in pairs on rocky, wooded hillsides, preferably near water. Has a curious habit: will sometimes sit parallel to the branch on which it perches. Found in the eastern and northern parts of Southern Africa, but not along the coast.

ROCK PIPIT (*Anthus crenatus*) (697). 18 cm. Above, a plain buffish brown with a *distinct light eye-stripe*, a faint blackish moustache-stripe and blackish lores. Wing-coverts, primaries and tail-feathers have thin, yellowish outer edges. Below, a light buff, finely streaked on the chin and throat. *Outer tail-feathers tipped not with white but with buff.* Prefers grass-covered hills and mountain slopes. Often perches on rocks, where male often sings, standing very erect and with his beak pointing upwards. Found in the southern and south-western parts of Southern Africa.

YELLOW-BREASTED PIPIT (*Anthus chloris*) (701). 16 cm. Above: buff-brown, heavily streaked and spotted with black. Eye-stripe a pale yellow. *Edge of wing a bright yellow;* wing-coverts and primaries edged with yellow. Outer tail-feathers mainly white. Below, chin to breast yellow; belly whitish; flanks buffish. *The relatively short tail, longish legs and boldly-patterned back* distinguish it from the Yellow Wagtail. Found singly or in pairs in the shortish grass of flats or valleys. Occurs in the inland mountainous regions of south-eastern Southern Africa.

Rarer species:
TREE PIPIT (*Anthus trivialis*) (698)
SHORT-TAILED PIPIT (*Anthus brachyurus*) (700)

ORANGE-THROATED LONGCLAW *Macronyx capensis*
(703)   p. 288
Afr Gewone kalkoentjie   *X* i-Ngilo
Z i-Qomfi

Identification: 20 cm. Above, including flight-feathers and tail, earth-brown. Heavy streaks on top of head and back. Edge of wing a bright orange-yellow. Flight-feathers have a narrow, paler yellow edge. Lores and stripe over eye orange-yellow. The four outer tail-feathers on each side are tipped with white. Below, *chin and throat a bright orange, bordered by a black gorget*. Breast and belly ochre to orange-yellow; flanks earth-brown. Eyes brown; bill a dark brown; legs paler. *Hind claw very long* and slightly curved. Sexes alike, but female has paler chin and throat. Subadult has chin and throat ochre-buff, and blackish spots instead of the black gorget.

A common, conspicuous resident, usually found in pairs. A truly terrestrial bird that only occasionally perches on tufts of grass and low bushes, and is hardly ever seen at any height above the ground. Not very shy: when flushed *flies only a short distance* before settling on the ground again. Flies rather heavily, with whirring wings, often giving a 'mewing' call. *White tips of fanned-out tail-feathers very conspicuous in flight.*

Voice: Gives a melancholy, whistled '*mewing*' call in flight or when perched, and short, lively '*chwirri-chwirri-chwirri-chwee*' on the wing.

Habitat: Open grassveld or grassy patches near perennial water. Also found on grassy hills beside the sea-shore.

Distribution: The eastern half of Southern Africa, but not in the north-eastern coastal regions. Also found in the southern coastal regions.

Allied species:

YELLOW-THROATED LONGCLAW (*Macronyx croceus*) (704). 20 cm. Above, similar to the Orange-throated Longclaw, except that edge of wing and eye-stripe are a bright yellow instead of an orange-yellow, and the edges of the flight- and tail-feathers are yellower and more distinct. *Chin and throat not orange but a bright yellow*; breast to belly a rich yellow. Flanks buff-brown and slightly streaked. Usually found in pairs in open patches in moist areas. Often perches on trees. Much more a bird of the bush than the Orange-throated Longclaw. Found along the south-eastern coastal belt and in the eastern and northern coastal regions.

Rarer species:

PINK-THROATED LONGCLAW (*Macronyx ameliae*) (705)

FÜLLEBORN'S LONGCLAW (*Macronyx fülleborni*)

SHRIKES: Laniidae

The shrikes are a family of medium-sized, conspicuously-coloured birds. They have stout bills, hooked at the tip, and most are insectivorous. The few carnivorous species have a small, toothlike projection behind the hook, and habitually impale part of their prey on thorns or the barbs of wire fences. Their habitats range from dense forest to savanna or desert, and from open plains with scattered trees to cultivated areas. Many species are skulkers and seldom seen, for they find their food in the dense foliage of trees and shrubs. Others perch freely on vantage-points from which they fly down to pounce on their prey on the ground.

Most shrikes are resident, but two species are palaeoarctic migrants. The resident shrikes have loud, clear, specific whistles, by which they can be identified. Their alarm-notes are generally harsh and scolding. A few shrikes have a fairly musical song. All build open, cup-shaped nests and lay speckled eggs.

FISCAL SHRIKE   *Lanius collaris* (707)   p. 289

Afr Fiskaallaksman (Janfiskaal)   *X* um-Xomi
Z   i-Lunga   *S* le-Tzoka

Identification: 23 cm. Top of head, sides of face, ear-coverts and mantle a dull black; scapulars white, *forming a white 'V' on the back*. Rump and upper tail-coverts grey. Wings black, with bases of primaries white. Long, thin, graduated tail black; tail-feathers broadly tipped with white. Below, white. Eyes brown; bill and legs black. Female has chestnut flanks. Sub-adult is ash-brown above; greyish brown below, and finely barred. (*The amount of black and white on the head and in the tail is variable, some birds having a conspicuous white eye-stripe.*)

The commonest and most familiar of the resident shrikes. Usually found singly on telegraph poles and other vantage-points, on the look-out for insects. Usually catches its prey on the ground. Has the habit of impaling part of its prey on thorns, or the barbs of wire fences. Is one of the carnivorous shrikes, and will take small birds, mammals and reptiles as well as insects. Usually carries its prey in its bill, but occasionally in its claws. Very careless about betraying the whereabouts of its nest, the fledglings being particularly noisy when being fed.

Voice: A harsh '*cheee-cheee-cheee*', often repeated. A variety of loud, harsh notes, and sometimes a not unpleasant song. Attempts at imitating other birds are rather poor.

Habitat: Found wherever there are indigenous or exotic trees but not in dense forest. Closely associated with human habitations and cultivated areas.

Distribution: Throughout Southern Africa.

RED-BACKED SHRIKE   *Lanius collurio* (708)   p. 289

Afr Rooiruglaksman

Identification: 18 cm. Adult male: above, narrow band on forehead, lores and ear-coverts black; head, neck and lower back grey; *mantle, scapulars, wing-coverts and inner secondaries chestnut*. Central tail-feathers black; remainder white, with broad black subterminal band. *Below, pinkish*; throat almost white. Eyes brown; bill and legs black. Female has *upper* *parts a dull rufous brown, with a buff eye-stripe*, dark ear-coverts and a lighter rump. *Below, a buffish white, with indistinct brown vermiculations*. Subadult similar to female but more distinctly vermiculated.

A common non-breeding palaeoarctic migrant. Usually found singly, perched on the top of small trees, bushes or fences, on the look-out for insects on the ground. Also sits on the bare lower branches of large trees. Is sometimes seen hovering not far from the ground and just above a spot where it has seen an insect. Wintering birds are sometimes seen.

Voice: Usual call a harsh '*chak-chak*'. Occasionally utters a subdued, warbling song.

Habitat: May be found wherever there are trees, but prefers the open savanna. If the Red-backed and the Fiscal Shrikes are found in the same area the former will inhabit the more densely-wooded parts.

Distribution: Over the greater part of Southern Africa, but not in the south-western regions.

COMMON BOU-BOU SHRIKE *Laniarius ferrugineus* (709) p. 289
Afr Gewone waterlaksman *X* i-Qubusha
Z i-Boboni *S* Pzempzete

Identification: 22 cm. Top of head, sides of face, ear-coverts, back and *relatively short, rounded tail black*, with a slight gloss. Rump buffish. *Wings black, with a white band across and along the wing*. Below, chin to upper belly white or creamy white; lower belly, flanks and under tail-coverts cinnamon-buff. Eyes brown; bill black; legs lead-coloured. Females similar to males but duller. Subadults indistinctly barred above and below; wing-bar buffish.

A common resident, more often heard than seen. Usually found in pairs, creeping about in tangled undergrowth or on the ground in search of insects. Its food includes berries. A skulking but inquisitive bird that will readily investigate any strange noise or alarm-note. Does not perch in the open but is sometimes seen in open glades, or even in gardens, hopping about in search of insects.

Voice: A vast array of duets that vary from place to place and are usually uttered in concealment. The most common is antiphonic: a loud, clear bisyllabic '*koko*' from the male, immediately followed by a '*weet*' from the female. Alarm-note a harsh, grating '*chirrr*'.

Habitat: Prefers tangled bush along water-courses, or any dense cover. Also found on mountain slopes.

Distribution: The north-eastern half of Southern Africa, and also the southern coastal belt. Also found in the far north-western region.

CRIMSON-BREASTED SHRIKE *Laniarius atrococcineus*
(711) p. 289
Afr Rooirborslaksman

Identification: 23 cm. Entire upper side, including tail and sides of face, a glossy blue-black; rump flecked with white. Wing-coverts and outer secondaries have white edges, so that there is a distinct *white bar along the wing*. Flight-feathers dusky. Below, *chin to under tail-coverts crimson*. Eyes brown; bill and legs black. Sexes alike. Subadult a dull black above, ash-grey below, and finely barred. The first feathers to become crimson are the under tail-coverts.

A common resident species, usually found singly or in pairs. Spends much time on the ground, hopping about in search of insects, and therefore readily seen. Inquisitive and not very shy, easily attracted if an alarm-call is given.

Voice: A loud clear whistling '*plip-plip*', repeated several times. Also has a number of duet-calls.

Habitat: The drier acacia thornveld, preferably regions in which there is dense, matted cover.

Distribution: The central and western northern half of Southern Africa.

PUFF-BACKED SHRIKE *Dryoscopus cubla* (712) p. 289
Afr Sneeuballaksman   *X* in-Taklembila
Z um-Hhlopekazi

Identification: 16 cm. Adult male: top of head, sides of face, mantle, scapulars and *short tail* a glossy blue-black. Wing-coverts, flight-feathers and edges of scapulars white. Rump mainly white, with a little grey. Remainder of underparts pure white. *Eyes red or orange*; bill black; legs slate-grey. Female a duller black above; lores and ear-coverts whitish; rump and underparts washed with buff. Subadult resembles female but is browner above, and more rust-coloured below and on the rump.

A common resident, usually found in pairs, hunting for insects in the foliage of large trees and creeping about in the branches. Often joins mixed bird-parties. Also catches insects on the wing. During the heavy display-flight of the male his wings make a buzzing, crackling sound. When a male is excited or displaying, the long, hair-like feathers of his back and rump are puffed out, almost enveloping the bird, and giving him the appearance of a snowball.

Voice: A loud, clear, bisyllabic whistle: '*chip-whee, chip-whee, chip-whee*', repeated a number of times, and often followed by a snapping sound. Alarm-note '*chak*', followed by a harsh '*skurr*'.

Habitat: Light bush and open savanna, as well as riverine forest. Sometimes also found near human habitations.

Distribution: The north-eastern half of Southern Africa and the south-eastern coastal belt.

BLACK-CROWNED SHRIKE   *Tchagra senegala* (715)   p. 289
   Afr Swartkroonlaksman   *X* um-Gupane
   Z i-Nqupane

Identification: 22 cm. Above, *top of head to nape and stripe through eye black*; stripe above the eye and face buff; mantle brown; rump a greyish brown; *wing-coverts and edges of primaries chestnut*. Scapulars and secondaries black with chestnut edges. Central tail-feathers ashy and distinctly barred; remaining tail-feathers black with white tips. Below, a creamy white; flanks and chest washed with grey. Eyes hazel; bill black; legs brown. Sexes alike. Subadult has a dull brownish black on head, and a horn-coloured bill.

A common resident, usually found singly or in pairs. Spends most of its time creeping about in dense vegetation, not far from the ground, in search of insects. Is sometimes seen on the ground. Flies low and with a hurried, heavy flight, from one tree to another. As it dives into cover, the chestnut on its wings and the white tips of its tail-feathers are conspicuous. Not particularly shy.

Voice: Alarm-call a prolonged '*chyrr*'. Normal call a loud, clear, from four- to six-syllabled whistle, variously rendered, e.g. as '*What did you DO that for?*' etc. Duet-calls not often heard.

Habitat: Prefers thorn bushes and areas with smaller trees. Often found in built-up areas.

Distribution: The north-eastern half of Southern Africa, and along the south-eastern coastal belt.

ORANGE-BREASTED SHRIKE   *Malaconotus*
   sulphureopectus (719)   p. 289
   Afr Oranjeborslaksman

Identification: 19 cm. Adult male: above, forehead yellow but becoming a greenish yellow towards the crown. Crown to mantle grey. Rump, wings and tail green; tail-feathers, secondaries and innermost primaries tipped with yellow. Lores to ear-coverts blackish; *eye-stripe yellow*. Below, a bright canary-yellow, except for *orange breast*. Eyes brown; bill and legs black. Female has sides of face greyish, not blackish. Subadult: forehead sides of face, eye-stripe and crown to nape grey, spotted with whitish. Wing-coverts tipped with yellowish. Flight- and tail-feathers have yellow edges. Below, whitish and yellow; chest has an orange wash and is more or less barred.

A not uncommon species, usually found in pairs. Less shy than most other shrikes. A rather slim-looking bird, often seen hopping about in the upper-level foliage of large trees, hunting for insects. Surprisingly inconspicuous, in spite of its bright colouring and often overlooked. Its presence is usually betrayed by its loud call.

Voice: A melancholy trisyllabic whistle '*who-who-whee*', with the last note slightly higher. This call is monotonously repeated, but the pitch of the whistle is sometimes altered. Also utters a liquid '*poo-poo-poo-poo*' and a harsh, grating alarm-note.

Habitat: Riverine forest and tangled thorn.

Distribution: The north-eastern half of Southern Africa and the south-eastern coastal belt.

GORGEOUS SHRIKE *Malaconotus quadricolor* (721)   p. 289
Afr Rooikeellaksman   *Z* u-Gongoni

Identification: 19 cm. Adult male: above, forehead and eye-stripe orange-yellow. Lores and thin black line running from under eyes and ear-coverts along sides of neck, black. Top of head to upper tail-coverts green. Flight-feathers blackish, with green edges. Tail black, except for the two central tail-feathers, which are finely barred and greenish, with blackish tips. *Below, chin and throat scarlet, with a broad black chest-band.* Breast, belly and under tail-coverts have a cinnamon-brown wash; breast slightly stained with scarlet. Flanks green. Eyes brown; bill black and legs slate-blue. Female similar to male but has sides of face a greenish yellow, throat scarlet and yellow and only a slight black chest-band. Tail not black but green. Subadult similar to female but has a yellow chin and throat, is finely barred with blackish and has no chest-band.

A not uncommon resident species, but so shy and retiring that it is rarely seen. Usually found in pairs. Territorial, and very hard to spot as they creep about in tangled bush, looking for insects. Seldom if ever found on the ground. Can be enticed to show themselves for a moment if their loud, distinctive whistle is imitated.

Voice: A loud, clear whistle '*kong-kong-koit*', often hard to locate.

Habitat: Dense riverine forest and low, matted thorn.

Distribution: In the more easterly regions of Southern Africa and all along the eastern coastal belt.

BOKMAKIERIE SHRIKE *Malaconotus zeylonus* (722)   p. 289
Afr Bokmakierielaksman (Bokmakierie)   *X* i-Ngqwani
S Pjempjete

Identification: 23 cm. Top of head to hind neck, sides of neck and ear-coverts an ashy grey. Eye-stripe yellow; lores and broadish line down side of neck black. Remaining upper parts green. Flight-feathers dusky, with green edges. Two central tail-feathers blackish, with a greenish wash and faintly barred; *remaining tail-feathers black, with broad yellow tips.* Below, *chin and throat bright yellow, with a broad black chest-band.* Rest of underparts sulphur-yellow; flanks washed with grey. Eyes brown; bill black; legs lead-coloured. Sexes alike. Subadult a greyish green above; throat a dirty white; rest of underparts a light buff, washed with yellowish and faintly barred; tail similar to that of adult.

A common, conspicuous, resident species. Usually found in pairs in more open country. Terrestrial in habits; often seen running about on the ground (always near sheltering trees), searching for insects. When the birds are giving their familiar duet-calls they sit within sight of one another, on the highest available perches. Fly low; black tail with broad yellow terminal band very conspicuous in flight.

Voice: Several loud, clear, whistled duets: *'bokmakierie'*, *'ko-ko-veet'*, etc. Alarm-note a softish *'tok-tok-tok'* or *'kwirrr-kirrr-kirrrr'*.

Habitat: Open savanna and scattered patches of bush. Also found in gardens and exotic plantations.

Distribution: The southern half and western coastal regions of Southern Africa, but not along the eastern coastal belt.

GREY-HEADED SHRIKE   *Malaconotus hypopyrrhus*
(723)   p. 289
Afr Spooklaksman   *X* u-Bamho
Z   u-Hlaza

Identification: 26 cm. *Top of head, sides of face and upper mantle grey;* lores white. Rest of upper parts green, tail included; wing-coverts and tail-feathers tipped with pale yellow. Flight-feathers dusky, edged with pale yellow. Below, a bright yellow; chest and breast washed with cinnamon. Eyes yellow; *heavy, hooked bill black;* legs brownish. Sexes alike. Subadult similar to adult but has a horn-coloured bill.

A *large*, somewhat uncommon resident species, found singly or in pairs searching for food in the foliage of large trees. Sometimes hunts on the ground and hawks from a perch. Often seen flying clumsily from one tree to another. Chiefly insectivorous, but will also take small birds, rodents and snakes.

Voice: An eerie, protracted, mournful whistle *'hooo-whoee'*, often heard during the hottest part of the day when other birds are silent. Also has a rattling call and a harsh, rasping alarm-call.

Habitat: Prefers riverine forest.

Distribution: The north-eastern third of Southern Africa and the southeastern coastal belt.

MAGPIE SHRIKE   *Corvinella melanoleuca* (724)   p. 289
Afr Langstertlaksman   *Z* i-Kongqeli
Ts mo-Tziloli

Identification: 41–50 cm. Top of head, mantle, wings and *long, graduated* *tail black. Scapulars and lower back white.* Flight-feathers tipped and spotted with white. Below, wholly black. Eyes brown; bill and legs black. Sexes alike. Subadult generally browner; lower back grey instead of white.

A common, conspicuous, resident species, usually found in small parties. Sit on the outer branches of trees, from which they pounce on insects and reptiles on the ground. Notwithstanding their long tails, their dipping flight is fast and straight. When displaying, raise the white feathers on the lower back like the Puffbacked Shrike. Very noisy and often call in chorus. **Voice:** A loud, '*too-wheep-toorl-wlioo*' and a higher-pitched '*see-er-ah*'. Alarm-call a harsh, scolding note.
Habitat: Thornveld savanna.
Distribution: The northern two-thirds of Southern Africa.

WHITE HELMET SHRIKE   *Prionops plumata* (727)   p. 289
    Afr Withelmlaksman   *Z* m-Timbazane
Identification: 20 cm. Head and *short crest of straight bristles greyish.* Blackish patch behind ear-coverts. Distinct white collar on hind neck. Mantle black, with slight greenish gloss; wings black. White tips to wing-coverts and white edges and tips to secondaries form a conspicuous white bar along the folded wing. White spots on primaries. Tail black; outermost feathers white; remainder tipped with white. Below, white, except for the chin and throat, which are greyish. *Eyes yellow, surrounded by yellow eye-wattle;* bill black; legs orange. Sexes alike. Subadults have brownish heads.

A common, resident, social species. Always found in parties of up to a dozen birds. Often join mixed bird-parties. Silent when flying from tree to tree but begin to chatter as soon as they start foraging for insects. Often drop to the ground to pick up food. As these birds follow one another or flit gracefully about their bold black-and-white flight-pattern is unmistakable. Extremely gregarious, nesting together and even sharing the incubation and feeding of the young.
Voice: A communal chattering and much bill-snapping. Normal alarm-note a low-pitched '*chow-chow*' that has considerable carrying power.
Habitat: Open woodland and acacia savanna.
Distribution: The north-eastern half and far northern parts of Southern Africa.

BRUBRU SHRIKE   *Nilaus afer* (731)   p. 289
    Afr Bontroklaksman
Identification: 15 cm. Adult male: above, forehead and stripe over eye white. Top of head a slightly glossy blue-black. Hind neck, mantle, scapulars and rump a mixed blue-black and white. Flight-feathers blackish. Broad white edges of secondaries and white tips of wing-coverts form a broad

272

PLATE 31

WARBLERS, CROMBEC, GRASSBIRD AND CISTICOLAS

1 **GARDEN WARBLER** *page* 235
Nondescript plump-looking bird.

2 **AFRICAN MARSH WARBLER** 236
No distinct eye stripe; light coloured legs.

3 **RATTLING CISTICOLA** 245
Pale rufous crown, blotched above.

4 **WILLOW WARBLER** 236
Distinct eye stripe, breast yellowish.

5 **GREY-BACKED WARBLER** 239
Wings green; crown, nape and back grey.

6 **NEDDICKY CISTICOLA** 245
Crown rufous, underparts greyish.

7 **YELLOW-BELLIED WARBLER** 236
Lower belly yellow; trace of white round the eye.

8 **GRASSBIRD** 237
Longish tail ragged-looking; tail feathers pointed, rufous head with distinct black markings.

9 **LE VAILLANT'S CISTICOLA** 246
Back blotched with black.

10 **FAN-TAILED CISTICOLA** 244
Rump rufous, chest unspotted, tail short.

11 **CLOUD CISTICOLA** 244
Tail very short, chest spotted.

12 **LARGER BARRED WARBLER** 237
Underparts barred neatly with blackish.

13 **RUFOUS-BELLIED CROMBEC** 238
Extremely short tail, bill longish and curved.

14 **CROAKING CISTICOLA** 246
Crown and hindneck streaked; crown *not* rufous. Large size unmistakable.

PLATE 32

FLYCATCHERS

1 **CAPE FLYCATCHER** *page 252*
Both male and female have rufous flanks.

2 **PARADISE FLYCATCHER** 254
Body colour reddish-brown, head bluish. Tail very long.

3 **CHINSPOT FLYCATCHER** 253
White flanks.

4 **COMMON TIT-BABBLER** 251
Under tail-coverts rufous, throat streaked and outer tail feathers
have white tips.

5 **FISCAL FLYCATCHER** 252
Centre tail feather black. Fanned tail shows broad terminal black
band.

6 **SPOTTED FLYCATCHER** 250
Breast finely streaked.

7 **FAIRY FLYCATCHER** 253
Thin white wing-bar, belly white with pink centre.

8 **BLUE-MANTLED FLYCATCHER** 254
Crest blue-black, broadish white wing bars.

9 **MARICO FLYCATCHER** 251
Breast whitish.

white longitudinal band on the folded wing. Tail blue-black; all except the central pair of tail-feathers have white tips and a certain amount of white on the outer webs. Below: sides of face, chin to under tail-coverts white; *sides of breast and flanks chestnut*. Eyes a reddish brown; bill black; legs slate. Female similar to male but is a dull, brownish black instead of a glossy blue-black. Subadult similar to female but mottled above; cheeks, throat and breast not barred but narrowly streaked.

This smallish shrike with the *relatively short tail* is a common resident, and is usually found in pairs, hopping about on the branches of trees and looking for insects among the leaves. Hunts like a tit, regularly giving its call. Often seen as a member of a mixed bird-party.

Voice: Bird derives its name from its clear, flute-like whistle: '*broo-broo-broo-broo*'. Also a '*kir-r-r-r*' that can be heard from afar.

Habitat: Prefers dry acacia veld and open bush.

Distribution: The northern two-thirds of Southern Africa.

Allied species:

LESSER GREY SHRIKE (*Lanius minor*) (706). 22 cm. Forehead, forecrown, lores and sides of face black. *Crown and back grey*. Wing-coverts and flight-feathers black; basal third of primaries white. Central pair of tail-feathers black; others black and white. Below, white; breast and flanks pinkish. A common palaeoarctic migrant, usually found singly, sitting on some exposed perch and catching its prey on the ground. Flight is much faster than that of the local shrikes. Found in the northern half of Southern Africa.

TCHAGRA SHRIKE (*Tchagra tchagra*) (713). 22 cm. *Top of head and back a dusky brown. Conspicuous white line over the eye, and a black line through it*. Wing-coverts and edges of flight-feathers chestnut. Central pair of tail-feathers ash-grey and finely streaked; remainder black, with white ends. Entire underside a greyish slate, with chin, throat and sides of face paler. A fairly common species, usually found in pairs, creeping about on the ground or in the lower parts of trees or bushes. A reluctant flier. Found in the southern parts of Southern Africa, and the south-eastern coastal regions.

THREE-STREAKED SHRIKE (*Tchagra australis*) (714). 20 cm. Top of head and back earth-brown (back paler). Like the Tchagra shrike it has a conspicuous black line through the eye, and a light buffish line above it, but this species also has a *narrow black line above the buffish line*. *Wing-coverts and flight-feathers a paler chestnut* than those of the previous species, but tail is similar. This slender-looking shrike is usually found in pairs, feeding on the ground. When disturbed, darts into cover near the ground During the breeding season the male flies just above the trees, with quivering wings, and then floats down whistling a melodious string of notes '*tui-tui-tui-*

tui . . .' on a descending scale. Generally found in the thornveld of the northern half of Southern Africa.

OLIVE SHRIKE (*Malaconotus olivaceous*) (717). 18 cm. *Two distinct phases.* (A) *Above*, a uniform moss-green; tail black, with all the outer tail-feathers broadly tipped and edged with yellow. Forehead and lores yellow. Line through eye and ear-coverts black. Chin to upper belly a yellowish cinnamon-brown; flanks and under tail-coverts sulphur-yellow. (B) Above: *forehead, crown and nape dark grey*; rest of back moss-green. Tail black and green; all the outer tail-feathers show only signs of yellow. Forehead and lores a light buff; line through eye and ear-coverts black, with a *thin whitish line above, and traces of white below the black ear-coverts.* Chin to breast a light cinnamon-brown; belly and under tail-coverts whitish; flanks washed with pale green. A furtive bird, usually found in pairs in the larger trees, along the south-eastern coastal belt and in the eastern and northern coastal regions of Southern Africa.

WHITE-TAILED SHRIKE (*Lanioturdus torquatus*) (726). 14 cm. Top of head black and white; back grey; wings black and white with a distinctive white patch on the folded wing. Flight-feathers tipped with white. *Short tail wholly white*, except for two black subterminal spots on the two central tail-feathers. Below, chin to chest white: broadish black band across the chest. Centre of breast, belly and under tail-coverts white; rest of underside grey. A shy and restless bird, found in pairs or small parties foraging for insects in trees or on the ground. Flies slowly and never covers long distances. Prefers open thornveld, and is found only in the far north-western parts of Southern Africa.

BLACK HELMET SHRIKE (*Prionops retzii*) (728). 23 cm. *Entire head, and underside to belly a glossy blue-black.* Back earth-brown. Flight-feathers blackish, with white spots on primaries. Tail-feathers tipped with white. Lower belly black and white; under tail-coverts white. *Yellow eye encircled by orange-red wattle*; *bill orange-red.* A common, social species, usually found in flocks of up to twelve. Active, noisy birds, continually chattering and snapping their bills. Found mostly in the larger trees of the north-eastern and central northern regions of Southern Africa.

WHITE-CROWNED SHRIKE (*Eurocephalus anguitimens*) (730). 24 cm. *Top of head to hind neck white;* chin to belly also. Lores, ear-coverts and sides of neck blackish. Back and belly ash-brown. Wings and tail a dark brown. This large, conspicuous shrike is usually seen perched on the outermost branches of trees, and catches most of its food on the ground. Found in small parties, scattered about within calling distance of one another. Their flight is straight, with short, rapid wing-beats, and they usually call when flying off. Found in the more open bush country. Distributed over most of the northern half of Southern Africa except the north-eastern coastal regions.

Rarer species:

WESTERN BOU-BOU SHRIKE (*Laniarius bicolor*) (710)

MARSH SHRIKE (*Tchagra minuta*) (716).

BLACK-FRONTED SHRIKE (*Malaconotus multicolor*) (720)

YELLOW-SPOTTED NICATOR (*Nicator chloris*) (725)

CHESTNUT-FRONTED HELMET SHRIKE (*Prionops scopifrons*) (729)

TROPICAL BOU-BOU SHRIKE (*Laniarius aethiopicus*) (709f)

SOUZA'S SHRIKE (*Lanius souzae*)

STARLINGS: Sturnidae

Starlings are medium-sized birds, most of whom are gregarious. They usually have strong, longish, slightly arched bills and fairly long, well-developed legs. The plumage of most of the species has a brilliant metallic sheen, in which blue and green predominate. They are noisy and conspicuous birds, and strong fliers. Some species are subject to local migration. They feed mainly on insects and fruit. Although they do a certain amount of damage to cultivated fruit this does not outweigh their value in controlling locust and insect numbers. Most nest in holes.

WATTLED STARLING   *Creatophora cinerea* (735)   p. 288

     Afr Vaalspreeu   *X* u-Wambu

     Z i-Ntetengwane   *S* le-Fokori

Identification: 22 cm. Adult male in *non-breeding dress*: general colour grey; rump usually paler. Whole head feathered, except for the shortish bare black streaks on either side of the throat. Flight- and tail-feathers black, with a slight greenish gloss. Primary wing-coverts white, forming a *distinct white patch on the folded wing*. Secondary coverts whitish in some cases. *Breeding dress*: top of head, face, chin and throat bare and black, *with black wattles on centre of crown, forehead and throat. Bare skin behind eye and on hind crown yellow*. Eyes a dark brown; bill pinkish; legs brown. Female similar to male in non-breeding dress but has no white patch on wing. Rump distinctly whitish. Subadult browner above.

A highly gregarious species that roams about restlessly in small parties or enormous flocks. Their irregular local movements depend on the food-supply, which consists chiefly of locusts. Large flocks perform remarkable aerial manoeuvres. Nest in large colonies, where their untidy stick-nests are crowded together in thorn-trees—usually near hatching locusts. In flight

the dark wings and tails and light rumps are unmistakable. Catch their prey on the ground as well as in the air.
Voice: A rather silent bird. Has a rasping, squeaky whistle and a short, subdued, rasping song. The noise made by the fledglings at a nesting-colony is shattering.
Habitat: Open savanna.
Distribution: Throughout Southern Africa.

PLUM-COLOURED STARLING   *Cinnyricinclus leucogaster*
   (736)   p. 288
   Afr Witborsspreeu
Identification: 18 cm. Adult male: entire head, chin to chest, back, wing-coverts, innermost secondaries and central tail-feathers a metallic violet-plum, shot with bronze. Rest of flight-feathers and tail black. *Chest to under tail-coverts white.* Eyes yellow; bill and legs black. Female mottled above with black and tawny; slightly rufous on head and wings; inner webs of flight-feathers a light chestnut. Below, white or buff and white, *heavily streaked and blobbed with blackish.* Subadult similar to adult female.

These beautiful starlings are gregarious when not breeding. They normally use natural holes, but sometimes also woodpecker or barbet holes, for nesting. Irregular in their movements, moving from place to place as berries and wild fruit ripen. Often the larger flocks consist mainly of females and subadults, with only a few adult males, and the smaller flocks mainly of adult males. They have an exceedingly swift flight, some-times hawking insects in the air. Rarely seen on the ground.
Voice: A soft, melodious, slurred whistle: *'tipu-tipu-teeeuu'*.
Habitat: Riverine forest and thick woodland during the breeding season, but otherwise found in the more open bush.
Distribution: The north-eastern half and far north-western regions of Southern Africa.

CAPE STARLING   *Lamprotornis nitens* (737)   p. 288
   Afr Gewone glansspreeu   *X* i-Byahili
   Z i-Kwezi
Identification: 25 cm. Entire plumage glossy. Head, including ear-coverts, steel-blue; rump, upper tail-coverts and tail violet-blue; rest of body a greenish blue. The bronze wing-shoulder and black subterminal spots on the wing-coverts are not readily seen in the field. Primaries blackish. *Eyes a bright orange;* bill and legs black. Sexes alike. Subadults duller; *eyes not orange but a dark grey.*

A fairly common species, usually seen singly or in pairs but also in *small loose parties.* Often seen on the ground; fly up and settle in the tree-tops when disturbed. Sometimes hawk insects in the air.

Voice: A fairly low-pitched '*turr-weeoo*'. Sings throughout the year, a slow, continuous series of warbled and whistled phrases. Does not as a rule sing in chorus.
Habitat: Mainly acacia thornveld.
Distribution: The greater part of Southern Africa but not in the far south-westerly regions.

BURCHELL'S STARLING *Lamprotornis australis*
(743)   p. 288
Afr Grootglansspreeu
Identification: 33 cm. Above, top of head to nape a metallic green. Ear-coverts and patch below eye a dark purple; hind neck and rump purple; remainder of upper side a metallic green. Wing-coverts have black sub-terminal spots. Wing-shoulders bronze. *Long, graduated tail purple, with underlying blackish bars.* Below, chin to breast a metallic green; belly purple. Eyes brown; bill and legs black. Sexes alike, but female is smaller. Subadult duller and browner below.

A large starling, found singly, in pairs or in flocks. Although its plumage is mainly a metallic green, the purple sheen predominates in the field, giving the impression of a purplish-black bird and not a bluish-green one like the Cape Starling. Feeds mainly on the ground, walking about in a crow-like manner. *Flies heavily, with a slow flapping of its broad wings.* In flight the long, *wedge-shaped tail* is unmistakable. Large flocks perform aerial manoeuvres before settling down to roost.
Voice: A loud, harsh, but not unmusical song. Very noisy when roosting.
Habitat: Large trees in bush country. Prefers the drier regions.
Distribution: The south-eastern, central and north-western parts of the northern half of Southern Africa.

RED-WINGED STARLING *Onychognathus morio* (745)   p. 288
Afr Rooivlerkspreeu   *Z* in-Somi
Identification: 28 cm. Adult male: general colour above and below a glossy blue-black. Tail blackish, with a slight greenish sheen. *Primaries chestnut, with blackish tips.* Eyes a dark brown; heavy bill and legs black. *Female has whole head and neck grey, with blue-black streaks, and breast streaked with grey;* otherwise similar to male. Subadults a sooty black, head included.

A common species, occurring as resident pairs, small straggling parties or large roving flocks. They have a dipping flight, in the course of which their melancholy whistle is constantly heard. In flight the *large chestnut window* is characteristic. In some areas these starlings cause a certain amount of damage to cultivated fruit.
Voice: A plaintive, long-drawn-out '*chi-wheeoo*'. Song a variety of warbled, whistled phrases. Alarm-call a harsh, jarring '*tchorr*'.

Habitat: Mountainous and hilly country. Also built-up areas, where they nest on the ledges of the taller buildings.

Distribution: The eastern half of Southern Africa and also the southernmost tip, but not found in the north-eastern coastal regions.

PIED STARLING   *Spreo bicolor* (746)   p. 288

Afr Witgatspreeu   *X* i-Giyogiyo
Z i-Gwayigwayi   *S* le-Holi

Identification: 25 cm. General colour above and below a dark earth-brown with a slight bronzy sheen, except for the tail, which has a greenish sheen. *Lower belly and under tail-coverts white, or buffish white.* Inner webs of flight-feathers a light ash-colour. Eyes a pale yellow; bill black, *gape yellow*; legs black. Sexes alike. Subadult duller; wing-coverts and secondaries have narrow whitish edges; base of bill buff.

A gregarious species, feeding mostly on the ground. Usually seen walking about, characteristically upright, among grazing cattle or in cultivated fields. Look black and white in the field. Nest in colonies in holes in sandbanks or in the walls of old mine-shafts. Sometimes congregate in very large numbers to roost in reed-beds.

Voice: A rather weak '*gwah-i, gwah-i*', repeated several times when bird is on the wing. Alarm-note a harsh, grating hiss.

Habitat: Open veld, especially where there are scattered trees (exotics included). Never found in thick bush or forest.

Distribution: The southern third and the central and eastern parts of Southern Africa, but not in the eastern coastal regions.

Allied species:

EUROPEAN STARLING (*Sturnus vulgaris*) (733). 20 cm. *Iridescent and spotted all over*, with a violet-green sheen predominating above and a blueblack sheen below. Flight- and tail-feathers ashy, edged and tipped with blackish. A common and familiar bird, found mostly in towns and villages, stalking about on the ground in small flocks or raiding fruit-trees. Gather in large flocks to roost on buildings or in tall trees, creating a terrific din that may be kept up all night. Introduced at the turn of the century and found only in the southernmost tip of Southern Africa.

INDIAN MYNA (*Acridotheres tristis*) (734). 24 cm. Whole head and neck a glossy black; back and chest to belly a rufous brown. Under tail- and under wing-coverts white. Flight-feathers blackish; basal half of primaries and primary wing-coverts white (*seen in flight as large, distinct white windows*). Tail black, tipped with white. *Bill, bare skin around the eyes, and legs a bright yellow.* Dependent on human habitations. Usually found in pairs or small parties during the day, in gardens, parks or market-places, but gather in larger numbers to roost and can then be very noisy, like the

European Starling. Introduced at the turn of the century and found mainly in the south-eastern coastal regions, but has begun to spread inland to the larger cities in small numbers.

GREATER BLUE-EARED STARLING (*Lamprotornis chalybaeus*) (738). 22 cm. General colour an iridescent blue-green. *Ear-coverts* and belly *violet-blue*. Lores black; eyes a bright orange. The magenta and bronze wing-shoulders are not conspicuous in the field. Black terminal spots on wing-coverts form distinct black spots on the folded wing. Similar to and of the same size as the Cape Starling, but the *violet blue ear-coverts form a strong contrast to the greenish colour of the head.* Found mostly on the ground. Fly off with a noisy swish of the wings. Gather in large flocks when not breeding. Found in the eastern and central northern regions of Southern Africa.

BLACK-BELLIED STARLING (*Lamprotornis corruscus*) (740). 19 cm. Top of head to nape a glossy blue-black; chin to breast a glossy green. Ear-coverts and rump a glossy violet. Flight- and tail-feathers blackish; *belly black*. No bronze shoulder-patch or black spots on the wing. A gregarious species found mainly in dense indigenous coastal bush. Noisy and conspicuous birds, flocks keeping up a continuous melodious chattering while feeding or at rest. Found in the south-eastern, eastern and northern coastal regions of Southern Africa.

LONG-TAILED STARLING (*Lamprotornis mevesii*) (742). 36 cm. Head, back and *very long graduated tail* have a purple sheen. Chin to breast a metallic green, shot with violet. Rump and belly purple with an old gold sheen; wings blackish, shot with green. A rather tame bird, usually seen in small flocks, feeding on the ground or flying about amongst the larger trees. Found in the central northern, and central eastern parts of Southern Africa.

PALE-WINGED STARLING (*Onychognathus nabouroup*) (744). 25 cm. A glossy blue-black all over, with a slight greenish sheen on the head. Basal two-thirds of primaries a light chestnut, seen as *large whitish windows in flight. Eyes a golden yellow or orange*, not dark brown like those of the Red-winged Starling. Found in flocks or small parties, usually in mountainous or hilly country. Occur in the more arid parts of the western third of Southern Africa, but not in the southernmost tip.

Rarer species:
LESSER BLUE-EARED STARLING (*Lamprotornis chloropterus*) (739)

SHARP-TAILED STARLING (*Lamprotornis acuticaudus*) (741)

OXPECKERS: Buphagidae

Oxpeckers are medium-sized birds with longish, slender tails, and are peculiar to Africa. Their relatively heavy bills are admirably suited to pulling ticks (their principal food) off animals. Their claws are strongly curved and very sharp, enabling them to cling to the skin of large game and domestic animals. They clamber all over these animals in every and any kind of posture, hopping about sideways, dropping forwards or backwards and with heads up or down. When resting, these birds squat on their tarsi. In pulling off ticks they sometimes cause wounds; these they may keep open by continually pecking at them. Nest in holes in trees or rock crevices; if not disturbed may roost under the eaves of farm buildings. Owing to the use of pesticides in combating ticks, these birds have been virtually exterminated except in the game reserves.

RED-BILLED OXPECKER   *Buphagus erythrorhynchus* (748)   p. 288
  Afr Rooibekrenostervoël   *X* i-Hlalanyati
  Z   isi-Hlalanyati   *S* Tsomi

Identification: 20 cm. Above, including wings, tail and rump, a uniform dark greyish brown. Below, chin to upper chest also a dark greyish brown; rest of underparts a pale greyish buff. *Eyes yellow to red; narrow wattle round the eye yellow; whole bill a waxy red;* legs blackish. Sexes alike. Subadult a more sooty brown above; and bill red only at the base, the rest being olive-yellow.

A common species, usually found in small parties and associated with the larger animals. Several hundreds are sometimes found with large herds of buffalo. If alarmed, move out of sight to the far side of the animal, or peer over the animal's back with upraised bill, giving a hissing alarm-note. Roost in flocks in reed-beds or trees.

Voice: A hissing '*tsssss*' or '*churrr*'; a '*tzik, tzik*'; and a shrill twittering, usually uttered in flight.

Habitat: Always found in association with the larger animals, and preferably in open thornveld.

Distribution: Mainly the eastern half of Southern Africa.

Allied species:

YELLOW-BILLED OXPECKER (*Buphagus africanus*) (747). 23 cm. Very similar to the Red-Billed Oxpecker, except that *the rump is a pale greyish buff*, like the belly (and not a dark greyish brown, like the back). Owing to the broad base of the lower mandible *the bill is heavier, and the basal part bright yellow, only the tip being red*. The eyes are a bright orange or scarlet, and *there is no eye-wattle*. Their call is a repeated '*tzirr-zurrp*', and is usually given as they fly off after having been disturbed. Not as common as the Red-billed Oxpecker. Also associated with the larger animals and found in the drier parts of the central and northern regions of Southern Africa.

SUGARBIRDS: Promeropidae

The sugarbirds are the only family of birds peculiar to Southern Africa. The non-metallic plumage of these medium-sized birds is dun-coloured, except for their under tail-coverts, which are a light lemon-yellow. They have long, thin, slightly down-curved bills and elongated tail-feathers. They are usually associated with protea bushes and trees, and suck the nectar from their flowers. Their main diet, however, consists of insects. Their nests are cup-shaped, not closed like those of the sunbirds.

CAPE SUGARBIRD   *Promerops cafer* (749)   p. 304
   Afr Kaapse suikerbosvoël

Identification: Male, 43 cm; female 23–28 cm. Adult male: forehead and crown buff, finely streaked with brown. Rest of upper parts a dusky brown, with olivaceous streaks, except for the rump, which is a yellowish green. Wings a dusky brown, with olivaceous edges; tail dusky. Below, chin and throat whitish; moustache-stripe blackish; chest and breast a slightly russet brown; belly and flanks whitish, streaked with dark brown. *Under tail-coverts lemon-yellow*. Eyes brown; bill and legs black. Sexes alike, except that the female has a much shorter tail. Subadult similar to female but browner above and less streaked on the flanks.

A locally common bird, seen in pairs during the winter months, which are their breeding season, but in small parties during the non-breeding season. The males are often seen perched on the tops of bushes, with their *long tails* blown about in the wind, calling and singing; now and again dashing off after other males intruding on their territory. During courtship the male performs a curious aerial dance over the nesting site. This display is accompanied by violent wing-clapping, and the long tail-feathers held over the back twist and turn during the performance. Their normal flight is straight and swift, and their tails are held straight out behind them. Spend much time hawking insects in the air.

Voice: A chattering, buzzing song, like that of the weavers. Alarm-notes a number of explosive '*chicks*', interspersed with chattering sounds.

Habitat: Only where proteas grow, and mainly on mountain slopes.

Distribution: The southernmost tip of Southern Africa.

Allied species:

GURNEY'S SUGARBIRD (*Promerops gurneyi*) (750). 23–28 cm. Similar to the Cape Sugarbird but much smaller, having the *forehead and crown a dark russet and the russet-brown from chest to belly much more decided.* Moustache-stripe usually very faint. Habits similar to those of the previous species; also dependent on proteas. Found inland, in the mountainous areas of the south-eastern and eastern parts of Southern Africa.

SUNBIRDS: Nectariniidae

Sunbirds are small birds with long, more or less curved bills, the fine points of which are used to puncture the tubes of certain flowers, so that the nectar that cannot be reached from the front may be extracted. Their tubular tongues can be slightly protruded. They feed on insects as well as nectar. In most species the males have a brilliant metallic plumage and the females are plain and drab. Female sunbirds are extremely difficult to identify in the field—in fact the males with whom they associate are the best clue to their identity. The males of some species have a female-like non-breeding dress, and a few subadult males assume an intermediate dress before putting on full breeding plumage. The males have yellow or orange pectoral tufts that are visible only when fanned out during court-ship displays, or when the birds are greatly excited. Their flight is swift and erratic, their wing-beats very fast. The usual song of most species is strident and very high-pitched. They sometimes utter a melodious warble, but this is so soft that it is heard only at close quarters. Sunbirds build oval closed nests with an entrance near the top. These are usually slung from the end of a drooping branch. Many of the species can best be observed if one watches flowering trees and waits for the birds to put in an appearance.

MALACHITE SUNBIRD   *Nectarinia famosa* (751)   p. 304

Afr Jangroentjiesuikerbekkie (Jangroentjie)   *X* i-Ncuncu

Z   i-Ncwincwi   *S* Taletale

Identification: Male 24 cm; female 15 cm. Adult male in breeding plumage: above, *entire head, neck and back a metallic green* washed with gold; upper tail-coverts a metallic emerald-green; wings and tail black. Secondaries have a blue sheen; the *two central tail-feathers are elongated* and the basal half is edged with a metallic emerald-green. Below, breast to belly a metallic golden-green; bluish under tail-coverts tipped with green. Pectoral tufts bright yellow. Eyes brown; bill and legs black. Adult female has sides of face and upper parts, including wings, an olivaceous brown. Short tail blackish. Slight eye-stripe whitish; moustache-stripe a pale yellow. Below, a mottled dusky yellow. Male in non-breeding plumage similar to female except that he retains his metallic upper wing- and tail-coverts and rump, as well as his black flight-feathers and two elongated tail-feathers. Subadult similar to female but greener above and more yellow below.

A common, conspicuous species that does not seem to be affected by strong winds, and can often be seen even when the wind is blowing at gale-force. The male is usually seen sitting on some prominent perch, giving his loud call or dashing after other males. Flies very fast and hawks insects in the air. Sometimes hovers in front of flowers while drinking their nectar, but usually perches on them. In his display-flight the male swoops down towards the female with slow, regular wing-beats. After settling near her he displays, revealing the bright yellow pectoral tufts that are otherwise so seldom seen.

Voice: Usual call an emphatic '*chipp*'. Song, '*chip, chip, chip*' in rapid succession and rather loud, followed by '*chee-chee-twistee, twistee, chee...*' Song often of short duration.

Habitat: Relatively open country. Often found in gardens.

Distribution: The southern half of Southern Africa. Also in the central and north-eastern regions, but not in the bushveld towards the east coast.

ORANGE-BREASTED SUNBIRD   *Nectarinia violacea* (753)   p. 304
Afr Oranjeborssuikerbekkie

Identification: 13–16 cm. Adult male: entire head, upper mantle, chin and throat a metallic green. Lower mantle to upper tail-coverts olive-green; wings and tail blackish. Flight-feathers have yellowish edges. *Central tail-feathers elongated.* Below, chest a metallic violet; *breast to under tail-coverts orange*, with a brownish wash on the breast. Pectoral tufts yellow. Eyes brown; bill and legs black. Female olive-green; belly slightly paler and tail-feathers dusky. Subadult similar to female.

A common, tame, conspicuous species, usually found in pairs. The males are noisy, often sitting on the tops of bushes, giving their characteristic call. Sometimes hawk insects in the air. Do not seem to be unduly affected by cold, wet, or windy conditions.

Voice: A harsh, almost wheezy '*tsearp*'; also a '*teer-turp*', twice repeated. During the breeding season the male has a short, high-pitched song.

Habitat: On mountain slopes and plateaus where heaths and proteas grow.

Distribution: The southernmost coastal regions of Southern Africa.

MARICO SUNBIRD *Nectarinia mariquensis* (755) p. 304

Afr Maricosuikerbekkie

Identification: 13 cm. Adult male: entire head and neck, mantle to upper tail-coverts and wing-coverts a metallic green, shot with gold and blue. Narrow band across the chest a metallic violet; *broad band across the breast maroon*, with some of the feathers tipped with metallic violet. Wings, tail and *belly black*. Eyes a dark brown; bill and legs black. Female an olivaceous ash-colour above; flight-feathers dusky, with narrow white edges; tail-feathers blackish, with white-tipped outer feathers. Below, a pale yellowish, finely mottled with dusky. Subadult similar to female but more olivaceous above.

A common sunbird, usually found in pairs. Has a more metallic plumage than most of the other sunbirds found in Southern Africa. Noisy and conspicuous, and feeds mainly on insects.

Voice: A loud, clear '*chip-chip*', often accelerated to form a staccato series. Also has a short, warbling song.

Habitat: Prefers the dry acacia thornveld but is also found in the open savannas of the more temperate regions.

Distribution: Over most of the northern half of Southern Africa, but not along the western coastal belt or in the north-eastern regions.

LESSER DOUBLE-COLLARED SUNBIRD *Nectarinia chalybea* (760) p. 304

Afr Kleinvaalpenssuikerbekkie

Identification: 11 cm. Adult male: entire head and neck, mantle to rump, wing-coverts, chin and neck a metallic golden-green. Upper tail-coverts a metallic blue. Wing and tail blackish. Below, a narrow blue metallic band across the chest and a *broadish scarlet band across the breast. Belly grey*. Pectoral tufts yellow. Eyes brown; bill and legs black. Female is sombre-coloured: a dusky ash above and slightly paler on the belly. Subadults similar to female but tend to be darker.

A common species, usually found in pairs, and visiting all kinds of flowers, including those of exotic trees. Tame as a rule and sometimes found in built-up areas. Swerves, jinks and dashes as it flies. Feeds mainly on insects and their larvae.

Voice: A high-pitched '*cheep-cheep*', rapidly repeated. Also a thin, pleasant, tinkling song, during which the yellow pectoral tufts are often displayed.

Habitat: Wherever there are trees, exotics included. Found in the scrub of very dry regions as well as in evergreen forests.

Distribution: The southern and eastern half of Southern Africa, but not in the north-eastern coastal regions.

WHITE-BELLIED SUNBIRD   *Nectarinia talatala* (763)   p. 304
   Afr Witpenssuikerbekkie

Identification: 11 cm. Adult male: entire head and neck, mantle to upper tail-coverts, wing-coverts and chin to chest a metallic green, shot with gold and blue. Flight-feathers dusky; tail-feathers blue-black, edged with metallic green. Below, *a broadish metallic violet band across the breast*, with a narrow, dull black band below it. Lower breast and *belly to under tail-coverts white*. Pectoral tufts lemon-yellow. Eyes a dark brown; bill and legs black. Female an ashy brown above and paler below, with indistinct streaks on chest and breast. Subadult similar to female but more olivaceous above, and yellower below.

These common, active sunbirds are usually seen in pairs. The males are noisy and conspicuous, usually sitting in the tops of the taller trees, uttering their characteristic calls. Partial to the nectar of *Loranthus*, a common parasitic plant found on acacia trees.

Voice: Common call a loud, clear '*tzick, tzick*', often repeated in quick succession. Has a bright, melodious little song during the breeding season.

Habitat: Prefers the more open acacia veld but is found in all types of open wooded country. Also in gardens in built-up areas.

Distribution: The north-eastern half of Southern Africa, and also the north-western regions.

DUSKY SUNBIRD   *Nectarinia fusca* (764)   p. 304
   Afr Namakwasuikerbekkie

Identification: 11 cm. Adult male: *top of head and mantle to upper tail-coverts a dark metallic brown*, faintly shot with green. Flight-feathers dusky; tail black. Below, chin to upper belly black, faintly shot with purple. *Lower belly and under tail-coverts white*. Pectoral tufts a bright orange. Eyes a dark brown; bill and legs black. Female a uniform ash-brown above; tail black. Below, a uniform brownish white. Subadult similar to female but more olivaceous yellow above, and tinged with yellow below.

A locally common species, often found in large numbers where food is available. A rather silent and inconspicuous little bird that feeds mainly on insects and their larvae.

Voice: A harsh '*chirrr-tchek-tchek*' and a twittering feeding call.

Habitat: The semi-arid and arid western regions.

Distribution: The western third of Southern Africa, but not the southernmost parts.

OLIVE SUNBIRD   *Nectarinia olivacea* (766)   p. 304
   Afr Olyfkleurige suikerbekkie

Identification: 15 cm. Adult male: *above, a uniform olive-green*. Flight- and tail-feathers dusky, with olive-green edges. Below, a uniform olivaceous green, some individuals having an orange wash from chin to chest. Eyes a dark brown; bill and legs black. Sexes alike, both male and female having yellow pectoral tufts. Subadult a brighter green below, with a paler throat and no pectoral tuft.

A locally common species, found singly or in pairs. The only sunbird found in Southern Africa that is *entirely without metallic plumage*. Not dependent on flowers; is often seen darting from shrub to shrub, and searching in their foliage for insects and their larvae in a tit-like fashion. Usually keeps to the lower levels. Male has a fluttering display-flight.

Voice: Normal call a sharp '*zipp-zipp*'. Alarm-note a harsh '*chirr-chiwee-chiwee-chiwee-chee-chee-chee*'. The loud, distinctive, warbling song of the males can be heard all the year round.

Habitat: Evergreen coastal bush and forest, especially in areas where wild bananas are abundant.

Distribution: In the eastern and north-eastern parts of Southern Africa. Also along the south-eastern coastal belt.

COLLARED SUNBIRD   *Anthreptes collaris* (771)   p. 304

   Afr Geelborssuikerbekkie   *X* u-Nohlozana

   Z i-Ntonto

Identification: 10 cm. Adult male: head, entire neck, mantle to upper tail-coverts and chin to chest a metallic green, shot with gold. Flight-feathers blackish with narrow yellowish edges; tail-feathers blue-black with metallic blue-green edges. *Below, a narrow metallic purple chest-band; breast to under tail-coverts yellow*. Pectoral tufts yellow. Eyes brown; *shortish bill* and legs black. Female similar to male above but *entirely yellow below*. Subadult similar to female but not entirely metallic above and having only the centre of the chest and belly yellow, the rest of the underparts being a greyish green.

These small sunbirds have *relatively straight, shortish bills* and are insectivorous. Usually seen in pairs, creeping about like white-eyes in flowering trees or creepers, hunting for insects. While foraging, they usually keep up a continuous twittering, and when alarmed, they have the habit of flicking their wings. Keep mainly to the lower levels of thick undergrowth.

Voice: A weakish '*tsssip*'. Male and female keep in touch with each other by frequently uttering a quiet twittering '*tswee, tswee*'. During the breeding season the male has a soft, sweet, warbling song.

Habitat: Moist forest and thick coastal bush.

Distribution: Along the entire coastal belt of the eastern half of Southern Africa. Also in the north-eastern regions.

PLATE 33

STARLINGS, OXPECKER, PIPITS, WAGTAILS AND LONGCLAW

1 **PLUM-COLOURED STARLING** *page* 277
  Male: breast white. Female: underparts heavily streaked.

2 **RED-BILLED OXPECKER** 281
  Bill orange-red.

3 **CAPE STARLING** 277
  Eyes of adults bright orange.

4 **WATTLED STARLING** 276
  Upper wing-coverts whitish. Male in breeding plumage has black
  wattles.

5 **RED-WINGED STARLING** 278
  Primaries reddish and tipped with black.

6 **BURCHELL'S STARLING** 278
  Tail relatively long and wedge-shaped.

7 **PIED STARLING** 279
  Lower belly and under tail-coverts white.

8 **RICHARD'S PIPIT** 261
  Outer tail-feathers mainly white, upper parts boldly patterned.

9 **CAPE WAGTAIL** 260
  Upper parts grey-brown, chest-band dark.

10 **BUSHVELD PIPIT** 262
  Breast heavily streaked.

11 **AFRICAN PIED WAGTAIL** 260
  Head black with distinct white eye-stripe. Upper wing-coverts white.

12 **ORANGE-THROATED LONGCLAW** 263
  Throat orange with black border.

PLATE 34

SHRIKES

1 **WHITE HELMET SHRIKE** *page* 271
Stiff greyish bristles covering part of bill, yellowish eye-wattle.

2 **BRUBRU SHRIKE** 271
Small; short-tailed with chestnut flanks.

3 **MAGPIE SHRIKE** 270
Long black tail, white 'V' on back.

4 **GREY-HEADED SHRIKE** 270
Large; grey head and enormous bill.

5 **GORGEOUS SHRIKE** 269
Scarlet throat, black bib.

6 **CRIMSON-BREASTED SHRIKE** 267
Crimson underparts, white wing-bar.

7 **RED-BACKED SHRIKE** 265
Male: red back and pinkish breast.

8 **COMMON BOU-BOU SHRIKE** 266
Underparts washed with chestnut (variable); white wing-bar, tail-feathers black.

9 **FISCAL SHRIKE** 265
White underparts, tail long and thin, white 'V' on back.

10 **PUFF-BACKED SHRIKE** 267
Medium-sized; red eyes, short tail.

11 **BLACK-CROWNED SHRIKE** 268
Black cap, wings chestnut.

12 **ORANGE-BREASTED SHRIKE** 268
Breast orange, throat and eye-stripe yellow.

13 **BOKMAKIERIE SHRIKE** 269
Black bib, throat yellow. Black tail-feathers tipped with yellow.

BLACK SUNBIRD *Nectarinia amethystina* (772)   p. 304
Afr Swartsuikerbekkie

Identification: 15 cm. Adult male: *forehead to crown a metallic green, shot with gold*; chin to throat and upper tail-coverts a metallic purple, shot with gold. (In the northern race the upper tail-coverts are a dull black.) Wing-shoulder a metallic violet and blue. *Rest of plumage, above and below, a dull black*. Eyes brown; bill and legs black. Adult female is a faintly streaked greyish olive above, including the sides of face and neck. Flight- and tail-feathers dusky. Slight eye-stripe and moustache-stripe a yellowish white. Lores, chin and throat black. Chest to under tail-coverts a very pale lemon; chest, breast and flanks heavily spotted and streaked with black. Subadult similar to female but yellower below; spots larger and extending to belly and under tail-coverts.

A common species, widely distributed and usually found in pairs. In the non-breeding season birds form small parties, largely consisting of subadult birds. Noisy and active, and continually on the move, foraging for insects. Subject to local migrations in search of suitable sources of food. A strong flier and can cover larger distances than most sunbirds. Has a fast, undulating, jinking flight. A very pugnacious bird that freely attacks other species.

Voice: Normal call a sharp, high-pitched '*tseet*', and a staccato '*chichichi*'. Alarm-note a rapid, '*tit, tit, tit*'. Male often sits inside a tree or bush singing a pleasant rather robin-like song, for long periods at a time.

Habitat: Open forest; wherever there are scattered trees (exotics included). Common in gardens in built-up areas.

Distribution: Mainly in the eastern half of Southern Africa.

SCARLET-CHESTED SUNBIRD *Nectarinia senegalensis* (774)   p. 304
Afr Rooiborssuikerbekkie

Identification: 16 cm. Adult male: *forehead to crown and chin a metallic green*, shot with gold. *Throat to breast scarlet*, finely spotted with a metallic blue; wing-shoulders a metallic violet. Rest of plumage, above and below, a sooty black, except for the wings and tail, which are a slightly glossy brown. Eyes a dark brown; bill and legs black. Adult female an olivaceous dusky above; flight- and tail-feathers brownish. Primary wing-coverts edged with white, forming an indistinct whitish spot on the folded wing. Below, an olivaceous yellow, very heavily streaked with blackish. Chin and throat a more uniform dusky colour. Subadult similar to female but has chin and throat blackish.

A very common species, usually found singly or in pairs. Conspicuous and noisy, especially when several are together. Hawks flying insects and catches larger insects than sunbirds usually do.

Voice: In flight, a sharp, high-pitched '*zit*'. Males have a piping four-syllabled call '*tip-teen-tip-tip*', with the second syllable lower in pitch. This call is often repeated at short intervals for long periods on end. The song of the male is a loud, trilling warble.

Habitat: Open forest and savanna. Also found in gardens in built-up areas.

Distribution: The northern third of Southern Africa and the eastern and south-eastern coastal regions.

Allied species:

PURPLE-BANDED SUNBIRD (*Nectarinia bifasciata*) (756). 10 cm. Adult male similar to male Marico Sunbird but *much smaller*; bill relatively short. The *metallic violet chest-band* is not narrow as in the Marico Sunbird but *as broad as the maroon band on the breast*. The female is less yellowish below than the female Marico Sunbird. Usually seen in pairs, in the larger trees of the open coastal bush. Found mainly in the north-eastern parts of Southern Africa, but in the eastern coastal regions its range overlaps that of the Marico Sunbird.

GREATER DOUBLE-COLLARED SUNBIRD (*Nectarinia afra*) (758). 15 cm. Adult male similar to male Lesser Double-collared Sunbird but *much larger* and with a longer, heavier bill. *Scarlet band across breast very distinct and about twice as broad* as in the Lesser Double-collared Sunbird. Female more yellow on the belly than in the smaller species. A common sunbird, usually found in pairs on the edges of forests or in forest scrub along the southern and south-eastern coastal belt, and also in the central eastern regions of Southern Africa.

YELLOW-BELLIED SUNBIRD (*Nectarinia venusta*) (762). 10 cm. Slightly smaller than the White-bellied Sunbird. Adult male very similar to the male of the White-bellied Sunbird on the upper side, but the metallic green of the forehead is shot with blue only. The metallic violet band across the breast is much broader, and the *belly is a bright yellow, not white*. A common species, usually found in pairs on the borders of patches of forest, but not in the forests themselves. Also found in kloofs overgrown with scrub. Found only inland, in the eastern and north-eastern parts of Southern Africa.

GREY SUNBIRD (*Nectarinia veroxii*) (765). 13 cm. Adult male a uniform brownish grey above, with a slight greenish gloss. Below, a *uniform buffish grey*, not olivaceous green like the Olive Sunbird. *Pectoral tufts not yellow but red*. A not uncommon bird of the coastal forest and bush, but not often seen as it usually keeps to the higher levels of the trees. A noisy bird, with a loud, distinctive call. Found in the eastern and south-eastern coastal regions.

Rarer species:

BRONZE SUNBIRD (*Nectarinia kilimensis*) (752)

COPPERY SUNBIRD (*Nectarinia cuprea*) (754)

BLACK-BELLIED SUNBIRD (*Nectarinia shelleyi*) (757).

NEERGAARD'S SUNBIRD (*Nectarinia neergaardi*) (761)

BLUE-THROATED SUNBIRD (*Anthreptes reichenowi*) (769)

VIOLET-BACKED SUNBIRD (*Anthreptes longuemarei*) (770)

WHITE-EYES: Zosteropidae

White-eyes are small, warbler-like birds with greenish or yellowish plumage and a conspicuous ring of small white feathers round the eyes. They feed on insects, berries and other soft fruit and nectar. They are gregarious for most of the year, and parties keep up a continuous twittering while foraging for insects on leaves and stems. Their movements are quick and restless, and members of a party fly off one after the other as they move from tree to tree. They are often associated with mixed bird-parties. Individuals of different populations vary greatly in colour, particularly the colour of the underside.

PALE WHITE-EYE   *Zosterops pallidus* (775)   p. 304
   Afr Gewone glasogie   *X* in-Tukwane

Identification: 11 cm. Upper parts and sides of face a dull olive-green. Lores black, *ring round eye white*. Below, chin and throat a canary yellow; remaining underparts variable, and may be: (1) a uniform grey; (2) a slightly olivaceous yellow (with flanks a more olivaceous green); (3) yellow (with flanks brownish); or (4) centre of chest to belly may be whitish, with a slight yellow wash and sides of chest and flanks buff-brown. Eyes brown; bill black; legs greyish. Sexes alike. Subadults a duller green above than the adults.

Very common and familiar little birds, usually found in pairs during the breeding season but otherwise in small loose flocks. Very active and noisy, calling continually to keep in touch with one another as they explore the foliage of trees, shrubs and even small plants for insects. Always on the move, playing 'follow-my-leader' as they fly from tree to tree.

Voice: Normal call a soft, low-pitched '*peep-peep*'. Song a subdued warble; sometimes a lively imitation of the calls of other birds, ending in a loud '*too-chee-titti-chee-chee*', several times repeated. This song is kept up for some time, different birds being imitated on each occasion.

Habitat: Different types of woodland, forest or bush; even exotic plantations. Common in gardens in built-up areas.

Distribution: The southern half of Southern Africa. Not found in the dry central regions.

(According to some authorities this should be divided into two distinct species: the Cape White-eye (*Z. virens*) and the Pale White-eye (*Z. pallidus*).)

Allied species:

YELLOW WHITE-EYE (*Zosterops senegalensis*) (777). 10 cm. Above, a greenish yellow; forehead yellow. Flight- and tail-feathers dusky, with greenish edges. Ring round the eye white, *thin black line from gape to below the eye. Below, canary yellow*; sides of breast and flanks washed with moss-green. Tail shorter than that of the Pale White-eye, and species apparently more insectivorous. Usually found in pairs or small parties in densely-foliaged trees, and often as members of mixed bird-parties, especially parties of sunbirds. Found in the north-eastern and central northern regions of Southern Africa.

SPARROWS, WEAVERS, WAXBILLS, WIDOW-BIRDS, WHYDAHS
and related species: Ploceidae

These small to medium-sized birds belong to the largest bird-family in Southern Africa. They are mostly resident, and the majority are seed-eaters, with short, hard bills. Some species, particularly those that are highly gregarious, may cause much damage in cultivated areas, particularly to grain. But since all these species feed their young mainly on insects they are probably more beneficial than harmful—at least at certain times of the year.

With the exception of a few hole-nesters, all these birds build closed nests, with the opening at the side, top or bottom. In many species the male in non-breeding dress is similar to the female. This makes it very difficult to identify them in the field, for the females of certain species are themselves very similar. Most of these species are polygamous. The whydahs are parasitic (mainly on waxbills), but differ from *true* cuckoos in that their young do not oust the young of the hosts but are reared together with them.

BUFFALO WEAVER *Bubalornis albirostris* (779) p. 305
    Afr Buffelwewer
Identification: 24 cm. Adult male: wholly black but with the white bases of the feathers giving the impression of irregular white flecks. Inner webs of flight-feathers mainly white and seen as *conspicuous white windows during flight*. Eyes brown; *bill red*; legs salmon. Female duller and browner than the male and has some greyish white on face and throat, and a red or

blackish bill. Subadult similar to female above but more strongly mottled below; bill horn-coloured.

These starling-like weavers are always found in smallish flocks. They are colonial breeders and build their large untidy communal nests mainly of thorny sticks. Several such nests may be found in a single tall tree, usually fairly high up. Feed mainly on the ground, often in the company of other birds. Very noisy when they forgather to roost.

Voice: A large variety of loud, unmelodious croaking and chattering calls, particularly at their nests.

Habitat: Dry tropical savannas with tall scattered trees.

Distribution: Most of the northern half of Southern Africa but not in the coastal, central, western or north-eastern regions.

WHITE-BROWED SPARROW-WEAVER *Plocepasser*
mahali (780)   p. 305
Afr Gewone dommossie (koringvoël)

Identification: 18 cm. Above: top of head, lores and moustache-stripe blackish; *broad, conspicuous eyebrow white.* Ear-coverts, mantle and scapulars a light brown; *rump and upper tail-coverts white.* Wings and tail dusky; flight-feathers have whitish edges. Broad white tips to upper wing-coverts form a distinct band on the folded wing. Below, whitish. Eyes brown; bill grey to blackish; legs a light brown. Sexes alike. Subadult similar to adult.

A common, conspicuous species, usually found in pairs or small parties. They feed mostly on the ground, their diet consisting mainly of insects (which probably makes them independent of water). Their untidy, round, loosely-woven nests are usually made of dry, pale-yellow grass stalks, and are placed in thorn trees. Those with two entrances are used for roosting, and the one entrance is blocked when the nest is required for breeding. Easily identified in flight by the *conspicuous white rump.*

Voice: Alarm-note a harsh '*chick-chick*'. Male has a pleasant, loud, challenging song, mostly heard at dawn and dusk and often continued after sunset. Birds are very noisy at their nesting colony.

Habitat: Dry acacia veld, with isolated patches of larger trees.

Distribution: The greater part of Southern Africa, but not in the southern and eastern third.

Rarer species:
RED-BACKED SPARROW-WEAVER (*Plocepasser rufoscapulatus*) (782)

SOCIABLE WEAVER *Philetarius socius* (783)   p. 305
Afr Versamelvoël

Identification: 14 cm. Above, top of head to nape earth-brown; feathers on sides of neck, mantle and scapulars blackish, with distinct buff edges giving *plumage a scaly appearance*; rest of upper parts earth-brown. Flight-feathers broadly edged with buff; all the outer tail-feathers blackish, with broad brown tips. *Lores and chin black*; rest of underparts stone-coloured, except for streak of black feathers edged with buff on the flanks. Eyes a dark brown; bill horn-coloured; legs a light brown. Sexes alike. Subadults have top of head faintly spotted with blackish; lores and chin a buffish white, not black.

A locally common species, found in flocks numbering from a few to several hundred birds. Feed only on the ground and are mainly insectivorous. Their enormous communal nests resemble haystacks and are usually built in the larger acacia trees, but smaller nests are sometimes seen on telegraph poles. These nests are continually repaired and one is known to have been in use for over a century. These nests are not only used for breeding and roosting; they are an integral part of the lives of these birds, who actually live in them. Compartments of active nests from which the rightful owners have been ejected are sometimes used by Pygmy Falcons and other species for breeding purposes.

Voice: Flight-call a chattering, staccato '*kick-kick-kick-kick*'. Also a rather nasal '*klok-klok*', sometimes rapidly repeated.

Habitat: Dry thorn country.

Distribution: The dry western regions of Southern Africa. Also found in the drier central parts.

HOUSE SPARROW *Passer domesticus* (784) p. 305

Afr. Dakmossie

Identification: 14 cm. Adult male: top of head grey; broad reddish-brown stripe from over eye down side of neck; rump and upper tail-coverts grey. Tail- and flight-feathers dusky, with buffish edges; rest of *back streaked with black and tawny*. Black around the eyes; ear-coverts and side of neck white. *Variable amount of black from chin to breast;* rest of underparts a buffish white. Eyes hazel; bill black; legs a pale brown. Female earth-brown above; *back streaked with black*. Light eye-stripe; sides of face and neck buff; underparts a buffish white. Subadult similar to female but more buffish above.

Introduced at the turn of the century and has spread rapidly from the coast to the interior. Always associated with human habitations. Relatively tame but wary. Usually seen hopping about on the ground. In flight and seen from the back the lower back is *grey and not chestnut* like that of the Cape Sparrow. Nests under eaves and in the horizontal pipes of electric poles (i.e. the pipes to which the insulators are attached). An aggressive and dominating species, often found in very large numbers at communal roosts.

Voice: A loud, penetrating '*chirrup*' or '*chissip*', becoming a harsh, rattling

twitter when bird becomes excited. Alarm-note a low-pitched 'teu-teu'.
Habitat: Cities, towns and homesteads.
Distribution: Is spreading rapidly over the greater part of Southern Africa.

CAPE SPARROW *Passer melanurus* (786)   p. 305
Afr Gewone mossie   *X* Nondlwane
S Tsiloane

Identification: 15 cm. Adult male: top of head and face black; broad white
line from above eye down side of neck. Hind neck earth-brown; *back to
upper tail-coverts a uniform chestnut*. Flight- and tail-feathers blackish,
edged with buff. Median wing-coverts tipped with white, forming a bar on
the folded wing. Sides of neck white; centre of throat and breast black.
Rest of underparts whitish, except for flanks, which are grey. Eyes brown;
bill black; legs brown. Female has entire *head greyish* (not black), *with
a white eye-stripe*. Band across breast and centre of throat a paler grey.
Upper parts similar to those of male, but the chestnut is paler. Below,
whitish. Subadult similar to adult female.

This tame and confiding bird has adapted itself to civilization. Usually
found in pairs, but congregates in fairly large flocks out of the breeding
season. These birds do a certain amount of damage to gardens in early
spring; on the other hand they destroy large numbers of insects. Do not
nest in holes but build large, untidy nests, usually in trees. It is perhaps
owing to this difference in nesting habits that this species has not yet been
ousted by the more aggressive House Sparrow.
Voice: A harsh 'chissip' or 'chirrup'. Alarm-note a strident 'chirrrr-chirrrr'.
Male has a simple, jerky song, in which short phrases are often repeated.
Habitat: Wherever there are suitable trees, indigenous or exotic. Even
found in very arid regions.
Distribution: Patchily distributed over the southern half and the north-
western parts of Southern Africa.

Allied species:
GREAT SPARROW (*Passer motitensis*) (785). 16 cm. Adult male: forehead
to mantle grey; black line through eye. Sides of neck tawny; back tawny,
streaked with black. Flight- and tail-feathers blackish. Sides of throat
white, with *conspicuous black bib*. Rest of underparts whitish and pale
grey. Adult female similar to male but has a white throat and a distinct
buff eye-stripe. A rather shy species, usually occurring in pairs where there
are tallish trees. Found in the central, northern and western parts of
Southern Africa.

GREY-HEADED SPARROW (*Passer griseus*) (787). 15 cm. *Entire head grey*;
no eye-stripe; upper back and wing-coverts tawny; lower back and upper
tail-coverts russet. *Conspicuous white bar on folded wing*. Flight- and tail-

feathers dusky. Below, a pale buffish grey. Bill black in breeding season, otherwise horn-coloured. Sexes alike. Usually found in pairs or small family parties in the dry savanna thornveld of the northern two-thirds of Southern Africa. Sometimes found near human habitations. Nest in holes.

YELLOW-SPOT SPARROW (*Petronia superciliaris*) (788). 15 cm. Above: including wings and tail, a dusky earth-brown. Mantle streaked with dark brown. *Conspicuous buff eye-stripe.* Wing-coverts tipped with buffish white, forming two bars (the upper being more conspicuous) on the folded wing. *The small yellow throat-spot is seldom seen in the field.* Below, a greyish white. Usually seen in pairs, searching for insects in the upper branches of trees. Seldom seen on the ground, but if it feeds on the ground does not hop like other sparrows but walks about like an insectivorous bird. Found in the eastern half of Southern Africa.

SCALY WEAVER *Sporopipes squamifrons* (789) p. 305
Afr Baardmannetjie *S* Sansakhane

Identification: 10 cm. *Feathers of forehead and crown are black, edged with white, producing a scaly effect.* Lores black; sides of head, neck and back an ashy grey. Wing-coverts, innermost secondaries and tail blackish, with broad white edges. *Primaries dusky. Heavy moustache-stripes black*; chin and throat white; rest of underside a pale ash-colour. Eyes brown; bill pink; legs flesh-coloured. Sexes alike. Subadult has a horn-coloured bill, no scaling on head, and the black feathers of the adult replaced by brown.

A very common gregarious species of the drier regions. Tame and confiding; often found near human habitations. Feeds chiefly on the ground; when disturbed, flies up into the shelter of tangled thorn-bushes. Keeps up a continuous chattering while feeding. In certain regions appears to be independent of water for long periods.

Voice: Normal feeding call a repeated '*tzir-zip*', '*tzir-zip*' or '*zeerp-zeerp-zeerp*'. Take-off call a soft '*zwirr-zwirr*', rapidly repeated. When flushed, a sharp, short '*zipp*'. Male utters a subdued canary-like song, with his head-feathers raised. Alarm-call a loud '*zeerrrp*'.

Habitat: Dry, open thorn-country.

Distribution: The central and north-western parts of Southern Africa.

FOREST WEAVER *Ploceus bicolor* (790) p. 308
Afr Bosvink *X* in-Takananja
Z i-Tilongo

Identification: 15 cm. Top and sides of head and whole upper side, including flight- and tail-feathers, a brownish black. Chin and throat whitish; rest of underparts chrome-yellow. Male has no non-breeding plumage.

Eyes brown; bill horn-coloured, legs pinkish. Sexes alike. Subadult has a speckled throat.

A common species, usually found in pairs or small parties and often attached to mixed bird-parties. Mainly insectivorous and feeds like a tit, scrutinizing dry foliage and the bark of trees and often hanging upside-down. Tough retort-shaped nest is built of coarse material and suspended from a high branch or creeper, usually overlooking a small clearing. Silent as a rule and therefore often overlooked.

Voice: Normal call '*tseet-tseet*' or '*spink-spink*'. Alarm-note '*tseet-tseet-tseet*' in rapid succession and run together. Has a sustained, flute-like song that is thin and reedy.

Habitat: Forest and thick coastal bush.

Distribution: The eastern and south-eastern coastal regions of Southern Africa.

SPECTACLED WEAVER *Ploceus ocularius* (791)   p. 308
> *Afr* Brilvink   *X* i-Heza
> *Z* i-Gelekele

Identification: 15 cm. Adult male: face saffron; *chin, throat, lores and line through eye black*; neck, mantle, scapulars and tail a yellowish olive. Flight-feathers dusky. Below, chrome yellow. (Male has no non-breeding plumage.) Eyes yellow; bill black; legs brown. Female similar to male except that chin and throat are saffron, not black. Subadult similar to female, except that bill is horn-coloured, not black.

A rather shy species, found singly, in pairs or with their young. Spends most of its time in trees, foraging for insects, and often joins mixed bird-parties. Its presence is often revealed by its melodious call. Its beautiful, finely woven, retort-shaped nest has a rather long entrance funnel and is usually attached to the end of a bough or creeper.

Voice: Individuals keep in touch with one another by means of a melodious '*tee-tee-tee-tee-tee*' on a descending scale. Alarm-note a harsh, staccato '*chit-chit-chit*'. No prolonged song recorded.

Habitat: Thick bush along rivers and streams, and in forest clearings.

Distribution: The south-eastern coastal regions and north-eastern third of Southern Africa.

RED-HEADED WEAVER *Malimbus rubriceps* (793)   p. 308
> *Afr* Rooikopvink

Identification: 14 cm. Male in breeding plumage has *entire head, neck and breast scarlet*; upper mantle sparsely streaked with black and scarlet: remainder of upper parts, including wings and tail, ash-grey. Yellow edges to flight-feathers conspicuous when wing is folded. Remainder of under-parts white. Eyes red-brown; *longish sharp bill orange-yellow;* legs brown.

Adult female similar to male but has top and sides of head a pale saffron; chin and throat yellowish. Male in non-breeding plumage resembles the female. Subadult similar to female but has a paler chin and throat.

A rather shy bird, usually found in pairs or small parties. Polygamous, the male building a separate nest for each female. Largely insectivorous and usually seen creeping silently about in the topmost branches of tall trees. Often joins mixed bird parties. The reddish brown nest is roughly woven out of tendrils, strips of bark and the midribs of leaves, and has a long entrance funnel. Usually built on a large tree overhanging a clearing or road.

Voice: Both male and female utter a continuous, high-pitched chattering at the nest.

Habitat: Bush country, especially where there are large trees. Even found near human habitations.

Distribution: The north-eastern third of Southern Africa.

CHESTNUT WEAVER *Ploceus rubiginosus* (796) p. 308

Afr Bruinvink

Identification: 16 cm. Male in breeding plumage has entire head black; rump and upper tail-coverts ashy and pale chestnut; tail- and flight-feathers blackish, with white edges; *rest of plumage chestnut*. In non-breeding plumage top of head is greenish, streaked with black; back also streaked with black; stripe above eye and sides of face and neck a yellowish buff. Below, white, with chest a dark buff. Eyes a reddish brown; bill horn-coloured; legs a bluish grey. Adult female similar to male in non-breeding plumage but has chest the same colour as remainder of underparts. Subadult also resembles non-breeding male but has chest faintly streaked.

Found in flocks and are probably polygamous. Males are said to desert the breeding colonies, leaving the females to rear the young. Their stout, kidney-shaped nests have no spouts, are made of grass and are untidy-looking, having spikes of grass protruding in all directions.

Voice: A loud, intense chattering at the nesting site.

Habitat: Acacia thornveld.

Distribution: The north-western parts of Southern Africa.

SPOTTED-BACKED WEAVER *Ploceus cucullatus* (797) p. 308

Afr Bontrugvink *Z* i-Hlokohloko

X i-Hobohobo

Identification: 16 cm. Male in breeding plumage has forehead yellow, tinged with saffron; crown and nape yellow, finely mottled with black; sides of face, chin and centre of throat black; *mantle and scapulars boldly mottled in black and yellow*; rump and upper tail-coverts grey, mottled with yellow. Flight-feathers blackish, edged with pale yellow; tail an olivaceous grey;

below, a golden yellow. In non-breeding plumage male resembles the female. Eyes red; bill black; legs flesh-coloured. Adult female has forehead to nape and sides of face a yellowish green, with fine, narrow, dark streaks; back a mottled earth-brown; rump earth-brown and tail an olivaceous grey. Wings blackish, edged with yellow. Below, chin to chest yellow; sides of breast and flanks a greyish brown; rest of underparts white; bill horn-coloured. Subadult similar to female, but browner above.

A common species, gregarious all the year round and usually found near water. Feeds mainly on seeds but sometimes on nectar also. Nests are built by males and suspended from the drooping branches of tall trees, both indigenous and exotic. Nesting colonies are sometimes found in reeds. The leaves are stripped from the branches to which nests are attached. If the colony is very large the tree may die as a result of being constantly defoliated. Colonies have the habit of suddenly flying off together, wheeling about for a while and then returning to the nests. These are kidney-shaped and usually have a short spout.

Voice: A husky sizzling. Extremely noisy at the nesting colony, but noise will sometimes stop as if cut off by a switch. Alarm-note a sharp 'zit'.

Habitat: Large trees near water; often on the banks of streams. Frequently found near human habitations.

Distribution: The eastern third of Southern Africa.

CAPE WEAVER *Ploceus capensis* (799)   p. 308
    Afr Kaapse vink   *X* i-Hobo
    S Talane

Identification: 18 cm: Male in breeding plumage has *forehead and crown a reddish brown*; nape and sides of face a light saffron; chin to chest a dark saffron; hind neck to rump a greenish yellow, with dusky centres to the feathers. Tail an olivaceous grey; wings blackish, their feathers edged with yellow; remaining underparts a bright yellow. Male in non-breeding plumage resembles the female. Eyes yellow (brown in female); *largish bill black;* legs flesh-coloured. Female an olivaceous green above, with indistinct dusky mottling; flight-feathers blackish, with yellow edges. Below, a uniform olivaceous yellow; bill horn-coloured. Subadult similar to female.

This large and robust species is also gregarious, but never found in very large colonies. Single nests are sometimes found. The males are polygamous and build a large, kidney-shaped nest for each female. The female lines the nest if she has accepted it. The male is often seen clinging to the entrance of a nest, fluttering his wings and calling to the female to inspect it. If she disapproves the nest is pulled to pieces by the male, and a new one is woven. Feeds on seeds and insects; also on the nectar of flowers, particularly aloes (the pollen of which often discolours the faces of these weavers).

Voice: A rapidly repeated '*a-zwit, a-zwit*' by the male, who also has a harsh, guttural, chattering song. Alarm-note a short '*chuk, chuk*'.

Habitat: Any type of country in which there are large trees, indigenous or exotic. Usually near water.

Distribution: The south-western tip and south-eastern parts of Southern Africa.

MASKED WEAVER   *Ploceus velatus* (803)   p. 308
Afr Geelvink

Identification: 15 cm. Male in breeding plumage has *forehead*, sides of face, chin *and pointed bib black*; crown saffron; nape and sides of neck yellow; mantle a yellowish green, streaked with dusky. Rump a bright yellow; tail an olivaceous green; flight-feathers blackish, edged with yellow. Below, a bright yellow. Male in non-breeding plumage similar to female. Eyes red; bill black; legs flesh-coloured. Adult female: above, a greenish grey, with dusky streaks; narrow eye-stripe yellowish. Chin to breast a pale yellow; belly white; bill horn-coloured; eyes brown. Subadult similar to female.

A common and abundant species, gregarious throughout the year. Often found breeding in small colonies, consisting of a male and several females. Not dependent on water. Very tame and confiding, and found in many urban gardens. Kidney-shaped nests have no spouts and are built at the ends of branches from which the leaves have been stripped. Feeds mainly on seeds and insects.

Voice: Noisy at the breeding colony. Male has a loud, sizzling song. Alarm-note a strident '*chitt . . . chitt . . . chitt chitt chitt chitt*'.

Habitat: Open woodland; exotic as well as indigenous trees.

Distribution: Throughout Southern Africa.

THICK-BILLED WEAVER   *Amblyospiza albifrons* (804)   p. 308
Afr Dikbekvink

Identification: 19 cm. Adult male: *forehead usually white*; entire head, upper mantle and upper chest chocolate. Rest of upper parts, including wings and tail, a blackish brown; white bases of flight-feathers conspicuous as a white bar in flight, and a white patch on the folded wing. Below, a blackish brown, with fine white edges to the feathers. Eyes brown; *deep, heavy bill black*, legs a dark grey. Adult female: above, slightly mottled with chocolate; below, a creamy white, heavily streaked with dark brown. *No white on wing; bill a yellowish horn.* Subadult similar to female but has a yellow bill.

A fairly common species, usually found in small parties or in pairs.

Their large, neatly-woven, thick-walled kidney-shaped nests are slung between two upright reeds. Nesting colonies usually comprise about half a dozen pairs. Out of the breeding season these weavers frequent trees on the fringes of forests and are often seen searching for food amongst the fallen debris in the undergrowth. Their flight is undulating, like that of the woodpeckers (active flying alternating with spells of gliding).

Voice: A rather silent bird that sometimes chatters at the nest. Male has a soft, bubbling song. Alarm-note a soft *'sweet, sweet'*.

Habitat: Marshy ground, reed-beds and forests.

Distribution: The south-eastern coastal belt, the eastern coastal region and the central northern parts of Southern Africa.

RED-BILLED QUELEA *Quelea quelea* (805) p. 308
Afr Rooibekvink   *S* le-Rhakane

Identification: 11 cm. Adult male in breeding plumage has crown and chest washed with old rose; *forehead, sides of face, chin and throat variable,* being a creamy white, pale buffish or black. Remainder of upper side ashy; back has heavy blackish streaks. Below: buffish, faintly streaked with brown. Male in non-breeding plumage resembles the female. Eyes brown: *bill red;* legs pink. Adult female has top of head a brownish grey, with fine dusky streaks; eye-stripe buffish and chin and throat whitish. Otherwise similar to male. During the breeding season the female's bill is a waxy yellow, not red. Subadult similar to female except that its bill is a pinkish horn-colour.

A common, gregarious and polygamous species. Since flocks often number tens of thousands these birds have become a pest in agricultural areas. From a distance these enormous flocks look, in flight, like rapidly moving clouds. A flock of queleas feeds in waves: while the one part of the flock is feeding on the ground the other will overfly it and settle ahead of it, only to be overflown again by the first group. The result is a sporadic wave-like movement. Because of the great damage they do to crops, queleas have been declared a pest, and are being exterminated on a large scale. Although a resident species they are subject to local migration, and large numbers invade the central regions from the west. Their flimsy, kidney-shaped nests are usually found in closely-packed colonies in relatively small thorn-trees, in the remoter areas.

Voice: A noisy chattering in the breeding colony. Alarm-call a shrill *'chack-chack'*.

Habitat: No preference; found wherever there are trees.

Distribution: The greater part of Southern Africa, but not in the western coastal regions or the southernmost tip.

Allied species:
CABANIS WEAVER (*Ploceus intermedius*) (792). 13 cm. Male in breeding

plumage similar to Masked Weaver except that *the black on the top of the head is not confined to the forehead but extends on the crown to behind the eye;* the black bib is not pointed, but rounded; the hind crown is not saffron but yellow; the rump is not a bright yellow but a greenish yellow; the eyes are a yellowish white and the *legs bluish.* Female and non-breeding male similar to Masked Weaver except that their legs are bluish. Semi-gregarious; usually found in small colonies. Their nests are kidney-shaped and have a short entrance funnel. Found mainly along streams and rivers; often also near human habitations in the northern half of Southern Africa.

GOLDEN WEAVER (*Ploceus xanthops*) (801). 18 cm. Male in breeding plumage has *forehead, sides of face and underside a golden yellow,* with a slight orange wash from chin to chest. Above, a uniform olive-green; flight-feathers blackish, with yellowish edges. Eyes a deep yellow; bill black; legs brownish. Male in non-breeding plumage duller. Female has more yellow below than most other female weavers. A non-gregarious species, usually found in pairs or small family parties. Large, loosely-woven nests are usually attached to reeds and have no entrance funnel. Found along streams and the borders of marshy ground in the north-eastern parts of Southern Africa.

Rarer species:

BAR-WINGED WEAVER (*Ploceus angolensis*) (795)

YELLOW WEAVER (*Ploceus subaureus*) (800)

BROWN-THROATED WEAVER (*Ploceus xanthopterus*) (802).

RED-HEADED QUELEA (*Quelea erythrops*) (806)

CARDINAL QUELEA (*Quelea cardinalis*) (807)

OLIVE-HEADED WEAVER (*Ploceus olivaceiceps*)

RED BISHOP *Euplectes orix* (808)   p. 309
   Afr Rooivink   *X* um-Lilo
   Z u-Bomvana   *S* Thaka

Identification: 13 cm. Male in breeding plumage has *forehead, forecrown, sides of face, chin and upper throat black*; hind crown, nape and sides of neck scarlet; mantle a reddish brown; lower back to upper tail-coverts scarlet; flight- and tail-feathers dusky, with buffish edges. Below, chest and under tail-coverts scarlet; rest of underside black. (Old males tend to become more orange on the upper side.) In non-breeding plumage male resembles female but is slightly darker. Eyes a dark brown; bill black; legs brown. Adult female has upper side buff, with heavy dusky streaks and a yellowish buff eye-stripe. Below: buffish; chin to chest and flanks narrowly streaked with brown; belly whitish. Bill horn-coloured. Subadult similar to female but feathers on upper parts have broader, paler edges.

PLATE 35

SUGARBIRD, SUNBIRDS AND WHITE-EYE

1 **CAPE SUGARBIRD** *page* 282
Under tail-coverts yellow, tail very long.

2 **COLLARED SUNBIRD** 287
Bill shortish. Under parts yellow. Male has green throat with narrow
purple chest-band.

3 **MARICO SUNBIRD** 285
Breast-band maroon, belly dark.

4 **ORANGE-BREASTED SUNBIRD** 284
Breast orange, centre tail-feathers elongated.

5 **SCARLET-CHESTED SUNBIRD** 290
Chest scarlet. General colour sooty black.

6 **BLACK SUNBIRD** 290
Chest black, crown iridescent green.

7 **LESSER DOUBLE-COLLARED SUNBIRD** 285
Belly grey, chest-band bright scarlet.

8 **OLIVE SUNBIRD** 286
Throat washed with orange. Plumage non-metallic olive-green.

9 **PALE WHITE-EYE** 292
Ring of white feathers round the eye.

10 **DUSKY SUNBIRD** 286
General colour dark brown, under tail-coverts white.

11 **WHITE-BELLIED SUNBIRD** 286
Belly white, chest band violet.

12 **MALACHITE SUNBIRD** 283
Male iridescent green, centre tail-feathers elongated.

PLATE 36

SPARROW-WEAVER, WIDOW-BIRDS, SPARROWS AND WEAVERS

1 **WHITE-BROWED SPARROW-WEAVER** *page* 294
  Eye-stripe white.

2 **LONG-TAILED WIDOW** 310
  Shoulder-patch red and off-white, tail very long and heavy.

3 **RED-COLLARED WIDOW** 307
  Collar red or orange, tail long and narrow.

4 **WHITE-WINGED WIDOW** 310
  Shoulder-patch yellow, tail relatively long and squarish.

5 **SCALY WEAVER** 297
  Long black moustache-stripes.

6 **CAPE SPARROW** 296
  Male: cheeks black with white border.

7 **BUFFALO WEAVER** 293
  Bill heavy and reddish.

8 **HOUSE SPARROW** 295
  Cheeks white, back reddish brown streaked with black.

9 **SOCIABLE WEAVER** 294
  Throat black, back heavily mottled.

10 **BLACK WIDOW-FINCH** 323
  Bill white or pinkish. Legs variable.

A common species, occurring in small or large flocks throughout the year. Conspicuous during the breeding season. Usually nest in bulrushes or reeds over water. Each male has a definite territory in which a flimsy, kidney-shaped nest is woven for each of his three or four females. Male puffs his feathers during his slow display-flights over the nesting site, and his wings make a buzzing sound. Now and again he will dart after an intruding male, or chase one of his females at high speed.

Voice: Courting call a sizzling '*zik-zik-zik*'; also a variety of wheezing, mewing calls.

Habitat: Open country, generally near water.

Distribution: Over the greater part of Southern Africa but not in the central and north-western regions.

YELLOW-RUMPED WIDOW *Euplectes capensis* (810)   p. 309
Afr Geelkruisvink   *X* isa-Homba

Identification: 15 cm. Male in breeding plumage wholly black, except for *wing-shoulders and lower back, which are a bright yellow*. Upper wing-coverts and flight-feathers have buff edges. Male in non-breeding plumage similar to female, except that he retains the yellow shoulders and has tail and wings darker. Eyes and legs a dark brown; bill black. Adult female streaked above with brownish and black; rump a brownish yellow; yellow feathers on wing-shoulders have black centres. Below, mainly a pale brown, with narrow dusky streaks; chin, throat and centre of breast whitish; bill horn-coloured. Subadult resembles female.

A common and widely distributed species, found in small flocks out of the breeding season. Males are polygamous and their display-flight is accompanied by thudding wing-beats. Often seen perched on the top of a bush, keeping watch over their territory and chasing away intruders. Nest is a large, semi-domed oval, slung between two upright stems, usually fairly low down.

Voice: A squeaky '*skeek*' or '*chinsk*'. When displaying above his territory male makes a sizzling, churring or buzzing sound.

Habitat: Tall grass and rank vegetation on marshy ground or near streams. Occasionally found in drier areas with fairly low scrub.

Distribution: The eastern half and southern tip of Southern Africa.

GOLDEN BISHOP *Euplectes afer* (812)   p. 309
Afr Goudvink   *S* Thakha

Identification: 11 cm. Male in breeding plumage has *forehead to nape a golden yellow*; hind neck black; mantle yellow in the middle and mottled with black on the sides; lower back to upper tail-coverts a golden yellow; wings and tail brownish, with narrow light edges to the feathers. Below, mainly black, with yellow patch on side of breast and yellow under tail-coverts. Male in non-breeding plumage similar to female but darker above. Eyes and legs brown; bill black. Adult female heavily streaked above with blackish and buff; *prominent whitish eye-stripe extends far behind the eye.* Below, a light buff; chin, belly and under tail-coverts whitish; breast and flanks finely streaked with brown; bill horn-coloured. Subadult similar to female but browner above; feathers have buff edges.

This fairly common species is not gregarious during the breeding season but gathers in small flocks during the winter, usually in the company of other weavers. Males are polygamous and perform display-flights over their nesting sites, erecting the golden-yellow plumes on their backs until they look like floating yellow balls, their wings beating so fast as to be almost invisible. Often seen perched on low bushes or tall grass. Their thin-walled, oval nests are placed fairly low down in grass or weeds, on moist or marshy ground.

Voice: '*Sip-sip-sip*' during the display-flight and '*chee-chee*' when alighting. When the males chase each other they utter harsh squeals. They also have a short, buzzing song.

Habitat: Rank vegetation on moist or marshy ground.

Distribution: The eastern half of Southern Africa.

RED-COLLARED WIDOW *Euplectes ardens* (813)   p. 305

    Afr Kleinflap   *X* u-Jabela
    Z i-Ntaka   *S* le-Tzoo

Identification: Male 36 cm; female 11 cm. Male in breeding plumage wholly black, except for a red or orange-red band on the lower neck in front. (Band varies in width and may be quite inconspicuous in some specimens.) Long black tail graduated, the central tail-feathers being the shortest. Non-breeding male is much larger than the female and more heavily streaked above with black and tawny; wings and longish tail black; conspicuous eye-stripe whitish and bill a dusky horn. Eyes and legs brown; bill black. Adult female streaked above with black and tawny; eye-stripe yellowish; flight- and tail-feathers blackish, edged with buff. Below, a uniform buffish; chin and throat washed with yellow; breast has a light tawny wash; bill horn-coloured. Subadult similar to female but feathers on back have broader buff edges.

A polygamous species, found in scattered breeding parties and, while feeding and in the non-breeding season, in small flocks. Male performs a display-flight, taking off from a prominent perch near the nesting territory, depressing and vertically fanning out his long tail. This is accompanied by heavy wing-beats. Nest is a semi-transparent oval, slung from grass stems, fairly low down. It is lined with softer grasses, the seed-heads of which protrude from the side entrance.

Voice: A staccato '*kizz-kizz-kizz* . . .'; during display-flight a rapidly-

308

PLATE 37

WEAVERS

1 **RED-HEADED WEAVER**   *page* 298
   Male in breeding plumage: head red.

2 **RED-BILLED QUELEA**   302
   Bill red. Male in breeding plumage usually has black mask, but colour
   variable.

3 **FOREST WEAVER**   297
   Head and back blackish, chest and belly chrome-yellow.

4 **MASKED WEAVER**   301
   Male in breeding plumage: mask and forehead black, crown saffron.

5 **SPOTTED-BACKED WEAVER**   299
   Male in breeding plumage: mask black, forehead and crown bright
   yellow. Back heavily spotted.

6 **CHESTNUT WEAVER**   299
   Breast chestnut, head black.

7 **CAPE WEAVER**   300
   Male in breeding plumage: head reddish brown, bill black and heavy.

8 **THICK-BILLED WEAVER**   301
   Bill very heavy. Male has small white wing-spot and usually a white
   forehead. Female has heavily streaked under parts.

9 **SPECTACLED WEAVER**   298
   Black stripe through eye. Male in breeding plumage has black bib.

PLATE 38

WHYDAHS, BISHOPS AND AMADINAS

1 **PIN-TAILED WHYDAH** *page* 321
Bill red, thin, long black tail.

2 **GOLDEN BISHOP** 306
Crown golden yellow, tail relatively short.

3 **SHARP-TAILED PARADISE WHYDAH** 322
Long, broad, pointed tail.

4 **SHAFT-TAILED WHYDAH** 322
Centre tail-feathers spatulate.

5 **YELLOW-RUMPED WIDOW** 306
Crown black.

6 **RED BISHOP** 303
Forehead black, crown scarlet.

7 **CUT-THROAT AMADINA** 312
Throat-band dark red.

8 **RED-HEADED AMADINA** 311
Male: head and throat crimson. Female: head has faint pinkish wash.

repeated '*zitt-titti-zitt-titti*' and a long-drawn-out '*chweee-chweee-chweee*'. Also a short, rasping, metallic song.

Habitat: Long grass, reeds, and coarse vegetation in marshy ground surrounded by trees.

Distribution: The eastern third of Southern Africa.

WHITE-WINGED WIDOW *Euplectes albonotatus* (814)   p. 305
    Afr Witvlerkvink

Identification: Male 18 cm; female 13 cm. Male in breeding plumage wholly black, except for *bases of flight-feathers, tips of upper wing-coverts and whole of under wing-coverts, which are white,* and the *wing-shoulder, which is yellow.* Male in non-breeding plumage similar to the much smaller female but retains the yellow shoulder-patch and the white of the wings. Eyes brown; bill a bluish grey; legs blackish. Adult female streaked with brown and black above; wing-shoulder finely mottled in yellow and black (not readily seen in the field); tail- and flight-feathers blackish, edged with buff; eye-stripe yellowish. Below: chin, throat, belly and under tail-coverts white, washed with yellow; breast and flanks buff, with faint brown streaks; bill horn-coloured. Subadult resembles female, but breast and flanks are darker.

A common species, gregarious and polygamous. Males display in their territories, sitting on an exposed perch, fanning their longish rounded tails and also twisting and turning them from side to side. Oval nest usually built in tall grass and has eaves overhanging the opening.

Voice: Rather silent, but sometimes utters a rustling sound followed by a throaty double chirp.

Habitat: Tall grass and weeds in moist localities in the open thornveld.

Distribution: The eastern half of Southern Africa, but not found in the north-eastern coastal regions.

LONG-TAILED WIDOW *Euplectes progne* (818)   p. 305
    Afr Gewone flap   *X* i-Baku
    Z i-Sakabula   *S* le-Phakha

Identification: Male 56 cm; female 15 cm. *Male in breeding plumage wholly black* except for the wing-shoulders, which are orange-red, and the median wing-coverts, which are whitish. *Tail very long and graduated,* the central feathers being the longest. Flight-feathers edged with light buff. Non-breeding male similar to much smaller female but retains the orange-red and white patches on the wing. Eyes and legs brown; bill blue-grey. Adult female heavily streaked above with light tawny and black. Wing-shoulders finely mottled in orange and black (not easily seen in the field). Tail-feathers narrow and pointed. Below, a pale buff; throat to breast streaked with brown. Bill horn-coloured. Subadult similar to female but has wing-shoulders mottled in buff and black (not orange and black).

A common species, polygamous but non-gregarious. During the breeding season male displays over his territory by fanning his tail vertically and depressing it, and flying low down with slow, deliberate wing-beats. During this flight the point of the tail is curved smoothly backwards. Male is in attendance only during the day and visits each of his nesting females in turn. Towards evening large numbers of males can be seen flying at speed, with their long tails compressed, towards communal nests in reeds. During the non-breeding season can be found in flocks. Nest is on the ground in a tuft of grass, the blades of which are woven into the nest to form an effective camouflage.

Voice: Alarm-note a peculiar, low-pitched churring. Male has a soft, sizzling song.

Habitat: Open grassveld and vleis where there is luxuriant growth.

Distribution: The south-eastern parts of Southern Africa, including the coastal belt.

Allied species:

RED-SHOULDERED WIDOW (*Euplectes axillaris*) (816). 18 cm. Male in breeding plumage wholly black, except for a red wing-shoulder and cinnamon upper wing-coverts. *Tail short.* In non-breeding plumage male is similar to female but retains the patches on the wing, the red becoming more orange. Adult female heavily streaked with black and tawny above and has a conspicuous buff eye-stripe. Below, a uniform buff, with breast slightly darker. A gregarious species found in coarse vegetation and long grass, on or near marshy ground. Mainly in the eastern parts of Southern Africa.

Rarer species:

CUCKOO-WEAVER (*Anomalospiza imberbis*) (854)
BLACK-WINGED BISHOP (*Euplectes hordeaceus*) (809)
YELLOW-BACKED WIDOW (*Euplectes macrourus*) (815)

RED-HEADED AMADINA   *Amadina erythrocephala* (820)   p. 309
    Afr Rooikopmossie

Identification: 14 cm. Adult male: *forehead to nape, sides of face, chin and throat crimson, with the underlying grey showing through.* Back, including flight-feathers, a pale earth-brown; upper tail-coverts have blackish bars; tail a dark earth-brown, all except the central tail-feathers being tipped with white. Upper wing-coverts also tipped with white and have narrow black subterminal bands. Below, chest grey and faintly barred; breast and flanks chestnut; feathers with white tips and black subterminal crescents give *plumage of underside a beaded appearance*; belly whitish. Eyes brown; bill horn-coloured; legs flesh-coloured. Adult female similar to male but has whole head earth-brown; underside pale grey and not chestnut, and barred instead of beaded. Subadult resembles female.

A common species, usually found in pairs or small flocks. Feeds on the ground but perches freely in trees. Occupies the nest-holes of other birds, in trees or buildings.

Voice: A harsh '*chuk-chuk*'; male has a characteristic song, similar to that of the mannikins.

Habitat: Dry open savanna.

Distribution: The central and north-western parts of Southern Africa.

CUT-THROAT AMADINA   *Amadina fasciata* (821)   p. 309
Afr Bandkeelmossie

Identification: 11 cm. Adult male: above, a light reddish brown; top of head heavily barred with black; back mottled in black and buff; dark tail tipped with white. Below, chin white; *dark red band across the throat;* rest of *underparts* light tawny and barred, *presenting a scaly appearance;* chocolate spot on belly. Eyes brown; bill a bluish horn; legs a pale flesh-colour. Female similar to male but has no throat-band; chin finely barred with black. Subadult resembles female.

Found in pairs during the breeding season but otherwise gather in large flocks, usually in the company of queleas or other weavers. Nest as a rule in weaver nests.

Voice: A high-pitched '*eee-eee-eee*' in flight; other calls similar to those of the Red-headed Amadina.

Habitat: Dry, open savanna.

Distribution: The central eastern and central parts of Southern Africa.

BRONZE MANNIKIN   *Lonchura cucullata* (823)   p. 316
Afr Gewone fret   *X* u-Nghenge
S se-Lyamoroka

Identification: 10 cm. *Top of head, sides of face and wing-shoulder a glossy dark brown, with a bottle-green wash;* back and wings brown; rump barred, *tail black*. Below, chin to breast a glossy bronzy black; flanks barred with brown; rest of underparts white. Eyes and legs brown; bill blackish. Sexes alike. Subadult a uniform pale brown, but lighter below.

A very common, tame, gregarious species. Spends most of its time on the ground or clambering about on grass-stalks, eating the seeds. When flushed, flies into the nearest tree, dropping back to the ground either singly or in small parties to resume feeding. Large, untidy grass nests are kept in repair throughout the year and used for roosting as well as breeding.

Voice: Alarm-note a sharp '*chick-chick-chicka*'. Also a wheezy twittering, uttered in chorus.

Habitat: Open bush and the edges of forests. Often found in cultivated fields.

Distribution: The eastern third of Southern Africa.

SWEE WAXBILL *Estrilda melanotis* (825) p. 316

Afr Swiesysie *X* u-Notswitswitswi

Identification: 9 cm. Adult male: forehead to nape blue-grey; *sides of face, chin and throat black*; back an olivaceous green; *rump a bright red*. Flight-feathers dusky; tail black. Below, mainly pale grey; belly and under tail-coverts buff. Eyes red; *upper mandible black, lower crimson*; legs black. Adult female similar to male but has sides of face, chin and throat a pale grey (not black). Subadult similar to female but entire bill is blackish and the general colouring is duller.

A common species, usually found in pairs or small family parties. Tame, but often overlooked because of its retiring habits. Feeds mostly on the seeds of growing grasses. Flimsy nests built in the forks of trees or shrubs.

Voice: A weak, gentle '*swee, swee, swee*'. Alarm-note a sharp '*tzwee*'.

Habitat: The rank undergrowth on the borders of forests (often riverine forests).

Distribution: The south-eastern parts of Southern Africa, including the southern and south-eastern coastal belt.

GREEN TWINSPOT *Mandingoa nitidulus* (827) p. 316

Afr Groenrobbin

Identification: 11 cm. Adult male: *face orange-red*; top of head, back, wings and tail olive-green; rump a golden olive. Below: *throat, chest* and under tail-coverts *olive-green, washed with orange*; breast, flanks and belly black, densely spotted with white. Eyes and legs brown; bill blackish, with an orange tip. Female similar to male but duller; face a pale orange. Subadult a dull olive-green above; grey below and has a buff face.

Retiring and not very common. Usually found in pairs, feeding on the ground near protective cover, into which it dives at the slightest sign of danger.

Voice: A chirping '*tzeet*'. Male also has a subdued little song.

Habitat: Forest undergrowth and thick coastal bush. Also found on the edges of cultivated fields.

Distribution: The eastern and south-eastern coastal regions of Southern Africa.

COMMON MELBA FINCH *Pytelia melba* (830) p. 316

Afr Melbasysie

Identification: 13 cm. Adult male: *forehead, cheeks, chin and centre of throat scarlet;* crown to upper back, sides of neck and ear-coverts grey.

Back and wings olive-green; *upper tail-coverts crimson*; tail black, washed with crimson. Below, breast a golden green; rest of *underparts barred with white and black*; under tail-coverts a light buff. Eyes red-brown; bill a dark pink; legs brownish. Adult female has entire head grey; chest to belly barred with white and blackish; back and tail similar to those of male. Subadult resembles female but is darker and more scaly-looking below.

A fairly common species, usually seen singly, in pairs or in small family parties. A restless bird that moves about continually and feeds in the lower parts of thickets. Does sometimes venture on to bare ground, usually in the late afternoon, but flies into cover when disturbed, the *dark tail and red rump* being clearly shown.

Voice: Alarm-note a single, softish '*wick*'. Male has a soft, pretty song, consisting of a long phrase that is repeated over and over again.

Habitat: In the undergrowth and thickets of the dry thornveld, usually near water.

Distribution: The northern half and the south-eastern regions of Southern Africa.

AFRICAN FIREFINCH *Lagonosticta rubricata* (833) p. 316
    Afr Kaapse robbin   *X* isi-Cibilili
    S mo-Salasopen

Identification: 10 cm. Adult male has entire head claret-coloured (crown and nape with underlying grey); *back and wings earth-brown*; rump claret-coloured; tail black. Below, throat to belly claret-coloured, with a few white pin-spots on side of breast; centre of belly and under tail-coverts black. Eyes and legs brown; *bill blue-black*. Adult female has top of head, back and wings earth-brown; rump and lores claret-coloured; tail black. Underside a pale claret with underlying pale brown; also has a few indistinct white spots (not easily seen in the field) on sides of breast. Subadult brownish above; belly dusky; upper mandible blackish and lower horn-coloured.

A common species, usually found in pairs or small parties. More often heard than seen, as they keep to the thick undergrowth. When flushed, fly from one bush to another, keeping low down. *Red rump conspicuous in flight*. Very inquisitive; are easily attracted if the alarm-notes of other birds are imitated.

Voice: A clear, metallic trill, often protracted and usually followed by '*wink-wink-wink*'. Alarm-note a sharp, staccato '*chit-chit-chit-chit*'.

Habitat: Thick bush on the borders of forests or beside streams. Partial to thorn scrub with tall grass.

Distribution: The eastern parts of Southern Africa and the south-eastern coastal belt.

ORANGE-BREASTED WAXBILL   *Amandava ubflava* (838)   p. 316
   Afr Rooiassysie

Identification: 9 cm. Adult male: top of head, sides of neck, back and wings earth-brown, with a faint greenish wash. *Rump crimson;* tail blackish; outer tail-feathers tipped and edged with white; crimson stripe from lores and above the eyes. Below: *chin, throat and centre of breast and belly a bright yellow;* sides of breast and flanks a dark olivaceous green, barred with yellow; *under tail-coverts a bright orange.* Eyes orange-red; bill red, with black spot at the base; legs brownish. Adult female: general colouring less bright than that of male; no eye-stripe; below, a pale dirty yellow, with indistinct bars on sides of breast and flanks. *Chin and throat whitish, instead of bright yellow.* Subadult similar to female but has a blackish bill.

A common bird, usually found in small flocks. Very lively; may be seen flicking their tails from side to side as they clamber up and down reed- and grass-stems or hop about on the ground. When disturbed the whole flock flies up simultaneously; flies a short distance, keeping low; then settles again. Always nest in abandoned weaver nests, especially those of the Red Bishop. Line the nests with feathers and soft material.

Voice: A soft, metallic, tinkling note, often uttered on the wing.

Habitat: Always in reed-beds and bulrushes, or the vegetation bordering marshes and streams.

Distribution: The eastern third of Southern Africa.

BLUE WAXBILL   *Uraeginthus angolensis* (839)   p. 316
   Afr Gewone blousysie

Identification: 11 cm. Adult male: top of head, back and wings earth-brown; rump and tail blue; *sides of face, chin to breast and flanks blue;* centre of belly and under tail-coverts buff-brown. Eyes red; bill lilac, with a black tip; legs a pale brown. Adult female similar to male above, but buff-brown, with a blue wash, below. (The blue is more concentrated on sides of face, chin and breast.) Subadult similar to female but paler, and has a blackish bill.

A familiar, common species, usually found in small flocks. Also found singly, but always within calling distance of other individuals. Feeds mainly on grass-seeds found on the ground. Very tame and inquisitive; usually the first to arrive when the alarm-call of some or other bird is imitated.

Voice: Alarm-note a harsh, high-pitched, metallic rattle. Feeding-call '*tse-tse-tseee*' or '*weet-a-weet*'. Males have a soft, lively little song.

Habitat: Dry thornveld near streams and rivers. Often found near human habitations.

Distribution: The north-eastern half of Southern Africa.

PLATE 39

WAXBILLS, FINCHES, TWINSPOT, FIREFINCH AND MANNIKIN

1 **SWEE WAXBILL** *page* 313
Rump bright red. Male has black throat and cheeks.

2 **ORANGE-BREASTED WAXBILL** 315
Under tail-coverts reddish orange, breast and throat bright yellow.

3 **AFRICAN FIREFINCH** 314
Bill blue-black, back brownish.

4 **BLACK-CHEEKED WAXBILL** 318
Face black, tail relatively long.

5 **VIOLET-EARED WAXBILL** 318
Ears violet.

6 **COMMON MELBA FINCH** 313
Throat and forehead of male bright scarlet; bill pinkish.

7 **GREEN TWINSPOT** 313
Chest and throat greenish.

8 **BLUE WAXBILL** 315
Chest and throat blue.

9 **BRONZE MANNIKIN** 312
Head and throat a glossy dark brown, tail black.

10 **COMMON WAXBILL** 318
Facial-stripe crimson, belly washed with pink.

11 **QUAIL FINCH** 319
Short tail. Male has black and white facial markings.

PLATE 40

CANARIES AND BUNTINGS

1 **YELLOW CANARY** *page* 328
Breast of male bright yellow; of female dirty white and heavily
streaked.

2 **FOREST CANARY** 325
Breast greenish-yellow and heavily streaked.

3 **YELLOW-EYED CANARY** 326
Eye-stripe and rump bright yellow.

4 **SISKIN CANARY** 324
Tips of tail and flight-feathers white.

5 **CAPE CANARY** 324
Nape bluish grey.

6 **WHITE-THROATED CANARY** 327
Throat white, rump yellowish.

7 **BULLY CANARY** 327
Heavy light-coloured bill, underparts bright yellow.

8 **PEACH CANARY** 326
Black marks on throat variable, rump yellow.

9 **STREAKY-HEADED CANARY** 328
Grey head streaked with white.

10 **ROCK BUNTING** 329
Cinnamon breast, striped head.

11 **GOLDEN-BREASTED BUNTING** 330
Orange-yellow breast, striped head.

12 **CAPE BUNTING** 330
Grey breast, striped head.

VIOLET-EARED WAXBILL *Uraeginthus granatinus* (840)　　p. 316
　　Afr Koningblousysie
Identification: 14 cm. Adult male: forehead blue; *sides of face violet;* chin and throat black; *back, sides of neck and chin to belly chocolate;* wings earth-brown; upper and under tail-coverts blue; tail black. Eyes red; bill crimson, with purple base; legs black. Adult female: forehead a pale blue, *sides of face a pale violet and tawny*; top of head to nape tawny; back and wings earth-brown; rump blue; tail black; chin to under tail-coverts a pale tawny. Subadult similar to female but duller.

A fairly common species, usually found in pairs and sometimes in small parties, but never in large flocks. Often associates with other waxbills, particularly the Blue Waxbill. *In flight the black tail looks broad and heavy.*
Voice: An often-repeated, trilling '*trriu-woo-wee*'. Male has a weak, canary-like song.
Habitat: Dry thorn scrub, even in very arid regions.
Distribution: The northern half of Southern Africa, but not in the extreme west or east.

BLACK-CHEEKED WAXBILL *Estrilda erythronotos* (841)　　p. 316
　　Afr Swartwangsysie
Identification: 13 cm. Top of head and back grey, very finely barred with blackish and faintly washed with claret; rump and upper tail-coverts claret-coloured; wing-coverts have distinct black and white bars. Flight-feathers dusky; longish tail black; *sides of face black*; chin blackish; throat to breast grey, finely barred with blackish and washed with claret. Belly and flanks claret-coloured; centre of lower belly and under tail-coverts black. Eyes reddish; bill blue-black; legs black. Female similar to male but colouring slightly duller; flanks a paler claret. Subadult resembles female but is greyer below and has brown eyes.

A common species, found in pairs during the breeding season but assembling in small flocks when not breeding. Feeds chiefly on the ground and flies into the nearest cover when alarmed. *General impression in the field is that of a small, long-tailed, blackish bird.*
Voice: The normal flocking call, by which members of a flock keep in touch with one another, is a melodious, quavering bisyllabic whistle '*fwoo-eee*', on an ascending scale. Male has a soft warbling song.
Habitat: Dry bush country.
Distribution: The central and north-western parts of Southern Africa.

COMMON WAXBILL *Estrilda astrild* (843)　　　　p. 316
　　Afr Rooibeksysie　　　*X* in-Tshiyane
　　Z in-Tiyane　　　*S* se-Tzetze
Identification: 11 cm. Adult male has entire upper side, including wings and

tail, a pale brown, closely and narrowly barred with dusky; *lores and stripe through eye crimson*. Sides of face and neck, chin and throat greyish; *centre of breast and belly a pinkish crimson;* under tail-coverts black; rest of underparts a pale brown, finely barred with buff and faintly washed with pink. Eyes and legs brown; *bill red*. Adult female similar to male but has less red below. Subadult has even less red, is faintly barred below and has a blackish bill.

A common and familiar species, usually found in small flocks. Often assemble in large numbers during the non-breeding season. Feed mainly on the ground and when flushed trail off one after the other, giving their flocking-call. Very lively; will flick their tails from side to side when disturbed; always on the move. Very tame and show little fear of man. *Red bill and facial stripe conspicuous in the field.*

Voice: Flocking-call a constant, reedy twittering. When excited, a '*chee-chee-churrr-chit*'. Call when taking off '*chairp-chairp-chairp*'. Male also has a subdued, melodious song.

Habitat: Marshy country, with reeds and tall grass; also found in the grass along streams and rivers.

Distribution: Throughout Southern Africa.

QUAIL FINCH   *Ortygospiza fuscocrissa* (844)   p. 316
Afr Kwartelsysie   *Z* u-Nonwhe
S le-Kolukotoane

Identification: 10 cm. Adult male: *forehead, sides of face and throat black; part round eyes and chin white*; top of head and back slightly mottled with grey and brown; flight-feathers brown, with narrow white edges; *short tail blackish, tipped with white*. Below: chest, breast and flanks distinctly barred with black and white; chestnut band on lower breast; belly a light tawny. Eyes brown; bill red; legs a light brown. Adult female paler and has forehead, face and throat earth-brown instead of black. Subadult similar to female; breast a uniform brown; flanks barred with dirty white; bill blackish.

Usually found in small parties or flocks during the non-breeding season. Almost entirely terrestrial; seldom perch on grass-stems. When disturbed, will fly up steeply in front of one's feet, with whirring wings, and giving their characteristic call. Keep up a continuous metallic chirruping while on the wing. Drop steeply when settling.

Voice: A high-pitched, bell-like '*tirrilink-tirrilink*'.

Habitat: Open grassland, especially the bare ground around pans and in swampy, tussocky areas.

Distribution: The north-eastern half of Southern Africa; also found in the south-western parts and the southernmost tip.

Allied species:

PIED MANNIKIN (*Lonchura fringilloides*) (822). 13 cm. Entire head and neck, patch on side of breast, rump and tail a glossy blue-black; rest of upper side brown: underside white. Stout, heavy bill black. A shy, gregarious species, usually seen in small flocks in riverine bush, or on the borders of evergreen coastal forest. *This large mannikin* is found in the eastern and south-eastern coastal belt of Southern Africa.

RED-BACKED MANNIKIN (*Lonchura bicolor*) (824). 10 cm. Entire head, neck (all round), breast and tail a glossy black. Flight-feathers and rump finely barred with black and white; *back and wing-coverts chestnut*. Sides of breast and flanks distinctly mottled in black and white; rest of underparts white. A fairly common species found in small parties feeding in open grassy patches in the bush. Similar to the Bronze Mannikin in size. Found in the eastern part of Southern Africa and also in the south-eastern coastal belt.

PINK-THROATED TWINSPOT (*Hypargos margaritatus*) (831). 13 cm. Top of head, back and wings russet-brown; tail black, washed with wine-red; *face, sides of neck and chin to breast a pinkish mauve;* lower breast, flanks and belly black, with pinkish-white spots. In the female the pinkish mauve is replaced by pale grey, and the spots on the underside are white. A fairly common species, usually found in pairs or small parties, feeding on the ground in tangled coastal bush. Found in the central eastern regions of Southern Africa.

JAMESON'S FIREFINCH (*Lagonosticta rhodopareia*) (835). 11 cm. Similar to the African Firefinch, but *top of head does not contrast strongly with back*, both being a uniform earth-brown, washed with pale claret. Entire underside a uniform light claret, with *little contrast between breast and back*. The female is also paler than the female African Firefinch. (Can be identified in the hand, since the second primary is *not* notched like that of the African Firefinch.) Usually found in pairs or family parties, feeding among bushes and shrubs overgrown with grass. Found in the north-eastern third of Southern Africa.

LITTLE FIREFINCH (*Lagonosticta senegala*) (837). 10 cm. This small firefinch differs from the others in having only *the centre of the crown earth-brown*. The claret on sides of face extends *above* the eye; that on sides of neck joins on the hind neck to form a collar. There is a marked contrast between the bright claret breast and the buffish belly. The *red bill* is unmistakable. In the female only the lores and rump are red, and the whole underside is a pale buff, with small white spots on the breast. A tame bird, usually found in pairs or small parties. Often found in urban areas. Distributed over the eastern half of Southern Africa, but not found in the southernmost parts.

GREY WAXBILL (*Estrilda perreini*) (842). 11 cm. General colour a dusky grey; throat to breast paler; *lower rump and upper tail-coverts a bright scarlet;* narrow black line through eye; chin and tail also black. An inconspicuous species, usually found singly or in pairs in thick bush with grass. Found in the south-eastern and eastern coastal regions of Southern Africa.

Rarer species:

NYASA SEEDCRACKER (*Pyrenestes minor*) (819)

NYASA CRIMSON-WING (*Cryptospiza reichenovii*) (828)

YELLOW-BACKED MELBA FINCH (*Pytilia afra*) (829)

RED-THROATED TWINSPOT (*Hypargos niveoguttatus*) (832)

BROWN FIREFINCH (*Lagonosticta rufopicta*) (836)

LOCUST-FINCH (*Ortygospiza locustella*) (845)

CINDERELLA WAXBILL (*Estrilda thomensis*)

PIN-TAILED WHYDAH   *Vidua macroura* (846)   p. 309
   Afr Rooibekkoninkie   *X* Hlekwe
   Z u-Hlegwane   *S* Mmamonoke

Identification: Male 33 cm; female 13 cm. Male in breeding plumage has head, mantle and flight-feathers black; white collar on hind neck; upper wing-coverts white, forming a large white patch on the folded wing. Rump and upper tail-coverts whitish; *four central tail-feathers black, narrow and considerably elongated;* other tail-feathers short and black, with inner webs white. Below: white, except for black patch on side of breast. Male in non-breeding plumage similar to female but more boldly streaked with black above. Eyes a dark brown; *bill red;* legs grey-black. Adult female has top of head black; centre of crown tawny, streaked with black. Entire upper side tawny, with broad, heavy blackish streaks. Sides of face a buffish tawny; moustache-stripe and line behind eye black; short tail blackish; inner webs of feathers white. Below, a uniform buffish white, slightly streaked on flanks; breast more tawny; bill a brownish red. Sub-adult earth-brown, with indistinct streaks above. Buff below; no white in the short tail; bill a reddish black.

A common, well-known species. During the breeding season male is usually seen in the company of half-a-dozen females or out-of-plumage males. Males very pugnacious and active, constantly chasing other birds or courting females, by hovering and displaying just above them. Display flight jerky and dipping. While feeding, males either drag their long tails on the ground or carry them arched in the air. Parasitizes the Common Waxbill and some cisticolas.

B.S.A.   x

Voice: During courtship flight, a thin, constantly-repeated '*tseet-tseet-tzip*', accompanied by quivering wing-beats. Male also has a shrill, sustained, twittering, laughing song. Alarm note a sharp '*chitt-chitt-chitt-chittchittchitt*'.

Habitat: Wherever there are trees, especially in built-up areas and near farmsteads.

Distribution: Throughout Southern Africa.

SHAFT-TAILED WHYDAH   *Vidua regia* (847)   p. 309

Afr Pylstertkoninkie

Identification: Male 33 cm; female 11 cm. Male in breeding plumage has top of head, lores, mantle to upper tail-coverts and wings black; primaries a dusky black; the short tail-feathers dusky with whitish tips; *the four central tail-feathers long, black and spatulate*. Collar on hind neck, sides of face and *whole of underside a light tawny*; under wing-coverts white. Male in non-breeding plumage similar to female but more boldly marked above; short tail black. Eyes brown; bill and legs orange-red. Adult female a warm buff or pale tawny, heavily streaked above with blackish. Buff eye-stripe and blackish line behind the eye but *no moustache-stripe*. Below a uniform buff. Short tail blackish, with off-white tips and edges to the outer tail-feathers. Subadult similar to female but general colour a more russet brown.

A fairly common species, usually found in small parties, consisting of a full-plumaged male and a number of plain-coloured birds (probably females and subadult males). Male is very pugnacious, like the male of the Pin-tailed Whydah. Undoubtedly polygamous. Known to parasitize the Violet-eared Waxbill.

Voice: Male has a sustained twittering song, softish and pleasant.

Habitat: The grassy parts of the dry thornveld; partial to cattle kraals.

Distribution: The central, northern and north-western parts of Southern Africa.

SHARP-TAILED PARADISE WHYDAH   *Steganura*
paradisaea (852)   p. 309

Afr Gewone paradyskoninkie

Identification: Male 38 cm; female 15 cm. Male in breeding plumage has entire head, back, wings and *broad, pointed tail black*; central tail-feathers broad with bare, elongated shafts; broad collar on hind neck a light tawny. Below: black bib on chestnut chest and breast; belly and flanks a light tawny; under tail-coverts black. Male in non-breeding plumage has entire head mottled in black and buff; wings and short tail blackish; rest of upper parts tawny, broadly streaked with black. Below, breast tawny; sides sparsely spotted with black; belly whitish. Eyes and legs brown; bill black.

Adult female similar to male in non-breeding plumage but generally duller and has a more distinct buffish stripe above and behind the eye. Broad stripe on centre of crown buff, with a few black spots. Below, earth-brown rather than tawny. Subadult brownish above; chest and breast a light earth-brown; belly whitish and bill horn-coloured.

A fairly common species; small flocks often seen feeding on the ground. During display-flight male flies straight up to a considerable height, then cruises about with the two broad central tail-feathers raised, almost at a right angle to the body. Can also be seen hovering above the females, with his wings moving slowly and rhythmically. Is usually seen sitting on a prominent perch such as the top of a bare tree, or a telegraph wire. Presumably polygamous, and parasitizes mainly Melba Finches.

Voice: A rather silent species. Male occasionally utters a sharp '*chip*'. Said to have a short, chirping, sparrow-like song.

Habitat: Open, dry thornveld savanna.

Distribution: The north-eastern half of Southern Africa.

BLACK WIDOW-FINCH   *Hypochera funerea* (849)   p. 305
   Afr Swartweduweetjie

Identification: 11 cm. Male in breeding plumage: *general colour a velvety black*, slightly shot with violet-purple; flight- and tail-feathers dusky. Male in non-breeding plumage similar to female. Eyes brown; *bill white or a pinkish white*; legs variable (from white to coral-red). Adult female has top of head blackish; broad stripe on centre of crown buff, with narrow black streaks; distinct buff stripe above and behind the eye. Rest of upper parts blackish, streaked with buff. Below: chin to breast and flanks a mottled earth-brown; belly whitish. Subadult similar to female.

A common species, rather inconspicuous except during the breeding season, when males may be seen on conspicuous perches, usually on the tops of bare trees. Males keep to specific perches for the whole of the breeding season. Feed on the ground in a characteristic fashion, hopping about actively, kicking up small puffs of dust and scattering grass seeds. Probably polygamous; parasitizes mainly firefinches.

Voice: Alarm-note a rasping chatter. While perched, male sings a sustained, melodious, chattering song.

Habitat: Open savanna.

Distribution: The eastern half of Southern Africa.

Allied species:

STEEL-BLUE WIDOW-FINCH (*Hypochera amauropteryx*) (851). 11 cm. Male in breeding plumage: general colour a velvety black, shot with steel-blue. Tail- and flight-feathers dusky; *bill and legs red*. Male in non-breeding plumage similar to female, which closely resembles the female of the

Black Widow-finch. Found in open bushveld, feeding in small flocks on bare patches. The north-eastern half of Southern Africa.

Rarer species:

BROAD-TAILED PARADISE WHYDAH (*Steganura orientalis*) (853)

CANARIES and BUNTINGS: Fringillidae

Canaries are smallish, seed-eating birds with short, stout bills. Most have green and yellow plumage. They differ from weavers in that they have only nine visible primaries and build open, cup-shaped nests. During the non-breeding season they gather in large flocks. They are renowned for their singing. Buntings differ from canaries in having more slender, pointed bills. Except for the Golden-breasted Buntings they have drab greyish-brown and black plumage, and no song to speak of.

SISKIN CANARY *Serinus tottus* (855)   p. 317

   Afr Pietjiekanarie

Identification: 13 cm. Adult male: forehead to nape brown, finely streaked with greenish olive; back a russet-brown. Rump a slightly yellowish olive; *tail and flight-feathers blackish, tipped with white;* slight yellowish streak above the eye; sides of face a yellowish brown. Below: chin finely spotted with black; throat to belly a yellowish olive; breast has a greenish wash; under tail-coverts earth-brown. Eyes, bill and legs brown. Female similar to male but has top of head and nape almost the same colour as back. Subadult similar to female but has faint dusky streaks on chin and chest.

Locally common and found in pairs or small parties. A rather shy and unobtrusive bird, usually seen feeding in bushes and shrubs; not often on the ground. *In flight, the dark back and white tips to the tail are conspicuous.*

Voice: Normal call a high-pitched, metallic '*tchwing-tchwing*', or '*pee-chee, pee-chee*'. Male has a typical but weak canary-song.

Habitat: Hilly and mountainous country.

Distribution: The extreme southern and south-eastern parts of Southern Africa.

CAPE CANARY *Serinus canicollis* (857)   p. 317

   Afr Kaapse kanarie   *X* u-Longi

   Z um-Zwilili   *S* Tsoere

Identification: 13 cm. Adult male: forehead and crown a bright orange-yellow; *nape, sides of neck and ear-coverts a bluish grey;* sides of face, chin, centre of throat and chest to upper belly a greenish yellow. Lower belly light grey; under tail-coverts lemon-yellow; back a greenish yellow, streaked with grey; rump a yellowish green. Slightly-forked tail a pale khaki; feathers have dark shafts and yellow edges; flight-feathers blackish, edged with yellow. Eyes brown; bill a dusky horn-colour; legs a greyish brown. Adult female generally duller; forehead yellow; more streaks on back. Subadult similar to female but paler, and streaked below as well as above.

A common species, usually found in large flocks, especially at roosting time. Flocks break up into pairs during the breeding season. Feed chiefly on the ground, where they can be seen hopping about. Have an undulating flight with frequent wing-beats. During the breeding season males have a flapping display-flight and often sing on the wing, though normally they sing while sitting in tall trees. *Grey nape and absence of eye-stripe characteristic.*

Voice: Normal call a loud, ascending, protracted *'zweeēt'*. Male has a typical canary-song, loud and melodious. Probably the best songster of the family.

Habitat: Wherever there are trees (exotics included), near open ground.

Distribution: The southern and eastern third of Southern Africa, but generally not in the north-eastern parts.

FOREST CANARY *Serinus scotops* (858)　　　　　　　p. 317
　Afr Streepborskanarie　　　　*X* u-Notswitswitswi

Identification: 13 cm. Adult male: above, a bright olive-green, streaked with blackish; rump a greenish yellow; flight- and tail-feathers blackish, edged with green; slight eye-stripe yellow; lores and chin black; ear-coverts green. Yellow patch on throat; chest and breast olive-green; belly, flanks and under tail-coverts a bright yellow; *entire underside except centre of belly heavily streaked with blackish.* Eyes brown; bill horn-coloured, with lower mandible paler; legs dusky. Adult female similar to male, but lores, chin and ear-coverts are greyish. Subadult similar to female but duller.

An active bird, not often seen as it usually keeps to the dense foliage of tall trees. Usually found in pairs or small parties. Never strays far from tall trees but may be seen feeding in glades or in the open, near the forest's edge.

Voice: Keep in touch with one another by means of constant call-notes: a plaintive *'tseetoo-tswee-ee'* and a rapid stuttering *'stit-ititit'*. Also a quiet *'tsik'*. Male has a brisk, warbling, trilling song, the opening phrase of which is *'sit-siddlwa-see'*.

Habitat: Dense evergreen bush and forest.

Distribution: The central south-eastern parts of Southern Africa and the southern and south-eastern coastal belts.

YELLOW-EYED CANARY   *Serinus mozambicus* (859)   p. 317
   Afr Geeloogkanarie   *X* u-Nyilelo
   Z u-Ntshingalothi

Identification: 11 cm. Adult male has *forehead, broad eye-stripe and rump a bright yellow;* rest of upper parts a dull green, streaked with blackish. Wings and tail dusky; tail-feathers tipped with white; lores and ear-coverts blackish. Below: *chin to upper belly a bright yellow; thin moustache-stripe black;* sides of neck and breast a greenish grey; lower belly and under tail-coverts a pale yellow. Eyes brown; bill horn-coloured; legs brownish. Adult female similar to male above, but much paler below. Subadult similar to female but duller; breast sometimes has dusky blotches.

A tame and very common species, usually found in small parties during the non-breeding season. Feeds chiefly on the ground, where it is often seen walking or hopping about. Flight undulating and erratic. When disturbed while feeding, flies into the nearest cover, clearly showing its *bright yellow rump.* Its *chubby shape and bright yellow eye-stripe* serve to distinguish it from the more slender and drab-looking Peach Canary, which also has a yellow rump.

Voice: A quiet, unmelodious '*chirrip*', '*chrup*' or '*zizzit*', Also sings a lively song, while sitting in or at the top of a tree.

Habitat: Open savanna and bushveld, often near human habitations.

Distribution: The eastern half of Southern Africa.

PEACH CANARY   *Serinus atrogularis* (860)   p. 317
   Afr Bergkanarie

Identification: 11 cm. Adult male: above, a light ashy brown, streaked with blackish; *rump yellow;* upper tail-coverts buffish; tail-feathers dusky, edged and tipped with white; flight-feathers blackish, edged with buff. Below: a buffish white, with *variable blackish spots on chin and throat.* Eyes brown; bill and legs horn-coloured. Adult female similar to male. Subadult resembles adult but more heavily streaked below with blackish brown.

A widely-distributed, locally common species, usually found in pairs or small parties, hopping about and feeding on the ground. Flight deeply undulating. *The yellow rump* of this drab-coloured little bird is unmistakable in the field.

Voice: A weak, reedy '*chee-oo, chee-oo*', '*tseek-tseek*' or '*tsee-tsee*'. Male has a lively, sustained song made up of short repeated phrases.

Habitat: Dry open savanna; never far from water.

Distribution: The northern two-thirds of Southern Africa, but not in the eastern or south-eastern regions.

BULLY CANARY   *Serinus sulphuratus* (863)   p. 317
   Afr Dikbekkanarie   *X* i-Ndweza eluhlaza
Identification: 16 cm. Adult male: above, yellow-green with dusky streaks; rump not streaked. Eye-stripe a bright yellow; sides of face and neck yellow-green; *moustache-stripe yellow*. Flight- and tail-feathers dusky, edged with yellow; *entire underside canary-yellow*. Eyes brown; *stout bill a light horn-colour* (upper mandible distinctly arched); legs brownish. Adult female similar to male but more heavily streaked above; facial markings less distinct; breast and sides of throat greener. Subadult paler than female, with broader streaks above. Streaked on side of breast and flanks.

An unobtrusive but fairly common bird; *rather heavily built*; usually seen singly or in pairs during the breeding season but forming small flocks during the winter months. Often seen in the company of mixed flocks of seed-eaters. Flight fairly rapid and less undulating than that of other canaries. While feeding on the ground, hops about briskly with body held erect; occasionally resorts to running. *Though the rump is slightly more yellow than the back there is not as strong a contrast as in the case of the other canaries.*
Voice: Normal call a rather rasping and unmusical '*swirri-wirrit*', '*pirrr-zip*' or '*chirr-irr-ree*'. Also has a rather soft song, husky and not very varied.
Habitat: Open bush or woodland; often found near farmsteads.
Distribution: The eastern half of Southern Africa and also the southernmost tip.

WHITE-THROATED CANARY   *Serinus albogularis* (865)   p. 317
   Afr Witkeelkanarie
Identification: 15 cm. Top of head and back an ashy brown, with faint dusky streaks; *rump yellowish;* tail- and flight-feathers dusky with narrow pale edges. Below: *chin and throat white, sparsely streaked with ash-brown;* sides of face and remaining underparts a uniform ash-brown, except for belly, which is whitish. Eyes brown; *stout bill a brownish horn;* legs blackish. Sexes alike. Subadult similar to adults but browner above and indistinctly streaked below.

Usually found singly or in pairs during the breeding season. Small flocks are seen during the winter, sometimes in the company of Bully Canaries. This is a thick-set bird and hops about when feeding on the ground. Flight rapid and more or less direct. *Its stout bill and yellowish rump distinguish it from the more slender* Streaky-headed Canary (which is also drab-coloured and also has a white chin and throat).
Voice: Call-note a low-pitched '*sqee-yik*'. Song powerful and melodious.
Habitat: Dry scrub country, particularly dry river-beds and hillsides.

Distribution: The south-western half of Southern Africa but not in the central western regions or south-eastern coastal belt.

YELLOW CANARY *Serinus flaviventris* (866) p. 317
Afr Geelkanarie

Identification: 15 cm. Adult male: forehead, cheeks and eye-stripe a bright yellow; *moustache-stripe and line through eye olive-green*, crown and back olive-green with dusky streaks; rump a bright yellow, contrasting strongly with the back; flight and tail-feathers dusky, with paler edges. Below, *whole underside canary-yellow.* Eyes hazel; bill horn-coloured; legs black-ish. Adult female a greyish olive above (sides of face, neck and moustache-stripe included); eye-stripe a buffish white. Below: *a dirty white;* flanks and breast tinged with yellow; *breast heavily streaked with dusky.* Subadult similar to female but generally duller, even on the rump; heavily streaked above and below.

A common and familiar species, usually found singly or in pairs during the breeding season and in small flocks during the winter. A lively bird that hops about while feeding on the ground. Rather restless, often flying into trees next to its feeding-ground and then dropping down to the ground again soon after. *The sexes are so different that both are readily identified in the field.*

Voice: Normal call a high-pitched *'tirriyip'* or *'tiyee'*. Its vigorous and sustained song is a series of simple phrases, interspersed with brief pauses.
Habitat: Open woodland, usually near water.
Distribution: The western two-thirds of Southern Africa, but not in the north-western tip.

STREAKY-HEADED CANARY *Serinus gularis* (867) p. 317
Afr Streepkopkanarie   *X* i-Ndweza

Identification: 13 cm. *Top of head to nape and sides of neck streaked with blackish and white;* remainder of upper parts ashy brown; back has faint dusky streaks. Eye-stripe whitish; sides of face ashy brown. Below: chin and throat white; rest of underparts a uniform earth-brown; belly paler. Eyes and legs brown; bill horn-coloured. Sexes alike. Subadult similar to adult but streaked below, and more heavily streaked above.

A common bird, but usually unobtrusive. Its presence is usually revealed by its song. May sometimes be seen in gardens, sitting on the seed-heads of flowers or pecking the seeds out of opening pine-cones. Usually seen in pairs, very seldom in flocks. Distinguished from the White-throated Canary by its *streaked head, longish weaver-like bill* and uniformly brown rump and back.

Voice: Contact-call, given either when perched or on the wing, a quiet husky *'chirrit'* or *'tseero-it'*. Song is pleasant, though simple and subdued.

Habitat: Open woodland and tall scrub. Often found in exotics in urban gardens.

Distribution: The south-eastern half of Southern Africa, but not in the southernmost tip.

Allied species:

BLACK-HEADED CANARY (*Serinus alario*) (861). 13 cm. Adult male: *entire head and chin to centre of breast black;* back, rump and tail a light chestnut; flight-feathers blackish; side of neck and remainder of underparts white. Female: above, a light brown with dusky streaks; wing-shoulders a light chestnut; chin to breast and flanks buff; belly whitish. A common bird of the drier regions, usually seen singly, in pairs or in small parties, feeding on the ground. Found mainly in the western third of Southern Africa, but not in the north-western tip.

Rarer species:

BLACK-EARED CANARY (*Serinus mennelli*) (868)

PROTEA CANARY (*Serinus leucopterus*) (869)

CHAFFINCH (*Fringilla coelebs*) (870)

LEMON-BREASTED CANARY (*Serinus citrinipectus*)

ROCK BUNTING *Emberiza tahapisi* (872)   p. 317
   Afr Klipstreepkoppie   *X* u-Ndenjenje
   S   Motoelitoeli

Identification: 15 cm. Adult male: entire head and throat black, with broken white lines down centre of crown and above and below the eye. Moustache-stripe white; rest of upper parts russet, streaked with black; flight- and tail-feathers a dark brown, edged with tawny. *Below, a uniform cinnamon.* Eyes brown; legs a yellowish brown; upper mandible dark brown and lower yellowish. Adult female similar to male but duller; head not black but russet, with blackish streaks on top; moustache-stripe and stripes above and below the eye not white but a pale buff. Subadult similar to female but faintly blotched below with darker brown.

A tame and confiding species, *of a slender build*; usually seen in pairs but occasionally in small family parties. Though partial to rocky ground it is found in all kinds of open country, perching freely on trees and bushes. When feeding on the ground, hops about with a jerky, shuffling action. Does not fly far when flushed but darts into the nearest cover. When disturbed, would rather run and keep out of sight than fly. Its *cinnamon underparts and conspicuous pale yellowish-brown legs* distinguish it from the Cape Bunting, which also has its head boldly striped.

Voice: Alarm-note a bleating, fairly high-pitched '*teh-rer-ray*'. Also has a soft, bubbling, repetitive song and a long-drawn-out '*pee-eeee*'.

Habitat: Prefers rocky ground, with scattered trees and bare patches. Occasionally ventures into small country towns.

Distribution: The eastern half of Southern Africa, and also the north-western regions.

CAPE BUNTING   *Emberiza capensis* (873)   p. 317

  Afr Kaapse streepkoppie   *S* Maborokoane

Identification: 14 cm. Forehead to nape earth-brown, streaked with black; back russet-brown, streaked with black; rump and upper tail-coverts a plain earth-brown. Sides of face and eye-stripes off-white; moustache-stripe and line through eye black; *wing-shoulders and broad edges of wing-coverts chestnut*; flight- and tail-feathers dusky, edged with chestnut. Below: chin and throat whitish, *chest and breast greyish*; belly light brown to light buff. Eyes brown; bill and legs a blackish brown. Sexes alike. Subadult paler and has dusky streaks on chest.

A common bird, comparatively tame and confiding. Sometimes found singly but more often in pairs or family parties. Looks squat and plump as it walks or hops on the ground, with bent legs and a shuffling action. When disturbed, flies for a short distance only, keeping low. Conspicuous when it sits on the top of a rock, singing and rhythmically opening and closing its wings. *Distinguished from the other buntings by its greyish breast and the chestnut on its wings.*

Voice: Normal call a sparrow-like chirp and a loud '*wheeoo-whee*' or '*cheriowee*'. Also has a shrill, jolly, canary-like song, consisting of a number of short phrases.

Habitat: Hilly and mountainous country; rocky, sandy coastal regions; often found near human habitations.

Distribution: The greater part of Southern Africa, excluding the south-eastern and eastern coastal regions and the central northern parts.

GOLDEN-BREASTED BUNTING   *Emberiza flaviventris* (874) p. 317

  Afr Goueborsstreepkoppie   *X* in-Tsasa

  Z um-Jamelonthi

Identification: 15 cm. Adult male: top of head to nape, sides of face and neck black; whitish lines down centre of crown to hind neck, above and below the eye; whitish collar on hind neck; back a dark chestnut, heavily streaked with greyish fawn. Rump and upper tail-coverts grey; upper wing-coverts broadly tipped with white, forming *two distinct white bars on the folded wing;* flight-feathers and two central tail-feathers blackish; rest of tail-feathers blackish, tipped with varying amounts of white (the outer ones being nearly all white). Below, chin white; *centre of throat a bright yellow;*

chest and breast cinnamon or orange-yellow; belly a bright yellow; flanks and under tail-coverts a pale grey. Eyes brown; bill horn-coloured (lower mandible paler); legs a pale brown. Female similar to male but generally duller. Subadult has buffish instead of white on head and is a paler yellow below.

A common, widely-distributed and conspicuous species, usually seen in pairs. Often seen perched in trees but feeds mainly on bare patches on the ground. Usually in a crouching position when not walking about. When flushed, flies up into the nearest cover, with *the white on the outer tail-feathers very conspicuous,* as in the honey-guides. When bird is perching, the two white bars on the folded wing are clearly seen. The boldly-striped head and brightly-coloured underparts are unmistakable.

Voice: Normal call a single plaintive '*droll-peer*', often answered by the mate, with a softish '*sitee*'. In flight a single '*chip*' is sometimes heard. Contact-call between male and female a quiet '*tsip, tsip, tsip*'. Also a simple, varied song.

Habitat: Open savanna: often found in country gardens.

Distribution: The north-eastern two-thirds of Southern Africa.

Allied species:

LARK-LIKE BUNTING (*Emberiza impetuani*) (871). 14 cm. Head and entire back a tawny buff with dusky streaks. Upper wing-coverts have tawny edges; flight- and tail-feathers dusky; eye-stripe a light buff; underparts a uniform tawny buff; belly paler. Sexes alike. Very common in the dry west; found in pairs or flocks, feeding on the ground. Congregate in very large numbers at water-holes in the dry season. Unlike the other buntings in that *the head is* **not** *boldly patterned in black and white, and therefore does not contrast with the back.* Differs from the smaller larks in that it has a *small head, short bill and longish tail, with no white on the outer feathers.* Found in the western two-thirds of Southern Africa.

Rarer species:

CABANI'S BUNTING (*Emberiza cabanisi*) (875).

BIBLIOGRAPHY

1. ALEXANDER, W. B.
   Birds of the Ocean.
   Putnam, London 1955.

2. BOLSTER, R. C.
   Land and Sea Birds of the South-West Cape.
   Speciality Press of S.A. Limited, Cape Town 1931.

3. BROWN, L.
   Eagles.
   Michael Joseph, London 1955

4. FITTER, R. S. R.
   Guide to Bird Watching.
   Collins, London 1963.

5. FITTER, R. S. R. and RICHARDSON, R. A.
   Pocket Guide to British Birds.
   Collins, London 1952.

6. FITZSIMONS, F.W.
   The Natural History of South Africa. Birds, Volumes I and II
   Longmans, Green, London 1923.

7. GILL, E. L.
   A First Guide to South African Birds.
   Maskew Miller, Cape Town 1936.

8. HAAGNER, A. and IVY, R. H.
   Sketches of South African Bird Life.
   Porter, London 1908.

9. HOESCH, W.
   Die Vogelwelt Südwestafrikas.
   John Meinert, Windhoek 1955.

10. HORSBRUGH, B.
    Game-birds and Water-fowl of South Africa.
    Witherby, London 1912.

11. LAYARD, E. L.
    The Birds of South Africa.
    Juta, Cape Town 1867.

12. MACDONALD, J. D.
    Contribution to the Ornithology of western South Africa.
    Trustees of the British Museum, London 1957.

13. MACKWORTH-PRAED, C. W. and GRANT, C. H. B.
    Birds of the Southern Third of Africa, Volumes I and II.
    Longmans, London 1963.

334   BIBLIOGRAPHY

14. PETERSON, R., MOUNTFORD, G. and HOLLOM, P. A. D.
A Field Guide to the Birds of Britain and Europe.
Collins, London 1954.

15. PRIEST, C. D.
The Birds of Southern Rhodesia, Volumes I to IV.
William Clowes, London 1933.

16. PROZESKY, O. P. M.
Uit ons Natuur: Ons Voëls.
Voortrekkerpers, Johannesburg 1965.

17. ROBERTS, A.
The Birds of South Africa.
Witherby, London 1940.

18. ROBERTS, A.
The Birds of South Africa, Revised edition by McLachlin and Liversidge.
Cape Times, Cape Town 1957.

19. SKEAD, C. J.
The Canaries, Seedeaters and Buntings of Southern Africa.
Trustees of the S.A. Bird Book Fund, Cape Town 1960.

20. SMITHERS, R. H. N.
A Check List of the Birds of the Bechuanaland Protectorate.
Trustees of the Natural Museums of Southern Rhodesia, 1964.

21. WILLIAMS, J. G.
A Field Guide to the Birds of East and Central Africa.
Collins, London 1963.

22. WINTERBOTTOM, J. M.
Field Handbooks series.
Longmans, Green, Cape Town 1952.

23. WOODWARD, R. B. and J. D. S.
Natal Birds.
P. Davis, Pietermaritzburg 1899.

INDEX

Entries in **bold** type refer to pages opposite illustrations

Accipiter badius	82
melanoleucos	77, **112**
minullus	77, **112**
ovampensis	82
rufiventris	82
tachiro	78, **112**
Achaetops pycnopygius	219
Acridotheres tristis	279
Acrocephalus arundinaceus	242
baeticatus	236, **272**
gracilirostris	242
palustris	243
rufescens	243
schoenobaenus	243
scirpaceus	243
Actophilornis africanus	107, **160**
Aegypius occipitalis	59, 80
tracheliotus	59, 80, **96**
Agapornis lilianae	150
nigrigenis	150
roseicollis	149, **177**
Alaemon burra	202
grayi	201
Albatross Black-browed	24, **65**
Grey-headed	25
Light-mantled Sooty	25
Shy	25
Sooty	25
Wandering	24, **65**
Yellow-nosed	25, **65**
Alcedo cristata	171, **209**
semitorquata	173
Alopochen aegyptiacus	51, 49, **64**
Amadina Cut-throat	312, **309**
Red-headed	311, **309**
Amadina erythrocephala	311, **309**
fasciata	312, **309**
Amandava subflava	315, **316**
Amblyospiza albifrons	301, **308**
Anas acuta	57
capensis	53, 49, **64**
clypeata	57
erythrorhyncha	53, 49, **64**
hottentotta	54, 49, **64**
querquedula	57
smithii	52, 49, **64**
sparsa	54, **64**
undulata	53, 49, **64**
Anastomus lamelligerus	41, **48**
Andropadus flaviventris	221
importunus	221, **241**
milanjensis	221
Anhinga rufa	35, **32**
Anomalospiza imberbis	311
Anous stolidus	138
Anthoscopus caroli	216
minutus	216, **241**
Anthreptes collaris	287, **304**
longuemarei	292
reichenowi	292
Anthropoides paradisea	102, **161**
Anthus brachyurus	263
caffer	262, **288**
chloris	263
crenatus	263
leucophrys	262
lineiventris	263
novaeseelandiae	261, **288**
similis	262
trivialis	263
vaalensis	262
Apalis Bar-throated	238, **257**
Black-headed	243
Rudd's	243
Yellow-breasted	238, **257**
Apalis flavida	238, **257**
melanocephala	243
thoracica	238, **257**
ruddi	243
Apaloderma narina	170, **192**
Aplopelia larvata	146
Apus aequatorialis	168
affinis	166, **208**
apus	167
barbatus	165, **208**
caffer	166, **208**
horus	167
melba	168
myoptilus	168
pallidus	168
Aquila dubia	73
fasciata	71, **81**
nipalensis	77
pennata	73
pomarina	77
rapax	70, **80**, **96**

Aquila [*continued*]
verreauxi 70, **80, 96**
wahlbergi 70, **80**
Ardea cinerea 35, **33**
goliath 36, **33**
melanocephala 36, **33**
purpurea 39
Ardeola ibis 38, **33**
ralloides 39
rufiventris 40
Arenaria interpres 117
Asio capensis 157, **193**
Aviceda cuculoides 67
Avocet 123, **145**

Babbler Arrow-marked 217, **240**
Bare-cheeked 219
Blackcap 219
Black-faced 218
Pied 217, **240**
White-rumped 218
Balearica pavonino 101, **161**
Barbet Black-collared 185, **225**
Crested 187, **225**
Green 188
Pied 186, **225**
White-eared 187
Whyte's 188
Batis capensis 252, **273**
fratum 259
molitor 253, **273**
pririt 259
Bee-eater Blue-cheeked 178
Boehm's 178
Carmine 174, **209**
European 174, **209**
Little 175, **209**
Swallow-tailed 178, **209**
White-fronted 175, **209**
Bias musicus 259
Bishop Black-winged 311
Golden 306, **309**
Red 303, **309**
Bittern Cape 39
Dwarf 39
Little 39
Booby Brown 29
Bostrychia hagedash 45, **48**
Botaurus stellaris 39
Boulder-chat 218
Bradypterus baboecala 242
barratti 243
sylvaticus 243
victorini 242
Broadbill African 195
Bubalornis albirostris 293, **305**

Bubo africanus 159, **193**
capensis 162
lacteus 162
Bucorvus leadbeateri 185
Bulbul Black-eyed 220, **241**
Cape 219, **241**
Red-eyed 219, **241**
Slender 221
Sombre 221, **241**
Stripe-cheeked 221
Terrestrial 220, **241**
Yellow-breasted 221
Yellow-streaked 221
Bunting Cabani's 331
Cape 330, **317**
Golden-breasted 330, **317**
Lark-like 331
Rock 329, **317**
Buphagus africanus 281
erythrorhynchus 281, **288**
Burhinus capensis 126, **145**
vermiculatus 126
Bustard Kori 103, **161**
Ludwig's 106
Stanley's 106
Buteo buteo 76, **81, 128**
rufinus 77
rufofuscus 75, **81, 128**
Butorides striatus 38, **33**
Button-quail Hottentot 93
Kurrichane 93, **113**
Buzzard Augur 76
Honey 69
Jackal 75, **81, 128**
Lizard 73, **81, 128**
Long-legged 77
Steppe 76, **81, 128**
Bycanistes brevis 185
bucinator 184

Calandrella cinerea 198, **240**
conirostris 199, **240**
fringillaris 220
ruddi 202
sclateri 202
starki 201
Calendula magnirostris 202
Calidris alba 124
alpina 125
bairdii 126
canutus 125
ferruginea 119, **144**
melanotos 126
minuta 120, **144**
ruficollis 125
Calonectris diomedia 27

Camaroptera brachyura 243
  brevicaudata 239, **272**
  fasciolata 237, **272**
  stierlingi 243
  subcinnamomea 243
Campephaga phoenicia 207, **240**
Campethera abingoni 194
  bennettii 191
  cailliautii 194
  notata 194
Canary Black-eared 329
  Black-headed 329
  Bully 327, **317**
  Cape 324, **317**
  Forest 325, **317**
  Lemon-breasted 329
  Peach 326, **317**
  Protea 329
  Siskin 324, **317**
  Streaky-headed 328, **317**
  White-throated 327, **317**
  Yellow 328, **317**
  Yellow-eyed 326, **317**
Cape Hen 26, **65**
Cape Pigeon 26, **65**
Caprimulgus europaeus 163, **193**
  fossii 164
  natalensis 165
  pectoralis 163, **193**
  rufigena 164
  tristigma 164, **193**
Centropus cupreicaudus 156
  senegalensis 156
  superciliosus 154, **192**
  toulou 156
Cercococcyx montanus 156
Cercomela familiaris 228, **256**
  schlegelii 230
  sinuata 230
  tractrac 230
Certhilauda albescens 200
  albofasciata 197, **240**
  curvirostris 200
Ceryle maxima 172
  rudis 170, **209**
Ceuthmocares aereus 156
Chaetops frenatus 218, **241**
Chaetura boehmi 167, **208**
  ussheri 168
Chaffinch 329
Charadrius asiaticus 117
  hiaticula 110, **129**
  leschenaultii 117
  marginatus 110, **129**
  mongolus 118
  pallidus 117

  pecuarius 111, **129**
  tricollaris 111, **129**
Chat Ant-eating 229, **256**
  Arnott's 230
  Buff-streaked 228, **256**
  Familiar 228, **256**
  Herero 231
  Karroo 230
  Layard's 230
  Mocking 228, **256**
  Mountain 226, **256**
  Sickle-winged 230
  Stone 229, **256**
Chlidonias hybrida 138
  leucoptera 137, **176**
  nigra 138
Chloroptera natalensis 258
Chrysococcyx caprius 154, **192**
  cupreus 153, **192**
  klaas 156
Ciccaba woodfordi 158, **193**
Cichladusa arquator 235
  ruficauda 235
Ciconia abdimii 43, **48**
  ciconia 43, **48**
  episcopus 44
  nigra 43, **48**
Cinnyricinclus leucogaster 277, **288**
Circaëtus cinerascens 77
  cinereus 73, **80**
  fasciolatus 77
  pectoralis 74, **80, 96**
Circus aeruginosus 85
  macrourus 83, **81, 112**
  maurus 83, **81, 112**
  pygargus 85
  ranivorus 82, **81, 112**
Cisticola aberrans 248
  aridula 247
  ayresii 247
  brachyptera 248
  brunnescens 248
  cantans 248
  chiniana 245, **272**
  erythrops 248
  fulvicapilla 245, **272**
  galactotes 248
  juncidis 244, **272**
  lais 247
  natalensis 246, **272**
  pipiens 248
  rufilata 247
  subruficapilla 247
  textrix 244, **272**
  tinniens 246, **272**
Cisticola Ayres' 247

Cisticola [*continued*]
Black-backed 248
Chirping 248
Cloud 244, **272**
Croaking 246, **272**
Dancing 247
Desert 247
Fan-tailed 244, **272**
Lazy 248
Le Vaillant's 246, **272**
Neddicky 245, **272**
Pale-crowned 248
Rattling 245, **272**
Red-faced 248
Shortwing 248
Singing 248
Tinkling 247
Wailing 247
Clamator glandarius 152, **192**
jacobinus 153, **192**
levaillantii 155
Colius colius 169
indicus 168, **209**
striatus 169
Columba arquatrix 146
delegorguei 147
guinea 141, **177**
Coot Red-knobbed 98, **145**
Coracias caudata 179, **224**
garrulus 179, **224**
naevia 180, **224**
spatulata 180
Coracina caesia 210, **240**
pectoralis 210
Cormorant Bank 34
Cape 34, **32**
Reed 34, **32**
White-breasted 31, **32**
Corncrake 99
Corvinella melanoleuca 270, **289**
Corvus albicollis 214, **161**
albus 214, **161**
capensis 214, **161**
Corythaixoides concolor 151, **192**
Cossypha caffra 232, **257**
dichroa 231, **257**
heuglini 231, **257**
humeralis 233
natalensis 233
Coturnix adansoni 91
coturnix 91
delegorguei 91, **113**
Coucal Black 156
Burchell's 154, **192**
Coppery-tailed 156
Green 156

Senegal 156
Courser Bronze-wing 131
Burchell's 127, **145**
Double-banded 130, **145**
Temminck's 130
Three-banded 131
Crake African 99
Baillon's 99
Black 94, **160**
Spotted 100
Striped 100
White-winged 100
Crane Blue 102, **161**
Crowned 101, **161**
Stanley 102, **161**
Wattled 102, **161**
Creatophora cinerea 276, **288**
Creeper Spotted 216
Crex crex 99
egregia 99
Crimson-wing Nyasa 321
Crombec Red-faced 243
Rufous-bellied 238, **272**
Crow Black 214, **161**
Pied 214, **161**
Cryptospiza reichenovii 321
Cuckoo African 155
Black 155
Didric 154, **192**
Emerald 153, **192**
Great Spotted 152, **192**
Jacobin 153, **192**
Klaas's 156
Lesser 156
Long-tailed 156
Red-chested 152, **192**
Striped-breasted 155
Thick-billed 156
Cuckoo-shrike Black 207, **240**
Grey 210, **240**
White-breasted 210
Cuckoo-weaver 311
Cuculus canorus 155
clamosus 155
poliocephalus 156
solitarius 152, **192**
Curlew 123, **145**
Cursorius rufus 127, **145**
temminckii 130
Cygnus olor 57
Cypsiurus parvus 167, **208**

Dabchick Cape 23, **32**
Daption capensis 26, **65**
Darter 35, **32**
Delichon urbica 207

Dendrocygna bicolor 55
  viduata 55, 49, 64
Dendropicos fuscescens 191, 225
Dicrurus adsimilis 211, 240
  ludwigii 211
Dikkop Cape 126, 145
  Water 126
Diomedea cauta 25
  chlororhynchos 25, 65
  chrysostoma 25
  exulans 24, 65
  melanophris 24, 65
Dove Blue-spotted 147
  Cape Turtle 142, 177
  Cinnamon 146
  Emerald-spotted 143, 177
  Laughing 142, 177
  Mourning 146
  Namaqua 143, 177
  Red-eyed Turtle 146
  Tambourine 146
Dromas ardeola 126
Drongo Fork-tailed 211, 240
  Square-tailed 211
Dryoscopus cubla 267, 289
Duck Black 54, 64
  Fulvous 55
  Knob-billed 51, 64
  Maccoa 56, 64
  White-backed 56
  White-faced 55, 49, 64
  Yellow-bill 53, 49, 64
Dunlin 125

Eagle African Hawk 71, 81
  Ayres' Hawk 73
  Bateleur 75, 80, 96
  Black 70, 80, 96
  Booted 73
  Crowned 72, 80, 96
  Fish 74, 80, 96
  Lesser Spotted 77
  Long-crested 72
  Martial 71, 80, 96
  Steppe 77
  Tawny 70, 80, 96
  Wahlberg's 70, 80
Egret Cattle 38, 33
  Great 37, 33
  Little 37, 33
  Yellow-billed 39
Egretta alba 37, 33
  ardesiaca 39
  garzetta 37, 33
  intermedia 39
Elanus caeruleus 69, 81, 128

Emberiza cabanisi 331
  capensis 330, 317
  flaviventris 330, 317
  impetuani 331
  tahapisi 329, 317
Ephippiorhynchus senegalensis 42, 161
Eremomela gregalis 243
  icteropygialis 236, 272
  scotops 239
  usticollis 239
Eremopterix australis 201
  leucotis 201
  verticalis 198, 240
Erythrocercus livingstonei 259
Erythropygia coryphaeus 234
  leucophrys 233, 257
  paena 232, 257
  quadrivirgata 234
  signata 234
Estrilda astrild 318, 316
  erythronotos 318, 316
  melanotis 313, 316
  perreini 321
  thomensis 321
Eudyptes cristatus 22
Euplectes afer 306, 309
  albonotatus 310, 305
  ardens 307, 305
  axillaris 311
  capensis 306, 309
  hordeaceus 311
  macrourus 311
  orix 303, 309
  progne 310, 305
Eupodotis afra 105, 161
  caerulescens 107
  cafra 107
  melanogaster 105, 161
  ruficrista 104, 161
  rüppelli 107
  vigorsii 104, 161
Eurocephalus anguitimens 275
Eurystomas glaucurus 180

Falco amurensis 62, 97
  ardosiaceus 67
  biarmicus 60, 97
  chicquera 62, 97
  columbarius 62
  cuvieri 62
  dickinsoni 63, 97
  fasciinucha 62
  naumanni 66, 97
  peregrinus 61
  rupicoloides 63, 97
  subbuteo 61, 97

Falco [*continued*]
tinnunculus 66, **97**
vespertinus 67
Falcon African Hobby 62
Cuckoo 67
Hobby 61, **97**
Lanner 60, **97**
Peregrine 61
Pygmy 67, **97**
Red-necked 62, **97**
Taita 62
Ficedula albicollis 259
Finch Common Melba 313, **316**
Locust 321
Quail 319, **316**
Yellow-backed Melba 321
Finch-lark Black-eared 201
Chestnut-backed 201
Grey-backed 198, **240**
Finfoot Peter's 100
Firefinch African 315, **316**
Brown 321
Jameson's 320
Little 320
Flamingo Greater 47
Lesser 47
Flufftail Buff-spotted 94, **160**
Chestnut-headed 100
Red-chested 99
Streaky-breasted 100
Striped 100
Flycatcher Black 258
Black and White 259
Blue-grey 255
Blue-mantled 254, **273**
Cape 252, **273**
Chat 258
Chinspot 253, **273**
Dusky 255
Fairy 253, **273**
Fan-tailed 255
Fiscal 252, **273**
Livingstone's 259
Marico 251, **273**
Mashona 259
Mouse-coloured 258
Paradise 254, **273**
Pririt 259
Spotted 250, **273**
Wattle-eyed 259
White-collared 259
White-tailed 259
Woodward's 259
Yellow 258
Yellow-bellied 259
Yellow-throated 258

Francolin Cape 89
Hartlaub's 89
Natal 88, **113**
Red-billed 88, **113**
Red-necked 90, **113**
Swainson's 89, **113**
Francolinus adspersus 88, **113**
afer 90, **113**
africanus 87, **113**
capensis 89
coqui 85, **113**
hartlaubi 89
levaillantii 87, **113**
levaillantoides 89
natalensis 88, **113**
rovuma 89
sephaena 86, **113**
shelleyi 89
swainsonii 89, **113**
Fregata minor 29
Fregetta grallaria 29
tropica 29
Frigate Bird 29
Fringilla coelebs 329
Fulica cristata 98, **145**
Fulmar Antarctic 29
Fulmarus glacialoides 29

Gallinago media 125
nigripennis 119, **160**
Gallinula angulata 100
chloropus 95, **145**
Gallinule American 100
Lesser 95, **160**
Purple 99
Gannet Cape 31, **32**
Garganey 57
Geocolaptes olivaceus 190, **225**
Geronticus calvus 45, **48**
Glareola nordmanni 130, **145**
nuchalis 131
pratincola 131
Glaucidium capense 162
perlatum 159, **193**
Godwit Bar-tailed 125
Black-tailed 125
Goose African Pygmy 51
Egyptian 51, **49, 64**
Spurwing 50, **49, 64**
Gorsachius leuconotus 40
Goshawk African 78, **112**
Black 77, **112**
Dark Chanting 82, **81, 112**
Gabar 78, **112**
Little Banded 82
Pale Chanting 79, **81, 112**

Grassbird 237, **272**
Grebe Black-necked 23, **32**
  Crested 22, **32**
Greenshank 122, **144**
Grus carunculatus 102, **161**
Guinea-fowl Crested 92
  Helmet 92
Gull Grey-headed 133, **176**
  Hartlaub's 134
  Lesser Black-backed 134
  Sabine's 134
  Southern Black-backed 133, **176**
  White-eyed 134
Guttera edouardi 92
Gymnogene Banded 84, **81, 128**
Gypaëtus barbatus 77
Gypohierax angolensis 60
Gyps africanus 58, **80**
  coprotheres 58, **80, 96**

Haematopus moquini 109, **129**
  ostralegus 109
Halcyon albiventris 172, **209**
  chelicuti 173
  leucocephala 173
  senegalensis 171, **209**
  senegaloides 173
Haliaëtus vocifer 74, **80, 96**
Halobaena caerulea 29
Hamerkop 40, **48**
Harrier African Marsh 82, **81, 112**
  Black 83, **81, 112**
  European Marsh 85
  Montagu's 85
  Pallid 83, **81, 112**
Hawk Bat 69
Heliolais erythroptera 243
Heron Black 39
  Black-headed 36, **33**
  Goliath 36, **33**
  Green-backed 38, **33**
  Grey 35, **33**
  Night 38, **33**
  Purple 39
  Rufous-bellied 40
  Squacco 39
  White-backed Night 40
Himantopus himantopus 124
Hippolais icterina 239
  olivetorum 243
Hirundo abyssinica 206
  albigularis 203, **208**
  atrocaerulea 207
  cucullata 204, **208**
  dimidiata 206
  griseopyga 206

rupestris 205, **208**
rustica 202, **208**
semirufa 203, **208**
senegalensis 207
smithii 206
spilodera 204, **208**
Honey-guide Greater 188, **225**
  Lesser 189
  Scaly-throated 189
  Sharp-billed 189, **225**
  Slender-billed 190
Hoopoe African 181, **240**
  Red-billed 181, **240**
  Scimitar-bill 182
Hornbill Bradfield's 185
  Crowned 184, **224**
  Grey 182, **224**
  Ground 185
  Monteiro's 185
  Red-billed 183, **224**
  Silvery-cheeked 185
  Trumpeter 184
  Yellow-billed 184, **224**
Hydrobates pelagicus 28, **65**
Hydroprogne caspia 134, **176**
Hyliota australis 259
  flavigaster 259
Hypargos margaritatus 320
  niveoguttatus 321
Hypochera amauropteryx 323
  funerea 323, **305**

Ibis Bald 45, **48**
  Glossy 46, **48**
  Hadeda 45, **48**
  Sacred 44, **48**
Ibis ibis 42, **48**
Indicator indicator 188, **225**
  minor 189
  variegatus 189
Ispidina picta 173
Ixobrychus minutus 39
  sturmii 39

Jacana African 107, **160**
  Lesser 108
Jynx ruficollis 195, **225**

Kaupifalco monogrammicus 73, **81, 128**
Kestrel Dickinson's 63, **97**
  Eastern Red-footed 62, **97**
  Greater 63, **97**
  Grey 67
  Lesser 66, **97**
  Rock 66, **97**
  Western Red-footed 67

Kingfisher Angola 171, **209**
  Brown-hooded 172, **209**
  Giant 172
  Grey-headed 173
  Half-collared 173
  Malachite 171, **209**
  Mangrove 173
  Pied 170, **209**
  Pygmy 173
  Striped 173
Kite Black 68, **81, 128**
  Black-shouldered 69, **81, 128**
  Yellow-billed 68, **81, 128**
Knot 125
Korhaan Black 105, **161**
  Blue 107
  Karroo 104, **161**
  Long-legged 105, **161**
  Red-crested 104, **161**
  Rüppel's 107
  White-bellied 107

Lagonosticta rhodopareia 320
  rubricata 314, **316**
  rufopicta 321
  senegala 320
Lammergeyer 77
Lamprotornis acuticaudus 280
  australis 278, **288**
  chalybaeus 280
  chloropterus 280
  corruscus 280
  mevesii 280
  nitens 277, **288**
Laniarius aethiopicus 276
  atrococcineus 267, **289**
  bicolor 276
  ferrugineus 266, **289**
Lanioturdus torquatus 275
Lanius collaris 265, **289**
  collurio 265, **289**
  minor 274
  souzae 276
Lark Botha's 202
  Calandra 202
  Clapper 197, **240**
  Dusky 200
  Fawn-coloured 200
  Flappet 200
  Gray's 201
  Karroo 200
  Long-billed 200
  Monotonous 199
  Pink-billed 199, **240**
  Red 202
  Red-capped 198, **240**

Rudd's 202
Rufous-naped 196, **240**
Sabota 196, **240**
Sclater's 202
Short-clawed 202
Singing Bush 199
Spike-heeled 197, **240**
Stark's 201
Thick-billed 202
Larus cirrocephalus 133, **176**
  dominicanus 133, **176**
  fuscus 134
  leucopthalmus 134
  novaehollandiae 134
  sabini 134
Leptoptilos crumeniferus 41, **161**
Leucanous albus 138
Limicola falcinellus 125
Limnocorax flavirostra 94, **160**
Limosa lapponica 125
  limosa 125
Lioptilus nigricapillus 219
Locustella fluviatilis 243
Lonchura bicolor 320
  cucullata 312, **316**
  fringilloides 320
Longclaw Fülleborn's 264
  Orange-throated 263, **288**
  Pink-throated 264
  Yellow-throated 264
Lophaëtus occipitalis 72
Lourie Grey 151, **192**
  Knysna 150, **192**
  Purple-crested 150, **192**
Lovebird Black-cheeked 150
  Lilian's 150
  Rosy-faced 149, **177**
Luscinia luscinia 235
Lybius leucomelas 186, **225**
  torquatus 185, **225**

Macheirhamphus alcinus 69
Macrodipteryx vexillarius 165
Macronectes giganteus 26, **65**
Macronyx ameliae 264
  capensis 263, **288**
  croceus 264
  fülleborni 264
Malaconotus hypopyrrhus 270, **289**
  multicolor 276
  olivaceus 275
  quadricolor 269, **289**
  sulphureopectus 268, **289**
  zeylonus 269, **289**
Malimbus rubriceps 298, **308**
Mandingoa nitidulus 313, **316**

Mannikin Bronze   312, **316**
  Pied   320
  Red-backed   320
Martin African Sand   205, **208**
  Banded Sand   207
  European Sand   207
  House   207
  Rock   205, **208**
Megalopterus minutus   138
Melaenornis infuscatus   258
  mariquensis   251, **273**
  pallidus   258
  pammelaina   258
  silens   252, **273**
Melanocorypha bimaculata   202
Melierax gabar   78, **112**
  metabates   82, 81, **112**
  musicus   79, 81, **112**
Melocichla mentalis   243
Merlin   62
Merops apiaster   174, **209**
  boehmi   178
  bullockoides   175, **209**
  hirundineus   178, **209**
  nubicoides   174, **209**
  pusillus   175, **209**
  superciliosus   178
Mesopicos griseocephalus   194
Microparra capensis   108
Milvus aegyptius   68, 81, **128**
  migrans   68, 81, **128**
Mirafra africana   196, **240**
  africanoides   200
  apiata   197, **240**
  cheniana   199
  chuana   202
  javanica   199
  rufocinnamomea   200
  sabota   196, **240**
Monticola angolensis   226
  brevipes   226
  explorator   226
  pretoriae   226
  rupestris   226, **256**
Moorhen Common   95, **145**
  Lesser   100
Motacilla aguimp   260, **288**
  capensis   260, **288**
  clara   261
  flava   261
Mousebird Red-faced   168, **209**
  Speckled   169
  White-backed   169
Muscicapa adusta   255
  caerulescens   255
  striata   250, **273**

Myioparus plumbeus   255
Myna Indian   279
Myrmecocichla formicivora   229, **256**

Namibornis herero   231
Nectarinia afra   291
  amethystina   290, **304**
  bifasciata   291
  chalybea   285, **304**
  cuprea   292
  famosa   283, **304**
  fusca   286, **304**
  kilimensis   292
  mariquensis   285, **304**
  neergaardi   292
  olivacea   286, **304**
  senegalensis   290, **304**
  shelleyi   292
  talatala   286, **304**
  venusta   291
  veroxii   291
  violacea   284, **304**
Neophron monachus   59
  percnopterus   60
Netta erythrophthalma   55, **49**, **64**
Nettapus auritus   51
Nicator chloris   276
Nicator Yellow-spotted   276
Nightingale Thrush   235
Nightjar European   163, **193**
  Freckled   164, **193**
  Mozambique   164
  Natal   165
  Pennant-winged   165
  Rufous-cheeked   164
  South African   163, **193**
Nilaus afer   271, **289**
Noddy Common   138
  White-capped   138
Numenius arquata   123, **145**
  phaeopus   125
Numida meleagris   92
Nycticorax nycticorax   38, **33**

Oceanites oceanicus   28, **65**
Oceanodroma leucorhoa   29
Oena capensis   143, **177**
Oenanthe bifasciata   228, **256**
  monticola   226, **256**
  oenanthe   231
  pileata   227, **256**
Onychognathus morio   278, **288**
  nabouroup   280
Oriole African Golden   212, **241**
  Black-headed   213, **241**
  European Golden   212, **241**

Oriolus auratus 212, **241**
  larvatus 213, **241**
  oriolus 212, **241**
Ortygospiza fuscocrissa 319, **316**
  locustella 321
Osprey 84, **81**, **128**
Ostrich 21
Otis denhami 106
  kori 103, **161**
  ludwigii 106
Otus leucotis 162
  scops 158, **193**
Owl Barn 157, **193**
  Cape Eagle 162
  Fishing 162
  Giant Eagle 162
  Grass 159
  Marsh 157, **193**
  Scops 158, **193**
  Spotted Eagle 159, **193**
  White-faced 162
  Wood 158, **193**
Owlet Barred 162
  Pearl-spotted 159, **193**
Oxpecker Red-billed 281, **288**
  Yellow-billed 281
Oxyura punctata 56, **64**
Oystercatcher Black 109, **129**
  European 109

Pachycoccyx audeberti 156
Pachyptila belcheri 29
  desolata 27
  turtur 29
  vittata 28
Pandion haliaëtus 84, **81**, **128**
Parisoma layardi 255
  subcaeruleum 251, **273**
Parrot Brown-headed 149
  Cape 148, **177**
  Meyer's 148, **177**
  Rüppel's 149
Parus afer 215, **241**
  niger 215, **241**
  rufiventris 216
Passer domesticus 295, **305**
  griseus 296
  melanurus 296, **305**
  motitensis 296
Partridge Coqui 85, **113**
  Crested 86, **113**
  Grey-wing 87, **113**
  Kirk's 89
  Orange River 89
  Red-wing 87, **113**
  Shelley's 89

Pelagodroma marina 29
Pelecanus onocrotalus 30
  rufescens 30
Pelican Pink-backed 30
  White 30
Penguin Jackass 21, **32**
  Rockhopper 22
Pernis apivorus 69
Petrel Antarctic 29
  Blue 29
  Giant 26, **65**
  Great-winged 29
  Pintado 26, **65**
  Schlegel's 29
  Soft-plumaged 29
  White-chinned 26, **65**
  White-headed 29
Petronia superciliaris 297
Phaëthon lepturus 29
  rubricauda 29
Phalacrocorax africanus 34, **32**
  capensis 34, **32**
  carbo 31, **32**
  neglectus 34
Phalarope Grey 125
  Red-necked 125
Phalaropus fulicarius 125
  lobatus 125
Philetarius socius 294, **305**
Philomachus pugnax 120, **144**
Phoebetria fusca 25
  palpebrata 25
Phoenicopterus minor 47
  ruber 47
Phoeniculus purpureus 181, **240**
Phyllastrephus debilis 221
  flavostriatus 221
  terrestris 220, **241**
Phylloscopus sibilatrix 243
  trochilus 236, **272**
Pigeon Delegorgue's 147
  Green 147, **177**
  Rameron 146
  Rock 141, **177**
Pinarocorys nigricans 200
Pinarornis plumosus 218
Pintail 57
Pipit Buffy 262
  Bushveld 262, **288**
  Nicholson's 262
  Plain-backed 262
  Richard's 261, **288**
  Rock 263
  Short-tailed 263
  Striped 263
  Tree 263

Yellow-breasted 263
Pitta Angola 195
Pitta angolensis 195
Platalea alba 46, 48
Platysteira peltata 259
Plectropterus gambensis 50, 49, 64
Plegadis falcinellus 46, 48
Plocepasser mahali 294, 305
  rufoscapulatus 294
Ploceus angolensis 303
  bicolor 297, 308
  cucullatus 299, 308
  capensis 300, 308
  intermedius 302
  ocularius 298, 308
  olivaceiceps 303
  rubiginosus 299, 308
  subaureus 303
  velatus 301, 308
  xanthops 303
  xanthopterus 303
Plover Blacksmith 115, 129
  Black-winged 115, 129
  Caspian 117
  Chestnut-banded 117
  Crab 126
  Crowned 114, 129
  Greater Sand 117
  Grey 118
  Kittlitz's 111, 129
  Lesser Golden 118
  Mongolian 118
  Ringed 110, 129
  Senegal 118
  Three-banded 111, 129
  Wattled 116, 129
  White-crowned 116, 129
  White-fronted 110, 129
  White-winged 118
Pluvialis dominica 118
  squatarola 118
Pochard Southern 55, 49, 64
Podica senegalensis 100
Podiceps cristatus 22, 32
  nigricollis 23, 32
  ruficollis 23, 32
Pogoniulus bilineatus 188
  chrysoconus 186, 225
  olivaceus 188
  pusillus 187
  simplex 188
Pogonocichla stellata 234
  swynnertoni 235
Poicephalus cryptoxanthus 149
  meyeri 148, 177
  robustus 148, 177

rüppellii 149
Polemaëtus bellicosus 71, 80, 96
  coronatus 72, 80, 96
Poliohierax semitorquatus 67, 97
Polyboroides radiatus 84, 81, 128
Porphyrio alleni 95, 160
  martinica 100
  porphyrio 99
Porzana marginalis 100
  porzana 100
  pusilla 99
Pratincole Black-winged 130, 145
  Collared 131
  White-collared 131
Prinia Black-chested 249, 257
  Forest 250
  Karroo 249, 257
  Namaqua 250
  Rufous-eared 250
  Tawny-flanked 248, 257
Prinia flavicans 249, 257
  maculosa 249, 257
  pectoralis 250
  robertsi 250
  subflava 248, 257
  substriata 250
Prion Dove 27
  Fairy 29
  Slender-billed 29
Prionops plumata 271, 289
  retzii 275
  scopifrons 276
Procellaria aequinoctialis 26, 65
  cinerea 27
Prodotiscus insignis 190
  regulus 189, 225
Promerops cafer 282, 304
  gurneyi 283
Psalidoprocne pristoptera 205, 208
Pterocles bicinctus 140, 160
  burchelli 140
  gutturalis 140
  namaqua 139, 160
Pterodroma incerta 29
  lessonii 29
  macroptera 29
  mollis 29
Puffinus assimilis 29
  carneipes 29
  gravis 27, 65
  griseus 28, 65
  puffinus 29
Pycnonotus barbatus 220, 241
  capensis 219, 241
  nigricans 219, 241
Pyrenestes minor 321

Pytelia melba 313, **316**
Pytilia afra 321

Quail African 91
　Blue 91
　Harlequin 91, **113**
Quelea Cardinal 303
　Red-billed 302, **308**
　Red-headed 303
Quelea cardinalis 303
　erythrops 303
　quelea 302, **308**

Rail Cape 98
Rallus caerulescens 98
Raven Cape 214, **161**
Recurvirostra avosetta 123, **145**
Redshank 125
Redshank Spotted 126
Rhinopomastus cyanomelas 182
Rhinoptilus africanus 130, **145**
　chalcopterus 131
　cinctus 131
Rhynchops flavirostris 138, **176**
Riparia cincta 207
　paludicola 205, **208**
　riparia 207
Robin Bearded Scrub 234
　Brown Scrub 234
　Cape 232, **257**
　Chorister 231, **257**
　Gunning's 235
　Heuglin's 231, **257**
　Kalahari Scrub 232, **257**
　Karroo Scrub 234
　Natal 233
　Starred 234
　Swynnerton's 235
　White-browed Scrub 233, **257**
　White-throated 233, **257**
Rock-jumper 218, **241**
Rock-jumper Damara 219
Rock-thrush Angola 226
　Cape 226, **256**
　Sentinel 226
　Short-toed 226
　Transvaal 226
Roller Broad-billed 180
　European 179, **224**
　Lilac-breasted 179, **224**
　Purple 180, **224**
　Racquet-tailed 180
Rostratula benghalensis 108, **160**
Ruff 120, **144**

Sagittarius serpentarius 57, **80, 96**

Salpornis spilonata 216
Sanderling 124
Sandgrouse Double-banded 140, **160**
　Namaqua 139, **160**
　Spotted 140
　Yellow-throated 140
Sandpiper Baird's 126
　Broad-billed 125
　Common 121, **144**
　Curlew 119, **144**
　Green 125
　Marsh 121, **144**
　Pectoral 126
　Terek 124
　Wood 122, **144**
Sarkidiornis melanotos 51, **64**
Sarothrura affinis 100
　ayresi 100
　böhmi 100
　elegans 94, **160**
　lugens 100
　rufa 99
Saxicola rubetra 231
　torquata 229, **256**
Schoenicola brevirostris 242
Scopus umbretta 40, **48**
Scotopelia peli 162
Secretary Bird 57, **80, 96**
Seedcracker Nyasa 321
Seicercus ruficapillus 258
Serinus alario 329
　albogularis 327, **317**
　atrogularis 326, **317**
　canicollis 324, **317**
　citrinipectus 329
　flaviventris 328, **317**
　gularis 328, **317**
　leucopterus 329
　mennelli 329
　mozambicus 326, **317**
　scotops 325, **317**
　sulphuratus 327, **317**
　tottus 324, **317**
Shearwater Flesh-footed 29
　Great 27, **65**
　Great Grey 27
　Little 29
　Manx 29
　Mediterranean 27
　Sooty 28, **65**
Shelduck South African 52, **49, 64**
Sheppardia gunningi 235
Shoveller Cape 52, **49, 64**
　European 57
Shrike Black-crowned 268, **289**
　Black-fronted 276

Black Helmet 275
Bokmakierie 269, **289**
Brubru 271, **289**
Chestnut-fronted Helmet 276
Common Bou-bou 266, **289**
Crimson-breasted 267, **289**
Fiscal 265, **289**
Gorgeous 269, **289**
Grey-headed 270, **289**
Lesser Grey 274
Magpie 270, **289**
Marsh 276
Olive 275
Orange-breasted 268, **289**
Puff-backed 267, **289**
Red-backed 265, **289**
Souza's 276
Tchagra 274
Three-streaked 274
Tropical Bou-bou 276
Western Bou-bou 276
White-crowned 275
White Helmet 271, **289**
White-tailed 275
Skimmer African 138, **176**
Skua Antarctic 132, **176**
Arctic 131, **176**
Pomarine 132
Smithornis capensis 195
Snake-eagle Banded 77
Black-breasted 74, **80**, **96**
Brown 73, **80**
Fasciated 77
Snipe Ethiopian 119, **160**
Great 125
Painted 108, **160**
Sparrow Cape 296, **305**
Great 296
Grey-headed 296
House 295, **305**
Yellow-spot 297
Sparrow-hawk Little 77, **112**
Ovambo 82
Red-breasted 82
Sparrow-weaver Red-backed 294
White-browed 294, **305**
Spheniscus demersus 21, **32**
Sphenoeacus afer 237, **272**
Spinetail Boehm's 167, **208**
Mottled 168
Spoonbill African 46, **48**
Sporopipes squamifrons 297, **305**
Spreo bicolor 279, **288**
Stactolaema leucotis 187
whytii 188
Starling Black-bellied 280

Burchell's 278, **288**
Cape 277, **288**
European 279
Greater Blue-eared 280
Lesser Blue-eared 280
Long-tailed 280
Pale-winged 280
Pied 279, **288**
Plum-coloured 277, **288**
Red-winged 278, **288**
Sharp-tailed 280
Wattled 276, **288**
Steganura orientalis 324
paradisaea 322, **309**
Stenostira scita 253, **273**
Stercorarius parasiticus 131, **176**
pomarinus 132
skua 132, **176**
Sterna albifrons 138
balaenarum 136, **176**
benghalensis 138
bergii 136, **176**
dougallii 138
fuscata 138
hirundo 135, **176**
paradisaea 137
sandvicensis 135, **176**
vittata 137
Stilt Black-winged 124
Stint Little 120, **144**
Red-necked 125
Storm Petrel Black-bellied 29
Common 28, **65**
Leach's 29
White-bellied 29
White-faced 29
Wilson's 28, **65**
Stork Black 43, **48**
Marabou 41, **161**
Openbill 41, **48**
Saddlebill 42, **161**
White 43, **48**
White-bellied 43, **48**
Wood 42, **48**
Woolly-necked 44
Streptopelia capicola 142, **177**
decipiens 146
senegalensis 142, **177**
semitorquata 146
Struthio camelus 21
Sturnus vulgaris 279
Sugarbird Cape 282, **304**
Gurney's 283
Sula bassana 31, **32**
leucogaster 29
Sunbird Black 290, **304**

Sunbird [*continued*]
Black-bellied 292
Blue-throated 292
Bronze 292
Collared 287, **304**
Coppery 292
Dusky 286, **304**
Greater Double-collared 291
Grey 291
Lesser Double-collared 285, **304**
Malachite 283, **304**
Marico 285, **304**
Neergaard's 292
Olive 286, **304**
Orange-breasted 284, **304**
Purple-banded 291
Scarlet-chested 290, **304**
Violet-backed 292
White-bellied 286, **304**
Yellow-bellied 291
Swallow Black Saw-winged 205, **208**
Blue 207
Cliff 204, **208**
European 202, **208**
Grey-rumped 206
Larger Striped 204, **208**
Lesser Striped 206
Mosque 207
Pearl-breasted 206
Red-breasted 203, **208**
White-throated 203, **208**
Wire-tailed 206
Swan Mute 57
Swift Alpine 168
Black 165, **208**
European 167
Horus 167
Little 166, **208**
Mottled 168
Pallid 168
Palm 167, **208**
Scarce 168
White-rumped 166, **208**
Sylvia borin 235, **272**
communis 243
Sylvietta rufescens 238, **272**
whytii 243

Tadorna cana 52, 49, **64**
Tauraco corythaix 150, **192**
porphyreolophus 150, **192**
Teal Hottentot 54, 49, **64**
Red-bill 53, 49, **64**
Teratophius ecaudatus 75, 80, **96**
Tchagra australis 274
minuta 276

senegala 268, **289**
tchagra 274
Tern Antarctic 137
Arctic 137
Black 138
Caspian 134, **176**
Common 135, **176**
Damara 136, **176**
Lesser Crested 138
Little 138
Roseate 138
Sandwich 135, **176**
Sooty 138
Swift 136, **176**
Whiskered 138
White 138
White-winged Lake 137, **176**
Terpsiphone viridis 254, **273**
Thalassoica antarctica 29
Thalassornis leuconotus 56
Thamnolaea arnotti 230
cinnamomeiventris 228, **256**
Threskiornis aethiopicus 44, **48**
Thripias namaquus 191, **225**
Thrush Groundscaper 223, **256**
Gurney's 223
Kurrichane 223
Natal 223
Olive 222, **256**
Palm 235
Rufous-tailed 235
Tinker Black-crowned 188
Green 188
Red-fronted 187
Yellow-fronted 186, **225**
Tit Black 215, **241**
Cape Penduline 216, **241**
Grey 215, **241**
Grey Penduline 216
Rufous 216
Tit-babbler Common 251, **273**
Layard's 255
Tockus alboterminatus 184, **224**
bradfieldi 185
erythrorhynchus 183, **224**
flavirostris 184, **224**
monteiri 185
nasatus 182, **224**
Trachyphonus vaillantii 187, **225**
Treron australis 147, **177**
Tringa erythropus 126
glareola 122, **144**
hypoleucos 121, **144**
nebularia 122, **144**
ochrophus 125
stagnatilis 121, **144**

terek	124
totanus	125
Trochocercus albonotatus	259
cyanomelas	254, **273**
Trogon Narina	170, **192**
Tropic Bird Red-tailed	29
White-tailed	29
Turdoides bicolor	217, **240**
gymnogenys	219
jardineii	217, **240**
leucopygius	218
melanops	218
Turdus fischeri	223
gurneyi	223
libonyanus	223
litsitsirupa	223, **256**
olivaceus	222, **256**
Turnix hottentotta	93
sylvatica	93, **113**
Turnstone	117
Turtur afer	147
chalcospilos	143, **177**
tympanistria	146
Twinspot Green	313, **316**
Pink-throated	320
Red-throated	321
Tyto alba	157, **193**
capensis	159
Upupa africana	181, **240**
Uraeginthus angolensis	315, **316**
granatinus	318, **316**
Vanellus albiceps	116, **129**
armatus	115, **129**
coronatus	114, **129**
crassirostris	118
lugubris	118
melanopterus	115, **129**
senegallus	116, **129**
Vidua macroura	321, **309**
regia	322, **309**
Vulture Black	59, **80, 96**
Cape	58, **80, 96**
Egyptian	60
Hooded	59
Lappet-faced	59, **80, 96**
Palm-nut	60
White-backed	58, **80**
White-headed	59, **80**
Wagtail African Pied	260, **288**
Cape	260, **288**
Long-tailed	261
Yellow	261
Warbler African Marsh	236, **272**

African Scrub	242
Bleating	243
Broad-tailed	242
Burnt-necked	239
Cape Reed	242
Cinnamon-breasted	243
European Marsh	243
European Reed	243
Forest Scrub	243
Garden	235, **272**
Greater Swamp	243
Great Reed	242
Green-capped	239
Grey-backed	239, **272**
Icterine	239
Karroo Green	243
Knysna Scrub	243
Larger Barred	237, **272**
Lesser Barred	243
Moustached	243
Olive-tree	243
Red-winged	243
River	243
Sedge	243
Victorin's Scrub	242
Willow	236, **272**
Wood	243
Yellow-bellied	236, **272**
Waxbill Black-cheeked	318, **316**
Blue	315, **316**
Cinderella	321
Common	318, **316**
Grey	321
Orange-breasted	315, **316**
Swee	313, **316**
Violet-eared	318, **316**
Weaver Bar-winged	303
Brown-throated	303
Buffalo	293, **305**
Cabanis	302
Cape	300, **308**
Chestnut	299, **308**
Forest	297, **308**
Golden	303
Masked	301, **308**
Olive-headed	303
Red-headed	298, **308**
Scaly	297, **305**
Sociable	294, **305**
Spectacled	298, **308**
Spotted-backed	299, **308**
Thick-billed	301, **308**
Yellow	303
Whale Bird	28
Wheatear Capped	227, **256**
European	231

Whimbrel   125
Whinchat   231
White-eye   Pale   292, **304**
  Yellow   293
Whitethroat   243
Whydah   Broad-tailed Paradise   324
  Pin-tailed   321, **309**
  Shaft-tailed   322, **309**
  Sharp-tailed Paradise   322, **309**
Widow   Long-tailed   310, **305**
  Red-collared   307, **309**
  Red-shouldered   311
  White-winged   310, **305**
  Yellow-backed   311
  Yellow-rumped   306, **309**

Widow-finch   Black   323, **305**
  Steel-blue   323
Wigeon   Cape   53, **49, 64**
Woodpecker   Bearded   191, **225**
  Bennett's   191
  Cardinal   191, **225**
  Golden-tailed   194
  Ground   190, **225**
  Knysna   194
  Little Spotted   194
  Olive   194
Wryneck   Red-breasted   195, **225**

Zosterops   pallidus   292, **304**
  senegalensis   293